The Cambridge Companion to *The Magic Flute*

Since its premiere in 1791, *The Magic Flute* has been staged continuously and remains, to this day, Mozart's most-performed opera worldwide. This comprehensive, user-friendly, up-to-date critical guide considers the opera in a variety of contexts to provide a fresh look at a work that has continued to fascinate audiences from Mozart's time to ours. It serves both as an introduction for those encountering the opera for the first time and as a treasury of recent scholarship for those who know it very well. Containing twenty-one essays by leading scholars, and drawing on recent research and commentary, this Companion presents original insights on music, dialogue, and spectacle, and offers a range of new perspectives on key issues, including the opera's representation of exoticism, race, and gender. Organized in four sections – historical context, musical analysis, critical approaches, and reception – it provides an essential framework for understanding *The Magic Flute* and its extraordinary afterlife.

JESSICA WALDOFF is Professor of Music at the College of the Holy Cross in Worcester, Massachusetts. She is the author of *Recognition in Mozart's Operas* (2006; 2011) and has published extensively on the music of Mozart and his contemporaries.

Cambridge Companions to Music

Topics

Composers

The Cambridge Companion to Bach
Edited by John Butt

The Cambridge Companion to Bartók
Edited by Amanda Bayley

The Cambridge Companion to Amy Beach
Edited by E. Douglas Bomberger

The Cambridge Companion to the Beatles
Edited by Kenneth Womack

The Cambridge Companion to Beethoven
Edited by Glenn Stanley

The Cambridge Companion to Berg
Edited by Anthony Pople

The Cambridge Companion to Berlioz
Edited by Peter Bloom

The Cambridge Companion to Brahms
Edited by Michael Musgrave

The Cambridge Companion to Benjamin Britten
Edited by Mervyn Cooke

The Cambridge Companion to Bruckner
Edited by John Williamson

The Cambridge Companion to John Cage
Edited by David Nicholls

The Cambridge Companion to Chopin
Edited by Jim Samson

The Cambridge Companion to Debussy
Edited by Simon Trezise

The Cambridge Companion to Elgar
Edited by Daniel M. Grimley and Julian Rushton

The Cambridge Companion to Duke Ellington
Edited by Edward Green

The Cambridge Companion to Gershwin
Edited by Anna Celenza

The Cambridge Companion to Gilbert and Sullivan
Edited by David Eden and Meinhard Saremba

The Cambridge Companion to Handel
Edited by Donald Burrows

The Cambridge Companion to Haydn
Edited by Caryl Clark

The Cambridge Companion to Liszt
Edited by Kenneth Hamilton

The Cambridge Companion to Mahler
Edited by Jeremy Barham

The Cambridge Companion to Mendelssohn
Edited by Peter Mercer-Taylor

Instruments

The Cambridge Companion to *The Magic Flute*

Edited by

JESSICA WALDOFF

College of the Holy Cross, Massachusetts

CAMBRIDGE
UNIVERSITY PRESS

Shaftesbury Road, Cambridge CB2 8EA, United Kingdom

One Liberty Plaza, 20th Floor, New York, NY 10006, USA

477 Williamstown Road, Port Melbourne, VIC 3207, Australia

314–321, 3rd Floor, Plot 3, Splendor Forum, Jasola District Centre, New Delhi – 110025, India

103 Penang Road, #05–06/07, Visioncrest Commercial, Singapore 238467

Cambridge University Press is part of Cambridge University Press & Assessment, a department of the University of Cambridge.

We share the University's mission to contribute to society through the pursuit of education, learning and research at the highest international levels of excellence.

www.cambridge.org
Information on this title: www.cambridge.org/9781108426893

DOI: 10.1017/9781108551328

First published 2023

A catalogue record for this publication is available from the British Library.

A Cataloging-in-Publication data record for this book is available from the Library of Congress

ISBN 978-1-108-42689-3 Hardback
ISBN 978-1-108-44684-6 Paperback

Cambridge University Press & Assessment has no responsibility for the persistence or accuracy of URLs for external or third-party internet websites referred to in this publication and does not guarantee that any content on such websites is, or will remain, accurate or appropriate.

For James Webster and Neal Zaslaw

Contents

Figures

These figures – including several in their original color versions – are also available in a Resources Tab at www.cambridge.org/9781108426893.

Tables

Musical Examples

Contributors

THOMAS BAUMAN is Professor Emeritus of Musicology at Northwestern University and taught previously at the University of Pennsylvania, Stanford, and the University of Washington. He has published extensively on eighteenth-century German opera, including the Cambridge Opera Handbook for Mozart's *Abduction from the Seraglio*, and also on Italian opera and musical institutions. More recently, he has written on Mahler, historiography, and African-American theater and film.

CATHERINE COPPOLA is Lecturer in Musicology and Chair of the Thomas Hunter Honors Program at Hunter College, where her teaching focus is on reframing canonic opera. She is published in *Musical Improvisation and Open Forms in the Age of Beethoven* (Routledge, 2018), *19th-Century Music*, the *Newsletter of the Mozart Society of America*, and *Text*.

LISA DE ALWIS is Teaching Assistant Professor at the University of Colorado, Boulder. She specializes in Viennese theatrical culture and censorship and is the editor and translator of the eighteenth-century document *Anti–Da Ponte*. She wrote the chapter on theatrical life in *Mozart in Context* (Cambridge University Press, 2019).

EMILY I. DOLAN is Associate Professor of Music at Brown University. She works on the music of the late eighteenth and nineteenth centuries, focusing on issues of orchestration, timbre, aesthetics, and instrumentality. She is the author of *The Orchestral Revolution: Haydn and the Technologies of Timbre* (Cambridge University Press, 2013).

DEAN DUNCAN is Associate Professor in the Department of Theatre and Media Arts at Brigham Young University. He has taught and published about narrative, documentary, media for and about families, and the use of classical music in film (*Charms that Soothe*, Fordham, 2003).

HAYLEY FENN is a musicologist who focuses on questions concerning materiality, audiovisual relationships, and aesthetics of performance. She completed her PhD at Harvard University in 2022 with a dissertation on music, puppetry, and their many varied encounters. She is currently Director of Music at Wilson's School in Croydon, United Kingdom.

MARK FERRAGUTO is Associate Professor of Musicology at the Pennsylvania State University. He is the author of *Beethoven 1806* (Oxford University Press, 2019), coeditor of *Music and Diplomacy from the Early Modern Era to the Present* (Palgrave Macmillan, 2014), and editor of *Franz Weiss: Two String Quartets, Op. 8 ("Razumovsky")* (A-R Editions, 2023).

AUSTIN GLATTHORN, University of Southampton, is a cultural historian of music focusing on interdisciplinary approaches to the intersections of music, politics, mobility, and communication in Central Europe ca. 1800. Austin is the author of *Music Theatre and the Holy Roman Empire* (Cambridge University Press, 2022) and currently editing, together with Estelle Joubert, "The Cambridge History of German Opera to the Early Nineteenth Century."

MATTHEW HEAD is Professor of Music at King's College London. He researches the cultural history of eighteenth-century music. He is the author of *Orientalism, Masquerade, and Mozart's Turkish Music* (Ashgate, 2000) and *Sovereign Feminine: Music and Gender in Eighteenth-Century Germany* (University of California Press, 2013).

KATE HOPKINS is the English-language editor (concert programs) for the Salzburg Festival. Her articles on opera have featured in program books produced by the Royal Opera House, Covent Garden, English National Opera, and Welsh National Opera, as well as in *The Wagner Journal*.

ESTELLE JOUBERT is Associate Professor of Musicology at the Fountain School of Performing Arts and Assistant Dean at the Faculty of Graduate Studies at Dalhousie University. Her research interests include computational musicology, especially graph databases and network science, as well as global histories of musics in the early modern period and eighteenth-century German opera.

SIMON P. KEEFE is J. R. Hoyle Chair of Music at the University of Sheffield. He is the author of five monographs, including *Mozart's Requiem: Reception, Work, Completion* (Cambridge University Press, 2012), which won the Emerson Award from the Mozart Society of America, and most recently *Haydn and Mozart in the Long Nineteenth Century: Parallel and Intersecting Patterns of Reception* (Cambridge University Press, 2023).

RICHARD KRAMER is Distinguished Professor Emeritus at the Graduate Center of the City University of New York. He is the author, most recently, of *From the Ruins of Enlightenment: Beethoven and Schubert in Their Solitude* (University of Chicago Press, 2022) and *Cherubino's Leap: In Search of the Enlightenment Moment* (University of Chicago Press, 2016). He was named a fellow of the American Academy of Arts and Sciences in 2001.

NICHOLAS MARSTON is Professor of Music Theory and Analysis at the University of Cambridge, where he is also a Fellow and Praelector of King's College. His work on Beethoven's sketches and compositional process, Schumann, and Schenker is internationally known and recognized. Current projects concern Beethoven's late quartets and Schumann's *Dichterliebe*.

DANIEL R. MELAMED is Professor at the Indiana University Jacobs School of Music and has written on the music of Bach and Mozart. He serves as president of the American Bach Society and as director of the Bloomington Bach Cantata Project.

ADELINE MUELLER is Associate Professor of Music at Mount Holyoke College and author of *Mozart and the Mediation of Childhood* (University of Chicago Press, 2021). She has published articles in *Eighteenth-Century Music* and *Frontiers in Communication*, guest-edited a 2012 issue of *Opera Quarterly* on the reception of *The Magic Flute*, and contributed two chapters to *Mozart in Context* (Cambridge University Press, 2019).

MARTIN NEDBAL, Associate Professor of Musicology at the University of Kansas, is the author of *Viennese Opera and Morality in the Age of Mozart and Beethoven* (Routledge, 2017) and translator and editor of *The Published Theoretical Works of Leoš Janáček* (Editio Janáček, 2020). His articles on Mozart, Beethoven, and Czech music have also appeared in many journals and books.

JOHN PLATOFF is Professor of Music at Trinity College in Hartford, Connecticut, where in 2016 he won the Thomas Church Brownell Prize for Teaching Excellence. His research focuses on the operatic music of Mozart and his contemporaries, but he has also written on subjects as diverse as late Beethoven string quartets and the controversial Beatles song "Revolution."

JULIAN RUSHTON, Emeritus Professor of Music (University of Leeds), has written widely on Mozart, including *New Grove* opera articles, handbooks on *Don Giovanni* and *Idomeneo*, a life and works in the Master Musicians series, an imagined conversation (*Coffee with Mozart* [Duncan Baird, 2007]), and more specialized articles on operas and wind music.

JESSICA WALDOFF, Professor of Music at the College of the Holy Cross in Worcester, Massachusetts, is the author of *Recognition in Mozart's Operas* (Oxford University Press, 2006; 2011). She has published mainly on issues of dramaturgy and representation in the late eighteenth century. She is also a past president of the Mozart Society of America.

IAN WOODFIELD is Professor of Historical Musicology at Queen's University Belfast. His monograph *Cabals and Satires*, an investigation into the political contexts of the Italian comic operas composed by Mozart in Vienna, was published by Oxford University Press in 2018. His recent study "Songs My Mother Taught Me: New Light on James Macpherson's *Ossian*" appears in the *Journal of the Society for Musicology in Ireland* (2021).

LAUREL E. ZEISS is Associate Professor of Musicology at Baylor University. Her research focuses on the operas of Mozart and his contemporaries. She has published articles in leading journals such as *Cambridge Opera Journal*, *Journal of Singing*, and *Ars Lyrica*, as well as in many edited collections, including the *Cambridge Companion to Opera Studies* (2012) and *Cambridge Haydn Encyclopedia* (2019).

Acknowledgments

To begin, I would like to thank my contributing authors for the splendid essays found within this volume and for many stimulating exchanges about Mozart and other topics. It has been a privilege to collaborate with such an extraordinary group of scholars. I would also like to thank many friends and colleagues for providing wise counsel and generous support at various stages: among them Alessandra Campana, Cathy Coppola, Paul Corneilson, Dan DiCenso, Mark Ferraguto, Simon Keefe, Daniel Melamed, Adeline Mueller, John Platoff, Karl-Heinz Schoeps, and Neal Zaslaw. At the College of the Holy Cross, I have received invaluable assistance from several colleagues. Robert Simon, our Fenwick Music Librarian, has been an extraordinary resource and help, especially with iconography, and deserves special thanks. Jared Rex (now at the Boston Public Library), Susan Skoog, and Patricia Chuplis were enormously helpful. I also feel a special debt of gratitude to all of the students in my seminars and courses over the years who asked challenging questions about Mozart and his world, and about this opera in particular.

I am grateful to several institutions for providing the images that appear in this volume and in the companion Resources Tab: the Albertina, the KHM-Museumverband, Theatermuseum Vienna, the Niederösterreichisches Landesarchiv/St. Pölten, the Österreichische Nationalbibliothek, and the Wien Museum.

A special word of thanks goes to Kate Brett, my editor at Cambridge University Press, for making this volume possible and for providing excellent advice and assistance along the way. I am also grateful to everyone at the Press who assisted with production, especially the volume's copy-editor Virginia Hamilton.

I owe a debt of gratitude beyond what words can express to my family: to my parents, Alice and Leon Waldoff, who have watched this volume come together with interest and have assisted in a variety of ways; and to my wonderful husband, Nathaniel Brese, who has watched this opera with me countless times, has often served as a sounding board, and has provided love and support through all of life's trials in recent years.

With admiration and gratitude, I dedicate this book to James Webster and Neal Zaslaw, who encouraged and shaped my first attempts to write about this opera when I was a student at Cornell. Thank you for a lifetime of support and friendship.

Abbreviations

COH   Peter Branscombe, *W. A. Mozart: "Die Zauberflöte."* Cambridge Opera Handbooks. Cambridge: Cambridge University Press, 1991.

FACS   Wolfgang Amadeus Mozart, *"Die Zauberflöte," K. 620: Facsimile of the Autograph Score.* With essays by Hans Joachim Kreuzer and Christoph Wolff. 3 vols. Los Altos, CA: The Packard Humanities Institute, 2009.

LMF   Emily Anderson, trans. and ed., *The Letters of Mozart and His Family.* 3rd edn. London: Macmillan, 1985.

MBA   Wilhelm A. Bauer, Otto Erich Deutsch, and Joseph Heinz Eibl, eds., *Mozart: Briefe und Aufzeichnungen, Gesamtausgabe.* 8 vols. Kassel: Bärenreiter, 1962–2005.

MDB   Otto Erich Deutsch, *Mozart: A Documentary Biography.* Translated by Eric Blom, Peter Branscombe, and Jeremy Noble. 3rd edn. London: Simon & Schuster, 1990.

MDL   Otto Erich Deutsch, *Mozart: Die Dokumente seines Lebens.* Kassel: Bärenreiter, 1961.

NMA   Wolfgang Amadeus Mozart, *Neue Ausgabe sämtlicher Werke.* Kassel: Bärenreiter, 1955–2007.

Introduction

JESSICA WALDOFF

A week after the premiere of *The Magic Flute*, Mozart wrote to his wife Constanze, "I have this moment returned from the opera, which was as full as ever. ... But what always gives me most pleasure is the *silent approval*! You can see how this opera is becoming more and more esteemed."[1] He could not possibly have imagined then, in October of 1791, how his opera's fortunes would rise in the years to come. *The Magic Flute* remained in the repertoire at the Theater auf der Wieden and by 1801 had received over 200 performances. It was staged in Prague in 1792, as well as in Leipzig, Munich, Dresden, and a host of other German cities in 1793 and the years immediately following. In his 1798 biography, Franz Xaver Niemetschek claimed, "Who in Germany does not know it? Is there a single theatre where it has not been performed? It is our national opera."[2] The opera soon reached stages in many European centers, including St. Petersburg (1797), Amsterdam (1799), Paris (1801), London (1811), and Milan (1816). Today, *The Magic Flute* is Mozart's most frequently performed opera around the globe. According to Operabase, which documents opera productions and performances worldwide for every season, *The Magic Flute* is consistently listed among the "10 Most Played Titles" (along with *The Marriage of Figaro* and *Don Giovanni*). In some seasons, including 2020/2021, 2021/2022, and 2022/2023, it has been the most performed opera by any composer.[3] The data available so far for 2023/2024 suggests that *The Magic Flute* will, once again, receive the most performances.

In the years since its premiere, *The Magic Flute* has been written about in a variety of contexts, by a multitude of authors, and from a dizzying range of perspectives. While it would be impossible for any single volume to adequately capture the range and complexity of more than two centuries' worth of research, commentary, and performance, this *Cambridge Companion to "The Magic Flute"* provides twenty-one essays on diverse topics, all newly written expressly for this collection. One important predecessor to this volume is Peter Branscombe's 1991 Cambridge Opera Handbook, *W. A. Mozart: "Die Zauberflöte."* Since that time, however, there have been significant documentary discoveries and developments.

A wealth of recent scholarship – ranging from books on Mozart and his contemporaries to studies of opera as a genre to explorations of Mozart's contemporary Viennese and German contexts – has broadened the ways in which we understand this opera. This Companion provides up-to-date commentary and interpretation in a single volume, with special emphasis on four key areas.

Part I, "Conception and Context," situates the opera in its immediate historical, cultural, and geographic context. As a German opera written expressly for Schikaneder's suburban Theater auf der Wieden with its tradition of magic operas and machine comedies, *The Magic Flute* was created for a particular place and time. The playbill announced "Eine grosse Oper" (A grand opera); newspapers reported extraordinary expense associated with costumes and scenery; Mozart and Schikaneder pulled out all the stops, including Italianate singing for the serious characters and Volkstheater humor for the comic ones. Four authors bring contemporary German opera in Vienna to life, situate the libretto in the context of German Enlightenment theater reform, offer a portrait of the Theater auf der Wieden and its players, and provide vibrant details and iconography associated with the premiere and early performances.

Part II, "Music, Text, and Action," is devoted to the opera's musical drama. Although no one would deny the centrality of music in opera, music has not always been the focus of studies of *The Magic Flute*, and even when it has been, discussion has tended to concentrate on select moments such as favorite arias and Tamino's colloquy with the Priest in the Act 1 finale. Essays in this section, individually and collectively, explore how Schikaneder and Mozart indicate dramatic action in text and music and with attention to the whole opera, providing a sense of character, plot, emotional life, mood, setting, stage direction, and special effects. Important topics, individual moments, and analytical questions are given new and illuminating treatment here.

Part III, "Approaches and Perspectives," addresses issues that might easily fill an entire volume. The five essays in this section explore essential thematic questions in *The Magic Flute*, all of which have taken on new significance in recent decades. Each is immersed in an interpretive tradition and its attendant assumptions, and each engages with that tradition to pose an important question. How should we understand the opera's search for Enlightenment? How should we understand its complex inclusion of exoticism and orientalism? How should we make sense of conflicting claims made about the work's sources and meanings? How should we understand and stage the opera's problematic representations of gender and race? Each of these essays opens a hermeneutic window through which we may view the work anew.

Part IV, "Reception, Interpretation, and Influence," offers five eclectic essays that trace *The Magic Flute* as it gained prominence, not merely on stages in Germany and across Europe but also in the cultural imagination. Readers may be surprised to discover the extensive material culture surrounding the opera, which emerged as early as 1792: from colorful prints and invitation cards to board games and fashion accessories to mechanical clocks and music boxes. In the decade following its premiere and in the early years of the nineteenth century, *The Magic Flute*, perhaps more than any other work by Mozart, played an unexpected role in shaping how future generations would think about Mozart and come to understand him. This may be seen in biography, criticism, literature, and art. A review of what the sources do and do not tell us and how they have influenced our collective understanding of the opera reads like a cautionary tale. This section also includes a brief, but sweeping, overview of the opera as it has been staged in productions ranging from the eighteenth century to the present day and concludes with a tribute to Ingmar Bergman's 1975 film.

For much of its 230-year history, critics and audiences have wanted to understand *The Magic Flute* as a theatrical entertainment with something for everyone, but also as one with a message. The exact nature of the message, however, has been much disputed over the years – at times, passionately. As early as 1794 the opera was read as a political allegory in pamphlets that advanced competing interpretations: pro-Jacobin and anti-Jacobin.[4] It has been understood as a Masonic allegory and as an allegory of Enlightenment. Mozart himself suggests the presence of a message in his letter of October 8–9, 1791, when he complains about the "know-all" who laughed at the "solemn scene" at the beginning of Act 2. "At first, I was patient enough to draw his attention to a few passages. But he laughed at everything. Well, I could stand it no longer. I called him a Papageno and cleared out."[5] Goethe made a comment when contemplating the possibility of staging the "Helena Act" from *Faust II* that similarly assumes a deeper significance: "I will be satisfied if most of the theater-goers enjoy the spectacle; the initiated will not miss the deeper meaning ... just as is the case with *Die Zauberflöte* and other such things."[6] George Bernard Shaw claimed, "*Die Zauberflöte* is the ancestor, not only of the Ninth Symphony but of the Wagnerian allegorical music-drama, with personified abstractions instead of individualized characters as *dramatis personae*."[7] Alfred Einstein described the opera in his biography as "on the surface a suburban machine-comedy, but in reality a piece for all mankind."[8] For many,

Bergman captured this sense of the work as a *theatrum mundi* at the beginning of his film when he panned the audience during the overture to highlight a diverse group of spectators: young and old, men and women, dark-skinned and white. Egil Törnqvist used this moment to argue that "*The Magic Flute*, transcending the boundaries of age, gender and race, has universal significance."[9]

Like all artworks for which such interpretations and claims have been made, *The Magic Flute* is the product of a particular time and place. Without question, the opera has significance, but we cannot be expected to all agree on what that significance is. It should not be made to bear the weight of universalizing claims. For one thing, with apologies to Foucault, the assumption of any dominant view attempts to assert a "principle of thrift in the proliferation of meaning."[10] For another, as many have pointed out in recent decades, the opera's misogyny and racism are significant problems. The Queen and Monostatos cannot be reconciled with such universalizing views. *The Magic Flute*, however, offers us something more valuable: a mirror in which we may see reflected the contradictions and complexity of human nature. The essays in this volume suggest many ways of understanding the opera and approaching its mysteries, allowing us to experience it anew with attention to questions that mattered in Mozart's time and still matter in ours.

Notes

1. Letter of October 7–8, 1791 (the emphasis is Mozart's: "*Stille Beifall!*"). LMF, 966–67; MBA, IV:157.
2. Franz Xaver Niemetschek, *Mozart: The First Biography*, trans. Helen Mautner, with an introduction by Cliff Eisen (New York: Berghahn Books, 2006), 73.
3. Operabase, "Statistics," www.operabase.com/statistics/en.
4. See Jay MacPherson, "*The Magic Flute* and Viennese Opinion," *Man and Nature* 6 (1987): 161–72; H. C. Robbins Landon, *The Golden Years, 1781–1791* (London: Thames & Hudson, 1989), 259–60; COH, 219–20; Rachel Cowgill, "New Light and the Man of Might," in *Art and Ideology in European Opera*, ed. Rachel Cowgill, David Cooper, and Clive Brown (Woodbridge: Boydell, 2010), 207–09.
5. LMF, 969; MBA, IV:160.
6. Cited in Robert Spaethling, *Music and Mozart in the Life of Goethe* (Columbia, SC: Camden House, 1987), 126.

7. From a centenary review in *The Illustrated London News*, December 9, 1891, in Bernard Shaw, *The Great Composers: Reviews and Bombardments*, ed. Louis Crompton (Berkeley: University of California Press, 1978), 97.

8. Alfred Einstein, *Mozart: His Character, His Work*, trans. Arthur Mendel and Nathan Broder (New York: Oxford University Press, 1962), 88.

9. Egil Törnqvist, *Bergman's Muses: Æsthetic Versatility in Film, Theatre, Television and Radio* (Jefferson, NC: MacFarland, 2003), 68.

10. Michel Foucault, "What Is an Author?" trans. Josué V. Harari, in *Foucault Reader*, ed. Paul Rabinow (New York: Pantheon Books, 1984), 118.

Conception and Context

1 | German Opera in Mozart's Vienna

ESTELLE JOUBERT

German Opera in Courtly and Urban Theaters in Vienna: From the National Singspiel (1778) to *Die Zauberflöte* (1791)

"Vienna has its share of all the genres: French comedy, Italian comedy, Italian opera, the grand Noverre ballets, German opera, and the like," writes Johann Pezzl in the first volume of his famous *Skizze von Wien* (1786).[1] German opera in Mozart's Vienna interacted with many other theatrical genres in what was widely celebrated as a rich cosmopolitan European center.[2] This is not to say that the genre did not have its own distinctive musico-dramatic features and theatrical history. Vienna boasts a rich and varied German-language theatrical tradition dating back at least to the late seventeenth century, including Jesuit drama, improvised comedy in folk theaters, often interspersed with song, and musical theater performed by traveling troupes. One of the formative moments for eighteenth-century German opera was Joseph II's 1776 announcement of the opening of the German National Theater, a spoken theatrical enterprise, which performed in one of the two court theaters, the Burgtheater, renamed the Nationaltheater. Two years later, its operatic counterpart, the German National Singspiel, was inaugurated in the same space with a new work, *Die Bergknappen* (The Miners), composed by the company's first music director, Ignaz Umlauf. Featuring accomplished singers such as Caterina Cavalieri (who would later create the role of Konstanze in Mozart's 1782 opera *Die Entführung aus dem Serail* [*The Abduction from the Seraglio*]), this court-operated company produced a number of successful works. Prominent examples include Umlauf's *Die Apotheke* (The Apothecary, 1778), *Die schöne Schüsterin* (The Beautiful Cobbler, 1779), and *Das Irrlicht* (The Will-o'-the-Wisp, 1782); Franz Aspelmayr's *Die Kinder der Natur* (The Children of Nature, 1778); and Salieri's *Der Rauchfangkehrer* (The Chimney Sweep, 1781).

Home of the National Singspiel company, the Burgtheater was regarded as one of the finest theatrical spaces in Europe. Contemporary book and art

9

collector Georg Friedrich Brandes, in a description from 1786, distinguishes it from Parisian theaters by its size and lighting:

It does not have a beautiful form, but it is fine, decorated in white with gold, and the fourth balcony undoubtedly much larger than those [theaters] in Paris. The lighting is also superior here. In Parisian theaters a crown hangs, which nearly fully blinds the audience members in the balconies. In Vienna two lights are installed for two balconies, through which the unpleasantness is much more dispersed, and the amphitheater is better illuminated.[3]

Lighting was costly and the Burgtheater's luxury is revealed through its illumination, where candlelight glistened against the gold and white interior. Brandes emphasizes the opulence of the Viennese court, explaining that "the court here pays for everything, and has the income to do so."[4] During this initial period of the German National Singspiel, the genre was well supported and composers were provided with sufficient resources to create a distinctive German-language operatic repertory. Crucially, Joseph II was not interested in establishing a *Singspiel* troupe in the manner of earlier North German traditions – most notably that of Johann Adam Hiller – in which the performers were actors first, singers second. While a simple folk-like style certainly appears in late eighteenth-century Viennese *Singspiel*, efforts were made to recruit top singers for the National Singspiel enterprise, and a fine orchestra of at least thirty-five players was established, including strings, flutes, oboes, bassoons, horns, and, by 1782, trumpets and a kettledrum player.[5] As a result, the musical writing for Viennese *Singspiel* from 1778 onwards does not shy away from featuring virtuosic singing and lavish orchestral timbres to paint particular scenes or situations.

Though initially successful, the German troupe at the Burgtheater proved difficult to sustain. It was disbanded in 1783 and replaced by a company that produced Italian *opera buffa*, one of the more popular and financially sustainable repertories. When a German company was reinstated in 1785, Emperor Joseph II issued a decree that withdrew performing privileges for all other troupes at the second royal theater, the Kärntnertortheater,[6] making it the new home for the German company, a practice which lasted until 1788. In 1787 Pezzl offered the following explanation for the reinstatement of the German company: "Since a large part of the public does not understand Italian, and one wishes to also entertain them with *Singspiele*, a German opera is established at the same time, which performs primarily at the Kärntnertortheater."[7] The new troupe included singers such as Caterina Cavalieri and Aloysia Lange, and this period witnessed the production of *Singspiele* such as Franz Teyber's *Die Dorfdeputierten* (1785), Mozart's *Der Schauspieldirektor* (1786), Umlauf's *Die glücklichen Jäger* (1786), and Dittersdorf's *Doktor und Apotheker* (1786), among other works.

German opera in late eighteenth-century Vienna was not limited to the two royal theaters. Alongside the opening of the German National Theater in 1776, Joseph II also declared *Spektakelfreiheit*, literally meaning "freedom of spectacle," which allowed new permanent private theaters to operate commercially. Three suburban theaters opened within a decade: the Theater in der Leopoldstadt, which was established in 1781 by Karl Marinelli; the Theater auf der Wieden, which opened in 1787 and was under the direction of Emanuel Schikaneder by 1788; and the Theater in der Josephstadt, which opened in 1788 and was run by Karl Mayer. Even with this *Spektakelfreiheit*, theater in Vienna was heavily censored at both the court and suburban theaters.[8] Each suburban theater specialized with respect to repertory. Marinelli's Theater in der Leopoldstadt was best known for its popular comedy in the Hanswurst tradition – popular entertainment, often improvised comedy, featuring the comic figure of "Hans Sausage." Though of older origins, this type of entertainment had distinctly Viennese roots, which could be traced back to Hanswurst roles created by Josef Anton Stranitzky earlier in the century.[9] Undoubtedly the most famous theatrical fixture of this type in Mozart's day was the comic character Kaspar, who is described here by a contemporary:

But who, then, is Kaspar? He is the comedian at Marinelli's theater in Leopoldstadt. I might almost say [he is] an original genius, the only one of his kind. He knows the public's taste; with his gestures, face-pulling, and his off-the-cuff jokes he so electrifies the hands of the high nobility in the boxes, the civil servants and citizens on the second balcony, and the masses crammed together on the third floor that there is no end to the clapping.[10]

The actor playing Kaspar was Johann La Roche, and he appeared in many spoken plays and German operas, perhaps most famously as Pizichi in Wenzel Müller's *Kaspar der Fagottist* (1791). Like Mozart's *Die Zauberflöte*, this *Singspiel* finds its roots in August Jacob Liebeskind's fairytale "Lulu, oder Die Zauberflöte" (1789). Emanuel Schikaneder's Theater auf der Wieden (renamed the Theater an der Wien after a renovation in 1801) specialized in magic opera (*Zauberoper*) and machine theater (*Maschinentheater*). The space was outfitted with state-of-the-art technology and might well have been the only theater that could have accommodated *The Magic Flute's* elaborate stage transformations.[11] Finally, the Theater in der Josephstadt was perhaps less important for German opera at the time of Mozart but gained importance in the nineteenth century. German opera in Mozart's Vienna thus traversed various theatrical venues, where it interacted with a wide range of theatrical genres, including French and Italian opera performed in translation, spoken theater, ballet, machine theater, and melodrama. This chapter offers an overview of German opera in Mozart's Vienna by considering moments in three seminal works: Ignaz Umlauf's *Die Bergknappen* (1778), which opened Joseph II's National Theater; Wranitzky's *Oberon*, a magic opera performed at the Theater auf der Wieden in 1789; and, finally, Wenzel Müller's *Kaspar der Fagottist*, performed at the Theater in der Leopoldstadt in 1791.

Joseph II's Sonic Jewel at the Nationaltheater: Ignaz Umlauf's *Die Bergknappen* (1778)

Mining featured prominently in Enlightenment scientific, cultural, and political ideals. It served, as Jakob Vogel illustrates, to showcase the economic development of individual states and territories, embodied in "patriotic visions" of mineral collections open to the public.[12] It is no surprise, then, that the *Singspiel* Paul Weidmann and Ignaz Umlauf created to inaugurate Joseph II's German National Singspiel was *Die Bergknappen* (The Miners). Mining was not merely a regional enterprise that would add local color to an operatic work but a matter of patriotic pride. The Hapsburg Empire competed with other European states to expand its royal mineralogical collections and knowledge, and riches particular to geographic regions were fervently excavated and displayed. The premiere of *Die Bergknappen* on February 17, 1778, put Viennese *Singspiel*, like its prized geological stones, on the map of cultural activities in Europe. Musically diverging from previous German *Singspiele* sung by actors in traveling troupes, the royal company invested in star singers and secured a top-quality orchestra to ensure the venture's success. The libretto lists the four soloists alongside their dramatic roles: Walcher, a mining officer, played by Hr. Fux; Sophie (his ward), played by Mlle Caterina Cavalieri; Fritz, a young miner, played by Hr. Ruprecht; and Zelda, a gypsy, played by Madam Stierle.[13] The main plot concerns the young lovers, Sophie and Fritz, whose union is initially prevented by the older Walcher, who intends to marry Sophie himself. After the lovers thwart Walcher's rendezvous with

Sophie, he ties her to a tree, where the gypsy Zelda takes her place at night. Walcher is terrified at what he believes is an evil transformation, and Zelda reveals to Walcher that Sophie is his daughter. When the miners return to work the following morning, singing about retrieving gold for the state, Fritz warns Walcher of a dream in which the mineshaft collapses, but is ignored. The earth trembles, and Fritz's vision comes true. He bravely enters the mineshaft to save Walcher, who is trapped below, and following a safe return, Walcher blesses Fritz and Sophie's union.

One of the most striking musical forms in Viennese *Singspiel* is a highly virtuosic coloratura aria sung by the lead female character. In the first years of the National Singspiel, these roles were sung by Caterina Cavalieri and included Sophie in *Die Bergknappen*, Nannette in *Die Apotheke*, and, perhaps most famously, Konstanze in *Die Entführung aus dem Serail*. This aria represents a significant departure from earlier *Singspiele*, in which virtuous female characters sang simple folk-like tunes to reveal their purity; such arias distinguished these heroines from noble characters singing in a virtuosic style that exemplified the artificiality and excessive luxury of court life. Typically set in a natural realm and often compared to birdsong, this coloratura aria type employs one or two obbligato instruments with which the voice interacts, resembling an instrumental concerto.[14] In a previous scene, Walcher has punished young Sophie by tying her to a tree for the night. An engraving of the scene shows Walcher shining a light on Sophie from a second-story window, enhancing the picturesque effect of the dark scene (Figure 1.1). Sophie's isolation in the garden at night, captured in the image, contributes to the sheer theatrical effect of two arias sung in the garden. The second of these is the coloratura aria "Wenn mir den Himmel." It features a lengthy orchestral introduction with oboe solo, effectively halting the plot and drawing all attention to Cavalieri's agile voice. The oboe opens with what seems at first to be a simple melodic phrase in C major. Yet when the opening figure is repeated, it is transformed into a virtuosic scalar passage, displaying the technical prowess of the performer. Sophie enters with the same melody and her coloratura passages are immediately echoed by the obbligato oboe, fusing into a double display of sonic artistry (Example 1.1a).[15] This bravura passagework draws to a close in the orchestra in the manner of an instrumental concerto, though the aria is not over. The audience is treated to another virtuosic display of dexterity as the second section commences with a repeat of the opening theme. The second installment is even more spectacular than the first, as the voice and oboe intermingle, sometimes passing scalar passages back and forth, and sometimes executing sixteenth-note passages a third apart

Figure 1.1 Scene from *Die Bergknappen* showing Caterina Cavalieri as Sophie. Ink drawing by Carl Schütz, 1778. Courtesy of The Albertina.

(Example 1.1b). Sophie sings of the heavens granting her new life, and, in the manner of an instrumental concerto, this second section is brought to a close by a fermata on the dominant, indicating free vocal embellishment, followed by closing material in the tonic by the entire orchestra. Her heartfelt plea seems to have been heard – she is set free and Zelda takes her place tied up against the tree.

Whereas an aria such as Sophie's emphasizes the importance of star singers in Viennese *Singspiel*, the scene in which the mine shaft collapses underscores the role of the orchestra. At first glance, one might surmise that Umlauf employs various instruments to paint natural phenomena, thereby creating a sonic play-by-play of the event. Yet a closer examination, coupled with aesthetic documents on musical painting, reveals an alternate approach. Orchestral timbre is used in conjunction with descriptions by Fritz and members of the chorus of miners. This enables the audience to experience the disaster from various human perspectives. In other words, the orchestra does not merely paint nature, it paints how humans experience natural phenomena. This aesthetic is in keeping with contemporary writings such as Johann Jakob Engel's "On Painting in Music" (1780).[16] The opening of

Example 1.1a Umlauf, *Die Bergknappen*, Sophie's aria "Wenn mir den Himmel,"
mm. 29–46.

Example 1.1a (cont.)

Example 1.1b Umlauf, *Die Bergknappen*, Sophie's aria "Wenn mir den Himmel," mm. 64–78.

Example 1.1b (cont.)

Example 1.2 Umlauf, *Die Bergknappen*, Fritz and the miners' recitative "Die Erde bebt," mm. 6–17.

the accompanied recitative "Die Erde bebt" (The earth shakes) features fast repeated notes on the strings, which paint the shaking ground (Example 1.2).

Once the chorus of miners alerts Fritz (and the audience) that Walcher is trapped, the texture shifts to slower unison writing; Fritz comments on his decision to risk his life to save his rival. As he descends, the orchestral writing features rapid scalar passages culminating in a tremolando effect; here, two chorus members sing, "Consider the danger, how we trembled." In other words, the audience is being asked to put themselves in the miners' shoes, and Umlauf's orchestral writing assists with this process of identification. It is no coincidence that we also hear from Sophie in an accompanied recitative, "Ein klägliches Geschrei klingt in mein Ohr" (Example 1.3). The oboe solo paints her anxiety as she awaits the outcome of her lover's brave rescue mission. The orchestral writing changes to rapidly repeated thirty-second notes as she describes her shaking limbs. Here, as in the earlier scene with the miners, we are privy to Sophie's physiological responses, which are painted by the orchestra; there is little sonic rendition of the natural disaster.

Joseph II's decision to secure both highly trained singers and orchestral players for the National Singspiel enabled composers such as Umlauf to produce first-rate operatic works in the German language. While many authors have emphasized the *Singspiel*'s apparent reliance on genres such as French *opéra comique* and Italian *opera buffa*, a closer examination of this little-known German repertory suggests a more complex situation. Viennese *Singspiel* engaged with other genres while at the same time rapidly striving to forge its own distinct musico-dramatic forms and conventions. The establishment of this institution served an important purpose: it made the production of German opera a matter of national urgency. The ability to hire star singers such as Caterina Cavalieri allowed for the creation of highly virtuosic concerto-like arias, which featured prominently in Viennese *Singspiel* for several decades. Joseph II's National Singspiel project may not have lasted very long, but it created an impetus for, and influenced, a German operatic repertory that would flourish in urban theaters across Vienna.

Magic Opera at the Theater auf der Wieden: Wranitzky's *Oberon* (1789)

Of the three main suburban commercial theaters in Mozart's Vienna, Schikaneder's Theater auf der Wieden exhibited the strongest predilection for theatrical works that incorporated magical themes, often featuring elaborate stage machines.[17] One of the most popular fairytale *Singspiele* prior to *Die Zauberflöte* was written by composer Paul Wranitzky and

Example 1.3 Umlauf, *Die Bergknappen*, Sophie's recitative "Ein klägliches Geschrei klingt in mein Ohr," mm. 1–15.

librettist Karl Ludwig Giesecke. *Oberon, König der Elfen* premiered on November 7, 1789, and the work was quickly disseminated across the German-speaking realm, with performances in Frankfurt am Main in 1790, Mainz in 1791, Berlin and Augsburg in 1792, and Lemberg, Buda,

Example 1.3 (cont.)

and Pest in 1794; it spread to Linz, Krakow, Prague, Bratislava, Warsaw, and Hamburg during the mid-1790s.[18] Its popular appeal can be attributed not only to its spectacular visual effects but also to various musico-dramatic features, which may be familiar to admirers of Mozart's last opera.

Hüon, a German knight, is sent by King Charlemagne to rescue the Sultan of Bagdad's daughter, Amande. Because the reunion of the fairy king and queen depends on the fidelity of Hüon and Amande, Oberon and Titania are keen to assist in the mission. Together with his father's squire, Scherasmin, Hüon successfully navigates a forest and is guided by Oberon's two genies in his search for Amande. The lovers escape Bagdad on a ship, but a strong storm renders them unexpectedly shipwrecked in Tunisia, where they become captives of Sultan Alamansor and his wife Alamansaris. Despite attempts by the Tunisian rulers to seduce Hüon and Amande, the two remain faithful even in the face of death. Oberon arrives just in time to save the pair, who have withstood all their trails, and Hüon and Amande are freed.

While it is tempting to focus exclusively on musical forms and devices, it is worth keeping in mind that *Singspiel* is an operatic genre that intersperses extended spoken dialogue with song. The dialogue between characters is therefore an essential component of generic analysis. And, as we shall see, theories of comedy in German opera are distinct from its Italian and French counterparts, and these differences often come to the foreground when the spoken dialogue is considered. The opening scene features the serendipitous encounter between Hüon and the comic character Scherasmin: the German knight finds himself lost in a forest, while the local has gathered a bundle of wood and is wearing "wild attire."

(While Scherasmin wants to leave, Hüon holds him back from behind.)

HÜON Stop!

SCHERASMIN *(falls to the ground)* Oh, oh! Wrathful Mr. Death! I called you only because my bundle of wood became too heavy, so that you can help me carry it.

HÜON Simple-minded person!

SCHERASMIN Pardon me for my naïveté. Let me regale on roots and herbs for another five years, maybe I'll improve by then.

HÜON Stupid, who wants to harm you! Just look at me, I am a human being, like you.

SCHERASMIN *(remaining turned away from him)* Someone else might believe you. I know very well that you disguise yourself every day with a different garment from your wardrobe.

HÜON Not true. I am an unfortunate one who has got lost here. Show me the way out of this forest and I will show you my gratitude.

SCHERASMIN *(straightens up)* Well, I will take a risk on your gratitude. But if you take me, poor devil, for a ride, then I'll cry out and woe to you.[19]

This comic encounter between the young knight and the Rousseauian natural man, soon to become his companion on a mission, is designed to amplify the differences in cultivation, social class, and kinds of knowledge. Scherasmin, for instance, has gained sufficient natural knowledge to survive in this hostile environment, whereas Hüon is very much in need of assistance. The two men also recognize their common humanity, and, implicitly, the scene drives home Enlightenment ideals of human equality and freedom. As the conversation unfolds, Scherasmin (and the audience) learns that Hüon is of noble descent and that he is on an impossible mission to travel to Bagdad, where he is to collect a handful of hair from the Sultan's beard, retrieve four of his back teeth, and take his daughter as a bride. Hüon discovers that Scherasmin used to serve his (now deceased) father and has been living in a cave in the forest for some fifteen years. Upon learning of the brave knight's mission, Scherasmin vows to serve him. This outcome alone is a paradigmatic example of typical interactions between working and noble classes in German opera.

Whereas Italian *opera buffa* revels in servants "uncrowning the King,"[20] often through feats of deceit, comedy in late eighteenth-century *Singspiel* is often generated by bringing together the most unexpected characters from vastly different social classes and backgrounds. These "unexpected encounters," such as the one between Hüon and Scherasmin (as well as Tamino and Papageno), showcase both noble and lower-class everyday life experiences and perspectives. More often than not, they feature productive collaboration between social classes. Put another way, comic lower-class characters in *Singspiel* often assist, rather than derail, noble characters in achieving their missions. It is well worth noting that *Singspiel* performers such as Emanuel Schikaneder were superb actors, whose comic gestures especially for characters such as Scherasmin and Papageno kept audiences returning to theaters.[21] In effect, the performative and comic dimensions of *Singspiel* came alive in the spoken dialogue, and they were reinforced by gesture, perhaps signaling the genre's debt to the heritage of the Hanswurst.

Comic Antics and Folklike Music: *Kaspar der Fagottist* (1791) at the Theater in der Leopoldstadt

"One is now hungry for spectacular pieces [*Specktakelstücken*] ... and, as such, this *Magic Zither* was taken up in Vienna and Prague, and was performed numerous times," an anonymous editor writes in the 1794 preface to librettist Joachim Perinet and composer Wenzel Müller's *Kaspar der Fagottist, oder Die Zauberzither* (1791).[22] Marinelli's aforementioned Kaspar figure appears as a comic sidekick named Kaspar Bita, accompanying Prince Armidoro on a mission to rescue Princess Sidi.

Daughter of the radiant star-queen Perifirime, the beautiful Sidi is held captive by an evil sorcerer, Bosphoro. Following their initial encounter in an enchanted forest, Perifirime endows Prince Armidoro with a magic ring and zither, and Bita with an enchanted bassoon, to ensure the success of their mission. While the opera certainly features magical sounds and visual spectacle, including a balloon ride toward the end of the opera, the comic character Bita is undoubtedly one of its main attractions. From his comic encounters with Perifirime – when, for example, he asks if he may drown in her wine cellar if he must die – to lighthearted songs celebrating women and wine, Bita's comic episodes are accentuated by the sound of a bassoon. Like Papageno in *The Magic Flute*, he needs nothing more than bread, wine, and a woman to love, and is easily scared by the sudden, spectacular transformations prevalent in magic operas. For instance, on one occasion, as he and Prince Armidoro approach Bosphoro's castle high on a cliff, the prince turns a magic ring, thunder and lightning ensue, and the prince disappears. Terrified, Bita runs for cover, turns motionless, and then runs to the back of the stage, only to dash back out as flames emerge from the earth. As it happens, the prince has transformed himself into a little old grey man, and Bita recognizes him only by his voice.

Once the pair meet Bosphoro, Armidoro demonstrates his musical talents with the magic zither and, eventually, sings "Es hielt in seinem Felsennest," a *Romanze* (a well-known song type in German opera), in the presence of Princess Sidi. This strophic song form sums up the moral of the story. While it is self-reflexive – it presents the crux of the tale at hand – it is performed within the diegesis of the opera as though it had nothing to do with the plot and is typically set in the distant past. In this instance, Armidoro sings the ancient tale of a young girl held captive in a castle tower high on a rocky cliff. A young knight passes by, hears her screaming, and promises to return at midnight to free her. That night at twelve o'clock the knight returns, throws up a rope for the girl to descend, and the story ends with a romantic kiss. Musically, the *Romanze* features a lilting melody in 6/8, typically beginning in the minor mode, with a turn to the major for the middle portion of the song (Example 1.4 shows the opening of the aria in a contemporary vocal score with an altered verse of unknown origin).[23] First appearing in mid-eighteenth-century French comic opera, the *Romanze* frequently appears in North- and South-German *Singspiel*, often telling the tale of a young woman being rescued from captivity. The simple, repeatable, songlike quality of this form fueled its popularity, and these tunes were disseminated well beyond theaters as folksongs and circulated in popular piano-vocal scores.[24] Armidoro's performance is

Example 1.4 Müller, *Kaspar der Fagottist*, Armidoro's *Romanze* "Es hielt in seinem Felsennest," mm. 1–20 (from a contemporary vocal score with altered text).

followed by Bita teaching Princess Sidi to dance, and naturally in Vienna she would be taught a waltz. Self-reflexive commentary ensues as Bita sings that "a waltz is in keeping with German ways" ("ein Waltz ist so nach deutscher Art") in his Act 2 song "Ein Walzer erhitzet den Kopf und das Blut," thereby celebrating German musical and cultural identity.

The popular folklike quality of Viennese *Singspiel* was not limited to solo numbers. Choruses, especially men's choruses, feature prominently in the genre and are often sung by groups of individuals easily recognizable in society. Whereas Umlauf's *Die Bergknappen* features a chorus of miners, *Die Zauberzither* showcases a group of hunters at the opening of the opera. Their presence is announced with hunting horns – a sound typically limited to the nobility in Italian opera – now appropriated by the bourgeoisie to showcase everyday German life. The opening chorus "Hau hau hau, auf Jäger seyd wach," featuring the echoing sound of working men singing in the forest, presents an idealized image of working-class German citizens contributing to society through manual labor, including mining, forestry, and hunting. Initially populating eighteenth-century *Singspiel*, these character groups would continue to appear in operas such as Carl Maria von Weber's *Der Freischütz* and in nineteenth-century German lieder.

Conclusion

Joseph II's inauguration of the National Singspiel in 1778 provided an impetus for the production of high-quality German-language opera that would rival its French and Italian counterparts. German opera in the decade leading up to *The Magic Flute* (1791) was forged in a transnational context and featured a rich array of musico-dramatic forms that we encounter in Mozart's last opera. Lavish orchestral writing, especially for scenes of heightened emotion, and concert-like virtuosic arias for the female heroine in Umlauf's *Die Bergknappen*, set the stage for Mozart's deployment of the orchestra and the Queen of the Night's arias. Spoken dialogue inspired by German comedic practices featuring encounters between lower-class comic characters and princes enrich our understanding of Papageno and Tamino's first exchange. The comic features of Kaspar, along with the memorable, folklike singing style, made Papageno a familiar and beloved figure. These musico-dramatic forms and features, well established in the decade leading up to *The Magic Flute*, clearly resonated with the public. They likely also contributed to the opera's enduring success and can bring new insights for our enjoyment of Mozart's last opera even today.

Notes

1. Johann Pezzl, *Skizze von Wien*, vol. 1 (Vienna: Kraußische Buchhandlung, 1786), 421.
2. By German opera, I am referring to works originally composed in the German language. It should be noted that Vienna also had an established tradition of performing German translations of French and Italian operas, which, while important in Viennese theatrical life, are not considered in this chapter.
3. Georg Friedrich Brandes, *Bemerkungen über das Londoner, Pariser und Wiener Theater* (Göttingen: Johann Christian Dieterich, 1786), 240.
4. Brandes, 237.
5. For a more detailed discussion of sources relating to the number of orchestral players and instrumental parts in the early years of the National Singspiel company, see Elizabeth Manning, "The National Singspiel in Vienna from 1778 to 1785" (PhD dissertation, Durham University, 1975), 50–51.

6. Manning, 109.

7. Johann Pezzl, *Skizze von Wien*, vol. 3 (Vienna: Kraus, 1787), 425.

8. For a study on morality and censorship in late eighteenth-century Vienna, see Martin Nedbal, *Morality and Viennese Opera in the Age of Mozart and Beethoven* (London: Routledge, 2017).

9. COH, 5.

10. Johann Pezzl, *Skizze von Wien*, vol. 4 (Vienna: Kraus, 1788), 795–96.

11. For a discussion of Vienna's theaters, see John Warrack, "The Viennese Singspiel," in *German Opera: From the Beginnings to Wagner* (Cambridge: Cambridge University Press, 2001), 124–43, at 128–29; W. Edgar Yates, *Theater in Vienna: A Critical History, 1776–1995* (Cambridge: Cambridge University Press, 1996).

12. Jakob Vogel, "Stony Realms: Mineral Collections as Markers of Social, Cultural and Political Spaces in the 18th and Early 19th Century," *Historical Social Research* 40/1 (2015): 301–20.

13. Paul Weidmann, *Die Bergknappen: Ein Originalsingspiel von einem Aufzuge* (Vienna: Logenmeister, 1778), 2.

14. Gretchen A. Wheelock first compared Konstanze's "Martern aller Arten" from Mozart's *Die Entführung aus dem Serail* to an instrumental concerto. See Gretchen A. Wheelock, "Staging Mozart's Women," in *Siren Songs: Representations of Gender and Sexuality in Opera*, ed. Mary Ann Smart (Princeton: Princeton University Press, 2000), 50–57.

15. I would like to thank Harrison Brooks for creating the musical examples for this chapter.

16. Johann Jakob Engel, "On Painting in Music," in *Source Readings in Music History*, ed. Oliver Strunk, rev. edn. Leo Treitler (New York: Norton, 1998), 954–64.

17. For a study on magic operas, see David J. Buch, *Magic Flutes & Enchanted Forests: The Supernatural in Eighteenth-Century Musical Theater* (Chicago: Chicago University Press, 2008).

18. Performances recorded in Austin Glatthorn, "The Theatre of Politics and the Politics of Theatre: Music as Representational Culture in the Twilight of the Holy Roman Empire" (PhD dissertation, Southampton University, 2015); supplemented with findings from the *Annalen des Theaters* and the *Allgemeines europäisches Journal.*

19. See Johann G. C. L. Giesecke, *Oberon, König der Elfen: Eine romantisch-komische Oper in drey Aufzügen, nach Wielands Oberon* (Vienna: Wallishausser, 1806), 3 (translation by the author). The frontispiece on the piano-vocal score also depicts him as a natural man, wearing an animal skin and walking with a large wooden walking stick. See Austrian National Library, Vienna, Ms. 12538, http://data.onb.ac.at/rep/10024A79.

20. See Mary Hunter, *The Culture of Opera Buffa in Mozart's Vienna: A Poetics of Entertainment* (Princeton: Princeton University Press, 1999), 73–84.

21. David Buch writes that "Schikaneder may have sung the role of Scherasmin, although he did not participate in the May 1790 revival, which provides the earliest surviving cast list." Buch, *Magic Flutes & Enchanted Forests*, 293.

22. Joachim Perinet, *Die Zauberzither: Eine komische Oper in drey Aufzügen, Neubarbeitet* (Leipzig: Friedrich August Leo, 1794), 5.

23. For a landmark study on the *Romanze*, see Daniel Heartz, "The Beginnings of the Operatic Romance: Rousseau, Sedaine, and Monsigny," *Eighteenth-Century Studies* 15/2 (1981): 149–78.

24. See Estelle Joubert, "Songs to Shape a German Nation: Hiller's Comic Operas and the Public Sphere," *Eighteenth-Century Music* 3/2 (2006): 213–30.

2 | *The Magic Flute*'s Libretto and German Enlightenment Theater Reform

MARTIN NEDBAL

Most of the operas Mozart produced in Vienna in the last decade of his life, including *The Abduction from the Seraglio*, *The Marriage of Figaro*, *Don Giovanni*, and *Così fan tutte*, were premiered at the Burgtheater, the imperial court theater in the city center. *The Magic Flute*, by contrast, was produced at the Wiednertheater (also known as the Theater auf der Wieden), a private and commercial institution in the Viennese suburbs. The author of *The Magic Flute*'s libretto, Emanuel Schikaneder, was not only the Wiednertheater's director, but also one of its greatest stars, as epitomized by the role of Papageno, which he created specifically for himself. Schikaneder became the director of the Wiednertheater in 1789, when he was approached by his ex-wife Eleonore Schikaneder after the death of Johann Friedel, her codirector and the Wiednertheater's founder. Prior to his directorship at the Wiednertheater, Schikaneder led several theater troupes in Southern Germany and Austria, including in Augsburg, Regensburg, and at Vienna's Kärntnertortheater. *The Magic Flute*'s libretto, therefore, reflects Schikaneder's experience both with the German theater repertoire presented by regional theater companies in the 1770s and 1780s and with the conventions of the repertoire presented on Viennese commercial suburban stages around 1790. At the same time, the libretto reveals Mozart's own sensibilities with respect to German-language theater and his wide-ranging experience with opera at the Vienna court theater.

To what extent Mozart himself may have contributed to the opera's libretto is not entirely clear. What makes the search for Mozart's textual contributions particularly problematic is how little is known about the libretto's inception. In an effort to clarify the enormous richness of subjects and themes in *The Magic Flute*, many previous studies have explored literary and theatrical works that critics and scholars believe influenced the conception and construction of the libretto. Emphasis has also been placed on Mozart's and Schikaneder's personal involvement with Masonry and with the contemporaneous repertoire of the Viennese suburban theaters. A substantial literature attempts to identify the sources from which many specific elements in the libretto derive. At the same time, *The Magic Flute* appears distinct and original, in ways that emerge from its libretto, when compared to many of the works produced by court and commercial theaters of the period.

This essay focuses on *The Magic Flute*'s links to theatrical aesthetics of the Vienna court theater, as well as debates surrounding late eighteenth-century calls for the establishment of a German national theater tradition, and suggests that Schikaneder's and Mozart's experiences with the world of late eighteenth-century German theater traditions shaped *The Magic Flute*'s libretto significantly. At the end, I will attempt to show that Mozart's contributions to Schikaneder's libretto in fact enhance the work's status as both a culmination of decades-long debates about German national theater and a harbinger of a future course for German national opera.[1]

German National Theater Reform

The Magic Flute's libretto reflects numerous ideas that German theorists had been debating since the 1730s in connection with a reform of the national theater. Among the many contexts for understanding the libretto, this may be one of the most important. Mid-eighteenth-century German aestheticians, such as Johann Christoph Gottsched, wanted to raise German theater to the level of the theatrical traditions of other countries, especially France and Italy. To achieve this end, German playwrights focused on works that were fully written out (as opposed to partially improvised), adhered to the principles of French neoclassical drama (such as the Aristotelian unities), and were both morally upright and didactic. One of the goals of the German reformers was to gain financial backing from German states and principalities in order to make German works more competitive with Italian and French operas and dramas, which represented the main fare at most German court theaters in the early 1700s. Through a repertoire of didactic national works, German intellectuals wanted both to transform German audiences into cultivated and well-behaved subjects and to express emerging notions of German national uniqueness (or moral superiority).[2]

Schikaneder and Mozart were both well versed in this tradition. Prior to taking over the directorship of the Wiednertheater in the fall of 1789, Schikaneder had directed German theater companies in various cities that produced elevated German dramas, including works by Goethe and

Lessing. Schikaneder's own spoken and musical dramas also subscribed to reformist viewpoints.[3] Mozart, too, participated in this cultural movement and famously expressed support for German national opera in his letter of February 5, 1783, to Leopold Mozart: "Every nation has its own opera and why not Germany? Is not German as singable as French and English? Is it not more so than Russian?"[4] Several of the works that scholars cite as important sources for *The Magic Flute*'s libretto in fact originated within the tradition of German reform drama. Most prominent among these is Tobias Philipp von Gebler's play *Thamos, König in Ägypten* (Thamos, King of Egypt), which premiered at the Vienna court theater (the Burgtheater) in April 1774. Like *The Magic Flute*, this play involves a conflict between a benevolent high priest/king (Sethos, a deposed Egyptian king) and a power-hungry, manipulative, and cruel priestess (Mirza), who stabs herself when she realizes her evil plan to help her nephew (Pheron) usurp the throne of Egypt has failed. *Thamos* certainly belongs to the tradition of German reform drama because of its elevated plot and didactic ending (the evil characters die, the virtuous ones are rewarded, and righteous behavior is exalted and commented upon throughout the play).

For Gebler's play, Mozart wrote three choruses and five instrumental numbers (four interludes and one postlude). Early versions of two of Mozart's three choruses were performed as part of the first production of Gebler's play at the Vienna Burgtheater in 1774.[5] Mozart revised these two choruses, added a third one, and wrote the instrumental music sometime between 1775 and 1780.[6] Unfortunately, we do not know for certain for which performance this additional incidental music was intended. The similarity between *Thamos* and *The Magic Flute* led early twentieth-century Schikaneder biographer Egon Komorzynski to speculate that Mozart revised and expanded the *Thamos* music for a production by Schikaneder's itinerant troupe, which performed in Salzburg between September 17, 1780 and February 27, 1781.[7] Since there is no record of a Schikaneder production of *Thamos* in Salzburg, however, later scholars connected Mozart's revision to the documented Salzburg performance of the play with an unspecified composer's music by Karl Wahr's company on January 3, 1776.[8] Whether it was performed by Schikaneder's or Wahr's company, Mozart's *Thamos* music does illustrate the composer's exposure to and artistic interactions with German reform drama in the 1770s. We know from a letter to his father of February 15, 1783, that Mozart thought well of this work and was disappointed when the national company in Vienna refused to perform Gebler's *Thamos*, and thus his choruses and interludes.[9]

Although *Thamos* quickly disappeared from German stages, Mozart's choruses and interludes were eventually repurposed for Karl Martin Plümicke's *Lanassa*, another reform German drama. *Lanassa* was performed throughout the 1780s by the troupe of Johann Böhm, including during Mozart's visit to Salzburg in September and October 1783.[10] According to a poster dating from September 17, 1790, Böhm's troupe performed *Lanassa* with Mozart's choruses and interludes in Frankfurt, and Mozart may have attended a performance during his visit to the city for the coronation of Leopold II.[11] Like many German dramas of the 1770s and 1780s, *Lanassa* contains elements that clearly prefigure *The Magic Flute*: The exotic plot takes places in an unspecified Indian port and is filled with depictions of religious rites; the drama's main theme is the criticism of religious fanaticism and human sacrifice (the main heroine's much older husband dies and she is supposed to be burnt alive on his funeral pyre). The most prominent connection to *The Magic Flute* is the claim of the main hero, General Montalban, that he is no conqueror but simply a human ("Kein Überwinder bin ich, ich bin ein Mensch"), which prefigures the Speaker's and Sarastro's statements that Tamino is not just a prince but a human (Speaker: "Er ist Prinz." Sarastro: "Noch mehr – er ist Mensch!").[12]

In Vienna, the most powerful endorsement of the reformist movement occurred in 1776, when Emperor Joseph II transformed the court theater into a National Theater devoted solely to presenting German spoken plays; the German opera troupe, or National Singspiel, was added in 1778. Shortly after his move to Vienna, Mozart became involved with the National Singspiel, for which he composed *The Abduction from the Seraglio*, which premiered in 1782. In two famous letters to his father dating from the fall of 1781, Mozart provides numerous details about his working relationship with Viennese playwright Gottlieb Stephanie the Younger on *The Abduction*'s libretto. For example, Mozart asked Stephanie to reorder the musical numbers and rework the plot, which led to the creation of a new, moralistic finale at the end of the second act.[13] It is possible (likely, even) that Mozart was similarly involved in the inception and development of *The Magic Flute*'s libretto. The libretto of *The Abduction* in many ways prefigures that of *The Magic Flute*, particularly in its reformist intensity (the opera presents exemplary actions that are explicitly promoted by text and music) and its variety of styles (a libretto that combines simple, strophic songs with more complex arias; a quartet resembling an Italian comic opera finale; and a vaudeville conclusion akin to those in contemporary French *opéra comique*).[14]

After Joseph II decided to replace the National Singspiel with an Italian opera company in 1783, German opera in Vienna moved into the hands of private entrepreneurs. Remnants of the reformist attitude toward opera was at times rekindled at the state-supervised Kärntnertortheater, which was rented out to private theater companies and for a brief period (1785–88) accommodated a variant of the court-supported National Singspiel.[15] At the request of Joseph II, Schikaneder became one of the temporary tenants at the Kärntnertortheater between November 5, 1784 and January 6, 1785, and during his brief stay in Vienna his company featured numerous German operatic works originally introduced by the National Singspiel. He even opened his brief Viennese *stagione* with *The Abduction*.[16] Before returning to Vienna in 1789, Schikaneder traveled through various parts of Southern Germany, and his longest director position was in Regensburg (between February 1787 and August 1789), where he featured both *The Abduction* and *Lanassa*.[17] German reform drama therefore represents a crucial context for Schikaneder's and Mozart's work on the libretto for *The Magic Flute*.

Fairy-Tale Operas in the Viennese Suburbs

In creating the libretto for *The Magic Flute*, Schikaneder also drew from a number of magical, fairy-tale operas that were particularly popular with the Viennese public. Such works were already prominent in the repertoire of the National Singspiel and its Kärntnertortheater variant. Among the most popular ones were the Viennese German adaptation of André Grétry's *Zemire et Azor* (1778), Ignaz Umlauf's *Das Irrlicht* (Will-o'-the-Wisp, 1782), and Joseph Martin Ruprecht's *Das wütende Heer* (The Wild Army, 1787). But it was the suburban operatic repertoire that had the most direct influence on *The Magic Flute*'s libretto. German opera flourished in commercial theaters that began appearing after 1776 in the Viennese suburbs. In the late 1780s and early 1790s, productions of magical operas shifted to the Leopoldstadt Theater and, after Schikaneder's assumption of the directorship there, also to the Wiednertheater.

A particularly important prototype of Viennese magical, fairy-tale opera is *Oberon, König der Elfen*, premiered by Schikaneder's troupe on November 11, 1789, with a libretto by Wiednertheater actor and playwright Karl Ludwig Giesecke and music by Paul Wranitzky. For the Viennese *Oberon*, Giesecke adapted (or, according to some commentators, plagiarized) the North German text written in 1788 and published in 1789 by the actress Friederike Sophie Seyler, who in turn based her work on Christoph Martin Wieland's 1780 epic poem *Oberon*. In his revision, Giesecke executed many changes that closely resemble those found in earlier Viennese librettos that also adapt preexisting texts (such as Stephanie's libretto for *The Abduction*). Wranitzky was no doubt closely familiar with these earlier Viennese operas, since in the late 1780s he served as the orchestral director, first at the Kärntnertortheater during the National Singspiel revival, and later at the Burgtheater. Giesecke reduced passages of spoken dialogue and the number of arias, ultimately allowing for fewer but longer musical numbers (with more of a sense of contrast): the first act of Seyler's original libretto, for example, features two arias for both the Papageno-like servant Scherasmin and the Tamino-like hero Hüon, whereas the corresponding first act of Giesecke's text features only one aria for each, allowing for greater stylistic distinction.[18] Giesecke also created numerous ensembles, either from Seyler's solo numbers or from her dialogues. At the very beginning, for example, Giesecke transforms a spoken monologue and an aria for Scherasmin into an introductory multisectional action duet for Scherasmin and Hüon, in which Scherasmin complains about his lonely existence in the woods (where he retired after the death of his master, Hüon's father), is scared by the approaching Hüon (whom he mistakes for the bringer of death), and then hides and is discovered by Hüon. Also commensurate with Viennese German libretto adaptation is Giesecke's creation of multisectional finales for the first and second acts. Just as in *The Abduction* and other Viennese works from the National Singspiel era, Giesecke's finales alternate musical dialogue with moments of reflection, which are often moralistic.[19] In the first-act finale, for instance, Oberon exhorts Hüon to be brave and virtuous, and Hüon promises to be just that. Oberon then addresses a group of dervishes, whom he had earlier punished for religious hypocrisy, urging them to be true to their religious beliefs. As Oberon flies away, the finale concludes with a section in which Hüon, Scherasmin, and the dervishes celebrate Oberon, thank him for his "teachings," and promise to devote themselves to virtue. The finales of *Oberon* and its Viennese predecessors likely served as models for the finales of *The Magic Flute*, where passages of dialogue alternate with communal, reflective (and often moralistic) moments. Many passages come to mind: the first-act finale opens with the Three Boys preaching virtue to Tamino, and the second-act finale opens with an episode in which the Three Boys prevent Pamina from stabbing herself. Mozart usually introduces striking shifts in tempo, dynamics, and style to emphasize these maxims – in particular, he often employs the pastoral style in connection with moralistic and utopian ideas.[20]

Following the production of *Oberon*, Schikaneder's company produced several magical operas, which recent studies have identified as the closest precursors of, and models for, *The Magic Flute* libretto. Many of these works were heavily indebted to another work of Wieland's (written in collaboration with his son-in-law, J. A. Liebeskind): the three volumes of fairy tales titled *Dschinnistan*, published between 1786 and 1789. Three musical works based on *Dschinnistan* premiered in Vienna in the seasons leading up to *The Magic Flute*. The earliest one, *Der Stein der Weisen, oder Die Zauberinsel* (The Philosopher's Stone, or The Magic Island), premiered a little over a year after *Oberon*, on November 11, 1790, with a libretto by Schikaneder. The work became particularly prominent in 1996, after musicologist David Buch found that a manuscript score of *Der Stein der Weisen*, newly returned to the Hamburg State and University Library from Russia, contained attributions of two segments of the second-act finale to Mozart. (Even before this discovery, the second-act duet "Nun liebes Weibchen" [K. 625] had been generally considered Mozart's work because of the existence of a partial autograph).[21] *Der wohltätige Derwisch, oder Die Schellenkappe* (The Beneficent Dervish, or The Fool's Cap) was also composed to a text by Schikaneder by a collection of composers. Premiered in early 1791, just a few months before *The Magic Flute*, its musical numbers are not as extensive as those in *Der Stein der Weisen*. This is reflected in its genre designation: Whereas surviving printed librettos referred to *Der Stein der Weisen* as "eine heroisch-komische Oper" (a heroic-comic opera), *Der wohltätige Derwisch* was designated a "Lust- und Zauberspiel" (comedic and magical play). (The third *Dschinnistan* opera was *Kaspar der Fagottist, oder Die Zauberzither* and will be discussed in the section below.)

Composed by the same author for the same company and theater, the texts of *Der Stein der Weisen* and *Der wohltätige Derwisch* share numerous similarities with *The Magic Flute*. All three works are infused with aspects of the *Dschinnistan* tales, including supernatural elements, magical objects, religious ceremonies, exotic settings, princely couples accompanied by comical servant ones, and wise, Sarastro-like figures. Scholars have identified numerous elements of *The Magic Flute*'s libretto that originated in the tales of *Dschinnistan*, one of which was in fact titled "Lulu, oder Die Zauberflöte" (Lulu, or The Magic Flute). Other characters and plot devices Schikaneder most likely derived from *Dschinnistan* include the Three Boys ("Die klugen Knaben" [The Clever Boys], volume III, story 3); the tests of flood and fire and the ancient Egyptian setting ("Der Stein der Weisen," volume I, story 4); a villainous slave who spies on the heroine and is punished rather than rewarded for it ("Adis und Dahy," volume I, story 2); and a hero who falls in love with the heroine's portrait ("Neangir und seine Bruder" [Neangir and his Brothers], volume I, story 3).[22] Whereas the German reform drama represents an important general context for the libretto of *The Magic Flute*, many specific elements of the opera were clearly derived from fairy-tale *Singspiele* of the Viennese suburban theaters and late eighteenth-century fairy-tale literature.[23]

Suburban Subversion and Parody

To fully understand *The Magic Flute* libretto, we must consider both how it resembles and how it differs from the works that immediately preceded it in the suburban theaters. *Der Stein der Weisen* and *Der wohltätige Derwisch* served as models in some respects; however, they do present a slightly different tone from *The Magic Flute* in that they partially abandon the reformist zeal that characterized the German reform repertoire at the Viennese National Theater. In these pre-*Magic Flute* works, Schikaneder seems to reference works produced at the Leopoldstadt Theater, his main competitor in Vienna at this time. According to Buch, the Leopoldstadt Theater started producing a lot of magical works after 1784, and this trend continued into the 1790s.[24] The aesthetic principles pursued in these works differed substantially, however, from those at the National Theater. The Leopoldstadt Theater to a large extent continued the traditions of earlier Viennese popular theater. Although Leopoldstadt plays were no longer improvised, as was the case throughout the first half of the eighteenth century, they still contained risqué humor, coarse language, and often engaged in parodies of more serious dramas. These elements often centered around the stock character of a comical male servant figure, called Hanswurst in the early part of the eighteenth century and Kaspar (or Kasperl) in the Leopoldstadt productions.[25]

One Leopoldstadt opera with coarse comedy that scholars have cited as related in content to *The Magic Flute* is *Das Sonnenfest der Braminen* (The Brahmins' Sun Festival), an exotic opera with a plot related to that of *The Abduction*, which premiered on September 9, 1790. Several scenes of *Das Sonnenfest* explicitly ridicule elevated situations from reform dramas, such as *Lanassa*. The plots of both works center on righteous Europe and heroes who rescue heroines in distress from either a harem (*Das Sonnenfest*) or an inhumane religious ritual (*Lanassa*). But the Leopoldstadt work upends the virtuous borrowed plot. In *Lanassa*, the European hero is aided by the long-lost brother of the heroine, who, even before recognizing his relationship to the heroine, decides to save her for humanistic reasons ("Menschenliebe"). In *Das Sonnenfest*, by contrast, the main hero is nearly seduced by his long-lost sister in a suggestive duet.[26]

The same irreverent ethos dominates another pre-Mozart *Dschinnistan* opera, *Kaspar der Fagottist, oder Die Zauberzither* (Kaspar the Bassoonist, or The Magic Zither), premiered at the Leopoldstadt Theater on June 8, 1791.[27] In the nineteenth century, this work became a source of yet another controversy surrounding *The Magic Flute*'s libretto: in an 1841 article, Friedrich Treitschke suggested that after the premiere of *Kaspar der Fagottist* Mozart and Schikaneder transformed the initially sympathetic Queen of the Night into a villainess to avoid replicating the plot of this Leopoldstadt opera, which featured a sympathetic fairy queen Perifirime. This theory is generally discredited nowadays.[28] The operas do share numerous features, including a prominent use of "magic" instruments. This particular shared feature, however, illustrates the different aesthetics guiding the two works. In *The Magic Flute*, Tamino's flute and Papageno's magic bells tame wild animals, give Tamino and Pamina encouragement and strength at crucial moments, and pacify Monostatos and his crew. The opera's celebration of music's ethical powers creates a connection to the Orpheus story, the subject of numerous operas and ballets featured at court theaters in Vienna and elsewhere.[29] Gluck's *Orfeo ed Euridice*, which premiered in Vienna in 1762, became the most celebrated representative of this elevated type of court opera; it was performed several times at the National Theater in 1782 and 1783. *Der Fagottist*, by contrast, ridicules rather than emulates the Orpheus myth and *opera seria*.[30] *Der Fagottist*'s counterpart to the magic flute is a magic zither presented by Perifirime to Tamino-like Prince Armidoro, but it is mainly used in various amorous adventures. Even less like its *Magic Flute* counterpart is the eponymous magic bassoon. Throughout the opera it is associated with sexual innuendo, such as when Kaspar uses it to impress the servant Palmire or when he complains about his broken "Blasinstrument" (blowing horn) after returning from a tryst with Palmire. Also peculiar is the duet in which Kaspar gives a bassoon lesson to the Monostatos-like character Zumio, in which quite explicit references to oral sex abound.[31]

Elements of similar fairground humor, quite distant from the preferences of German reformists, can also be found in *Der Stein der Weisen* and other magical operas by Schikaneder and his team. For example, *Der Stein der*

Weisen plays humorously with the topic of marital infidelity when it presents how the evil magician Eutifronte abducts the Papagena-like character Lubanara, who was earlier heard praising infidelity in an aria, and places a pair of gilded antlers (a prominent symbol of cuckoldry) on the head of Lubano, the Papageno-like husband of Lubanara. Schikaneder and his compositional team further ridicule Lubano's unhappy marriage by bringing in a chorus of hunters, who mistake Lubano for a stag and chase him around.

Reformist Qualities of *The Magic Flute*'s Libretto

Even though *The Magic Flute* libretto emerged from, and is closely associated with, the world of Viennese popular suburban theater, it differs from that tradition significantly in that it mainly avoids the parodistic elements featured in the Leopoldstadt operas and Schikaneder's other Wiednertheater librettos, such as *Der Stein der Weisen*. In fact, a few scenes in *The Magic Flute* appear to engage *Der Stein der Weisen* directly in a moralistic dialogue. For example, the padlock the Three Ladies place on Papageno to punish him for pretending to be the killer of the serpent that threatened Tamino at the beginning of the opera has a parallel in the padlock that Lubano places on the door of his cabin to prevent the unfaithful Lubanara from meeting other men. But such parallels also point to ways in which the librettos of these operas differ significantly. In *Der Stein der Weisen*, the locking of the door occurs within a duet for Lubano and Lubanara (No. 5, "Tralleralara! Tralleralara!"), and the two characters react to it with a communal utterance of nonsensical syllables: "Mum, mum! Dideldum!" In *The Magic Flute*, the first-act quintet (No. 5, "Hm! Hm! Hm!") begins with the unlocking of Papageno's padlock and then leads to a communal statement, a maxim that explains the moralistic significance of the episode:

Dies Schloss soll deine/meine Warnung sein.	This padlock is to warn you/me.
Bekämen doch die Lügner alle	If the lips of all liars
Ein solches Schloss vor ihren Mund;	Could be padlocked like this:
Statt Hass, Verleumdung, schwarzer Galle	Instead of hate, slander, and black bile,
Bestünde Lieb und Bruderbund.	Love and brotherhood would reign.

Mozart launches the maxim with the musical phrase that introduced the nonsensical reflection in *Der Stein der Weisen*, as if he wanted to point out the striking difference between the neglect of the padlock's moralistic potential in the earlier work and the didactic significance of the maxim in the later opera.

The attention to communal, moralizing statements in *The Magic Flute* exemplifies calls for such statements in German reformist theater criticism of the time. For example, a 1789 essay in the *Kritisches Theater-Journal von Wien* complains that Karl Friedrich Hensler's Leopoldstadt play *Das Glück ist kugelrund, oder Kasperls Ehrentag* (Happiness is Fickle, or Kaspar's Day of Honor, premiered on February 17, 1789) does not present clear moral truths and should not be performed any longer; according to the critic, only fairy-tale works with clear moral statements are worthy of presentation.[32] *The Magic Flute*'s libretto is governed by ideas similar to those expressed in the critique, as demonstrated by an actual link to the quite popular *Das Glück ist kugelrund*.[33] In both works, characters attempt to commit suicide by hanging themselves. In Hensler's play, Kasperl's suicide attempt leads to magical comedy: first, when the ladder that he climbs to reach a tree branch disappears; and second, when a door with a nail to hold the noose transforms into a cloud from which a fairy appears to tell him she is bringing him happiness.[34] In the second-act finale of *The Magic Flute*, Papageno is prevented from hanging himself by the Three Boys who, unlike Hensler's fairy, draw a moralistic warning from the situation: "Stop, Papageno! And be smart! / Life is lived only once, let that be sufficient for you." ("Halt ein, o Papageno! und sey klug. / Man lebt nur einmal, dies sey dir genug.")

The subtle, yet significant, differences between *The Magic Flute* and its most immediate predecessors (the fairy-tale operas of Schikaneder and the Leopoldstadt authors) bring us back to the question of Mozart's involvement in the libretto's production. The opera's adherence to the principles of a reformed, didactic German national theater contrasts with most other Schikaneder librettos from the Wiednertheater era, and this in turn suggests that Mozart may have been responsible for the difference. That Schikaneder would be willing to make concessions to Mozart's suggestions about the overall aesthetic character of the libretto is not surprising, since, compared to the other composers working for the suburban theaters in Vienna, Mozart was an international celebrity. Mozart was also the first composer writing for the Viennese suburban stage who also had experience with both the National Theater and the court theater in Vienna. In the works created with his long-term creative team, Schikaneder seems to be concerned about competing with the parodistic and risqué productions at the Leopoldstadt Theater and heeding the principle, which he himself mentioned in prefaces to his own works, that morals and reformist uprightness are not good for the box office of his commercial institution.[35]

However, in his collaboration with Mozart, Schikaneder clearly emphasizes elements associated with genres, such as the German reform drama and *opera seria*, produced predominantly by state- or court-supported institutions. This includes engaging in moralizing statements, especially on the part of Sarastro and the Priests. Some of these statements are reprehensible – among the most straightforwardly racist or sexist utterances in all of eighteenth-century opera – and are usually censored in present-day productions of *The Magic Flute*, although we can assume that they were widely accepted in the eighteenth century. These statements, however, do contribute to the unique quality of the opera's libretto and its combination of aesthetic viewpoints associated with suburban, commercial, and popular theatrical traditions on the one hand, and reformist, national, state- and court-sponsored traditions on the other.

The Magic Flute is a notoriously complex work that accommodates a large number of different theatrical and musical styles. The opera's connection to the ideals of German reform drama is particularly significant, because it illustrates that even within the confines of a private, commercial theater Mozart and Schikaneder aimed at the creation of a high-minded work. In the handwritten list of his compositions, Mozart famously referred to *The Magic Flute* as a "teutsche Oper" (German opera), an unusual designation since the titles of most other contemporary Viennese operas referred to the works' dramaturgical features, not their language or national character (e.g., *heroisch-komische Oper* or *lustiges Singspiel*). The resonance between *The Magic Flute* and the moralistic concepts of German national theater suggests that the designation might have had a symbolic meaning – that for Mozart *The Magic Flute*, with its didacticism, represented a truly German national work.

Notes

1. The double-sided nature of *The Magic Flute* as both a crowning achievement and a step in a new direction is discussed in Christoph Wolff, *Mozart at the Gateway to His Fortune* (New York: Norton, 2012), 107–33.
2. For a more detailed discussion of these developments, see Martin Nedbal, *Morality and Viennese Opera in the Age of Mozart and Beethoven* (New York: Routledge, 2017), 1–11.
3. Anke Sonnek, *Emanuel Schikaneder: Theaterprinzipal, Schauspieler und Stückenschreiber* (New York: Bärenreiter, 1999), esp. 23–84.
4. LMF, 839; MBA, III:255.

5. See Dexter Edge, "Mozart's Choruses for *Thamos, König in Ägypten* (20 April 1774)," in *Mozart: New Documents*, ed. Dexter Edge and David Black, first published June 12, 2014, www.mozartdocuments.org/documents/20-april-1774/ (accessed March 22, 2023).

6. Wolfgang Plath and Alan Tyson date the orchestral numbers to 1776–77 and the revised choruses to 1779–80. See Alan Tyson, *Mozart: Studies of Autograph Scores* (Cambridge, MA: Harvard University Press, 1987), 24–25.

7. Egon Komorzynski, *Emanuel Schikaneder: Ein Beitrag zur Geschichte des deutschen Theaters* (Vienna: Doblinger, 1951), 56–58.

8. Neal Zaslaw, "Mozart's Incidental Music to *Lanassa* and His *Thamos* Motets," in *Music Libraries and the Academy: Essays in Honor of Lenore Coral*, ed. James P. Cassaro (Middleton, WI: A-R Editions, 2007), 57–58.

9. It is easy to imagine that Mozart approached Böhm during his visit to Salzburg later in 1783 and that he perhaps arranged the *Thamos* music for Böhm's production of *Lanassa*, though there is no evidentiary support for such a supposition.

10. Zaslaw, "Mozart's Incidental Music," 60.

11. Joseph Heinz Eibl, ed., *Mozart: Die Dokumente seines Lebens: Addenda und Corrigenda* (Kassel: Bärenreiter, 1978), 64. The way in which Mozart's music was fitted to the choruses from the fifth act of Plümicke's drama becomes clearer from the orchestral score preserved in the Frankfurt University Library and described in Wolfgang Plath, "Mozartiana in Fulda und Frankfurt," *Mozart-Jahrbuch* 1968–70, 366–67.

12. *Lanassa* (Vienna: Hartmann and Logenmeister, 1786), 33.

13. Nedbal, *Morality and Viennese Opera*, 64–72.

14. Ibid., 48–58.

15. Ibid., 112–16.

16. Sonnek, *Emanuel Schikaneder*, 60–66.

17. Ibid., 75–84.

18. A chart of Giesecke's changes in Seyler's libretto can be found in Paul Wranitzky, *Oberon: König der Elfen*, ed. Christoph-Hellmuth Mahling and Joachim Veit (Munich: Henle, 1993), II:546–51. The vocal numbers in the first act of Giesecke's libretto are: an introductory action duet for Hüon and Scherasmin, Hüon's aria, a duet for Hüon and Scherasmin, Titania's aria, an oracle's accompanied recitative, a chorus of nymphs, Oberon's aria, Oberon's recitative, a chorus of the dervishes, and a multisectional finale.

19. On the structures of Viennese German opera finales in the early 1780s, see Nedbal, *Morality and Viennese Opera*, 64–79.

20. On maxims in *The Magic Flute*'s first- and second-act finales, see Nedbal, *Morality and Viennese Opera*, 135–45.

21. David J. Buch, "Mozart and the Theater auf der Wieden: New Attributions and Perspectives," *Cambridge Opera Journal* 9/3 (1997): 195–232. The Viennese copyist of the Hamburg manuscript score, and author of the attributions, was the

actor and singer Kaspar Weiß. See Dexter Edge, "Mozart's Viennese Copyists" (PhD dissertation, University of Southern California, 2001), chap. 10; David Buch, "*Der Stein der Weisen*, Mozart, and Collaborative Singspiels at Emanuel Schikaneder's Theater auf der Wieden," *Mozart-Jahrbuch* 2000, 89–124.

22. COH, 26–27.

23. On the idea of hierarchical levels of influence on the libretto of *The Magic Flute*, see David J. Buch, *Magic Flutes & Enchanted Forests: The Supernatural in Eighteenth-Century Musical Theater* (Chicago: University of Chicago Press, 2008), 332ff.

24. Buch, 282.

25. See Beatrix Müller-Kampel, *Hanswurst, Bernadon, Kasperl: Spaßtheater im 18. Jahrhundert* (Vienna: Schöningh, 2003).

26. This duet is discussed in Nedbal, *Morality and Viennese Opera*, 126–27.

27. Rommel uses the words "grob-burlesker Art" (coarsely burlesque manner) when describing this work. Otto Rommel, *Die Alt-Wiener Volkskomödie: Ihre Geschichte vom barocken Welt-Theater bis zum Tode Nestroys* (Vienna: Schroll, 1952), 551.

28. Friedrich Treitschke, "*Die Zauberflöte, Der Dorfbarbier, Fidelio*: Beitrag zur musikalischen Kunstgeschichte," *Orpheus: Musikalisches Taschenbuch für das Jahr 1841*, ed. August Schmidt (Vienna: Riedls Witwe und Sohn, 1841), 239–64. For an argument against the plot-shift theory, see COH, 29–34. Buch also points out that a similar plot reversal occurs in *Der Stein der Weisen*, where the Tamino-like hero Nadir is temporarily turned by the evil Queen-of-the-Night-like Eutifronte against the Sarastro-like Astromonte. Buch, *Magic Flutes & Enchanted Forests*, 334–35.

29. For an overview of recent literature on *The Magic Flute* and the Orpheus myth, see Simon P. Keefe, *Mozart in Vienna: The Final Decade* (New York: Cambridge University Press, 2017), 578n108.

30. Several parodies of Gluck's second reform opera, *Alceste*, in fact appeared at the Leopoldstadt Theater in 1782 and 1783, probably in response to the Italian production of the opera at the National Theater in 1782. The most popular of these was *Alceste: Opera seria, wobey Kasperle den Höllengott spielen wird* (Alceste: Opera seria, in which Kasperle will play the God of the Underworld). See Rommel, *Die Alt-Wiener Volkskomödie*, 533.

31. See Nedbal, *Morality and Viennese Opera*, 142–45.

32. *Kritisches Theater-Journal von Wien*, February 28, 1789 (Vienna: Mathias Ludwig, 1789), 72–80. See also Buch, *Magic Flutes & Enchanted Forests*, 273.

33. The play was performed fifty-seven times between 1789 and 1798; see Rommel, *Die Alt-Wiener Volkskomödie*, 543.

34. *Das Glück ist kugelrund, oder Kasperl's Ehrentag* (Vienna: Goldhann, 1792), 11–12.

35. See Nedbal, *Morality and Viennese Opera*, 146.

Emanuel Schikaneder and the Theater auf der
Wieden

LISA DE ALWIS

The Magic Flute was conceived and created specifically for the Theater auf
der Wieden and its company of players, under the direction of Emanuel
Schikaneder. Despite its status today as a work of genius, Schikaneder and
Mozart's opera was not conceived in a vacuum, so understanding its
vibrant theatrical context can help us avoid subscribing to what David
Buch has called "the myth of singularity."[1] Like all works of art, *The Magic
Flute* was a product of its time and place: Schikaneder and other librettists
had written magical operas for the Theater auf der Wieden in the years
immediately preceding 1791; Mozart and Schikaneder created roles with
specific singers and their talents in mind; and other theaters were also
presenting operas featuring similar characters and plotlines. Certain features of *The Magic Flute* adhere to traditions that were already in place at
this theater – a plot that includes a serious couple as well as a comic one, for
example, or the simple style of Papageno's entrance aria. And musical
aspects of the opera, such as the role of the choruses, bear more resemblance to the works of the theater's regular or "house" composers than they
do to the works of other composers that were also performed there.[2] The
personnel of the Theater auf der Wieden were also influenced by other
theaters in the city, particularly by the Theater in der Leopoldstadt, their
main competitor. This chapter provides an overview of the Theater auf der
Wieden under Schikaneder's directorship in the years leading up to the
premiere of *The Magic Flute*, in order to situate the opera in its original
performance venue.

The Freihaus auf der Wieden and Its Theater

Until 1850, the city of Vienna comprised only the area that is today's first
district. It was encircled by a massive, defensive wall, which, in turn, was
surrounded by a flat area called the glacis, which served to expose invading
armies to the city's defenders. Abutting the glacis were the various suburbs
or *Vorstädte*, all of which are today a part of the city of Vienna. In 1781, five

years after Joseph II announced his *Spektakelfreiheit*, which allowed private theaters to put on performances for profit, Karl Marinelli opened his Theater in der Leopoldstadt, the first suburban theater in Vienna. Schikaneder, who in 1786 was employed at the Burgtheater, appealed to Joseph for special permission to open a theater just like Marinelli's, but on the glacis, in a location where people living in three suburbs would have had easy access to it. Joseph turned down the request, but agreed that Schikaneder could open a theater within a Viennese suburb instead. In the end, it was a German actor and director, Christian Rossbach, who received permission from Joseph in 1787 to build a theater in the suburb of Wieden (which was incorporated as Vienna's fourth district in 1850).

The Theater auf der Wieden, as it came to be called because of its location in the eponymous suburb and its proximity to the Wieden river, was a two-story rectangular theater that could seat about 800 people and operated from 1787 to 1801. It was sometimes referred to as the Wiednertheater or the Schikanedertheater, but should not be confused with the Theater an der Wien, which replaced it in 1801 and still exists today. Although the Theater auf der Wieden was a free-standing building, it was situated within the perimeter of an enormous apartment complex in greater Vienna called the Starhembergisches Freihaus, after the Starhemberg family, which had owned the land as a fief since 1643. Four years later, upon payment of a thousand gulden to the court, the family was released from owing property taxes in perpetuity, hence the name "Freihaus."[3] After several fires and much subsequent rebuilding, it became, by the end of the eighteenth century, the largest privately owned apartment complex in Vienna. The Freihaus encompassed 25,000 square meters (269,098 square feet), with 402 buildings of various sizes, and housed around 10,000 people. The floorplan of the building gives a sense of how large the Freihaus was, particularly if we note how the 800-seat theater, located below the third courtyard (*Hof*), comprises a small fraction of the total space (see Figure 3.1.). We know that by the mid-nineteenth century the complex boasted a concert hall, a library, a dance school, a sports center, and the businesses of countless artisans. With excellent drinking water to be had from its many wells, the Freihaus was essentially a self-contained city within the city. Tailors and shoemakers provided their services, and small shops sold everything from textiles, needles, and nails, to socks, pens, ink, and even violin strings.[4] By adding a theater to the Freihaus, Rossbach, the first director, was probably hoping to take advantage of the patronage of a built-in audience.[5]

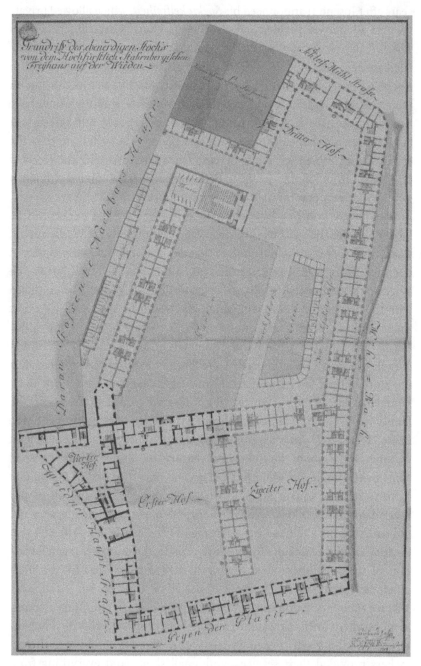

Figure 3.1 Plan of the ground floor of the Hochfürstlich Starhembergischen Freihaus auf der Wieden in Mozart's day. The Freihaus Theater can be seen above the garden. Andreas Zach, landscape architect, 1789. Pen, ink, and watercolor. Courtesy of the Niederösterreichisches Landesarchiv/St. Pölten, Nö. Regierung (vor 1850), E 1 Zl. 22924 bei 19798 ex 1789.

The theater building commissioned by Rossbach (in which *The Magic Flute* would eventually premiere) was built by Andreas Zach, who was also responsible for renovations of the entire Freihaus. According to Michael Lorenz, the original plans for the theater show that its walls were of masonry, but the interior was made of wood, in keeping with the conventions of such buildings at the time. While it was not physically connected to the surrounding, far larger Freihaus building (it stood in the middle of a field), its tiled roof was taller than the apex of the Freihaus's roof.[6] The plans for the theater also show a wooden passageway – one of six in the Freihaus – which was likely intended to allow audience members to cross the courtyard and arrive at the theater without muddying their feet.[7] The theater's dimensions were thirty by fifteen meters, with almost half of that space occupied by the twelve-meter-deep stage area, presumably to allow for elaborate sets.[8] Surviving engravings from some productions as well as descriptions of sets in contemporary press reports attest to their grandeur. Tall buildings and realistic trees flank singers as they descend into the ground on a moving platform in *Der Stein der Weisen* (The Philosopher's Stone), and a review of *Babylons Pyramiden* (The Pyramids of Babylon) refers to the theater's technical capability to surprise the audience with a rustic, hut-like exterior that gives way to show a large, impressive temple, or an enormous haystack that opens up to reveal many beautifully rendered rooms.[9] As to the appearance of the interior of the theater, it was painted simply and included a proscenium arch flanked by life-size statues of a knight with a dagger and an elegantly masked lady, but it is unclear whether it looked this way from its early days. Entrance to the theater cost seventeen kreutzer to the parterre and seven to the upper floor.[10]

Lorenz's extensive research on the history of the theater building shows that there were several attempts to expand its capacity of 800 seats by building either a new wing or an entirely separate building in a different courtyard of the Freihaus. A map of the planned expansion that Lorenz discovered shows what the actual second floor of the theater looked like, including private boxes and a spiral staircase.[11] These more ambitious plans, which date from around 1790, were probably curtailed due to financial problems, when the main backer of the theater, Joseph von Bauernfeld, faced financial ruin in 1793.[12] Schikaneder, the director at the time, had to pay off the creditors, and the owner of the theater, Anton von Bauernfeld, Joseph's brother, gave the building to his wife as part of a divorce settlement in 1794. The list of items from the theater that were transferred to Antonia von Bauernfeld includes everything from the walls and the number of private boxes to the locations of the various benches and whether or not they were upholstered.[13]

Early Directors of the Theater auf der Wieden

Rossbach was already running performances of plays, ballets, and some operas in a temporary, wooden structure in the city center, when, on September 29, 1787, he announced in the *Wienerzeitung* that his new theater would be opening on October 7 and that, hoping to please all theater friends and benefactors, he would spare no expense and present a play with songs, a related *opera buffa*, and a plot-appropriate ballet of national character.[14] Such mixtures of pieces were common for traveling troupes and catered to the taste of the Viennese public.[15] We do not know the exact repertoire Rossbach presented on his stage, but there could not have been much of it since his directorship lasted a mere six months.

The next director, Johann Friedel, a writer and the leader of his own traveling acting troupe, took over, together with Eleonore Schikaneder (a member of the troupe and the estranged wife of Emanuel), in 1788. A number of oft-quoted reports claim a romantic relationship between these two, but since there are no primary sources to confirm it, this may be a result of theater gossip handed down through the generations.[16] We do know that Emanuel and Eleonore were apart during this time, because he was in Augsburg with his troupe of opera singers. Friedel was better known and more successful as a writer, and his tenure as director was largely unsuccessful. His preference for Lessing and Schiller over more standard comic fare did not endear him to contemporary audiences, although it coincided with Emperor Joseph II's intention to elevate and promote German-language spectacles as part of his larger plan to unify German-speaking nations.

In a speech given on March 24, 1788, at the premiere performance of his directorship, Friedel begged the audience to be patient with him and not to expect too much.[17] Reviewers criticized Friedel as inexperienced because of various directorial missteps; these included offering too many different shows in a row, with the result that the actors were underprepared, and scrambling to find enough performers to cover each type (*Fach*) of role – even assigning women to play male roles, as one outraged report notes.[18] One writer acknowledged that these lapses might have been due to Friedel's ill health, but added that this was no excuse for subjecting audiences to ill-prepared actors reading rather than performing their parts from memory or for reducing the role of reviewers to commenting on whether these parts were read poorly or relatively well.[19]

Thus far, Friedel's troupe had performed only plays, but in January of 1789 he made plans to introduce German-language opera. A German opera troupe was engaged to begin after Easter; the goal was to offer a wider variety of entertainment.[20] Even prior to Easter, Friedel brought opera, mainly in the form of a few German translations of Italian comic works, to the Theater auf der Wieden for the first time. The press deemed this move a financial calculation, comparing it to Schikaneder's earlier engagement with the state theaters and writing that although Schikaneder's previous performances in a Viennese theater had been mediocre at best, they nevertheless filled the house with a charmed Viennese public, always eager for more German-language opera.[21] German opera, in other words, was immensely popular but panned by the critics. As the *Kritisches Theater Journal von Wien* damningly put it, "The theater was full, but the actors were empty."[22] Friedel ran the theater for just a year and died after an extended illness on March 31, 1789, at the age of thirty-eight. Since she was female, the codirector, Eleonore Schikaneder, may have thought it unrealistic to run the theater by herself, so she sought the assistance of her husband, Emanuel. The years of his directorship represented a golden age, the most important period in the story of the Theater auf der Wieden and the one that produced *The Magic Flute*.

Characters and Repertory

The first work to premiere under Schikaneder's directorship of the theater was his own *Der dumme Gärtner im Gebürge, oder die zween Anton* (The Stupid Gardner in the Mountains, or The Two Antons), with music by Johann Baptist Henneberg and Benedikt Schack. Schikaneder himself played Anton, a character intended as competition for the popular Kasperl, a comic figure who reigned at the rival Theater in der Leopoldstadt. Anton never achieved Kasperl's level of acclaim in Vienna, but both characters represent a tradition in Viennese comedy that originates in the much older Hanswurst figure, popularized by Josef Anton Stranitzky in the first half of the eighteenth century. With roots in the Italian *commedia dell'arte*, this largely improvised comic type allowed Stranitzky and later performers the freedom to create a witty lower-class or servant character, who could outmaneuver his aristocratic or bourgeois masters while improvising lines that were relevant to, or even critical of, contemporary society. Much of the appeal of such comedy lay in making the upper classes look ridiculous. It was for this reason that Empress Maria Theresia had attempted to control improvised comedy in 1752, finally banning it in 1770, at which time a protocol for censoring theatrical works was established.[23] Nevertheless, improvised comedy continued in full force through the reign of Joseph II. Even a theater reviewer was shocked by what Kasperl was able to get away with on the stage of the Theater in der Leopoldstadt in 1789 as he offended morals and religion, to say nothing of good taste.[24]

Papageno is the most famous of these lower-class characters, whose lineage continued into the nineteenth century. Having inherited their main features, he is generally bumbling, good-hearted, cowardly, and ruled by his appetites, but he deviates from them in that he says nothing in *The Magic Flute* that is particularly subversive. Characters such as Leporello in *Don Giovanni*, also share Hanswurstian features. Whereas in Mozart's time such figures were associated more with silliness and coarse humor, the nineteenth-century successors of Hanswurst returned to criticizing authority, not only through improvised lines they might have sneaked into the written text but also in the development of a type of metalanguage that was an unexpected by-product of the censorship process – a censor struck an offensive word from a libretto and replaced it with an innocent one – and the performer, through nuance, could convey the original offensive meaning, presumably much to the delight of the audience.[25]

On a visit in 1768, Leopold Mozart was unamused by the undying popularity of Hanswurst and characters of his ilk among the Viennese and called their antics "foolish stuff."[26] But the elitist opinion of Mozart, senior, was in the minority. The Viennese loved their Hanswursts, Antons, and Kasperls.[27] Wanting to capitalize on the popularity of *Der dumme Gärtner*, Schikaneder created six sequels featuring Anton over the next six years. In 1791 Mozart wrote his Variations K. 613 on "Ein Weib ist das herrlichste Ding auf der Welt" (A woman is the most wonderful thing in the world), a popular aria from the second Anton opera, *Die verdeckten Sachen* (The Obscured Things).[28]

On November 7, 1789, Schikaneder presented Paul Wranitzky and Karl Ludwig Gieseke's opera, *Oberon, König der Elfen* (Oberon, King of the Elves), initiating a new era in Viennese popular theater that culminated in *Die Zauberflöte*.[29] *Oberon* was enormously successful, and Schikaneder's rival Karl Marinelli, director of the Theater in der Leopoldstadt, took notice and began presenting competing magical operas in his theater. *Oberon* was novel, not only because it was a magically themed and newly written German-language opera, but also because magical aspects were a central rather than an incidental part of the misadventures of an Anton or Kasperl figure.[30] There had been magical operas in Vienna before this time, of course, but the subject of the supernatural was treated differently then. During the reign of Maria Theresia (1740–80), magic on the stage had been frowned upon because it was thought to encourage superstition and to detract from religious teachings.[31] But under her son Joseph, censorship around magic on the stage was loosened, and later operas such as *Oberon* and *The Magic Flute* employed aspects of the supernatural to transmit Enlightenment morals. For example, Sarastro's powers of good are related to the sun, the Queen of the Night's evil powers are connected to the moon, and the rites undergone by Pamina and Tamino emphasize fortitude and wisdom. The religious-seeming ceremonies and even quasi-religious figures like Sarastro would not have made it past the censor prior to 1780. Joseph's successors (Leopold II and Francis II) tightened censorship laws again, but with more emphasis on eradicating political and sexual content than magical or anti-religious material.[32]

The centrality of magic was not the only similarity between *Oberon* and *The Magic Flute*. Both operas include a couple subjected to various difficult trials, a magical instrument (in *Oberon* it is a horn), music that compels villains to dance, and the use of coloratura to indicate supernatural power. Oberon is a trouser role, written for soprano and premiered by one of the central figures of Schikaneder's troupe, Josepha Hofer, who, in addition to being Mozart's sister-in-law, was also the first Queen of the Night.[33] Other than *The Magic Flute*, *Oberon* was perhaps the best-known magical opera of its time, and it was performed widely outside Vienna, for example in Frankfurt and Hamburg.[34] One reason so many other Viennese magical operas, both those contemporary with and especially later than *The Magic Flute*, never captured the imagination of audiences outside the city could be their connection to the so-called *Lokalstück* (local farce). This tradition of popular comic pieces included numerous references to either Viennese landmarks or local incidents that someone in Vienna would have understood, but that made them less accessible to people living elsewhere.[35]

Since theaters and their offerings were a major source of entertainment for the public, people frequently attended the same show multiple times. In Mozart's day, even the upper echelons of society attended the Theater auf der Wieden and its rival houses. Leopold II and his wife, Maria Luisa, for example, brought the visiting Sicilian court to a performance of *Der Stein der Weisen* (1790), having also attended a performance of the same opera nine days earlier. The nobility often rented boxes for an entire season, sometimes in more than one theater, which gave them (or their friends) the opportunity to attend all performances of all the works in any given season. The theater provided a place of entertainment, and repeated attendance could bring great familiarity with the repertoire, but it was also a useful venue for conducting business deals and pursuing romances – eighteenth-century opera audiences were hardly as quiet and polite as twenty-first-century ones.

Schikaneder's Troupe

The Theater auf der Wieden's performing troupe easily numbered fifty people without counting the supporting staff, which included subdirectors (dance master and prompter, for example), composers, orchestral players, administrative staff, set builders, and painters.[36] Life in the theater was very much a family affair: there were many married couples within the troupe, and children often began participating at a young age. Schikaneder, in addition to his work as director and librettist, continued as performer, most famously playing Papageno in *The Magic Flute* and, true to this type, other rustic, comic characters, notably the lead role in *Der Tiroler Wastel* (Wastel from Tyrol), which became another one of the theater's most popular offerings.[37] Schikaneder's older brother, Urban, was also a member of the troupe and originated the role of the First Priest in *The Magic Flute*; Urban's daughter, Anna, may have played the role of the First Boy, although that is not indicated on surviving playbills.

In 1796, the theater's performing personnel could be divided into three separate troupes, consisting of eight male and eight female singers (including Emanuel Schikaneder), ten male and five female actors (including Eleonore Schikaneder), and five male and three female dancers, as well as two grotesque dancers and twelve *Figuranten* or extras. Grotesque dancers, or *grotteschi*, combined French ballet techniques with pantomime and more daring, acrobatic movements that came from Italy.[38] There could be overlap between these three groups, as perhaps one actor was also an accomplished dancer, and some actors may also have filled out the chorus, which is listed as having only five members between 1793 and 1794.[39] A performer could, for example, have played kindly older men and funny servants but might also have sung tenor roles in opera. The listings of personnel from closer to Mozart's time seem to mainly divide the performers by gender rather than métier, which implies that over time there was less overlap and more specialization, perhaps as the theater became more successful and could hire more personnel.

Not much is known about the men responsible for how the sets looked: on the playbill for the premiere of *Die Zauberflöte*, Joseph Gail is listed as the set painter and someone named Nesslthaler as the designer. Contemporary reviews of this and other shows at the theater frequently indicate that sets and decorations were magnificent, but offer few details. Reviewers tended to comment if something was particularly unusual, such as when, in 1797, actual cannons were rolled onto the stage during the second part of Schikaneder's *Der Tiroler Wastel* to honor Archduke Karl's military achievements. The librettos of most of the operas from the Theater auf der Wieden describe the scenery in some detail, and the *Allmanach für Theaterfreunde* from 1789 to 1790 includes twelve engravings by Ignaz Albrecht of scenes from operas or plays that confirm the variety of sets used in this theater. All of the scenes show that great attention was paid to perspective and giving the illusion of depth: they show details, for example, of the interior of a house, depicting its row of decorative plates above the door, or of an outdoor scene with a realistic-looking mill wheel; and two illustrations from *Der Stein der Weisen* show the use of a platform on which performers could stand if they needed to sink into or rise from the depths. Albrecht's engravings are also important because they provide the only known images of some of the main performers at the theater.[40]

Suburban Theaters in Contemporary Reviews

With the exception of *The Magic Flute*, much of the music in works performed at the Theater auf der Wieden earned a reputation for being third-rate. That may be partly due to confusion about chronology and which works were being reviewed. Reviews from the years around 1791, the year of *The Magic Flute*, were frequently positive, and some writers were even impressed by the quality of the music. In the earlier period (for instance, under Friedel), shows at the theater had generally earned less favorable reviews, in which critics objected to the quality of the performances rather than to the music itself. And later, in the nineteenth century, as the repertoire tended toward lighter fare, in which music played a more ancillary role, there was a marked increase in negative reviews that commented on the banality of the plots and the simplicity of the music. But Mozart's Viennese decade (1781–91), which corresponds roughly to the reign of Joseph II, was a unique and particularly creative time in the city.

Since censorship was loosened during this time, there were more creative possibilities to explore, particularly in operas and plays, the texts of which were generally more heavily censored than those in books.

Schikaneder's decision to hire two singers who could also compose – Schack and Gerl – as well as the influx of highly qualified court musicians, who came to the theater due to the closure of one of the court theaters, resulted in musical performances of particularly high quality. The overlap of métiers, as troupe members frequently took on duties other than their official or major ones, was important in creating the special environment that was the Theater auf der Wieden. David Buch has pointed out that people like Schack and Gerl helped set this theater apart from the other suburban houses.[41] Certainly, the collaborative approach to composition that produced *Der Stein der Weisen* seems more pronounced at the Theater auf der Wieden than elsewhere in Vienna. But we should not overstate the success of the theater simply because of *The Magic Flute*.

Other suburban houses, and most especially the Theater in der Leopoldstadt under the direction of Karl Marinelli, easily enjoyed as much acclaim for their shows as did the Theater auf der Wieden. Of course, we might do well to consider acclaim and quality separately, and the wide-ranging tastes of Viennese audiences are important to consider: one reviewer, after noting the success of the premier of *The Magic Flute* and the magnificence of its decorations and costumes, commented in his subsequent sentence on the success of the competing play that same night at the Theater in der Leopoldstadt, which featured an actor dressed as an orangutan as its main character.[42] More serious examples of well-crafted works at the Theater in der Leopoldstadt are Wenzel Müller's *Das Sonnenfest der Braminen* (The Brahmins' Sun Festival, 1790) and *Das Donauweibchen* (The Nymph of the Danube, 1798), with music by Ferdinand Kauer. At least one prominent scholar holds that, apart from *The Magic Flute*, the quality of the pieces at the Theater in der Leopoldstadt was higher than those at the Theater auf der Wieden.[43] It seems that throughout this period Schikaneder paid close attention to the Theater in der Leopoldstadt and frequently modeled aspects of his works on those of its best-known writers, Joachim Perinet and Karl Friedrich Hensler.

Recipes for Success

Suburban theaters were important entertainment venues for the Viennese public, and their personnel were expected to continually produce new works. As such, it is unsurprising that Schikaneder wrote sequels or reused plot structures that he knew would be successful; *The Magic Flute* and some of Schikaneder's other important magical operas derive source material from Christoph Martin Wieland's collection of fairy tales entitled *Dschinnistan*. One of these, *Der Stein der Weisen*, was a particularly important model for *The Magic Flute*. Much of the plot of *The Magic Flute* rests on the twist that the Queen of the Night is not the wronged mother she at first appears to be, but a vengeful, power-hungry sorceress, and that Sarastro is not a throne-usurping child abductor, but a unifying ruler governed by reason. Similarly, *Der Stein der Weisen* presents two powerful magician brothers, one of whom (Eutifronte) convinces the hero (Nadir) that he must kill the other brother (Astromonte) to save his beloved Nadine. Eventually, Nadir realizes that Astromonte is actually the good brother.[44] In both operas, it is an initially wronged party who turns out to be evil: since he was the second-born son, Eutifronte was denied the philosopher's stone by his father, and it is presumably because she is a woman that the Queen of the Night was denied her husband's throne, which was given instead to Sarastro. The similar, often rhyming names of the couples, as well as the pairing of an upper-class couple with a lower-class one, are common features of fairytales; Pamina and Tamino are equivalent to Nadir and Nadine, while Papageno and Papagena are equivalent to Lubano and Lubanara.[45] In scenes involving Eutifronte, Lubanara, and Lubano, Eutifronte's evil (in this case he kidnaps Lubanara) is augmented by his blackness, just as Monostatos was considered more threatening to Pamina because of his dark skin.

Further evidence of a type of house efficiency is the composition of the music by more than one composer. The first of the *Anton* series is one example, but the best known of the theater's collaboratively written *Singspiele* is *Der Stein der Weisen*. The most obvious composer for this work is Henneberg, who, as the official composer and *Kapellmeister* of the theater, would have been expected to write the music for any new pieces to be performed and to conduct the orchestra, but Gerl (the first Sarastro) and Schack (the first Tamino) also composed parts of the opera. There is evidence that Mozart composed a duet and two sections of the finale for it.[46] This collaborative approach speaks to the speed and efficiency with which new works needed to be written, so that they could be rehearsed quickly and then performed. A contemporary Viennese author likened the process of composing at the theater to building a house, where each person contributes a different part to create a whole. Composition and performance were intimately intertwined in a manner quite foreign to present-day notions of opera – most often understood as the creative product of one person brought to life by interpreters. As the Viennese author noted, this older process was certainly the fastest way to bring a work to the stage.[47]

Schikaneder's method of creating new works for his theater can be understood as a template that included similar sets of characters and then allowed for the adjustment of plot and setting and the addition of new music. This was a profitable way to run the business because performers could be placed into roles that were written to emphasize their individual strengths, thereby appealing to the audience. The focus, musically speaking, was always on writing for the appropriate voice types available within the troupe, but it was also important to keep the type of character (e.g., comic, old, lower-class) and audience expectations in mind.

Operas presented at rival theaters, particularly at the Theater in der Leopoldstadt, clearly influenced *The Magic Flute*, although it is difficult to determine with certainty whether the source of influence was a plot feature, a type of stock character, or a particular example of that feature or character in a single work. *Das Sonnenfest der Braminen*, set to Müller's music with a libretto by Karl Friedrich Hensler, was first performed on September 9, 1790, at the Theater in der Leopoldstadt, and is an excellent case in point. The preface to the libretto emphasizes that the work was intended to honor the upcoming double wedding of Archduke Francis, the future emperor, and his younger brother, Archduke Ferdinand. Although the plot is different from that of *The Magic Flute* and rather like other operas of the period – long-lost family members are rediscovered and cross-dressing leads to an amusing mix-up – several of its other features remind us of Schikaneder and Mozart's work. Worship of nature, including the sun, is central, and there are many solemn, priestly choruses with prayers directed at two deities, Brama and Wistnu. Importance is placed on the relative unworthiness of those who do not belong to this priestly caste and on a belief that people can only truly be trusted once they have been initiated. There are two main lower-class characters in *Das Sonnenfest der Braminen*, one a gardener and the other a comic servant, who resemble Monostatos and Papageno, respectively. There is confusion at their initial meeting, and their subsequent conversation concerns Black Hottentots stealing their master's beloved; the gardener mentions stealing kisses and that his urges keep leading him to the hut of two female characters. The Papageno figure discusses girls and wine – the good things in life – and is particularly cowardly when faced with anything serious or life-threatening. He also makes light of the priestly traditions and sings an aria, "Adieu! du schnöde, böse Welt!" (Farewell! you disdainful, wicked world!), when he thinks he is going to die. There are other similarities as well: the male lead character's first sung words are "zu Hülfe" (prefiguring Tamino's "Zu Hilfe"); one main female character begs the highest figure of authority for her freedom (as when Pamina asks Sarastro for hers); and the other leading female sings about whether the feeling she is experiencing is love and decides "Ja ja, nein nein, die Liebe muß es seyn" (very much as Tamino sings in "Dies Bildnis ist bezaubernd schön").

How should we understand this partial list of similarities between *Das Sonnenfest der Braminen* and *Die Zauberflöte*? We could look to stock characters and situations to explain them (servant characters are always ruled by their base instincts), or we could assume that some similarities are more specific than general (in 1790 and 1791, sun-worshipping priests might have been just the right enticement to bring audiences to the theater). Either way, this example of *Das Sonnenfest der Braminen* invites us to consider just how cognizant of each other's productions Schikaneder and his rivals were. Character types, plot lines, and literal lines from operas were easily absorbed and transferred to others. In this brief overview of the Theater auf der Wieden, I have tried to set *The Magic Flute* in the immediate context of the stage on which it premiered. It may not be possible to recover or entirely recreate this theatrical culture, but knowing more about the Theater auf der Wieden, its company of singers and actors, and other operas produced on its stage and in rival theaters can help us to understand *The Magic Flute* not merely as a work of "singularity" but as part of a repertory. It should be clear that the messy collection of works being performed around *The Magic Flute* both at the Theater auf der Wieden and at rival theaters can be considered an important source for understanding Mozart and Schikaneder's opera.

Notes

1. David J. Buch, "The House Composers of the Theater auf der Wieden in the Time of Mozart (1789–91)," *Min-Ad: Israel Studies in Musicology Online* 5/2 (2006): 14.
2. Ibid., 18.
3. Michael Lorenz, "Neue Forschungsergebnisse zum Theater auf der Wieden und Emanuel Schikaneder," *Wiener Geschichtsblätter* 4 (2008): 2; Andrea Harrandt and Christian Fastl, "Freihaustheater auf der Wieden," Oesterreichisches Musiklexikon online article, http://dx.doi.org/10.1553/0x00020888 (accessed July 26, 2021).
4. Else Spiesberger, *Das Freihaus* (Vienna: Paul Zsolnay Verlag, 1980), 61–62.

5. Franz Hadamowsky, *Wien, Theatergeschichte: Von den Anfängen bis zum Ende des Ersten Weltkrieges* (Vienna: Jugend und Volk, 1988), 504.

6. Lorenz, "Neue Forschungsergebnisse," 4; Spiesberger, *Das Freihaus*, 42.

7. Lorenz, "Neue Forschungsergebnisse," 5.

8. Ibid., 4.

9. David Buch, "'Der Stein der Weisen,' Mozart, and Collaborative Singspiels at Emanuel Schikaneder's Theater auf der Wieden," *Mozart-Jahrbuch* 2000, 114; "Recensionen," *Allgemeine musikalische Zeitung* 1/5 (October 31, 1798): cols. 72–80, at col. 73.

10. Lorenz, "Neue Forschungsergebnisse," 4.

11. Ibid., 7.

12. Spiesberger, *Das Freihaus*, 50.

13. Ibid.

14. Christian Rossbach, *Wienerzeitung*, September 29, 1787. The theater actually opened a week later, on October, 14, 1787; Hadamowsky, *Wien, Theatergeschichte*, 505.

15. Hadamowsky, *Wien, Theatergeschichte*, 505.

16. Lorenz, "Neue Forschungsergebnisse," 5–6.

17. Johann Friedel, *Antritsrede bei Eröfnung des Theaters im hochfürstl. Stahrembergischen Freihause auf der Wieden* (Vienna: Joh. Jos. Jahn, 1788).

18. Otto Erich Deutsch, *Das Wiener Freihaustheater* (Vienna: Deutscher Verlag für Jugend und Volk, 1937), 9, 11.

19. Kritisches Theater-Journal von Wien, February 19, 1789 (Vienna: Mathias Ludwig, 1789), 53–55.

20. Deutsch, *Das Wiener Freihaustheater*, 10.

21. Ibid.

22. Kritisches Theater-Journal von Wien, January 8, 1789 (Vienna: Mathias Ludwig, 1789), 232.

23. James Van Horn Melton, "From Image to Word: Cultural Reform and the Rise of Literate Culture in Eighteenth-Century Austria," *Journal of Modern History* 58/1 (1986), 121–23.

24. Kritisches Theater-Journal von Wien, March 14, 1789 (Vienna: Mathias Ludwig, 1789), 119–28.

25. Lisa de Alwis, "Censorship and Magical Opera in Early Nineteenth-Century Vienna" (PhD dissertation, University of Southern California, 2012), 37.

26. "That the Viennese, generally speaking, do not care to see serious and sensible things [performances], have little or no understanding of them, and only want to see foolish stuff, dances, devils, ghosts, magic, Hanswurst, Lipperl, Bernardorn, witches and apparitions is well known, and their theaters prove it every day." Lipperl and Bernadorn are two other characters derived from Hanswurst. Leopold Mozart to Lorenz Hagenauer, January 30, 1768, in MBA, I:254.

27. Egon R. von Komorzyński, *Emanuel Schikaneder* (Berlin: Behr'sVerlag, 1901), 27.

28. David J. Buch, *Two Operas from the Series* Die zween Anton, *Part 2:* Die verdeckten Sachen *(Vienna, 1789)* (Middleton, WI: A-R Editions, 2016), 301–06.

29. Peter Branscombe has noted that Gieseke's libretto is "hardly more than a mild revision" of a libretto entitled *Hüon und Amande* by Friederike Sophie Seyler. COH, 28.

30. De Alwis, "Censorship and Magical Opera," 112.

31. Ibid., 2–3, 10–12.

32. Ibid., 55, 58.

33. COH, 28; David J. Buch, *Magic Flutes & Enchanted Forests: The Supernatural in Eighteenth-Century Musical Theater* (Chicago: University of Chicago Press, 2008), 292–93.

34. Deutsch, *Das Wiener Freihaustheater*, 16. *Oberon* was performed in Frankfurt in 1790 as part of the festivities surrounding the coronation of Leopold II as the new Holy Roman Emperor, which Mozart also attended. According to Deutsch, the opera was given twenty-four times over the next six weeks.

35. De Alwis, 110–11.

36. *Wiener Theater Almanach für das Jahr 1796* (Vienna: Joseph Camesina, 1796), 46–50.

37. Wastel is a shortened form of Sebastian.

38. Kathleen Kuzmick-Hansell, "Eighteenth-Century Italian Theatrical Ballet," in *The Grotesque Dancer on the Eighteenth-century Stage: Gennaro Magri and His World*, ed. Rebecca Harris-Warrick and Bruce Alan Brown (Madison, WI: University of Wisconsin Press, 2005), 20–23.

39. Joseph Sonnleithner, *Wiener Theater Almanach für das Jahr 1795* (Vienna: Joseph Camesina, 1795), LIV.

40. David Buch, "Newly-Identified Engravings of Scenes from Emanuel Schikaneder's Theater auf der Wieden," *Maske und Kothurn* 48/1–4 (2002): 370.

41. Buch, "House Composers," 15.

42. Dexter Edge, "The earliest published report on the premiere of *Die Zauberflöte* (1 October 1791)," in *Mozart: New Documents*, ed. Dexter Edge and David Black, first published March 16, 2015, updated December 6, 2017, www .mozartdocuments.org/documents/1-october-1791/ (accessed March 22, 2023).

43. Peter Branscombe, "The Singspiel in the Late Eighteenth Century," *Musical Times* 112, no. 1537 (1971): 228.

44. For David Buch's extensive work on this and other operas at the Theater auf der Wieden, see Buch, *Magic Flutes & Enchanted Forests*, 294–314.

45. For more on the aspects of his operas that Schikaneder tended to repeat, see
    Buch, "*Die Zauberflöte*, Masonic Opera, and Other Fairytales," *Acta
    Musicologica* 76/2 (2004): 207–08.

46. David Buch, ed., *Der Stein der Weisen* (Middleton, WI: A-R Editions, 2007),
    xii.

47. *Wiener Theater Almanach für das Jahr 1794* (Vienna: Kurzbeck, 1794), 188;
    Buch, "House Composers," 16.

4 | *The Magic Flute* in 1791

AUSTIN GLATTHORN[*]

Vienna, October 1 (from private letters):

Yesterday a Singspiel, *Die egyptischen Geheimniße*, for which Hr. Mozart composed the music and himself directed the orchestra, was performed in the Wiednertheater to unanimous acclaim. Hr. Schikaneder went all out to present this opera in accurate costume, with appropriate splendor in dress and scenery. On the same evening in the Leopoldstadt a new play was given, *Die Indianer*. An orangutan that appeared in the piece received the greatest applause.[1]

Thus reported the *Münchner Zeitung* on October 7, 1791. This excerpt – placing the success of Mozart's *Singspiel* alongside that of a spoken play featuring an orangutan – is the earliest known account following the premiere of *The Magic Flute*. To be sure, the opera, which is referred to by the alternative title *Die egyptischen Geheimniße* (The Egyptian Mysteries), was first given on September 30, 1791, in a performance that was well received according to this correspondent.[2]

Yet, despite the "unanimous acclaim" – not to mention the popularity and canonic status that *The Magic Flute* would achieve in the decades that followed – little can be said with certainty about its first performance. Not much is known about the opera's commission, preparation, and production as the correspondent of the *Münchner Zeitung* would have experienced it. Although the sources available simply do not provide a full picture of the premiere, this chapter draws on existing documentary evidence to consider how audiences may have experienced *The Magic Flute* in 1791. More than that, however, this chapter attempts to contextualize the conception and earliest performance(s) by approaching the work not as Mozart's final opera informed by over two hundred years of reception history, but rather as the product of a specific historical moment.

Toward the German Theater: Mozart in 1791

Understanding Mozart's circumstances in the period leading up to the premiere of *The Magic Flute* is key to understanding the work itself. To be sure, the Mozart of 1791 was not the Mozart listeners know today.

K. M. Knittel's distinction between Beethoven and "Beethoven" is equally applicable here: Mozart was not yet "Mozart" when *The Magic Flute* first appeared, meaning that his romantic hagiography only emerged posthumously.[3] Understanding his circumstances in the years before the premiere helps explain why Mozart might have taken on the project – one quite unlike any other he had previously undertaken – in the first place.

In the decade between his relocation to Vienna in 1781 and the appearance of *The Magic Flute*, Mozart had composed four operas specifically for the city's theatergoers: *Die Entführung aus dem Serail* (1782), *Der Schauspieldirektor* and *Le nozze di Figaro* (1786), and *Così fan tutte* (1790).[4] Granted, *Don Giovanni* also appeared on the Viennese stage (1788), but Mozart had composed this opera for audiences in Prague (1787). Despite what the disproportionate attention on Mozart in secondary literature might suggest, data from Vienna indicates that he was less successful than some of his contemporaries, when measured by the number of performances his operas received.[5] If it is true that "the more popular an opera was, the more it was repeated," then Mozart's works were not as well received as those of his peers, at least by the standards of the theatergoers for whom they were intended.[6] For example, *Die Entführung*, Mozart's most successful work for the German stage prior to *The Magic Flute*, was given twelve times in the Kärntnertortheater and Burgtheater (the Viennese court theaters) the year it was premiered, whereas another popular contemporary German opera, *Der Apotheker und der Doktor* (1786) by Carl Ditters von Dittersdorf (1739–99), was given twenty times in these theaters in the year of its premiere. In total, during Mozart's lifetime *Die Entführung* would go on to be staged in the court theaters on only about ten more occasions than *Der Apotheker*, despite having had a four-year head start.[7] So far as Italian operas for the Viennese court theaters are concerned, between the premiere of *Figaro* in 1786 and Mozart's death in 1791, works by Vicente Martín y Soler (1754–1806), Antonio Salieri (1750–1825), and others were performed significantly more often than Mozart's "Da Ponte" operas.[8] Performance data from this period are clear on this point and provide an important sense of the operatic world in the years before *The Magic Flute*.

These figures are supported by contemporary opinion. When Johann Pezzl (1756–1823) listed Vienna's most beloved operas in 1787, he named works by Dittersdorf, Martín, Paisiello, Salieri, and Giuseppe Sarti.[9] Mozart and his music are conspicuously absent. What is more, Mozart was the second choice of composer for *Così* and *La clemenza di Tito* (1791), both having been offered first to Salieri.[10] In short, Mozart's contemporary status and fortunes as a composer were anything but certain in 1791.

The period immediately prior to *The Magic Flute*'s premiere had been particularly difficult for the composer for other reasons as well. From 1788 until at least mid-1791, Mozart had borrowed significant sums of money from friends to pay pressing debts and make ends meet.[11] Hoping to turn around his precarious fortunes, he invested significant amounts in two performance tours: one to Dresden, Leipzig, and Berlin between April and June 1789 and another to Frankfurt am Main, Mainz, and Mannheim from September to October 1790.[12] His financial situation was no secret. In a letter dated April 7, 1791, the Mannheim actor Heinrich Beck (1760–1803) – whose wife Josepha Beck (unknown–1827) played the role of the Countess in a performance of *Die Hochzeit des Figaro* during Mozart's 1790 visit wrote to the dramatist Friedrich Wilhelm Gotter (1746–97) in Gotha.[13] Even though Beck was well aware that "Mozart ... is in very limited circumstances," he recommended Dittersdorf – known for his works for the German stage – as a potential composer for Gotter's latest text.[14]

Uncertain professional success, financial instability, and missed opportunities may have led Mozart to begin exploring the possibilities that the German theater had to offer. After all, the vast majority of audiences throughout the Holy Roman Empire and wider *Kulturkreis* encountered operas set in Italian as German-language adaptations for their local stages. As was the case in Mannheim, far more Central European theatergoers experienced *Le nozze di Figaro* in German adaptation as *Die Hochzeit des Figaro* and *Don Giovanni* as *Don Juan*, for instance. And, specifically in Vienna, the court theater was not attracting theatergoers as it once had.[15] It is little surprise, then, that Schikaneder and Mozart began to collaborate professionally in 1790 and 1791. When Mozart agreed to compose *The Magic Flute*, he acknowledged the German stage as a source of both potential recognition and income and decided to try his luck there.

Toward *The Magic Flute*: The Schikaneder Company and Viennese Theater in the Reign of Leopold II

Of the hundreds of German-language theater companies active in the last quarter of the eighteenth century, Schikaneder's was one of a few that operated continuously throughout the period. The troupe was experienced, for it had visited roughly ten cities and towns within the southern half of the empire by the time it reached Vienna.[16] Like many other companies, Schikaneder's actors staged both spoken and musical theater. Among the troupe's musico-theatric repertoire in this period were such works as Dittersdorf's *Der Apotheker und der Doktor*, Salieri's *Die Höhle des Trofonius* (*La grotta di Trofonio*, 1785), Martín's *Lilla* (*Una cosa rara*, 1786), and Johann Ernst Hartmann's *Balders Tod* (1788), to name but a few.[17]

Schikaneder and Mozart had first met when his company visited Salzburg in 1780, and within a year of his troupe's relocation to Vienna, in 1789, they were working together. The first evidence of collaboration was *Der Stein der Weisen* (1790). This *Singspiel* was written by Schikaneder and set to music by the Wiednertheater *Kapellmeister* Johann Baptist Henneberg (1768–1822), company actor-singers Franz Xaver Gerl (1764–1827) and Benedikt Schack (1758–1826), Schikaneder, and Mozart, who probably set the duet "Nun liebes Weibchen" (K625) and assisted with the second-act finale.[18] Building on the success of earlier works, including *Oberon, König der Elfen* (1789) by Paul Wranitzky (1756–1808), *Der Stein der Weisen* was the latest of Schikaneder's so-called magic operas (*Zauberopern*) and machine comedies – terms used to denote pieces that drew heavily on stage machinery and effects to enhance the spectacle. The vogue for such *Zauberopern* resulted in steady competition between the Wiednertheater and the nearby Theater in der Leopoldstadt. When the latter theater premiered the incredibly successful *Kaspar der Fagottist* by Joachim Perinet (1763–1816) and Wenzel Müller (1767–1835) in June 1791, Schikaneder's Wiednertheater was already preparing its response: *The Magic Flute*.[19]

One of the reasons very few documents survive concerning the commission and early composition of *The Magic Flute* is almost certainly because Mozart and his collaborators were together in Vienna, so they had no need to correspond. Writing in the early 1990s, Peter Branscombe suggested that "it is unlikely that the details of Mozart's contract with Schikaneder (if there was one) will ever be known, or when he began to write the score."[20] His prediction remains true thus far. The earliest known reference to *The Magic Flute* is found in one of Mozart's letters to Constanze (1762–1842), his wife, thought to have been written on June 11, 1791. Mozart expresses here his anxiety about finances and mentions having "composed an aria from the opera."[21] Given what is known about Mozart's compositional practices, he was most likely hard at work on *The Magic Flute* by this point, as he typically set ensembles first and composed arias only later.[22] Subsequent references to the *Singspiel* appear in the postscript of a letter written sometime around late June or early July and in yet another dated July 2. These missives confirm that Mozart's work on the opera was advanced, as he asked Constanze to ensure that Franz Xaver Süßmayr (1766–1803) was making progress with the short score, so that he could begin orchestrating numbers from the first act.[23] Meanwhile, evidence found in correspondence dated between July 3 and 12 indicates that Mozart was also well into the second act by this point.[24] All but a few numbers of *The Magic Flute* were complete when Mozart departed for Prague, at which time he shifted most of his attention to *La clemenza di Tito*, an opera designed to celebrate the coronation of Emperor Leopold II as king of Bohemia.

While Mozart was in Prague, it is assumed that Henneberg took over rehearsals for *The Magic Flute*.[25] Exactly how Henneberg and the troupe's other actor-musicians – Gerl, Schack, and Schikaneder – may have shaped its music remains uncertain. But given that Mozart had collaborated with them before, set three of *The Magic Flute*'s leading roles for them, and was later feverishly occupied with *Tito*, it is possible that they made contributions that shaped the work throughout its creation. To be sure, collaboration may help to explain the fact that Henneberg's song "Das Veilchen und der Dornstrauch," printed in the *Liedersammlung für Kinder und Kinderfreunde am Clavier* (1791), included music that would later appear in the final section of the Act 1 quintet "Hm! Hm! Hm!"[26]

In mid-September, Mozart departed from Prague and returned to Vienna, where he resumed work on the *The Magic Flute*, just in time for the premiere. He entered the March of the Priests (Act 2, scene 1, no. 9) and the overture in his thematic catalogue on September 28. Such late additions – his last documentable work on the opera – were common for the period. As Mozart's frenzied labor composing *The Magic Flute* and *La clemenza di Tito* in the summer and autumn of 1791 suggests, composers often continued working on pieces right up to the opening night.

The Premiere of *The Magic Flute*

The Magic Flute was first brought to the stage in the Theater auf der Wieden at 7:00 p.m. on Friday, September 30, 1791. The principal roles were created for and by veteran actors of Schikaneder's company. Many of these singers had been active on other German-language stages across Central Europe before joining the troupe and each filled one of the era's stock character types. As was standard for the period, the playbill advertising this performance lists the cast on the opening night (see Figure 4.1).

Figure 4.1 Playbill for the premiere of *The Magic Flute*. Courtesy of the KHM-Museumsverband, Theatermuseum Vienna. *Die Zauberflöte*, Uraufführung, Faksimile des Theaterzettel (ÖTM PA_RaraG286).

Heading the bill was Franz Xaver Gerl, the first Sarastro, particularly known for comic roles and a former student of Leopold Mozart (1719–87) in Salzburg before joining the companies of Ludwig Schmidt (unknown–1799) in Franconia and Gustav Friedrich Wilhelm Großmann (1746–96) in the Rhineland. A former *Kapellmeister* to the prince of Schönaich-Carolath, Benedikt Schack became a member of Schikaneder's troupe in 1786. Schack was the leading tenor by the time Schikaneder took over the Theater auf der Wieden, and it was for him that Schikaneder and Mozart created the part of Tamino. Josepha Hofer (1758–1819), Mozart's sister-in-law and first Queen of the Night, performed in Graz before joining the troupe at the Theater auf der Wieden in 1789, for which she sang many leading parts, including Titania in Wranitzky's *Oberon, König der Elfen*. The first Pamina, Anna Gottlieb (1774–1856), was a native of Vienna, where she grew up in a family of actors. Gottlieb was young, but experienced. Active on the stage from the age of five, she had also created the role of Barbarina in Mozart's *Le nozze di Figaro* when she was only twelve years old. Schikaneder, in writing the text, created the part of Papageno for himself. Barbara Gerl (1770–1806) specialized in leading female parts and created the role of Papagena. These actor-singers were supported by other actors as well as the company's orchestra, comprising about thirty-five musicians.

It is clear that the opera featured novel costumes and sets. This was a common practice employed by theater companies to draw audiences: investing in bespoke decorations and clothing to supplement more common and universal sets – like gardens, palaces, chambers, and temples – that could be reused from earlier productions.[27] Sources differ on exactly how much these items cost, though it is clear that Schikaneder's company spent a significant amount on *The Magic Flute*. In early October, a Hamburg newspaper printed a report from Vienna written a week before the premiere claiming the costumes and scenery cost 5,000 florins.[28] An account in the *Münchner Zeitung* reported an even higher estimate on October 8:

For the past few days at the Wiednertheater, a new machine comedy called *Die Zauberflöte* has been performed, for which the scenery cost 7,000 florins and for which our famous Kapellmeister Mozart produced the music. On account of the latter two circumstances, the piece is also receiving universal acclaim.[29]

It is significant that this correspondent attributes the opera's "universal acclaim" equally to its scenery and its music. Production value, including costumes, scenery, and spectacle, were apparently vital to its success.

The original libretto, which was available for purchase, provides important descriptions about how characters in the first performances may have
appeared. Tamino sported "splendid Japanese hunting clothes," for
example, while the Three Ladies were veiled and carried spears.[30]
Papagena was "dressed exactly as Papageno" when she removed her disguise at the conclusion of Act 2, scene 23; the two men who lead Tamino to
his trials appeared in black armor with fire blazing from their helmets; and
Tamino and Pamina were dressed in priestly clothes at the conclusion of
the second act.[31] The libretto also included two engravings, one of which
depicted a costume as it allegedly appeared in the premiere. Specifically
mentioned in the playbill, it shows "Schikaneder in the role of Papageno
according to [his] true costume," covered in feathers and with a birdcage
on his back (see Figure 4.2).[32] This image of Papageno and another
included in the *Allgemeines europäisches Journal* in 1794 (based on the
costume that appeared in "Mannheim and on other large, nonlocal stages")
are nearly identical: both are covered in feathers, with a feather headdress,
panpipes, and birdcage.[33] Both costumes also include a feather tail, which,
according to a description in the journal, could be made to swing by pulling
on a string.[34] The same journal included only one other engraving of
a single character's costume from the *Singspiel*. It shows the Queen of the
Night during her famous Act 2 aria, dagger in hand and arm raised in
vengeful anger, wearing a dress bedecked with stars and an elaborate star-
covered veil.[35]

Descriptions of the scenery included in the original libretto are more
detailed and more prevalent than those of the costumes, providing valuable
clues regarding what audiences may have seen in 1791. Many examples
come to mind: mountains that separate to reveal the starry throne room of
the Queen of the Night (Act 1, scene 6); the later change of scene to a grove
revealing the Temples of Wisdom, Reason, and Nature (Act 1, scene 15);
Sarastro's entrance in a chariot drawn by six lions (Act 1, scene 18); and the
palm grove, where silvery trees are covered with golden leaves and seats
await eighteen priests, that opens the second act. Indeed, as was often the
case with *Zauberopern*, *The Magic Flute*'s action included many expensive
scene changes and was accompanied by stage effects to heighten the
spectacle. Some involved stage machinery, such as lifts and cloud carts
for seemingly magical appearances and exits (e.g., Act 2, scene 16). Other
scenes sought to intensify the dramatic effect by replicating tumultuous
weather, such as that caused by a combination of wind, thunder, and
lightning (e.g., Act 2, scene 5). Others still included spewing fire, as did
the trials by fire and water in Act 2, scene 28.

Figure 4.2 Emanuel Schikaneder as Papageno in an engraving by Ignaz Alberti, opposite page 4 of the original libretto as printed by Alberti (Vienna, 1791).

In some cases, contemporary iconography confirms exactly the descriptions in the text. The backdrop for Papageno's entrance (Act 1, scene 2), for instance, is described as "a rocky area, here and there overgrown with trees, on both sides are accessible hills; there is also a round temple." This idealized scenery appears in the engraving of Schikaneder in his

Papageno costume found in the libretto (Figure 4.2). The rocks, trees, and a round temple are present, but represented more closely, as they might have appeared on stage in another engraving from the early 1790s. This image (Figure 4.3) captures the moment when the Three Ladies return to punish Papageno for claiming that he saved Tamino from the serpent (Act 1, scene 3). It thus provides an idea of how Tamino's hunting attire and the costumes of the veiled Three Ladies (albeit without their spears) might have appeared on stage.

This image and others created sometime around 1794 deserve special consideration as the most detailed early depictions of scenes from the opera yet known. At least six engravings – three scenes from each act – were created by Joseph Schaffer, and some scholars believe they may preserve some details of the original production – an oft-repeated assertion that is made without much discussion.[36] The reasoning behind this, and even the date of their creation, are unclear. What is certain is that they were later revised slightly and included in the Brno monthly *Allgemeines eurpäisches Journal* as hand-colored foldouts between the months of January and July 1795. Given the similarities of costumes in Vienna, Mannheim, and

Figure 4.3 Act 1, scene 3. Papageno: "Here, my beauties, here are my birds." Engraving by Joseph Schaffer, ca. 1794. Courtesy of Wien Museum.

elsewhere discussed above, as well as descriptions of the sets found on playbills advertising the Augsburg and Innsbruck premieres (1793) that are remarkably similar to those in Schikaneder's text, it seems that early stagings resembled one another closely. Even though it cannot be determined to what degree these images reflect scenes from the opera as it may have appeared on any particular stage on any particular night, their value as contemporaneous iconographic evidence is beyond doubt. For this reason, all six scenes are included in this chapter (Figures 4.3, 4.4, 4.5, 4.6, 4.7, and 4.8); and they are available in full color in the Resources Tab for this volume.[37]

It is worth comparing the frontispiece in the original libretto to a related scene depicted in one of the Schaffer engravings. Ignaz Alberti's engraving reveals a large vaulted hall in the background; in the foreground sits an obelisk with pseudo-hieroglyphics across from a large urn (Figure 4.9).[38] A shovel and pick are propped up in the bottom right, as if they had just been abandoned after being used to uncover this long-forgotten location. Not serving any obvious function in the opera, these tools may have been

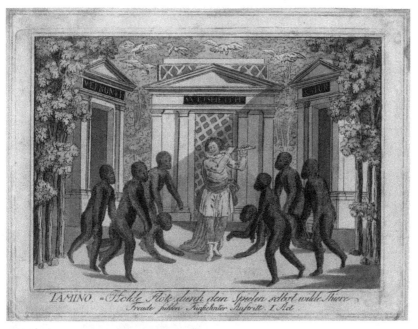

Figure 4.4 Act 1, scene 15. Tamino: "Dear flute, through your playing even wild animals [*wilde Thiere*] feel joy." Engraving by Joseph Schaffer, ca. 1794. Courtesy of Wien Museum.

Figure 4.5 Act 1, scene 18. [Chorus:] "Long live Sarastro!" Engraving by Joseph Schaffer, ca. 1794. Courtesy of Wien Museum.

Figure 4.6 Act 2, scene 18. Pamina: "You here! – Benevolent Gods." Engraving by Joseph Schaffer, ca. 1794. Courtesy of Wien Museum.

Figure 4.7 Act 2, scene 25. Speaker: "Away with you, young woman, he is not yet worthy of you." Engraving by Joseph Schaffer, ca. 1794. Courtesy of Wien Museum.

Figure 4.8 Act 2, scene 28. Tamino: "Here are the terrifying gates." Engraving by Joseph Schaffer, ca. 1794. Courtesy of Wien Museum.

Figure 4.9 Engraving by Ignaz Alberti showing hieroglyphics, ruined columns, and the "vault of pyramids" associated with scenery in Act 2, frontispiece of the original libretto as printed by Alberti (Vienna, 1791).

added by the artist as a means of inviting the audience into this distant realm, for the engraving appears just before the title page (Alberti was also the printer and a Mason). Schaffer's depiction of Act 2, scene 25, which shows the Speaker leading Papagena away from the not yet worthy Papageno, reproduced a more stage-friendly version of this scene (compare Figures 4.7 and 4.9). Many of the features included in the text's engraving are also visible here: a marked obelisk on the left, a large urn surrounded by ruins or rocks, and a star dangling from the two central arches.

Sources related to early performances indicate that individuals closest to the original production made alterations very early on. A copy of the printed libretto annotated by Karl Ludwig Giesecke (1761–1833), stage manager and actor in this run, still provides fresh insight into stage directions, lighting, scenery, and props.[39] It reveals, for instance, that the second act duet "Bewahret euch vor Weibertücken" may have been replaced by other music or omitted altogether.[40] Performance parts from the archive of the Theater auf der Wieden presumed to have been based on the theater's copy of Mozart's autograph support this possibility. Most of these early instrumental parts indicate that the duet was indeed omitted.[41] They also include music not present in the autograph. Such is the case in the opening bars of the duet "Bei Männern, welche Liebe fühlen."[42] The parts also reveal that the wind chords immediately preceding Pamina's entrance were in most cases four eighth notes rather than the dotted rhythm most commonly heard today and notated in the *Neue Mozart-Ausgabe*.[43] Considering that Mozart left this music blank in the autograph, these parts may reveal an alteration that he or a collaborator made during rehearsals or very early in its run.[44]

Schaffer's depiction of Act 2, scene 18 (Figure 4.6) may also shed new light on early performances. In the original libretto, this scene, where Pamina discovers Tamino and Papageno during the trial of silence, takes place in "a hall in which the Boys' flying machine can operate." Just why this engraving appears to depict a moonlit garden as opposed to the hall as described in the libretto – at the beginning of scene 13 – is uncertain. It could be a simple mistake on the part of the engraver, but this seems unlikely given that other details in the image are accurate and that all of the other engravings in this series are remarkably faithful to the depictions in Schikaneder's text. It is possible that early performances of this scene did indeed take place in a moonlit garden, a possibility that Giesecke's annotations may support.[45] As Branscombe notes, Giesecke includes the heading "Mondtheater" (moon theater) at this point in his copy of the libretto. Parts of Schikaneder's original stage direction are then crossed out, though it is uncertain whether Giesecke made the deletion or what exactly it meant.[46] The details of Branscombe's speculation aside, discrepancies such as these are significant, because they indicate that alterations were made during some of the earliest performances of *The Magic Flute.*

Even though there are some contemporary sources concerning the composition and first performances of *The Magic Flute*, they are not enough to reconstruct the opera as audiences might have experienced it in 1791. In any event, the nature of eighteenth-century opera renders such an effort moot. The concept of an "ideal" opera – that is, one that represents definitively a creator's intentions – was foreign to the eighteenth century. This was not only because such works were collaborative, but also because almost all pieces were at some point altered to suit local circumstances.[47] Then, as now, musicians and dramatists often emended works in response to the first few performances and for subsequent productions with different casts. *The Magic Flute* was no different. Sources closest to the original production indicate variety in early performances, including possible changes that involved the composer, performers, and theater management. It is the contemporary moment – that is, the context, not so much the opera itself – that helps to make sense of how music for the stage was performed and received in its moment.

Initial Reception

Early reactions to *The Magic Flute* provide some clues about its initial reception. In a letter to Constanze dated October 7, for example, Mozart reports:

> It was just as full as always. – the Duetto *Mann und Weib* etc.: and the Glöckchen Spiel in the first Act was as usual encored – also in the 2nd Act the Boys' Terzett – but what pleases me most, is, the *Silent approval!* – one can see well how much, and increasingly so, this opera is gaining esteem.[48]

In a letter dated October 8 and 9, Mozart once again speaks of the work's enthusiastic reception, as well as of his disappointment with an acquaintance who "laughed at everything."[49] In his last surviving letter, he told Constanze how Salieri and the soprano Caterina Cavalieri (1755–1801) showered his opera with praise after seeing it together on the evening of October 13.[50]

Mozart might have claimed audiences praised the music, but contemporary reception was not entirely favorable. On November 6, 1791, the avid music enthusiast and diarist Count Karl von Zinzendorf (1739–1813) claimed that "the music and the sets are pretty, the rest an incredible farce. An immense audience."[51] Another early report published in the Berlin-based *Musikalisches Wochenblatt* that December, but dated October 9, is more critical:

The new comedy with machines, *Die Zauberflöte*, with music by our Kapellmeister *Mozard* [sic], which is given at great cost and with much magnificence in the scenery, fails to find the hoped-for success, because the contents and the language of the piece are altogether too wretched.[52]

Three newspaper reports published outside of Vienna and recently uncovered by Dexter Edge offer valuable information about the early reception. The first is that which opens this chapter. Published in the *Münchner Zeitung* and dated October 1, this earliest known report following the premiere referred to *The Magic Flute* by the alternative title "*Die egyptischen Geheimniße*" and stated that it earned unanimous acclaim and that Schikaneder spared no expense on the costumes and scenery.[53] The second of these new sources, found in the *Bayreuther Zeitung*, transmits the words of a Viennese correspondent dated October 5. Its anonymous author states that the weather had turned unexpectedly cold, causing more people to attend the suburban theaters than either the court theaters or outdoor entertainments such as those hosted in the Prater.[54] Referring to the work by the more familiar title *Die Zauberflöte*, this source further noted that the opera depicted an ancient initiation as depicted in *Sethos* (1731) by Jean Terrasson (1670–1750) and that it had been given three times to full houses. The report also states that Mozart "directed it himself, for which he was granted the third [night's] receipts by Herr Schikaneder."[55] This is currently the only evidence of Mozart's compensation for his work on the *Singspiel*. Edge has calculated that this sum may have been around 400 florins, a not insignificant amount, which may have been on top of a flat fee Mozart received from Schikaneder.[56] The final, recently uncovered, newspaper source – mentioned earlier but worth repeating here – is the claim found in the *Münchner Zeitung* dated October 8 that the opera's scenery cost 7,000 florins. This correspondent confirms once again that *The Magic Flute* was a hit with Viennese audiences, specifically attributing its success to Mozart's music as well as the scenery: "On account of the latter two circumstances," the correspondent writes, "the piece is also receiving universal acclaim." Schikaneder's decision to invest a significant sum in new sets paid off in the end, as they helped to attract theatergoers to his machine comedy.

Within weeks of the premiere, audiences could also encounter *The Magic Flute* outside of the theater. Arrangements of operas for smaller performing forces provide an invaluable source of gauging contemporary reception. Musicians hurried to adapt the most popular works for the lucrative market of domestic and public music-making. As early as November 1791, arrangements of unidentified numbers from the *Singspiel* for keyboard and voice were advertised in the *Wiener Zeitung* within a collection that also included arias from Wenzel Müller's *Kaspar der Fagottist*.[57] The printing house Artaria advertised Papageno and Pamina's "Bei Männern, welche Liebe fühlen" and Sarastro's "In diesen heil'gen Hallen" – alongside "12 new variations on the duet: Bei Männern welche Liebe fühlen from the new opera *Die Zauberflöte*" by Anton Eberl (1765–1807) – in keyboard arrangements on November 23.[58] Versions of the trio "Seid uns zum zweitenmal willkommen" were listed on December 3.[59] That these works were so quickly made available suggests that they were among the opera's earliest hits. To be sure, "Bei Männern, welche Liebe fühlen" and "Seid uns zum zweitenmal willkommen" were among the numbers that Mozart claimed were usually encored in his letter of October 7. By early December, Artaria had twelve numbers from the opera on offer.[60]

Arrangements for larger ensembles soon followed. Roughly a month after announcing that *Kaspar* was available in arrangement for wind ensemble (*Harmonie*), the *Wiener Zeitung* likewise advertised *Die Zauberflöte* for eight- or six-part *Harmonie*.[61] Although transcriptions for piano were important in propagating the opera's music during the critical weeks following its first appearance, the nature of the instrument confined these arrangements to the homes of those wealthy enough to own one. Even though the creation of *Harmonie* transcriptions was more time-consuming and expensive than those for keyboard, these ensembles held a special place in the musical life of the late eighteenth century: *Harmonien* performed in every space that audiences could expect to encounter music, including the church, court, home, inn, theater, and pleasure garden, among others. Through such versatile and mobile ensembles, *The Magic Flute* was able to escape the boundaries of the theater, allowing its music to be heard by all strata of society across the city and eventually beyond.[62]

The popular success of *The Magic Flute* was due to many factors, including such arrangements. When the *Singspiel* first appeared on the Viennese stage in the autumn of 1791, no one could have foreseen just how enduring a work it would become. Alongside performances of its music in private homes and pleasure gardens, it was produced on German-language stages across Central Europe countless times within the next decade. Sequels soon followed, though none came close to replicating the success of the original.[63] Few contemporaries could have predicted how the appearance of this work at a critical juncture in music history contributed to its subsequent triumph: the ca. 1800 moment marks the rise of the public as a musical force, the emergence of the Romantic image of the composer, and the nascent foundations of a musical canon. All of these factors helped to ensure performances of *The Magic Flute* beyond 1791 and well into the future.

Notes

* I am grateful to Mark Everist, Sterling E. Murray, Adeline Mueller, and Jessica Waldoff for their invaluable comments on earlier versions of this chapter.

1. As translated in Dexter Edge, "The earliest published report on the premiere of *Die Zauberflöte* (1 October 1791)," in *Mozart: New Documents*, ed. Dexter Edge and David Black, first published March 16, 2015, updated December 6, 2017, www.mozartdocuments.org/documents/1-october-1791/ (accessed March 22, 2023).

2. On the alternative title, see ibid.

3. See K. M. Knittel, "The Construction of Beethoven," in *The Cambridge History of Nineteenth-Century Music*, ed. Jim Samson (Cambridge: Cambridge University Press, 2001), 118–50.

4. Mozart abandoned two operas, *L'oca del Cairo* (1783) and *Lo sposo deluso* (1785), and composed two for Prague, *Don Giovanni* (1787) and *La clemenza di Tito* (1791).

5. See, for example, the recent claim that the "greatest success" of Emperor Joseph II's National Singspiel was "Mozart's *Die Entführung aus dem Serail*," an assertion seemingly made owing to Mozart's status today rather than historical observation. Lisa de Alwis, "Theatrical Life in Mozart's Vienna," in *Mozart in Context*, ed. Simon P. Keefe (Cambridge: Cambridge University Press, 2018), 162.

6. Lisa de Alwis, for one, makes the former argument in "Theatrical Life in Mozart's Vienna," 162. Other scholars have argued that box office returns are a more appropriate indication of success than number of performances alone. See John Platoff, "Sarti's *Fra i due litiganti* and Opera in Vienna," *Journal of the American Musicological Society* 73/3 (2020): 539.

7. These figures are based on performances listed in MDB, 201; MDL, 179; and Dorothea Link, *The National Court Theatre in Mozart's Vienna: Sources and Documents 1783–1792* (Oxford: Oxford University Press, 1998), esp. 72–183.

8. Link, *National Court Theatre*, 72–183.

9. "Wälsche und deutsche Oper," *Skizze von Wien* 3 (1787): 421–26.

10. See John A. Rice, *Antonio Salieri and Viennese Opera* (Chicago: University of Chicago Press, 1998), 474–79, 505–07.

11. Jessica Waldoff, "Mozart and Finances," in *Mozart in Context*, ed. Simon P. Keefe (Cambridge: Cambridge University Press, 2018), 177–80.

12. Christoph Wolff, *Mozart at the Gateway to His Fortune: Serving the Emperor, 1788–1791* (New York: Norton, 2012), 44–73; see also Austin Glatthorn, "The Imperial Coronation of Leopold II and Mozart, Frankfurt am Main, 1790," *Eighteenth-Century Music* 14/1 (2017): 89–110.

13. Dexter Edge and Martin Nedbal, "The premiere of *Die Hochzeit des Figaro* in Mannheim (24 October 1790)," *Mozart: New Documents*, ed. Dexter Edge and David Black, first published July 6, 2019, www.mozartdocuments.org /documents/24-october-1790/ (accessed March 22, 2023).

14. Forschungsbibliothek Gotha der Universität Erfurt, Chart. B 1915 II, fol. 47r. See also Austin Glatthorn, *Music Theatre and the Holy Roman Empire: The German Musical Stage at the Turn of the Nineteenth Century* (Cambridge: Cambridge University Press, 2022), 76.

15. See Dexter Edge, "Mozart is awarded the third receipts from *Die Zauberflöte* (5 October 1791)," in *Mozart: New Documents*, ed. Dexter Edge and David Black, first published March 16, 2015, updated December 9, 2017, www .mozartdocuments.org/documents/5-october-1791 (accessed March 22, 2023).

16. For a list of reported destinations, see Glatthorn, *Music Theatre and the Holy Roman Empire*, 287.

17. *Theater-Kalender* 15 (1789): 205.

18. See *Der Stein der Weisen*, ed. David J. Buch, Recent Researches in the Music of the Classical Era 76 (Middleton, WI: A-R Editions, 2007).

19. Both *Singspiele* draw on the same source, August Jacob Liebeskind's "Lulu, oder Die Zauberflöte," published in Christoph Martin Wieland's *Dschinnistan* (1789). See COH, 4–34, especially 25–34.

20. COH, 73.

21. MBA, IV:136–37; COH, 73.

22. COH, 75. For a detailed account of the creation of the work, see also 67–86.

23. MBA, IV:143–44; COH, 76.

24. See COH, 77.

25. Ibid., 78, 152.

26. See Alan Tyson, "Two Mozart Puzzles: Can Anyone Solve Them?," *Musical Times* 129/1741 (1988): 127; and Placidus Partsch, *Liedersammlung für Kinder und Kinderfreunde am Clavier (1791): Frühlingslieder and Winterlieder*, ed. David J. Buch (Middleton, WI: A-R Editions, 2014).

27. On costumes and sets as a means of attracting audiences to the theater (and the first Augsburg production of *Die Zauberflöte*), see Glatthorn, *Music Theatre and the Holy Roman Empire*, 82–86.

28. Edge, "The earliest published report."

29. As quoted in Dexter Edge, "An early report on *Die Zauberflöte* (addendum) (8 October 1791)," in *Mozart: New Documents*, first published March 16, 2015, updated December 3, 2017, www.mozartdocuments.org/documents/ 8-october-1791/ (accessed March 22, 2023).
30. Emanuel Schikaneder, *Die Zauberflöte: Eine große Oper in zwey Aufzügen* (Vienna: Alberti, 1791), 1.
31. Ibid., 90, 95, 106.
32. The playbill may also be found in the Austrian National Library (Österreichische Nationalbibliothek, Bildarchiv und Grafiksammlung 117.804-D).
33. "Theaterkostums," *Allgemeines europäisches Journal* 1/3 (1794): 530 and plate IV.
34. Ibid., 530.
35. "Theaterkostums," *Allgemeines europäisches Journal* 1/4 (1794): 153 and plate IIII (*sic*).
36. Among others, see Carloyn Abbate, *In Search of Opera* (Princeton: Princeton University Press, 2001), 83, 262; and Daniel Heartz, *Mozart, Haydn, and Early Beethoven: 1781–1802* (New York: Norton, 2008), 283.
37. On the genesis and early history of these images, see Walther Brauneis, "Wolfgang Amadé Mozarts 'Zauberflöte' und Innsbruck: Neue Quellen zum Erstaufführungsdatum im National-Hoftheater gegenüber der Innsbrucker Hofburg und zu den sechs Szenenbildern des Innsbrucker Zeichners und Kupferstechers Joseph Schaffer," *Wissenschaftliches Jahrbuch der Tiroler Landesmuseen* 2/43 (2009): 43–61.
38. Schikaneder, *Die Zauberflöte*, unpaginated.
39. Giesecke's elaborately bound text is preserved in the Austrian National Library (Österreichische Nationalbibliothek, Musiksammlung 685928-A); for an analysis, see COH, 92–98.
40. COH, 94.
41. David J. Buch, "Eighteenth-Century Performance Materials from the Archive of the Theater an der Wien and Mozart's 'Die Zauberflöte,'" *Musical Quarterly* 84/2 (2000): 297.
42. See ibid., 300–02.
43. Ibid., 300; NMA II/5/19, 122.
44. Buch, "Eighteenth-Century Performance Materials," 300.
45. See Brauneis, "Wolfgang Amadé Mozarts 'Zauberflöte' und Innsbruck," 56.
46. COH, 95.
47. See, for example, Glatthorn, *Music Theatre and the Holy Roman Empire*, 118–19.
48. As quoted in COH, 152; see also MBA, IV:157.
49. Letter to Constanze Mozart. MBA, IV:159–61.
50. Letter of October 14, 1791. MBA, IV:161–63.
51. As quoted in COH, 154.

52. As quoted in ibid.

53. *Münchner Zeitung*, no. 158 (October 7, 1791), 843. See also Edge, "The earliest published report."

54. *Bayreuther Zeitung*, no. 121 (October 11, 1791), 947. See also Edge, "Mozart is awarded the third receipts."

55. As quoted in Edge, "Mozart is awarded the third receipts."

56. See ibid.

57. "Die Zauberflöte," *Wiener Zeitung*, no. 89 (November 5, 1791), 2848–49.

58. "Neue Musikalien," *Wiener Zeitung*, no. 94 (November 23, 1791), 3006.

59. "Neue Musikalien," *Wiener Zeitung*, no. 97 (December 3, 1791), 3102.

60. "Neue Musikalien," *Wiener Zeitung*, no. 98 (December 7, 1791), 3134.

61. "Musikalienankündigung," *Wiener Zeitung*, no. 100 (December 14, 1791), 3198; "Neue Musikalien," *Wiener Zeitung*, no. 6 (January 21, 1792), 185.

62. For example, see Joseph Sonnleither, *Wiener Theater Almanach für das Jahr 1794* (Vienna: Kurzbeck, 1794), 172–89.

63. Schikaneder's own sequel was entitled *Das Labyrinth* (1798) and was set to music by Peter von Winter (1754–1825).

PART II

Music, Text, and Action

5 | Music as Stagecraft

JULIAN RUSHTON

Unless we count his modest contribution, along with four other composers, to *Der Stein der Weisen*, *The Magic Flute* was a new type of opera for Mozart, at least in its handling of word-music-drama relationships.[1] It was less new in other ways; its moral content is anticipated in *Die Entführung aus dem Serail*, where, as again in *La clemenza di Tito*, the characters' fate lies in the hands of a benevolent autocrat (here Sarastro). The Introduction, arias, ensembles, and multisection finales followed naturally from Mozart's recent Viennese comedies, but with significant differences. Spoken dialogue bears much of the weight of action and characterization conveyed in *opera buffa* by simple recitative. At dramatic high points, Italian opera uses orchestrally accompanied recitative (the voice supported by expressive instrumental gestures), usually leading to an important aria. In *The Magic Flute*, orchestrated recitative occurs mainly in the finales, which would be unusual in *opera buffa*.[2]

The variety of forms and the passages in finales that are neither recitative nor aria look ahead to the more continuous opera of the next century. From a post-Wagnerian standpoint, linking stage action to musical design may seem unremarkable. But closed, fully cadenced forms were the eighteenth-century norm, despite the example of Gluck's later operas, where recitative, arioso, and aria come closer thanks to his abandonment of simple recitative. The long finales of *The Magic Flute* are unlike those of the Viennese comedies; they do not follow Lorenzo Da Ponte's prescription for few if any scene-changes, the music accelerating as characters fill the stage. The finales of *The Magic Flute* require several scene-changes, and the spectacle assumes greater importance. Another novelty is that two "characters" are multivoiced, but sing as a unit: the Three Ladies attendant on the Queen, and Three Genii or "Knaben" (boys, although the original singers were female). And unlike Viennese *opera buffa*, the opera makes serious use of a chorus.

Overture and Introduction

Overtures are the composer's domain, without text and with the stage as yet unseen. Yet, perhaps following Gluck's precedent, Mozart linked his overtures to the dramatic action, to the point of prequotation (the overtures were written last).[3] So, although the dramaturgy of *The Magic Flute* is remote from that of Gluck's late operas, the overture shows what must be deliberate connections to what follows. The overture offers a sense of the numinous, of energy, and of intellectual engagement – all elements that play a significant role in the unfolding action – but it is not a symphonic précis of the opera, unlike the overture written shortly before, to *La clemenza di Tito*, which has been subtly interpreted by Daniel Heartz as a "dramatic argument."[4]

Schikaneder's public may have expected comedy, sentiment, and fantasy, but the overture prepares for higher styles. The Adagio "alla breve" (two half-note beats per measure rather than four quarters) is not so slow, and is short but solemn. The opening is rhythmically related to the "three-fold chords" ("dreimalige Akkord"). In the Allegro, these are "quoted" from Act 2, dividing the sonata exposition from the development. The rest suggests mystery: strings, their dotted rhythm a hushed reminder of the opening, introduce minor coloring, punctuated by soft trombone chords. In the second finale, trombones present a similar dotted rhythm to introduce the chorale and "learned" (imitative) texture of the scene with two Armored Men. This full orchestration with trombones – which retain their association with religion and the supernatural – is unique in Mozart's overtures (in *Don Giovanni*, trombones play in the "statue" scenes, but not when the same music opens the overture; his other Vienna operas use no trombones). Fugue, not a standard component of comic opera (despite the ending of *Don Giovanni*), is a principal topic of the Allegro, which combines fugue and sonata form – a procedure new to Mozart's overtures but anticipated in the finale of the String Quartet in G, K. 387.[5] Unlike that movement, however, the overture has only one well-defined theme, the fugue subject, which is also used for a brilliant *tutti*, then combined in the secondary key area with graceful woodwind solos (from mm. 57 and 74). The "threefold chords" intrude on the sonata design, bringing the music virtually to a halt (mm. 96–102). The development responds by further resourceful handling of the theme, largely in minor keys, with some strict canonic imitation (basses and violins, from m. 116). The retransition, and Mozart's compositional resourcefulness in combining the recapitulation with fresh developments (from m. 144), add to the surpassing quality of this overture, which remains a concert favorite despite the oddly intrusive "threefold chords."

Sarastro's last words (Act 2 finale) assert that as sunrise expels night, so does virtue overcome wickedness. The breakthrough from night into day is the central metaphor for progress toward enlightenment, and is repeatedly reflected in the music: already in the overture (Adagio–Allegro; stormy development–recapitulation), and in No. 1, headed "Introduction" (*sic*). The scene presents a rugged, hence dangerous, terrain as Tamino runs on, pursued by a monstrous serpent. The key, C minor, is the dark shadow of the overture's E-flat. Marked rhythms, tremolo, and sweeping scales represent terror, using the topic identified as *tempesta*.[6] As Tamino faints, a harmonic interruption (m. 40) brings release; the Ladies slay the monster and their "Triumph!" restores the overture's E-flat. Such harmonic strokes are a feature of later scenes, marking significant turning points in the plot. The Ladies cannot trust one another, if left alone, not to be too affectionate toward the unconscious prince. Thus the dark (*tempesta*) turns not to light but to the first passage of comedy, with a mild sexual charge. The keys follow the action: E-flat modulates to closely related G minor (by m. 119), followed by a lively G major in 6/8 and a furious *stretta*, closing in the tonic C, but in the major, at a faster tempo.[7] No. 1, therefore, is an introduction to dramatic contrasts – terror; triumph; popular, if slightly misogynist, comedy – and to the opera's principal tonalities.

A Tonal Overview

After E-flat, C, and G, the principal keys used in *The Magic Flute* are F and B-flat, neither of which frames a finale; nor does G, but its association, in major and minor modes, with Pamina and Papageno gives it an importance comparable to the framing tonalities.

A word of caution is needed in connection with keys. The subject offers more than the usual temptation to search for key symbolism, but while E-flat, the overall frame, has been associated with Freemasonry partly because it has three flats, it is also used for the servants of the evil Queen (Introduction). Mozart also employed C, major and minor, for "Masonic" works. C minor (also with three flats) reappears in the second finale for the solemn chorale before the trials of initiation, but also for the last entry of the Queen and her minions, intent on violence. C major frames the first finale and reappears in the second for the trials (and so for both "magic flute" solos), but C is also the key of Monostatos's aria as he prepares to rape Pamina. A composer's hands cannot be tied by fixed connotations of keys, even within a single work.

Tonality on its own cannot distinguish truth from falsehood, good from evil. Mozart's choice of keys reflects practical considerations, instrumental (since only a few were then available for natural trumpets) and vocal, reflecting Mozart's concern to "fit the costume to the figure."[8] His chosen keys place notes from the tonic chord, normally the third (mediant) or the fifth (dominant), high but comfortably within his singers' ranges. These are usually exceeded by no more than one degree, at moments of climax or intense expression.

C and E-flat suited Benedikt Schack (the first Tamino); as Abert remarks, "It is doubtless largely thanks to Schack that the role of Tamino is of such high quality."[9] In his aria (No. 3), high G (g′) is the mediant in the tonic chord, E-flat, and the highest notes are all a-flat′. His first-finale solo is in C, using both a-flat′ and a-natural′ above the dominant, g′.[10] The keys of G and F suited the actor-singer (baritone) Schikaneder (the first Papageno); both his arias and his solo in the second finale (also in G) exceed the dominant by one degree, reaching e, d, and in the finale a poignant e-flat′ borrowed from the minor mode as he contemplates suicide. B-flat (the Queen's first aria, No. 4) and F (within the second, D minor, aria) invited Josepha Hofer's top note (f‴), approached by a leap, and probably attained by a vocal harmonic; it is noticeable that in her second aria (No. 14) f‴ does not reappear in the final section. But B-flat is not the Queen's personal key; it is used for the stern "threefold chords" and the Act 2 trio (No. 19) for Pamina, Tamino, and Sarastro. The keys of Sarastro's principal utterances exploit the vocal resources (low notes, wide intervals) of Franz Xaver Gerl. His aria (No. 15) is in E, reaching c-sharp′, one degree above the dominant; his deepest note is F, the keynote of "O Isis und Osiris" (No. 10) and the fifth (dominant) in the trio. Mozart appreciated that Anna Gottlieb (once little Barbarina in *Figaro*) could now, as Pamina, ascend expressively to high B-flat and pitch wide intervals in her aria (No. 17). In each finale she sings important passages in F. In the first (from m. 395), kneeling, she explains her escape to Sarastro (whose kindly response brings his first low F).[11] In the second finale (from m. 277), embracing Tamino, she leaps to the high mediant, a″. Such instrumental and vocal considerations were more likely to have been at the forefront of Mozart's choice of keys than symbolism or larger structural questions.

Musical Styles

The variety of musical styles in *The Magic Flute*, and the separation of musical numbers by lengthy dialogues, gave rise to a study whose title queries whether it is more muddle than masterpiece.[12] *The Magic Flute* overture prepares us for grand ideas, and for storm and stress, but not for the sufferings of the characters; the Introduction (No. 1) combines terror and high comedy. Papageno's entry introduces a new stylistic element, for "Der Vogelfänger bin ich ja" (No. 2) is headed "Aria" but is essentially a popular song.

Seeing the dead serpent, Papageno flinches, but (in speech) he is soon lying glibly to Tamino. This first passage of spoken dialogue introduces elements – comedy, deceit, friendship – that recur throughout the opera, in speech and in musical numbers. The strophic song form used by Papageno (twice) reappears in arias for Monostatos and Sarastro; Mozart also found strophic forms useful in arias that are not popular in character. The central plot is launched when, in the first true aria (No. 3, "Dies Bildnis ist bezaubernd schön"), Tamino contemplates Pamina's portrait. Like most arias in *The Magic Flute*, it is in one tempo throughout. Although Mozart composed several important arias in two or more tempi (e.g., those for Fiordiligi in *Così fan tutte*), only two in *The Magic Flute* change speed: the Queen's first, grandly operatic in style, and Papageno's second, popular in style. This usage corresponds to *Der Stein der Weisen* (written for – and, indeed, partly by – some of the same singers).

Mozart's aria forms, like their keys, were selected to suit the strengths of the singers. But, in turn, these choices may affect our understanding of character. In a strophic song or a single-tempo aria the dramatic situation remains essentially unchanged; rather than advancing the action, the music explores the singing personality. Correspondences with characters in other works by Mozart, not necessarily of the same voice type, also contribute to the context in which we listen today: Heartz revealingly juxtaposes passages from *The Magic Flute* and *La clemenza di Tito*.[13] When Tamino rises in his first phrase to g' (the mediant), and develops it with its upper neighbor, the resulting gentle tension suggests comparisons to Mozart's song "Das Traumbild" and the Countess's E-flat aria ("Porgi amor") in *Figaro*.[14]

The arias in Act 2 richly develop the varied characters: Monostatos intent on rape (No. 13), the Queen chastising her daughter (No. 14), Sarastro comforting Pamina (No. 15), her despair at Tamino's obdurate silence (No. 17, "Ach ich fühl's"), and Papageno's second strophic song (No. 20, the stanzas progressively elaborated by the "magic bells"). Each form suits characters whose feelings at this stage are concentrated on one thing only. This makes the two-tempo aria for the Queen in Act 1 (No. 4) a significant exception. We hear her approach before we see her; the libretto mentions a "hideous chord with music" ("erschütternde Akkord mit Musik"), for which Mozart provided no notation. Her arrival should be spectacular, and her appearance visibly alarms Tamino, for her first words, in recitative, are "Do not tremble" ("O zittre nicht"). McClelland identifies her entry music as *tempesta*, pointing to its "veiled" reappearance in the brilliant B-flat major Allegro that concludes the aria.[15] The first, slow section of the aria is a plaint in G minor, the key Mozart favored for women in distress.[16] The voice rises with almost overdone sincerity to a semitone above the keynote (a-flat″), foreign to the G minor scale, and the harmonized cadential descent (mm. 59–60) employs all twelve pitches of the chromatic set.

At this point, the Queen appears sympathetic, and Tamino is easily persuaded to attempt Pamina's rescue; but her music – including another unusual feature: aria sections in different keys – may allow us to question her sincerity. The difference from Pamina's G minor aria is telling. The 6/8 meter of "Ach ich fühl's" is more lilting than the Queen's 3/4, but the phrasing is hesitant, the vocal line divided by rests. The Queen's line is more sustained and controlled (indeed controlling, of Tamino). Pamina's coloratura (many notes to a syllable) is slower, gentler, and not strato-spheric like the Queen's, and her wide intervals (one and a half octaves: m. 34) are agonized where those of Sarastro seem authoritative, secure. Wide vocal intervals for Fiordiligi are sometimes misinterpreted as satirical, but they were part of every prima donna's technique.[17]

Chromatic saturation does not in itself imply insincerity. In the Queen's aria, it provides information which, with hindsight, suggests that, if not actually lying, she is operating on Tamino for her own selfish ends. Pamina's closing phrases use ten of the possible twelve notes (lacking only F and B), but her final cadences are straightforwardly diatonic. She is less complex than her mother, but the distribution of musical elements suggests the genuineness of her love and consequent misery. Pamina's entry in the second finale adopts C minor and then intensifies tonally to G minor (from m. 80); all twelve pitches are in play at the cadence (mm. 92–93). Yet this cadence is deceptive; the music, like her suicide, is inter-rupted when the Genii intervene, and G minor is displaced by E-flat, which the Genii adopt for the Allegro. Thus the course of Pamina's life, like Tamino's in the first finale, is turned round by a harmonic deception.

Whereas in Mozart's *opera buffa* finales, the linked sections consist mostly of ensembles that usually run their course to a cadence, those of *The Magic Flute* include various kinds of declamation, recitative-like or in tempo, and sections of music that are "open" in form, without a final cadence. This freedom enabled him to include the complex scene of Tamino's realization that all may not be as it seemed prior to his arrival at the temples. Following solemn, if nonspecific, advice from the Genii, he

Example 5.1 The Queen's "O zittre nicht" (No. 4) and Tamino's "O ew'ge Nacht" (No. 8).

is left alone to express his puzzlement in recitative. Rejected at two of the temple gates, he is confronted at the third by the "Elderly Priest" (also sometimes called "Sprecher" [Orator][18]) whose entry, which changes Tamino's life, is signaled by a change of harmonic direction when A-flat follows the descending C minor arpeggio (m. 85, Adagio). Recitative allows Mozart to distinguish orchestrally between Tamino's impetuosity and the Priest's grave, if cryptic, responses. When Tamino grows agitated, with tremolo (m. 109, "Sarastro herrschet hier"), the harmony implies resolution into F minor; as if in reproof, the Priest contradicts this expectation with a C minor chord (m. 110), rather than C major, the dominant of F. More sustained harmonies, as if to calm the young man, introduce the Priest's last words, sung in tempo (m. 137), in A minor, to a distinct melodic shape – a minuscule arioso.

Still more perplexed about what is truth and what deceit, Tamino invokes the night ("O ew'ge Nacht!"), retaining the key of A minor, but with an unmistakable echo of the Queen's first words (Example 5.1). Can this be coincidence? Perhaps it was intentional; by harmonizing with the voice (the Queen's a' and Tamino's g-sharp: her "nicht" and his "Nacht"), the chords in the upper parts clash with the retained bass note.[19] Other musical cross-references, making connections across the spoken dialogues, suggest that in this opera Mozart, or his unconscious, may have been working that way. The scene is concluded in A minor, when the Priest's miniature arioso is twice repeated on cellos, accompanying the unseen male chorus.

Tamino has recourse to the magic flute, playing solo in a section unlike anything in Mozart's other finales.[20] "Wie stark ist nicht dein Zauberton" is an open form; after a reprise and a darkening to C minor, the flute scale is answered by Papageno's pipe and the song breaks off. Tamino's excited response (m. 212, Presto) ascends to f', then a', on a pause (m. 216); there follows one measure only of Adagio, then Presto, this time with a cadence in C. He exits to a recitative-style punctuation figure, very much like that with which he had approached the temples. Unfortunately, Pamina and Papageno enter from the other direction, as if to remind us that *The Magic Flute* is, among other things, a comedy. The last part of the finale, framed by choruses in praise of Sarastro, proceeds swiftly and flexibly through confrontations and the noble couple's moment of recognition. The key scheme is simple (C major and near relations G and F), without deceptive tonal shifts, for good and evil are now distinct; Sarastro's speech to Pamina is all benevolence, he punishes Monostatos, and although he parts the lovers before their trials, trumpets and drums in C major proclaim his dignity and strength.

When Mozart went to Munich to work on *Idomeneo* in the presence of the singers, he engaged in an epistolary battle with the librettist (by way of his father) and exerted further control by composing the final ballet, which could have been left to a local composer. In Vienna Mozart lived near his poets, so there is no comparable record of their collaboration. But given his intimacy with Schikaneder and his troupe, it seems likely that he helped shape elements of the libretto and stage action and was happy with the freedom these offered to select appropriate musical forms without having to bend to the will of the highly paid singers at the court theater. Schikaneder, as impresario, no doubt took a controlling hand in ensuring the variety and brilliance of the spectacle, but it was surely Mozart who decided to set the various trials to strikingly original music that eschews the invitation to melodramatic excess.

Pamina, unlike Tamino and the reluctant Papageno, seems not to know that she is being subjected to trials, which she mostly has to face alone. The men receive specific advice after the solemn hymn ("O Isis und Osiris"), when two Priests interrogate them in dialogue, concluding with a very short duet (No. 11). The words are an invitation to critics of the opera seeking out misogyny. But Mozart does not present this stern advice to beware of the wiles of women in severe, minor key music, nor in the martial style already associated with Sarastro. Instead, the music is fast, light in tone and texture, in a comic vein, the flowing, *galant* melody incorporating a chromatic innuendo (on the words "er fehlte"). True, the orchestra includes trombones. But even the march-like conclusion (from m. 18) is sung *sotto voce*, with the orchestra *piano* and *staccato*. Mozart seems to imply that although the men must follow the Priests' injunction, we – the audience – should not take it too seriously.

Tamino is given no music to correspond to the pain he must feel on hearing Pamina's aria ("Ach ich fühl's"), and his flute, even if it is heard during the dialogues (as sometimes happens, without notation from Mozart), is of no service here. The use of dialogue, rather than recitative, contributes directly to characterization when the Queen, who does not speak in the first act, confronts Pamina before her tempestuous "Der Hölle Rache" by talking – like an ordinary person. In this justly celebrated aria, requiring her to hit the top note four times (against once in Act 1), Mozart again shows his resourcefulness in handling tonal form, which requires a return to the original key, D minor, and also to the passagework heard in the subsidiary key, F major. So her rage now overflows in running triplets (from m. 69), before the passagework resumes, compensating for its lower pitch (reaching d''' rather than f''') by a sequential extension (from m. 77). The conclusion is an incisive recitative ("Hört der Mutter Schwur!"), with eleven pitches (missing only C) in the last few measures.

Another trial for Pamina is that she is reintroduced to Tamino (in dialogue), only to be told by Sarastro (speaking) that they are meeting for their "letzte Lebewohl" (final farewell). When the music starts (Trio, No. 19), Sarastro contradicts himself, singing that they will meet again ("Ihr werdet froh euch wiedersehn"). The lovers seem not to hear, even at the end where Sarastro's deep notes reassure us: "We'll meet again" ("Wir sehn uns wieder"). Pamina's deafness to Sarastro's *words* leads to further despair and her resolve to die if she must lose Tamino. The trio's music is serene (Andante moderato in B-flat, with few woodwind instruments but no brass or percussion) and may represent the truth of the situation, but not the whole truth, for it leaves the lovers in uncertainty. In the interests of dramatic suspense, Mozart is careful not to express this too obviously.

The lovers' reunion within the finale is in F major, the key of the solemn march that opened Act 2. Now Pamina takes control; after an outburst of joy, she becomes grave on recognizing the magic flute. As in the parallel scene with the Elderly Priest in the first finale, Mozart turns to near-recitative, moving fluidly (m. 317) to G minor, before returning to the local tonic, F, for a quartet in which Pamina soars above Tamino and the two Armored Men. After each trial the lovers' voices join, their personalities merged as if in matrimony; their silence in the last scene at their moment of glorification marks their absorption into the community, and with it, perhaps, a loss of autonomy.

For the final trials Mozart hit on something extraordinary. Did Schikaneder ask him not to make the music too exciting, in case it distracted from the visual representation of the perils of fire and water? For in this scene the spectacle (as in the French "merveilleux") should indeed be wonderful. Mozart makes no attempt to parallel what the stage machinery offers; fire and water are alike in the music. Not every late eighteenth-century composer would be so reticent; compare the collapse of the magic palace and gardens in Lully's *Armide* (a simple, major key flourish) with the D-minor histrionics to which Gluck set the same libretto (1777). Mozart created a unique sound-world; it sufficed to provide the flute with its second solo, over basic harmony from a brass choir, the phrases softly punctuated by timpani. Taken out of context, this might appear dry, unresponsive, and not a little weird; within the opera it is utterly compelling.

Apotheosis of Papageno

When the chorus proclaims "Triumph!" the opera might have ended, except that the key is still C major, not E-flat, and Papageno's story is incomplete. He seems to have failed the trials, but he is otherwise worthy and does no harm. He has glimpsed a youthful Papagena, cruelly snatched away. He becomes worthy of her through his willingness to die. The scene is in G major, like his first song, but the musical form is far from simple. He calls her name, with a fanfare shape resembling the choral "Triumph!" of the Act 1 finale, and pipes in vain to summon her. Then comes new melodic material that forms the basis of a sonata rondo of 130 measures, a thoroughly modern (though usually instrumental) form that cannot be called popular. Mozart takes full control by imposing a musical design on a shapeless text. The rondo theme involves stuttering calls and the smoother phrase first heard at measure 418. When this phrase returns at measure 444, the two-note anacrusis will not fit the words, so Mozart uses a three-note anacrusis instead; at measure 468 the original anacrusis is restored (Example 5.2).

The rondo episodes are Papageno's only extended minor-mode music, though his tragicomic "O Weh!" ended the first-act quintet in G minor. The first episode uses the relative, E minor, with an agitated running figure

Example 5.2 Papageno in the Act 2 finale, comparison of mm. 443–47 and 468–71.

[443]

und drum ge - schieht es mir schon recht,___ drum ge - schieht es mir__ schon recht.

[467]

Ster - ben macht der Lieb' ein End',___ wenn's im Her - zen noch__ so brennt.

Example 5.3 Papageno in the Act 2 finale, motives from the same section, mm. 415–17
and 447–49.

Papageno (*pfeift*)

Oboes, horns

[415]

Violins

[447]

[*p*]

inverting his piping motif (Example 5.3); chromatic runs further expand
Papageno's musical lexicon.

In the second episode, as if in empathy with Pamina, Papageno adopts
G minor, relating the episode material to the main keynote. His tonal
domain is further enriched by cadences in its relative, B-flat (to m. 493).
Papageno is an allegro character, but now he falters, with sensitive chromatic
touches (G minor, with "Neapolitan" A-flat, m. 539), in a passage that could
almost be inserted into her aria. Again, harmonic interruption signals
a change of fortune; a G-minor cadence seems to have been prepared, but
is displaced by a dominant seventh on G, pointing to C (m. 543). In a new
tempo and meter, the Genii remind Papageno of the magic bells, which ring
out again in C major before the scene is rounded tonally by returning to
G for the duet with Papagena.

This is the climax of the comic element in *The Magic Flute*, but with all
Papageno has gone through, it is an epiphany he thoroughly deserves,
prepared by the relative complexity of his sonata rondo. With the ensembles in which he takes part, this scene confirms that Schikaneder was an
accomplished musician as well as a versatile actor and ambitious impresario. This apotheosis of the bird couple is remote from the world of the
temple, but the authors' enlightenment conception seems to have been that

simple folk, without ambition and represented mainly in a comic mode, should receive their due as real people who can also suffer. Papageno's actions are a potent critique of the initiates who have brought him to this pass. Mozart's music is pitched at a level that makes it possible to interpret it as simultaneously comical and essentially serious. We may laugh at Papageno's counting one-two-three before accepting his destiny, but it is through tears – unless we withhold those for the sudden incursion of the Genii, whose music throughout is among the most beguiling of the whole opera.

The Genii and the Ending

The Genii ("Knaben") embody the comical sublime that binds the disparate strands of the opera – not, mercifully, into a "unity" but into a more interesting kind of wholeness. They are purely musical; they are only heard in song. Their first entry (Act 1 finale) is heralded by an imposing slow march, using trombones for the first time since the overture, in marked contrast to their high voices. On their last appearance, they toss Papagena onto the stage in a scene of pure fun. These entries may be made on foot, but for one delicious ensemble (No. 16), they should appear in a flying machine ("Flugwerk"). Their words echo the Priests in command-ing the initiates to silence, distinguishing Tamino from Papageno, but the music is the same for each; the dancing A major Allegretto in 6/8 has some of the lightest orchestration even for this opera, so that, as with the Priests' duet, we are encouraged not to take the next trial too much in earnest. Sounding graver in the second finale, counseling Pamina (from m. 94), the Genii nevertheless sing in a delicately orchestrated *galant* style. Less indi-vidualized than the Queen's Ladies (the first of whom has a few solo passages and who do speak), the Genii affect the action more and touch the extremes of the opera's dramatic and musical range.

At the end, a scene heralded by a glorious sunrise, the Genii and the noble lovers are on stage, but silent. The Queen's futile attempt at a coup is followed by a final transition from darkness to light and to the framing key, E-flat major. The brittle C-minor march of the Queen and her minions and the violence of their overthrow are slowed by whole-measure harmonies in tremolo (Example 5.4). The transition emerges onto F, which, with an added seventh, brings temporary closure in B-flat. The chain of suspen-sions (mm. 820–21) invites a slight relaxation of the tempo, not indicated

Example 5.4 Act 2 finale, the Queen and her entourage, mm. 812–22.

by Mozart but an invitation to conductors that is sometimes accepted to good effect.

As the stage fills with light, orchestral gestures give Sarastro's short recitative the incisive character of his entry in Act 1. His speech overlaps with a steadily unfolding cadence, in tempo (Andante), settling in E-flat. The chorus enters with more intertextual references. Within the Act 2 finale, the scene of the two Armored Men already recalled the overture by its imitative counterpoint (albeit with a different theme) and the first finale by its solemn introduction. The latter is more literally redeployed to start the final two-section chorus that proceeds from solemn thankfulness to festive joy (Example 5.5).

The glorification of Pamina and Tamino is followed by an Allegro *contredanse* of the kind often used in symphonic finales, its pointed first theme (m. 847) contrasted with a lyrical phrase (m. 787), which may remind us that this work was intended to entertain as much as, if not more than, edify.

The Magic Flute, in sum, is not a muddle, but an inspired synthesis of stylistic elements. Joseph Kerman endorsed Edward J. Dent's "appreciation of the impeccable dramatic structure," in which "the music sums up the dramatic situation and illuminates it" in every number.[21] In this respect, the music also justifies the dialogues which Dent's edition curtailed, while resisting any temptation to subvert the work's nature by substituting

Example 5.5 Act 2 finale comparison: mm. 190–96 (Adagio of the Armored Men) and 829–34 (in the opera's last scene).

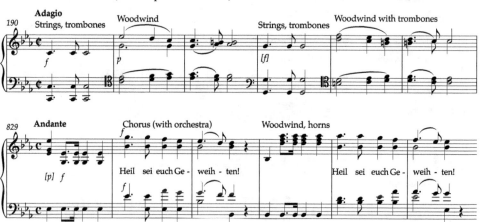

recitative.[22] Antonio Salieri, no mean composer of opera, serious and comic, and Caterina Cavalieri, the first Konstanze in *Die Entführung*, rightly called *The Magic Flute* an "operone" (grand opera).[23] There is no need to apologize for its stylistic mixture which, on the contrary, is an essential part of its strength.

Notes

1. Structural parallels with *The Magic Flute* are detailed in *Der Stein der Weisen*, ed. David J. Buch (Middleton, WI: A-R Editions, 2007), xiv.
2. *Così fan tutte* contains more orchestral recitative than is usual in *opera buffa*, but not in finales. Mozart's longest orchestral recitatives are in *Idomeneo*, a serious opera without multisection finales.
3. The dedicatory preface to *Alceste* (1769) states that the overture should prepare the audience for the drama to follow, an intention most fully realized in *Iphigénie en Aulide* (1774).
4. Daniel Heartz, "The Overture to *La clemenza di Tito* as Dramatic Argument," in *Mozart's Operas*, ed. Thomas Bauman (Berkeley: University of California Press, 1990), 319–41.
5. On "learned style" and other topics, see Leonard G. Ratner, *Classic Music: Expression, Form, and Style* (New York: Schirmer, 1980).
6. Clive McClelland, *Tempesta: Stormy Music in the Eighteenth Century* (Lanham, MD: Lexington Books, 2017), 135–37 (on *The Magic Flute*).

7. The time-signature implies a half-note beat, like the overture, not the quarter-note beat of the opening.
8. See Leopold Mozart's letter to his wife, November 24, 1770. LMF, 171; MBA, I:405.
9. Hermann Abert, *W. A. Mozart*, trans. Stewart Spencer, ed. Cliff Eisen (New Haven, CT: Yale University Press, 2007), 1265.
10. In *Der Stein der Weisen*, the composition of a tenor aria also in E-flat (No. 9) is attributed to Schack.
11. This is also the first use of basset horns, low clarinets pitched in F; the hieratic association of these mellow instruments is confirmed in the opening scene of Act 2 and in Mozart's Requiem.
12. H.-K. Metzger and R. Riehn, "Ist die Zauberflöte ein Machwerk?," *Musik-Konzepte*, no. 3 (1978).
13. Daniel Heartz, "La Clemenza di Sarastro: Masonic Beneficence in the Last Operas," in Heartz, *Mozart's Operas*, 255–76, at 265, 273–4.
14. Virginia Rushton, "Mozart's Lieder: A Survey," *Studies in Music from the University of Western Ontario* 14 (1993): 105–130, at 122–27.
15. McClelland, *Tempesta*, 135–36.
16. Steven Jan, *Mozart's Music in G Minor* (New York: Garland, 1995).
17. Julian Rushton, "*Così fan tutte*: Mozart's Serious Comic Opera," *Studies in Music from the University of Western Ontario* 14 (1993): 49–78, at 56–64.
18. On the designation of this priest, see NMA II/5/19, xvi.
19. Abert calls Tamino's phrase "clearly reminiscent" of the Queen's (*W. A. Mozart*, 1275), without remarking on the dissonance, implicitly a dominant chord superimposed on the keynote in the bass.
20. Animals come to listen, and the stage direction adds "Birds sing along," for which, again, Mozart provided no notation.
21. Joseph Kerman, *Opera as Drama*, 2nd edn. (London: Faber & Faber, 1988), 107.
22. As did Franz Lachner with Cherubini's *Médée* and Ernest Guiraud with Bizet's *Carmen*.
23. Mozart's letter of October 14, 1791. LMF, 970–71; MBA, IV:161–63.

6 | Enduring Portraits: The Arias

LAUREL E. ZEISS

The arias in Mozart's *The Magic Flute* are undoubtedly some of the most recognizable in the operatic repertoire. What factors influenced their creation? The same ones that shaped practically all opera arias in the eighteenth century: poetic structures, musical and dramatic conventions, as well as the abilities of the singers who originated the roles. Staging and other practical considerations also played a part. What, then, makes these arias so enduring and memorable? Mozart's ability to create vivid music that portrays the character and dramatic situation might be one answer. How the arias explore and stretch customary operatic practices and musical language could be another. The composer seems to have taken great care to make each aria distinctive. The arias' diversity of style, color, and affect is striking, especially when we hear and see them in the context of the drama. Moreover, most contain something unusual or extravagant – a musical element or moment that extends beyond the ordinary. As a result, the arias offer a compelling demonstration of one of the opera's main themes: the power of music.

What Shapes an Aria?

All arias involve multiple components – what some analysts refer to as "domains."[1] Poetic structures and literary devices within the text often shape the vocal line's phrases as well as the aria's musical meter and overall musical form. The composer can opt to adhere closely to the text's poetic form (to set the text line by line, for example) or s/he can choose to repeat words, sentences, or entire stanzas. The vocal line can be primarily syllabic or melismatic (multiple notes present one syllable of text); it can be more declamatory in nature, lyrical and tuneful, or florid. As we shall see, how the orchestra interacts with the vocal line can vary a great deal. The instruments can double the voice, utter comments in between the vocal phrases, or be quite independent. The orchestral material itself may encompass interlocking rhythmic layers, and certain instruments may carry semantic associations. In addition, the dramatic situation and a character's social status and gender can also influence an aria's musical content.[2] Finally, the strengths and proclivities of the initial cast actively shaped the music. Eighteenth-century composers knew the singing and acting abilities of the performers who would premiere their works and composed with those in mind. The original singer's range and technical prowess could influence an aria's tonality, orchestration, and, most importantly, the scope and nature of the vocal line, including such things as the size and number of the leaps or runs it contained. As Mozart himself wrote in February 1778, "I love it when an aria is so accurately measured for a singer's voice that it fits like a well-tailored suit of clothes."[3]

In other words, even though arias combine music and text and use standard musical forms, many additional factors influence the end result, which in turn affects how and what the number reveals about the character who sings it. While many writers focus primarily on musical form when analyzing arias,[4] *The Magic Flute* contains examples in which overarching form is perhaps the least important and telling aspect. Frequently, other elements contribute more to the aria's expressivity and the dramaturgical role it plays. Our journey through *The Magic Flute*'s arias will begin with three examples that share the same form, to demonstrate how these other musical and dramatic components shape a number. It will then examine arias for each character, to show how Mozart responds to poetic content and structures, adapts conventions, "tailors" arias to the singers who created the roles, and infuses each number with delightful, extravagant touches.

Strophic Numbers for the Bird-Catcher, the Moor, and the Ruler

"Der Vogelfänger bin ich ja," "Alles fühlt der Lieben Freuden," and "In diesen heil'gen Hallen" share the same form. All are strophic; in each case, two stanzas of text are set to the same music. Because the poetic stanzas share the same meter and number of lines, the same music can be repeated for each verse of text. In all three arias, the rhyme scheme remains the same for both verses.

In addition to matching stanzas, the text for the first aria sung by the bird-catcher Papageno, "Der Vogelfänger bin ich ja," contains other poetic features that influence the musical form (see Table 6.1). Both eight-line strophes commence with exactly the same four lines. Each poetic line ends

Table 6.1 "Der Vogelfänger bin ich ja": text, translation, and rhyme scheme

Der Vogelfänger bin ich **ja**,	a	The bird-catcher am I, yes,
Stets lustig, heißa! hop**sasa!**	a	Always merry, *heißa! hopsasa!*
Ich Vogelfänger bin be**kannt**	b	I the bird-catcher am well known
Bei Alt und Jung im ganzen **Land**.	b	By old and young throughout the land.
Weiß mit den Locken umzu**geh'n**,	c	I know how to handle snares,
Und mich aufs Pfeifen zu ver**steh'n**.	c	And to make myself understood by piping.
Drum kann ich froh und lustig **sein**;	d	Thus, can I be happy and merry;
Denn alle Vögel sind ja **mein**. *(Pfeift.)*	d	For all the birds are mine. *(Plays the pipe.)*
Der Vogelfänger bin ich **ja**,	a	The bird-catcher am I, yes,
Stets lustig, heißa! hop**sasa!**	a	Always merry, *heißa! hopsasa!*
Ich Vogelfänger bin be**kannt**	b	I the bird-catcher am well known
Bei Alt und Jung im ganzen **Land**.	b	By old and young throughout the land.
Ein Netz für Mädchen möchte **ich**;	e	A net for maidens would I like;
Ich fing' sie dutzendweis für **mich**.	e	I would catch them for me by the dozens.
Dann sperrte ich sie bei mir **ein**,	f	Then, I would lock them up at my place,
Und alle Mädchen wären **mein**.	f	And all the maidens would be mine.
(Pfeift . . .)		*(Plays the pipe . . .)*

[Center column of letters = rhyme scheme. Bold = accented syllable & line ending.]

with an accented syllable. The text's straightforward meter and simple rhyme scheme (rhyming couplets) prompt end-oriented phrases in the music: regular four-bar phrases that begin on upbeats and cadence on strong beats.

Much else in the aria remains within a narrow scope. The vocal line spans a ninth, but many of its gestures move within a fifth or even a third. The upper strings largely double the voice. The limited range and doubling of the voice line may be due to the abilities and reputation of the singer who premiered the role. The first Papageno, Emanuel Schikaneder, was the opera's librettist and the star of the troupe. He was primarily an actor and impresario, not an opera singer, and had performed in a wide variety of roles; in Vienna, he had made a name for himself by playing comic, not too bright, peasant characters such as the gardener Anton (another role he wrote for himself).

Yet the aria's harmonic vocabulary is also limited, inordinately so. Most chords are in root position; tonic-dominant-tonic progressions dominate; many dominant chords lack a seventh. Mi-re-do (3–2–1) figures permeate the melody. In other words, the music is about as diatonic as it could possibly be. The key – G major – is simple, too.

Together, the limited verbal, melodic, and harmonic content gives the impression that Papageno is the unsophisticated "Naturmensch" (natural man) he later claims to be. What you hear is what you get. The strophic form, straightforward syllabic melody, and nonsense syllables in the text also give the aria what some commentators call a *Volkston* or folk tone.[5]

Monostatos's aria, "Alles fühlt der Liebe Freuden," also uses strophic form, but the aria's poetic and grammatical structures, irregular phrases, and musical conventions for portraying Otherness result in a very different-sounding aria. Like "Der Vogelfänger bin ich ja," the text consists of two eight-line stanzas that share the same meter and rhyme scheme, but in this case the rhyme scheme and metrical pattern are more complicated. Each poetic line begins with an accented syllable; thus, practically every vocal phrase starts on a strong beat. The ends of lines, however, alternate between accented and unaccented syllables. Some poetic lines, particularly in the second verse, contain incises or shorter phrases within the longer line, as in the stanza's opening lines:

Drum so will ich, weil ich lebe,	Thus, I wish, because I am alive,
Schnäbeln, küssen, zärtlich sein! –	To coo, kiss, to be tender! –
Lieber, guter Mond – vergebe	Dear, good moon – forgive [me]

In the 1791 libretto, Monostatos is described in the dramatis personae as "ein Mohr" (a Moor). Pamina calls him "Der böse Mohr" (the wicked Moor) during the Act 1 finale (scene 18). Monostatos refers to himself as "Ein Schwarzer" (a black man) during his aria, as does Papageno in Act 1, scene 14.[6] "Exotic," lecherous men were a specialty of singer-actor Johann Nouseul, who premiered the role. The poetry and the character depicted prompted Mozart to employ many of the musical devices associated with "Turkish" music in the 1700s, including duple meter, a fast tempo, and phrases that begin on a strong beat with a longer note followed by sixteenths or eighths and are uneven in length.[7] The aria opens with a lopsided nine-measure introduction (five measures plus four measures) rather than the customary four, eight, or two bars. Irregular phrase lengths continue throughout the aria. In fact, just as five-measure phrases seem to become the norm, two-measure or three-measure insertions interrupt the pattern (see mm. 25–34, for example).

The instrumentation also signifies Otherness. The piccolo (an unusual instrument for the time), flute, and first violin double one another, while the lower strings reiterate a single pitch for the first five bars. As Mary Hunter has argued, the *alla turca* style "represents Turkish music as a deficient or messy version of European music."[8] In this case, the sparse orchestration supports an equally sparse or "deficient" tune. The melody circles around a single pitch, the tonic. In fact, one could apply the epithet "too many notes" to this number – it has too many of the *same* notes, because so many pitches are reiterated. Even the aria's home key, C major, can be considered a sign of Otherness, as that tonality was commonly used to portray these types of characters. In short, much about "Alles fühlt der Liebe Freuden" is irregular, despite the regular rhythms of the text and the repetitive strophic form. Arguably, Monostatos's Otherness and the resultant musical irregularities have to be contained within a repetitive, predictable form.

Sarastro's "In diesen heil'gen Hallen" is also strophic, but differences in multiple domains distinguish it from the opera's other strophic numbers. The aria's text consists of two six-line stanzas whose scansion is more complex than the above examples. Lines 1–4 alternate rhymes and unaccented line endings with accented ones. Two lines that conclude with accented syllables close each stanza, forming a rhyming couplet. The stanzas themselves are linked by anaphora – beginning with the same word or phrase – in this case the words "In diesen heil'gen." This poetic device implies strophic form.

While the overall musical form of the aria is strophic, the strophe itself is through-composed. The vocal line does not conclude any of its phrases on the tonic until the strophe's final bars; instead, Mozart has the vocal phrases end on scale degrees 3 or 5. Both of these musical choices create a sense of forward momentum and continuity of thought. The shape of the vocal line does as well. In accordance with the prosody of the text and in contrast with Monostatos's aria, Sarastro's vocal lines all commence on an upbeat; most conclude on a downbeat on a more stable harmony. While the vocal line in all three strophic arias is largely syllabic, Sarastro's vocal line is more conjunct and thus sounds more lyrical. Appoggiaturas abound.

The relationship between the accompaniment and the vocal line also differs. Even a cursory glance at the score reveals more counterpoint between the voice and the orchestra than in the other strophic numbers, perhaps due to the skill of the original performer. The first Sarastro, Franz Xaver Gerl, was an accomplished musician, a composer and performer, who had studied under Mozart's father, Leopold, as a choirboy in Salzburg.

What does the use of strophic form for "In diesen heil'gen Hallen" imply? Perhaps that the character Sarastro and the values he espouses (friendship, forgiveness, love) are constant and unchanging. Together, the vocal line's low range, the stately tempo, and the aria's straightforward form depict Sarastro as a calm, reasonable person, particularly since the number contrasts starkly with the aria that immediately precedes it, the Queen's "Der Hölle Rache."

The Queen's Arias: Displays of Power and Rage

The Queen of the Night's numbers, "Der Hölle Rache" and "O zittre nicht ... Zum Leiden," exemplify how Mozart "tailors" numbers to a particular singer and adapts a variety of musical traditions to create two of the most celebrated arias ever written. The soprano who originated the role, Josepha Hofer, Mozart's sister-in-law, certainly had special capabilities. Judging from these arias and other music written for her, she must have had an agile voice and an impressive high register.[9] Both of the Queen's arias require the singer to ascend to an f''', the highest note on the Viennese piano at the time. Additionally, the character's status, musical conventions, and perhaps Mozart's desire to show off his compositional prowess converge in the Queen's music.

To take the second aria first, "Der Hölle Rache" is undeniably music fit for a Queen. The marchlike rhythms, full orchestration (strings, double winds, timpani, and trumpets), and extended coloratura passages that require exceptional vocal virtuosity signal that the character is a powerful person of high rank. Here, Mozart adapts a conventional aria type from *opera seria*. "Der Hölle Rache" has many of the hallmarks of a "rage aria." Its minor key, large leaps in the vocal line, bustling accompaniment, use of tremolo and sforzandi, and chromatic ascents and descents customarily conveyed great anger during the eighteenth century. But Mozart draws on a local Viennese tradition as well: that of spectacular arias for powerful supernatural characters. Other magical *Singspiele* written for the company that premiered *The Magic Flute* contain flashy, vocally demanding arias.[10] Paul Wranitzky's *Oberon* (1789), which also starred Hofer in a similar role, for example, includes numbers with elaborate coloratura that require the soprano to ascend to a d'''. Did competitiveness prompt Mozart to write an even higher and flashier aria?

The Queen's first aria, "O zittre nicht ... Zum Leiden," also presents extreme vocal demands and synthesizes several operatic traditions. Practical considerations shape the scene as well. Written for a theater that was celebrated for its spectacular staging, extravagant music complements extraordinary stage effects.[11] A lengthy and majestic orchestral prelude ushers the Queen onstage. Rising arpeggios over a B-flat pedal gradually increase the volume and tonal expanse. The orchestral introduction clearly portrays the Queen as a grand personage (mm. 1–10). It also allows time for the scenic transformation described in the original libretto to unfold:

> The mountains part and the theater transforms into a magnificent chamber. The Queen sits on a throne which is decorated with transparent stars.

Mozart draws on several other noble idioms to portray this character. An orchestrally accompanied recitative precedes the aria (mm. 11–20). Accompagnato in this repertoire, like coloratura and the grand prelude, also signified noble or supernatural characters. Motives from the orchestral introduction continue to frame the Queen's utterances as she reassures Tamino.

Recitativ	Recitative
O zittre nicht, mein lieber Sohn!	Do not tremble, my dear son!
Du bist unschuldig, weise, fromm;	You are innocent, wise, pious;
Ein Jüngling, so wie du, vermag am besten	A youth, such as you, can best
[Das] tief betrübte Mutterherz zu trösten.	Console this deeply saddened
	mother's heart.

"O zittre nicht … Zum Leiden" is perhaps an instance where the text's structure suggests one musical form and Mozart opted to employ another. The metered poetry of the aria commences with three quatrains, the second of which has shorter lines and a different rhyme scheme. A fourth stanza is marked Allegro. This combination of poetic structures suggests a two-tempo rondò (ABAC in form, with C being in a faster tempo), an aria type associated with upper-class heroines. While Mozart alludes to this conventional aria type, he fashions a number that is looser in form. The Andante section in particular (mm. 21–64) has an arioso-like character and is more formally ambiguous.

Arie	Aria
Zum Leiden bin ich auserkoren;	For suffering I am destined;
Denn meine Tochter fehlet mir,	For my daughter is missing from me,
Durch sie ging all mein Glück verloren –	With her all my happiness was lost –
Ein Bösewicht entfloh mit ihr.	An evil creature fled with her.
Noch seh' ich ihr Zittern	Still I see her trembling
Mit bangem Erschüttern,	With anxious shuddering,
Ihr ängstliches Beben	Her fearful tremors,
Ihr schüchternes Streben.	Her timid struggles.
Ich mußte sie mir rauben sehen,	I had to see her robbed from me,
Ach helft! war alles was sie sprach;	"O help!" was all that she spoke;
Allein vergebens war ihr Flehen,	Only in vain was her pleading,
Denn meine Hülfe war zu schwach.	For my help was too weak.

Allegro	**Allegro**
Du wirst sie zu befreien gehen,	You will go to free her,
Du wirst der Tochter Retter sein.	You will my daughter's rescuer be.
Und werd ich dich als Sieger sehen,	And if I see you as the victor,
So sei sie dann auf ewig dein.	Then shall she be yours forever.

The aria proper commences at measure 21 with a triple-meter section in G minor in the middle range of the voice. Mozart carefully crafts the opening paragraph to highlight the character's plight and the reason for it. Lightly orchestrated three-measure phrases underscore the Queen's sorrowful opening lines. In keeping with the accents of the poetry, most of the vocal phrases begin and end on weak beats, until the Queen's revelation that "an evil creature" took her daughter. Here, dotted rhythms and militaristic flourishes in the orchestra lead to the aria's first strong cadence (both the voice and bass land on the tonic) and a change of key to B-flat major (mm. 32–35).

Word painting permeates the next segment, as the Queen describes how her daughter was taken from her. Fluttering sixteenth notes in the violins depict Pamina's "trembling," "fearful tremors," and "timid struggles" (mm. 38–44). A chromatic countermelody in the bassoons and violas, which perhaps can be heard as representing Pamina, accompanies the Queen's narrative (mm. 36–44).

The aria's third verse returns to the soft dynamics, delicate scoring, and the key of G minor as the Queen describes Pamina's cries for help and her own inability to rescue her (mm. 45–61).[12] A lengthy series of minor and diminished harmonies, a deceptive cadence (m. 56), and a prolonged descent in the vocal line conclude her tale and lead into the Allegro moderato that follows.

Once the Queen completes her story, her speech shifts from past to future tense. She issues commands and promises rewards ("You will go to free her"). Mozart reflects the change to the imperative by composing it into the music. The meter, tonality, and tempo all shift – from triple to duple meter, G minor to B-flat major, Andante to Allegro moderato. Mozart also employs contrasting melodic contours. Decisive scalar figures and arpeggios in the vocal line replace the sighing figures and descending phrases that dominated the previous section. Most phrases now commence and conclude on strong beats. In fact, the composer sometimes ignores the prosody in order to do so.

The vocal line soars into the stratosphere (B-flat″ to f‴) as we approach the aria's conclusion. Extensive roulades (m. 79ff.) and the medium tessitura of the accompaniment highlight the power of the singer's (and the character's) voice. While Mozart has been criticized for setting the word "dann" (then) on a melisma lasting thirteen measures, such complaints ignore how the word contains a felicitous vowel for singing in the upper register.[13] The composer's choice also stresses the conditional nature of the Queen's promise. Melodically, the line becomes the equivalent of saying, "And if I see you as the victor, *then* she shall be forever yours." The vocal line's extensive sixteenth- and eighth-note runs broaden to half-notes to drive home the aria's final words "auf ewig dein" (forever yours). A harmonically decisive postlude that recalls the opening of the Allegro closes the entire scene.

The grand entrance music, the accompagnato, and the vocal pyrotechnics give the impression of a forceful being. The scene as a whole displays the breadth of the Queen's rhetorical arsenal as she uses three, very different musical styles to persuade Tamino to rescue her daughter. During the accompagnato she reassures and flatters; in the triple-meter Andante section she laments, narrates, and seeks empathy; during the melismatic Allegro she dispenses orders and makes promises. After such a compelling musical and rhetorical display, it is no wonder that Tamino believes she is telling the truth and undertakes his quest.

A Man of Feeling: "Dies Bildnis"

While the Queen's arias draw on traditional methods of depicting nobility, Tamino's aria "Dies Bildnis" draws on another prominent eighteenth-century dramatic convention: the portrayal of sensibility. The text's content and its punctuation indicate passionate emotions. Tamino's monologue contains repeated words, exclamation points, and dashes, particularly during its second half. The use of first person in eighteenth-century sentimental novels is often interrupted by similar pauses, exclamations, and heavily emphasized or repeated words, as in this excerpt from the quintessential sentimental novel, Samuel Richardson's *Pamela*:

This is indeed too much, too much for your poor Pamela! And as I hoped all the worst was over, and that I had the pleasure of beholding a reclaimed gentleman, and not an abandoned libertine. What now must your poor daughter do! O the wretched, wretched Pamela![14]

And this selection from J. W. von Goethe's *The Sorrows of Young Werther*:

Why I have not written to you?—You, who are a learned man too, ask a question like that. You might guess that things are well with me, and indeed—In a word, I have made an acquaintance who has touched my heart very closely. I have—I know not what. … I am unable to tell you how, and why, she is perfection itself; suffice it to say that she has captivated me utterly.

So much simplicity with so much understanding, so much goodness and so much resolve, and tranquility of soul together with true life and vitality.[15]

As James Webster points out, "Dies Bildnis" as a whole depicts how Tamino's feelings "progress … from [the character's] initial undifferentiated reaction to the portrait, through the realization that he has fallen in love, and the confusion engendered by awakened but unfulfilled passion, to conviction."[16] Mozart's music enhances the arc of Tamino's emotional journey in a number of ways. The composer matches Tamino's fragmented ruminations with irregular phrases, harmonic interruptions, rests, and pauses. For example, an unexpected harmony (an augmented sixth chord) on the downbeat of measure 12 underscores the "new emotion" Tamino feels. The musical setting increases the text repetition even more. To give but one instance, the prince asks himself, "Could this sensation be love?" twice (mm. 22–25), before responding, "It is love alone. Love, love, love alone" (mm. 27–34).

Dies Bildnis ist bezaubernd schön,	This image is enchantingly beautiful,
Wie noch kein Auge je geseh'n!	As no eye has ever seen!
Ich fühl' es, wie dies Götterbild	I feel it, how this godly portrait
Mein Herz mit neuer Regung füllt.	My heart with new emotion fills.
Dieß Etwas kann ich zwar nicht nennen;	This "something" to be certain I cannot name;
Doch fühl' ichs hier wie Feuer brennen.	Yet I feel it here like fire burning.
Soll die Empfindung Liebe sein?	Could this sensation be love?
Ja, ja! die Liebe ist's allein. –	Yes, yes! It is love alone. –
O wenn ich sie nur finden könnte!	O if only I could find her!
O wenn sie doch schon vor mir stände!	O if she already stood before me!
Ich würde – würde – warm und rein –	I would – would – warmly and purely –
Was würde ich? – Sie voll Entzücken	What would I do? – Full of delight,
An diesen heißen Busen drücken,	[I would] press her to this scorching breast,
Und ewig wäre sie dann mein.	And then for eternity would she be mine.

Harmonic arrivals and departures promote the sensation of emotional transformation. This surface variety is grounded in a clear tonal structure. A paragraph in the tonic (mm. 1–15) is followed by one in the dominant key (mm. 16–34). The aria's third paragraph prolongs the harmonic tension through extended dominant pedals (mm. 35–43) that lead to a grand pause. A full bar of silence precedes the tonic's unequivocal return at a crucial dramatic moment (discussed below).

The aria's melodic variety, complex orchestration, and through-composed form suggest that Tamino is a refined, more complicated person. Not surprisingly, the number was written for a sophisticated, multitalented musician, Benedikt Schack, who was praised by Mozart's father for his elegant singing.[17] In contrast to the arias written for Schikaneder, the orchestra here rarely doubles the voice; when it does, it presents embellished versions of the vocal line. At times, the orchestra paints the text; sixteenth- and thirty-second-note figures during the third paragraph, for example, portray Tamino's growing ardor and pounding heart. Simon P. Keefe suggests that the clarinets, bassoons, and horns included in the ensemble underscore (literally and figuratively) the character's aristocratic status and were chosen to enhance Schack's beautiful tenor voice.[18]

In addition to being an illustration of growing sentiment, "Dies Bildnis" can also be understood as a shift from ignorance to awareness – what Aristotelian poetics calls a scene of recognition. Musically, the aria meets Jessica Waldoff's criteria for recognition scenes. Her study of these pivotal dramatic moments shows that musical shifts prompt shifts in action or thought, which are then followed by an explanatory narrative. Musical recollections (references to prior material) also frequently occur.[19] "Dies Bildnis" encompasses all of these, albeit in miniature. A musical shift precedes Tamino's realization that he is in love. Winds and horns *sans* strings lead into his ecstatic "Ja, ja" (Yes! Yes! mm. 24–26). The modulation to the dominant is confirmed decisively in both the vocal and orchestral material shortly thereafter (m. 34). That in turn ushers in an extended dominant pedal as Tamino expounds upon his desires. The character then begins to fashion his own explanatory, self-predictive narrative, a narrative he later seeks to fulfill: "What would I do? I would press her to this scorching bosom, and then for eternity would she be mine." An entire measure of silence – comparable to the dashes in sentimental fiction – precedes his final declaration. The aria concludes with the richest accompaniment pattern yet (three interlocking gestures) and a musical recollection. The aria's closing figures repeat, decorate, and extend material that originally accompanied the words "my heart with new emotion fills" (compare mm. 10–15 to mm. 52–61).

Tamino repeats his final declaration five times. Regardless of whether we view this monologue as a sentimental statement or a scene of recognition, "Dies Bildnis" is an extremely end-oriented aria tonally, formally, and dramatically. More importantly, the sense of emotional discovery it conveys arises more from the music Mozart creates than the aria's text.

The Princess Laments: "Ach ich fühl's"

While Tamino's aria depicts blossoming love, Pamina's sole aria laments its loss. Arguably, this number is the most poignant and the most complex aria of the opera. The character sings "Ach ich fühl's" in response to Tamino's refusal to speak to her, mistakenly believing that he has rejected her.

The aria's home key and instrumentation set this number apart and lend it a "special intensity."[20] As Christoph Wolff notes, "Ach ich fühl's" is the only aria in the opera with three soli winds (flute, oboe, bassoon).[21] The home key of G minor is one Mozart used sparingly in his later operas. The other instances also involve distraught heroines (Ilia in *Idomeneo* and Konstanze in *Die Entführung aus dem Serail*, for example) and, as we have just discussed, the account Pamina's mother gives of her daughter's abduction ("Zum Leiden").[22]

"Ach ich fühl's" is replete with harmonic and rhythmic tension. The predictable and the unexpected rub against one another in almost every measure. The aria is notated in 6/8. An unrelenting, repeating rhythm in the strings (a march? a heartbeat?) underpins practically every bar. Yet, as William Braun points out, the characteristic 6/8 rhythm of "long-short-long … is nowhere to be found. In fact, it is about the only possible rhythm in 6/8 that Mozart does not use in the aria, and Pamina, almost unbelievably, sings a new rhythm in just about every bar."[23] Even though each line of the aria's text begins with an accented syllable, the vocal line never begins its phrases on the downbeat. Again, Mozart works against, ignores even, the scansion of the text.

Ach ich fühl's, es ist verschwunden –	Ah, I feel it, it has vanished –
Ewig hin der Liebe Glück!	Forever gone, the happiness of love!
Nimmer kommt ihr Wonnestunden,	Nevermore will come, hours of bliss,
Meinem Herzen mehr zurück.	Back to my heart.
Sieh Tamino, diese Thränen	See, Tamino, these tears [that]
Fließen Trauter, dir allein.	Flow, beloved, for you alone.
Fühlst du nicht der Liebe Sehnen,	If you do not feel love's longing,
So wird Ruh im Tode sein.	Then I must find tranquility in death.

What does occur on numerous downbeats is dissonance. Tritones and diminished sevenths abound within the vocal line and between it and the bass. Chromatic motion saturates the voice leading as well.

The vocal line begins with three descents in bars 1–4 (from 5 down to 1, from 1 down to 5, and then 6 down to sharp-7), setting up a pattern that permeates the aria. Extended descents and incomplete ascents pull against one another throughout the number. In measures 16–19, for example, the flute and oboe attempt, but cannot even manage, to scale the octave. Instead, they rise through the seventh and fall; their leap downward creates a tritone with their counterpart, the bassoon, whose half-step sighs belatedly resolve the dissonances two beats too late (mm. 17–18 and 19–20).

As Thomas Bauman writes, Mozart uses "silence . . . as expressively as the notes themselves" throughout Pamina's lament, but particularly near the end.[24] The aria's final measures contain small, but telling, details. The persistent rhythm subsides (mm. 36–37). The strings sound an eighth note while the voice sustains a quarter (m. 38). Pamina, it seems, is truly on her own, unsupported musically and dramatically. The voice utters its final phrase largely unaccompanied. It hovers on a flat-6 (E-flat, an implied ninth over the dominant) before tumbling down to the tonic again (mm. 37–38). A moment of silence precedes the postlude, whose melodic contours echo Pamina's earlier pleas but whose rhythms do not.[25] Syncopated descents laced with pungent dissonances cascade into the strings' lower ranges. The aria's final sonority barely whispers a third above the tonic G.

How are we to interpret the aria's postlude? Bauman points out that all previous postludes in the opera have a close rhythmic connection to important phrases in the numbers they close. This one does not.[26] Some authors have suggested that the postlude, and other passages that feature the flute in the opera, might represent the mute Tamino's inner thoughts. Braun and Webster, on the other hand, believe it depicts a devastated Pamina, her pleas unanswered, staggering away.[27] Another possibility exists. The postlude pairs instruments that have not partnered one another earlier in the aria – the bassoon and flute, oboe and second violin, viola and cello – which implies that the passage portrays the anguish both characters feel.

Papageno Improvises: "Ein Mädchen oder Weibchen"

The Magic Flute's final aria, "Ein Mädchen oder Weibchen," juxtaposes simplicity with opulence, as poetic structures, standard musical forms, and the skills of the original creators intertwine. Sung by Papageno, the number again inhabits the realm of the *Volkston*. Formwise, however, "Ein Mädchen oder Weibchen" is more complex than "Der Vogelfänger bin ich ja," the character's first aria. The number features two soloists, not one – the baritone and the magic bells – whose interplay captures both Mozart's and the original Papageno's gifts for improvisation.

"Ein Mädchen oder Weibchen" alternates between two contrasting sections: a refrain in 2/4 (labeled in Table 6.2 below as A) and verses in 6/8 (labeled B). The poetry, with its built-in refrain, clearly prompts the form: different line lengths and accentuations in the poetry inspire the meter changes. The iambs of the refrain fit neatly into 2/4; the verses, on the other hand, incorporate dactyls (an accented syllable followed by two unaccented ones), a pattern that suggests 6/8. The verses also incorporate two different types of line endings. The first couplet ends with an unaccented syllable, the second couplet with an accented one.

Table 6.2 "Ein Mädchen oder Weibchen": text, translation, rhyme scheme, and scansion

Music	REFRAIN [*Iambs*]		
A 2/4	Ein **Mäd**chen **oder Weib**chen	a	A maiden or a little wife
	Wünscht **Papageno sich!**	b	Papageno wishes for himself!
	O **so** ein **sanf**tes **Täub**chen	a	O such a tender little dove
	Wär **Selig**keit für **mich!** —	b	Would be bliss for me! —
B 6/8	VERSE 1 [*Dactyls*]		VERSE 1
	Dann **schmeck**te mir **Trin**ken und **Essen**	c	Then food and drink would taste good to me
	Dann **könnt'** ich mit **Fürs**ten mich **messen,**	c	Then I could compare myself with princes,
	Des **Lebens** als **Weiser** mich **freu'n,**	d	Enjoy life as a wise man,
	Und **wie** im **Elysium sein.**	d	And as if in Elysium be.
A'	REFRAIN		REFRAIN
	Ein Mädchen oder Weibchen . . .		A maiden or a little wife . . .
B'	VERSE 2		VERSE 2
	Ach **kann** ich denn **keiner** von **allen**	e	Ah, can't I then be pleasing to any of all
	Den **reizenden Mädchen** gefallen?	e	The charming maidens? If one
	Helf' **eine** mir **nur** aus der **Noth,**	f	Could only help me out of my need,
	Sonst **gräm** ich mich **wahr**lich zu **Tod'.**	f	Otherwise, I will really worry myself to death.
A''	REFRAIN		REFRAIN
	Ein Mädchen oder Weibchen . . .		A maiden or a little wife . . .
B''	VERSE 3		VERSE 3
	Wird **keine** mir **Lieb**e gewähren,	g	Will none grant me love,
	So **muß** mich die **Flamme** verzehren!	g	Then the flames must consume me!
	Doch **küßt** mich ein **weiblicher Mund,**	h	But if a feminine mouth should kiss me,
	So **bin** ich schon **wie**der gesund.	h	Then I would again be healthy.

[Bold = accented syllable. Center column of letters = rhyme scheme. Underlined letters = accented syllable at end of the poetic line.]

It is perhaps a bit unusual that the aria begins with a refrain. From the outset we hear an unexpected and distinctive tone color. Papageno's magic bells introduce the simple but catchy tune and then alternate with the voice during both the A and B sections. Like the character's first aria, the simple but memorable diatonic melody moves within a limited range. Root-position chords and tonic–dominant–tonic progressions dominate the harmony. As the aria progresses, however, the music for the bells becomes more and more florid. During the third repetition of the refrain, for instance, the bells play triplet sixteenths and thirty-second notes while the winds take over the tune; the bell part features continuous sixteenths during the aria's third and final verse (see Table 6.3).

Therefore, the aria melds strophic form with techniques commonly found in keyboard variations on popular tunes, one of Mozart's specialties. On one level, "Ein Mädchen oder Weibchen" can be analyzed as a strophic song with a refrain. On another, it can be viewed as a double or alternating variation, with variants that may have grown out of improvisations. Like Mozart, Schikaneder, the original Papageno, was known for his ability for extemporization, including adding strophes to popular arias.[28] A letter by Mozart from October 1791 indicates how one performance involved a bit more improvisation than Schikaneder anticipated:

[W]hen Papageno's aria with the Glockenspiel came on, at that moment I went backstage because today I had a kind of urge to play the Glockenspiel myself. – So I played this joke: just when Schikaneder came to a pause, I played an arpeggio – he was startled – looked into the scenery and saw me – the 2nd time he came to that spot, I didn't play – and this time he stopped as well and did not go on singing – I guessed what he was thinking and played another chord – at that he gave his Glockenspiel a slap and shouted "*shut up!*" – everybody laughed. – I think through this joke many in the audience became aware for the first time that Papageno doesn't play the Glockenspiel himself.[29]

The aria's significantly more complex form and the increasingly complicated accompaniment patterns suggest that the character Papageno has grown as a person. His simple rhetoric has been enriched.

Conclusion

The Magic Flute reveals Mozart's ability to tailor arias not only to singers, but also to the character portrayed and the dramatic situation. As stated earlier, the composer seems to have taken great care to make each of the opera's arias

Table 6.3 "Ein Mädchen oder Weibchen": overview of text and music

Form	A	B	A'	B'	A"	B"	B'''
Text	Lines 1–4 ABAB Iambs	Lines 5–8 CCDD Dactyls	Lines 1–4 ABAB Iambs	Lines 9–12 EEFF Dactyls	Lines 1–4 ABAB Iambs	Lines 13–16 GGHH Dactyls	
Meter	2/4	6/8	2/4	6/8	2/4	6/8	6/8
Tempo	Andante Refrain 1	Allegro Verse 1	Andante Refrain 2	Allegro Verse 2	Andante Refrain 3	Allegro Verse 3	Allegro Coda (orchestra alone)
Role of magic bells	Bells intro melody A (mm. 1–8) + flourishes in between vocal phrases (mm. 9–20)	Bells intro melody B (mm. 21–24) + flourishes in between vocal phrases (mm. 32–43)	Bells vary melody A + flourishes	Bells vary melody B + flourishes	Bells = 16th-note triplets & 32nd-note figurations + flourishes *Winds and horns take over melody* (mm. 1–8)	Bells = constant 16th notes & wider range + flourishes	Bells vary melody B: 16th notes (mm. 43–47) *Bells absent* (mm. 48–51) *Winds and horns double the melody* (mm. 43–51) + *Strings join in forte at the end* (mm. 47–51)

distinctive. All of the arias contain something unusual and/or extravagant. From the extreme high notes of the Queen's numbers, to the increasingly florid flourishes of the bells in "Ein Mädchen oder Weibchen," to the panoply of rhythms in "Ach ich fühl's," and the full measure of silence in "Dies Bildnis," each aria stretches the limits of eighteenth-century music in some fashion. As a result, Mozart's skill and creativity as a composer was and is on display, particularly his ability to compose in diverse styles and create nuanced timbres. Ironically, these arias, so deftly tailored to particular singers' strengths and to specific dramatic situations, have become some of the most well-known pieces of European art music. Therefore, the arias manifest the power of music on multiple levels, including its ability to endure and speak beyond its original context.

Notes

1. See Carolyn Abbate and Roger Parker, "Dismembering Mozart," *Cambridge Opera Journal* 2 (1990): 187–95; James Webster, "The Analysis of Mozart's Arias," in *Mozart Studies*, ed. Cliff Eisen (Oxford: Clarendon Press, 1991), 101–99.
2. Webster, "Mozart's Arias"; Mary Hunter, *The Culture of Opera Buffa: A Poetics of Entertainment* (Princeton: Princeton University Press, 1999), 95–155.
3. Letter of February 28, 1778. MBA, II:304. As translated in Robert Spaethling, *Mozart's Letters, Mozart's Life: Selected Letters* (New York: W. W. Norton, 2000), 135.
4. To give just two examples: Malcolm S. Cole, "*The Magic Flute* and the Quatrain," *Journal of Musicology* 3 (1984): 157–76; Nathan J. Martin, "Mozart's Sonata-Form Arias," in *Formal Functions in Perspective: Essays on Musical Form from Haydn to Adorno*, ed. Steven V. Moortele, Julie Pedneault-Deslauriers, and Nathan J. Martin (Woodbridge: Boydell & Brewer, 2015), 37–74.
5. Joseph Kerman, *Opera as Drama*, rev. edn. (Berkeley: University of California Press, 1988), 107; Erik Smith, "The Music," in COH, 128.
6. For discussions that place this character in a broader context, see Malcolm S. Cole, "Monostatos and His 'Sister': Racial Stereotype in *Die Zauberflöte* and Its Sequel," *Opera Quarterly* 21 (2005): 2–26; Jessica Waldoff, "*Zauberflöte, Die*," in *The Cambridge Mozart Encyclopedia*, ed. Cliff Eisen and Simon P. Keefe (Cambridge: Cambridge University Press, 2006), 540–53.
7. For a concise list of musical techniques eighteenth-century composers used to portray "Turkish" characters and settings, see Thomas Bauman, *W. A. Mozart: "Die Entführung aus dem Serail"* (Cambridge: Cambridge University Press, 1987), 62–65.

8. Mary Hunter, "The *Alla Turca* Style in the Late Eighteenth Century: Race and Gender in the Symphony and the Seraglio," in *The Exotic in Western Music*, ed. Jonathan Bellman (Boston: Northeastern University Press, 1998), esp. 43–71, 51, 60–61.

9. Paul Corneilson, "Josepha Hofer: First Queen of the Night," *Mozart Studien* 25 (2018): 477–88.

10. David J. Buch, *Magic Flutes & Enchanted Forests: The Supernatural in Eighteenth-Century Musical Theater* (Chicago: University of Chicago Press, 2008), 293–94, 302–07, 336, 343, 349.

11. Konrad Küster, *Mozart: A Musical Biography*, trans. Mary Whittall (Oxford: Clarendon Press, 1996), 358; Waldoff, "*Zauberflöte.*"

12. This portion of the aria includes some references to earlier material. Compare mm. 28–31 with mm. 45–47, for example.

13. See, for example, Carolyn Abbate, *Unsung Voices: Opera and Musical Narrative in the Nineteenth Century* (Princeton: Princeton University Press, 1991), 10–11, 68.

14. Samuel Richardson, *Pamela; Or, Virtue Rewarded*, ed. Peter Sober (London: Penguin Books, 1980), 262.

15. Johann Wolfgang von Goethe, *The Sorrows of Young Werther*, trans. Michael Hulse (London: Penguin Books, 1989), 36.

16. Webster, "Mozart's Arias," 192.

17. May 26, 1786, letter to Nannerl. MBA, III:549. For an English translation, see Daniel Heartz, *Mozart, Haydn and Early Beethoven 1781–1802* (New York: W. W. Norton, 2009), 272.

18. *Mozart in Vienna: The Final Decade* (Cambridge: Cambridge University Press, 2017), 573–74. Webster states that the instrumentation is typical for sentimental arias. Webster, "Mozart's Arias," 109, 187–96.

19. Jessica Waldoff, *Recognition in Mozart's Operas* (Oxford: Oxford University Press, 2006), esp. 44–45, 61–64.

20. Christoph Wolff, *Mozart at the Gateway to His Fortune: Serving the Emperor, 1788–1791* (New York: W. W. Norton, 2012), 127.

21. Christoph Wolff, "Musicological Introduction," in FACS, 23, 28.

22. Gretchen A. Wheelock, "*Schwarze Gredel* and the Engendered Minor Mode in Mozart's Operas," in *Musicology and Difference*, ed. Ruth A. Solie (Berkeley: University of California Press, 1993), esp. 201–21, 210–14, 218.

23. William R. Braun, "Measures of Greatness," *Opera News* 78/6 (December 2013): 20.

24. Thomas Bauman, "At the North Gate: Instrumental Music in *Die Zauberflöte*," in *Mozart's Operas*, ed. Daniel Heartz (Berkeley: University of California Press, 1990), 283.

25. Compare mm. 17–20 ("Sieh Tamino!") with mm. 38–41.

26. Bauman, "At the North Gate," 279–84.

27. Braun, "Measures of Greatness," 21; Webster, "Mozart's Arias," 196. It also should be noted that the postlude serves a practical purpose: it gives Pamina time to exit.
28. David Buch, "On the Context of Mozart's Variations on the Aria 'Ein Weib ist das herrlichste Ding auf der Welt,' K. 613," *Mozart-Jahrbuch* 1999, 79–80.
29. Letter of October 8–9, 1791, to Constanze. MBA, IV:160. As translated in Spaethling, *Mozart's Letters*, 441.

7 | "All Together, Now"? Ensembles and Choruses in *The Magic Flute*

NICHOLAS MARSTON

To be invited, as a music analyst, to explore the ensembles and choruses in *The Magic Flute* is at once both enticing and daunting. The enticement needs little explanation: Who would not rejoice at the chance to spend scholarly time with this work, the music of which is unquestionably as *bezaubernd schön* as the image of Pamina that launches Tamino's quest? As for what is daunting – aside from the very challenge to do verbal justice somehow to that *Schönheit* – part of the answer lies in the fact that the traditional concentration on ensembles, including finales (if not choruses), in analytical accounts of Mozart's operas has been subjected to harsh criticism, and in high places. Carolyn Abbate and Roger Parker, addressing (again) the opening duet from *Le nozze di Figaro*, argued more than thirty years ago that "the traditional concentration on ensembles in the Mozart literature may lie simply in professional habits. Writers on musical topics – analysts in particular – tend to turn to a small repertoire of much-analysed pieces whenever they wish to advance a new theory or to demonstrate a new prowess." And they note that *Figaro* in particular "has its share of these poor, battered and dismembered exemplars, brutally denied an opportunity to speak out against those who have assailed them."[1] One can at least reply that the ensembles in *The Magic Flute* have suffered less battering than those in *Figaro*, and in the Da Ponte operas more generally.

Abbate and Parker go on to suggest, more seriously, that the concentration on ensembles may be laid at the door of late nineteenth-century Mozart reception, and Wagnerism in particular, with its emphasis on unity of music and dramatic action, on the one hand, and purely musical unity, particularly in the shape of large-scale "symphonic" formal structures, on the other. And although eschewing a "call to arms," they invite consideration of the possibility that "coherence, symmetry or 'symphonic' sense" and "absolute correspondence between the unfolding of music, text and stage-action" may not be the only aesthetic criteria against which the Mozartian operatic ensemble may be fruitfully measured.[2] They trace the concern with large-scale formal processes, and thus ensembles and finales, back to the work of Alfred Lorenz in the 1920s, as also has James Webster, who notes that what Lorenz initiated was perpetuated in the work of writers such as Joseph Kerman and Charles Rosen.

This brings Webster to the importance given over by Kerman and Rosen to the role of sonata form, "both as a primary constituent of Mozart's operas and as a criterion of value."[3] Indeed, writing of the chief characteristics of the sonata style in his hugely influential *The Classical Style*, Rosen could state that "there is no question, however, that Mozart was the first composer to comprehend, in any systematic way, their implications for opera,"[4] before going on to develop an extended sonata-form analysis of the Act 3 sextet from *Figaro* that itself quickly became paradigmatic for later commentators. Yet, as Webster noted, only one of the sixteen nonduet ensembles in the Da Ponte operas "is unambiguously in sonata form!"[5] And already by 1996 Tim Carter could report that sonata-form analyses of Mozart ensembles were "coming under threat," while going on to remark that "the need for an adequate typology of Mozart's ensemble sonata (and other) forms has not yet been met by the literature."[6] More importantly, perhaps, in comparing *Figaro* to *Così fan tutte*, he suggested that Mozart may have become increasingly eager "to explore realistic alternatives to sonata-form organization," in particular adopting the "looser, more progressive structures" typical of finales to mid-act ensemble movements.[7]

The twenty-first-century ensemble analyst, then, can no longer take easy refuge in cozy formal strategies of earlier critics, which were already creaking at the end of the twentieth.[8] And even if one were to argue that the ensembles in *The Magic Flute*, a *Singspiel*, may not best be approached from the formal paradigm of Italian *opera buffa*, there remains the fact that the dramatis personae of *The Magic Flute* include unique groupings that materially affect the musical and dramatic conception of several ensembles. Most telling in this respect are the Three Ladies and the Three Boys, who function not as individuals but rather as what might be termed "ensemble characters." This point was noted as far back as 1956 by Gerald Abraham, in the context of a discussion of Mozart's preference for the operatic ensemble as a vehicle for the development of dramatic character. Given this purpose, it is not surprising that the composer tended to favor duets and trios, "the combinations which offer him one character to strike against another or two others. When more characters are introduced, problems begin to arise."[9] While in *Figaro* and *Don Giovanni*, and excluding finales, the trio texture is exceeded only by one quartet and two sextets, *The Magic Flute* boasts a quintet in each act, both set for the same characters (namely, Tamino, Papageno, and the Three Ladies). But since the Ladies "amount to only one character, their quintets . . . are, from the dramatic point of view, essentially trios."[10]

The lack of individuality of these two sets of characters is emphasized by the layout of some editions of the score (the Eulenburg version, edited from the autograph by Hermann Abert, being a case in point), in which the first two Ladies and two Boys are scored on one stave while the third (often functioning as what Abraham terms a "pseudo-bass"[11]) is scored separately. This does not reflect Mozart's practice in the autograph, in which he routinely provided a separate stave for each part.[12] But even in cases such as the Introduction (No. 1), measures 106–19, when the Ladies sing in contrapuntal dialogue with one another, their music, thoughts, and motivation are essentially all one. As for the multisection Introduction as a whole, it might logically be termed a quartet, in that the participating characters are the Three Ladies and Tamino. Even so, the entrance of the Ladies (m. 40) marks the end of Tamino's vocal contribution: he sings as a soloist and then remains unconscious for the rest of the number, so the four characters never sing together. This is an ensemble – and Introduction – in a quite different sense to that of the action- and character-filled "Introduzione" that opens *Don Giovanni*.

Tamino's presence in the Act 1 quintet is similarly compromised. It is notable that following his opening duet with Papageno, lamenting his inability to free Papageno's padlocked mouth, he is largely silent, except for those passages in which all five parts combine in "moralizing" state-ments (mm. 54–77, 111–32, 184–203).[13] Only after the last of these does Tamino make any contribution to plot development, in asking where he and Papageno are to find Sarastro's castle; remarkably, the Ladies' earlier gift of the magic flute (mm. 80–87) – a *sine qua non* of the entire action – brings forth no individual response from him. A good deal of this "quintet" actually operates as a vocal quartet for the Three Ladies and Papageno; or rather, by Abraham's logic, it functions as a duet. Similarly, the three constituent characters of the succeeding trio (No. 6) never sing as a trio: rather, the number is constituted of two duets, each tonally closed in G, one for Monostatos and Pamina, the other for Monostatos and Papageno. Even the duets (Act 1, No. 7; Act 2, No. 11) are not occasions for "one character to strike against another"; the Two Priests in "Bewahret euch vor Weibertücken" sing as one, like the Ladies and Boys, while Pamina and Papageno, highly differentiated characters in so many respects though they be, inhabit the same musical and emotional world in "Bei Männern, welche Liebe fühlen." This characteristic merging of characters perhaps reaches its apogee in the celebrated "duet" for the Men in Armor in the Act 2 finale (mm. 206–37), where both sing in unison at the octave, their music not even Mozart's but rather the chorale melody "Ach Gott, vom Himmel sieh' darein." Indeed, given that the chorale melody was substituted for an alternative melodic line initially sketched by Mozart, one can perhaps speak here not so much of the merging of characters but rather of the anonymization or even suppression of "character" itself.[14]

The Act 1 and 2 Quintets

The temptation to invoke classical instrumental forms in relation to the ensembles is well illustrated by Erik Smith's suggestion that the Act 1 quintet "could be described harmonically as a sonata rondo with coda, but not in the normal sense of a recurring melody, for Mozart constantly finds new words and new situations requiring new music."[15] Inasmuch as one cannot deny the overarching I–V–I–vi/modulatory–I tonal scheme, the formal comparison is at least intelligible; but to try to think of this music in terms of sonata rondo does little for one's experience of its unfolding. In particular, there is lacking the more dynamic transition between sections, and especially between dominant and tonic, that is so characteristic of the sonata style. Smith himself notes the "perfunctory" nature of the shift to V (mm. 33–35) for the beginning of his second section; and one might say the same of the return to I for the beginning of the third, measures 77–81 – essentially the same formula that links the penultimate and final sections of the Introduction, measures 151–53. Mozart's musical design is clearly indebted to the structure of the libretto: the move to V at measures 34–35 corresponds to the scene shift introducing the Three Ladies, for example; and the "moralizing" statements directed to be sung by "Alle Fünf" in Schikaneder's libretto evidently dictated the location of the close to Smith's second and third sections.

  Smith's suggestion that measures 133–71 form a section "in G minor" in which "Papageno is ordered to accompany Tamino" is also open to question, in that it fails to acknowledge the strong turn toward D minor (iii) that sets in as the Ladies tell Papageno what the Queen of the Night requires of him, including the emphatic V pedals with neighboring augmented-sixth harmonies in measures 150–57. Only after the passage has come to a full cadence in D minor with the Ladies' closing instruction at measure 163 is there a return to the realm of G minor, where Papageno is speaking "für sich" rather than engaging with those around him.[16] If one were to defend Smith's G-minor reading, however, one could point to the detail that as he begins this

private speech, Papageno reiterates the VI#6–V/g progression that concluded his attempted leave-taking of the Ladies at measures 138–39. In this
sense, then, the D-minor passage, for all its musical and dramatic prominence, might be considered musically subordinate, or parenthetical, to a more
overarching tonal continuity. There will be occasion to return to the notion
of parenthesis below.

Schikaneder's "Alle Fünf" directions in the libretto are absorbed into the
close of the second and third sections of Smith's sonata rondo scheme, as
already remarked. But the third such direction ("Silberglöckchen,
Zauberflöten") is treated by Smith as the *beginning* of his sixth section,
which would implicitly function as the "recapitulation" in his sonata rondo
scheme. Prior to this, he identifies measures 172–83 as a conspicuously
"short E flat section in which Papageno is presented with the glockenspiel."
(Only the beginning is "in" E-flat; by its conclusion, this section has
returned to V/I.) It is not difficult to recognize that this event parallels
the presentation, earlier and in the tonic B-flat, of the magic flute to
Tamino. If we allow our analysis to be guided as much by the construction
of the libretto and the events on stage as by abstract, tonic-driven tonal and
formal schemes, it makes sense to read the arrival at B-flat in measure 184
as an ending rather than a beginning. And an ending it clearly is, as the
words of farewell and the stage direction "Alle wollen gehen" make clear.

This returns us to the idea of parenthesis, which may serve to critique the
weakest aspect of Smith's analysis – namely, that "the Andante in B flat
forms the coda." (It is not even dignified with its measure numbering, 214–
47, in Smith's table.) The coda designation is reasonable, in that all five
characters had been preparing to leave the stage following their farewells
and the strong tonic closure in measures 196–203. On the other hand, the
dominant preparation for the Andante (measures 207–13), the last of the
four sections in this quintet to open in the tonic, is far more emphatic – and
more characteristic of sonata style – than any heard previously, including
particularly that (measures 180–83) which sets up the preceding section,
presumed to be a conclusion. This, at last, feels like a "willed" arrival of the
tonic key rather than a chance re-encounter with it. Registrally, however,
and in terms of its (gorgeous) scoring, it does not follow seamlessly from
that preparation; only gradually, once Tamino and Papageno begin to
repeat what the Ladies have told them about the Three Boys, is the lower
register and eventually full scoring retrieved.

To the extent that a coda can be regarded as a tonal and formal
afterthought, an appendix to the main action, the label here is singularly
inappropriate on both counts. This is a distinct moment, at which musical

Example 7.1 Act 1 quintet (No. 5), formal overview.

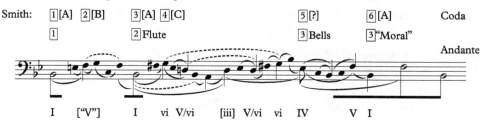

and dramatic considerations clearly align in some senses but not in others. Tonally speaking, one can argue that this is the goal of the entire design; dramatically, it marks the introduction of the Boys, a new "ensemble character," but without their being physically present. In his music for the Three Ladies here, Mozart brilliantly evokes the ensemble singing style of these extraterrestrial beings and the role they will later play. Schikaneder directed that Tamino and Papageno repeat only the first two ("Drei Knäbchen ... Reise") of the Ladies' four lines and that following these all five characters repeat the lines of farewell that had seemed to be bringing the quintet to its end at measure 192. Mozart follows suit: the Ladies repeat the second half of their verse after Tamino and Papageno have sung their lines, following which – counterintuitively, perhaps – the latter begin the words of farewell, but borrow the Ladies' music referring to the Three Boys, the end of which is then taken up by all, closing at measure 241. The remaining six measures may properly be described as a coda, but they might just as easily have performed the same function in relation to the first farewell close, back at measure 203. It is in this sense that the main body of the Andante may be regarded as parenthetical to a larger continuity. Accordingly, the tonic arrival at its beginning is at once a significant tonal goal, in an immediate sense, and yet an interpolation in a larger scheme. This quintet ends, after all, with an interpolated vision of characters yet to be seen. That is why we might think of the B-flat tonic as in some sense "there" and yet not quite *being* there at all (see Example 7.1).

If this last claim seems far-fetched to some, as an attempt to suggest that for dramatic and musical reasons the tonal closure of the Act 1 quintet may not be as definite as it appears on the pages of the score, the relative openness of the ending of the Act 2 quintet, which cannot be dealt with at such length here, is much less debatable, closing as it does in the minor mode of its G tonic, a dramatic and sudden shift brought about

by the surprise imprecations of the unseen Priests.[17] In fact, the Priests'
entry here ("Entweiht ist die heilige Schwelle") at first seems to wrench
the tonality not toward G minor but rather C minor, itself the parallel
minor of their C-major duet (No. 11), which is separated from the quintet
by only the briefest passage of spoken dialogue. There is thus a close
musical and dramatic continuity between these two numbers: the Priests
quit the stage after No. 11, but they may be understood as (initially) silent
participants in the quintet; overhearers of the Ladies' claims of their
falsehood and of the unavoidable descent into hell of those who join
their brotherhood, the Priests eventually intervene to cast down the
Ladies themselves.[18] The universalized moralizing warning against
"Weibertücken" in No. 11 finds its specific target here at the end of the
quintet. And the closing shift to G minor is cleverly prefigured in
Papageno's unexpected D–E-flat ascent at "unerhört!" in measures 71–
72; indeed, the Priests (note also the similar *forte* unison accompani-
ments) pick up the very same pitch, though approached now from g a
minor sixth below, at their entry in measures 151–52, and Papageno will
repeat his original semitonal ascent at the first of his three "O weh!" cries
(measures 160–61) before he falls to the ground.[19]

Eschewing a detailed comparison, Smith claims that this number "shows
a similar construction" to that of the Act 1 quintet, while noting that it
differs in setting "a single situation throughout."[20] There are indeed super-
ficial similarities: the opening tonic section is followed by one in the
dominant and then a return to the tonic, even (as is not the case in
Act 1) with a reprise of the "recurring instrumental phrase" [flute, violin
I]) associated by Smith with "the sweet blandishments of the Ladies" and
latterly Tamino's "rather platitudinous refusals" – though the reprise, if not
"purely" musical, might as well have been prompted by the similar words of
the Ladies, "Tamino, dir ist Tod geschworen!" (mm. 11–13) and "Tamino,
hör! Du bist verloren!" (mm. 47–49), which also draw from Mozart a repeat
of their earlier music. Compared to the Act 1 quintet, though, what is
importantly different here, from the musical point of view, is the greater –
more "sonata"-like? – space and energy given to the securing of the
dominant key (mm. 21–29; note the extended root dominant pedal, compared to the "perfunctory" first-inversion harmony at mm. 34–35 in the
Act 1 quintet) as Tamino enjoins Papageno to silence. And unlike in Act 1,
the return to the tonic at measures 41–45 is not aligned with a new thought
or action, but rather closes off Tamino's exasperated question to Papageno.

The ensuing modulatory section, touching on IV and ii, again has its
loose parallel in Act 1; but the second return to I at measures 64–65

Example 7.2 Act 2 quintet (No. 12), formal overview.

(equivalent to the *tutti* "Silberglöckchen," Smith's "recapitulation," at measure 184 in the earlier quintet) is reached merely through sequential repetition of the two preceding measures (g-sharp–e–a/f-sharp–d–g) and is again embedded within the ongoing confrontation between Tamino and the Ladies rather than initiating some new stage in the proceedings, which now lead musically to another extended dominant harmony that will provide the backdrop to Papageno's intrusive E-flat (the pun on "unerhört!" is delicious) and what it portends. The "recurring instrumental phrase" ("motive" in Example 7.2) appears again to connect this dominant quietly forward to the tonic at measures 76–80; again, and in contrast to the Act 1 quintet (compare the dominant pedal leading to the Andante there), there is no obvious dramatic motive for this tonal return. The final reassertion of the tonic, at measure 112, is motivated by the single passage of the libretto set for "Alle Fünf" – thus, the only piece of genuine quintet writing in the whole number – but it essentially falls within the sway of the earlier arrival at measure 80 (see Example 7.2).

As superficially similar (irrespective of appeals to conventional instrumental forms) as the tonal schemes of these two extended numbers may be considered to be (compare Examples 7.1 and 7.2[21]), what is more important to grasp is their different dynamics or qualities; this has much to do with the treatment of the tonic in each, especially in relation to the libretto and dramatic action. Also different is the more emphatic "staging" of the initial move to V (identified in Example 7.2 as the "structural" V, in contrast to Example 7.1) in the Act 1 quintet, and the second move toward that harmony (mm. 67–71), which has no counterpart in the Act 2 quintet. Most different of all, of course, are the two endings, the one interrupted by an ethereal vision and the other by an all too real peripeteia that has clearly audible musical consequences: the tonic is now unquestionably "there" at the end, but it is no longer the tonic that we have known.

Those Magnificent Boys in Their Flying Machine . . .

Reference has already been made to the special, and in some respects unique, nature of the ensembles in *The Magic Flute*. For Christoph Wolff, "compared to all of Mozart's other operas, any attempt to classify the duets, trios and quintets likewise [as with the arias] reveals an unparalleled variety."[22] That variety is particularly plain to see if one compares the large structures of the quintets with one of the shortest numbers in the opera, the trio "Seid uns zum zweiten Mal willkommen" from Act 2, in which the Boys greet Tamino and Papageno and return their magical instruments to them. Its thirty-six measures parse effortlessly into 9x4-measure phrases; the harmony is stunningly simple, consisting of little more than alternating tonics and dominants. (Wolff's "variety" can also be gauged in the comparison between this and the succeeding trio, No. 19, for Pamina, Tamino, and Sarastro, which at 78 measures has much more the tonal design of the Act 1 quintet, with which it shares both its key and its closing farewell wish.) The light, high-register accompaniment is not identical to that of the Andante "vision" in the Act 1 quintet, but serves similarly to transport us off ground and into the ether.

For all its manifest simplicity, though, this miniature harbors some fascinating subtleties. Mozart's 6/8 meter could have accommodated Schikaneder's iambic tetrameters in the manner of No. 7, the duet "Bei Männern," also in 6/8 (though to imagine singing the words of one of these numbers to the music of the other is an object lesson in Mozart's sense for text-music proprieties). As the autograph shows, he completely rebarred "Bei Männern," shifting the barline by half a measure, which alters the words that take the main musical accent at line ends.[23] The accommodation of the text to the music in No. 16, however, creates sometimes inappropriate stresses at line beginnings ("*Seid* uns" rather than "Seid *uns*"; "*die* Flöte," rather than "die *Flöte*," m. 11).[24]

Schikaneder's ten lines of text comprise two quatrains and a closing couplet. At the outset, Mozart's four-measure phrase accommodates two lines of text (mm. 5–8, 9–12, 13–16, 17–20). But because the setting of lines 5–6 (mm. 13–16) prolongs the dominant harmony reached at measure 12, the musical reprise at measures 17–18 corresponds to the second half of the second quatrain, rather than the first, as was the case at measures 5–6. That is, the musical and textual structure have drawn apart from one another. Furthermore, measures 19–20 do not reprise measures 7–8 but rather repeat measures 17–18, remaining on V at the close. The remaining two lines of the couplet are now each accommodated within a four-measure phrase, which again results in a change – a kind of augmentation – of the hypermetrical correlation between text and music. A further subtlety is that the pitch content of the first measure of these two phrases (measures 21 and 25) is closely related to that of the second measure of the initial four-measure phrase: the violin part in each case spans e2–d3. Finally, the overall metrical regularity of this little number is briefly disturbed, as the setting of the couplet is completed at measure 28. Here, as hitherto in all cases, the final cadence falls on the second beat of the fourth measure of the phrase. But Mozart's decision to repeat "still, schweige still" in a further four-measure phrase has the effect of shifting the barline back by one beat (the autograph in this case shows no indecision on Mozart's part, however), so that the tonic arrivals in measures 28 and 30 feel like downbeats. The original, correct metrical scheme is restored by the closing repetition of the very first phrase: as the Boys came, so they go.

All Together, Now!

Outside of the two act finales, examined elsewhere in this volume, the role of the Chorus is limited to two numbers, both in Act 2, and both scored for male voices only: No. 10, Sarastro's aria with Chorus, and No. 18. That both of them begin with the words "O Isis und Osiris" is an obvious link; and while the libretto identifies the former as "Chorus" and the latter as "Chor," Mozart's autograph specifically identifies the characters as the "Chor der Priester" (or "Priestern") in both instances.[25] What is particularly revealing here in the libretto directions is that Schikaneder envisaged No. 10 as a Chorus only; together with the March of the Priests (No. 9), which opens Act 2, and the dramatically and textually related No. 18, these numbers would have formed two imposing choral pillars at either end of the act prior to the finale. It was Mozart's idea, then, to use Schikaneder's text as an aria for Sarastro, the role of the chorus eventually being merely to echo the closing words of each of his two stanzas.

The scoring of the two numbers is similar, but not identical. The chorus is in four parts (TTBB) in No. 10, but in only three (TTB) in No. 18, which, together with the addition of flutes, oboes, and trumpets not found in No. 10 (this, however, uses the distinctive timbre of two basset horns along with the trio of trombones), gives this number a brighter, tessiturally higher character, naturally enhanced by the key of D rather than F major (No. 10). The instrumentation of both (including the all-male vocal texture) is crucial to the evocation of an appropriately antique, ecclesiastical tone, as also is the adoption of the hymn topos, which needs little elaboration in words. To compare this music to that of the Boys' trio, No. 16, is to witness again that "unparalleled variety" in the music of this opera of which Wolff writes. And the comparison to No. 16, in fact, is perhaps even more instructive. All in all, No. 18, in its brevity (42 measures, admittedly at an adagio pace), its transparent binary form, and its three-part chordal texture, stands in close but starkly obverse relation to No. 16; it is, as it were, the "dark" side of that earlier number, from which it is musically divided by Pamina's aria, No. 17. Equally, the Chorus of Priests extends that welcome return into Sarastro's realm uttered by the Boys, but importantly preempts, too, the banishing of that "düst're Nacht," which will in due course hold no terrors for the finally united Pamina and Tamino; see measures 330–52 of the Act 2 finale, where not only the switch to homophonic writing but also the marked neighboring diminished harmonies in the last five measures invite one to recall the Priests' earlier hieratic utterances.

"Nacht," "Osiris," and "Isis" all reappear in the final four lines of the libretto, at the very end of Act 2 (mm. 830–46). In a curious reversal of the earlier situation, the libretto specifies, for the first and only time, that these lines are sung by the "Chor von Priestern," while Mozart's autograph identifies only a "Chor."[26] Moreover, this is no longer a male chorus, but one scored SATB. Mozart's concluding ensemble in The Magic Flute eschews individual characters in favor of the collective; by extension, it is an ensemble that ultimately includes us all.

Notes

1. Carolyn Abbate and Roger Parker, "Dismembering Mozart," Cambridge Opera Journal 2 (1990): 190.
2. Ibid., 194, 195.
3. James Webster, "Mozart's Operas and the Myth of Musical Unity," Cambridge Opera Journal 2 (1990): 200.
4. Charles Rosen, The Classical Style: Haydn, Mozart, Beethoven, rev. edn. (London: Faber & Faber, 1976), 289.
5. Webster, "Mozart's Operas," 201.
6. Tim Carter, "Mozart, Da Ponte and the Ensemble: Methods in Progress?," in Wolfgang Amadè Mozart: Essays on His Life and His Music, ed. Stanley Sadie (Oxford: Oxford University Press, 1996), 242–43.
7. Ibid., 247.

8. See further John Platoff, "Myths and Realities about Tonal Planning in Mozart's Operas," *Cambridge Opera Journal* 8 (1996): 3–15; Mary Hunter, *The Culture of Opera Buffa in Mozart's Vienna: A Poetics of Entertainment* (Princeton: Princeton University Press, 1999). While Platoff's and Hunter's principal concern is *opera buffa*, James Webster, in "To Understand Verdi and Wagner We Must Understand Mozart," *19th-Century Music* 11 (1987): 175–93, includes (at 185–92) a detailed analysis of the "colloquy in recitative between Tamino and the Priest" from the Act 1 finale of *The Magic Flute.*

9. Gerald Abraham, "The Operas," in *The Mozart Companion*, ed. H. C. Robbins Landon and Donald Mitchel (London: Faber & Faber, 1965), 309–10.

10. Ibid.

11. Ibid., 311.

12. See FACS.

13. On moralizing maxims in *The Magic Flute*, see Martin Nedbal, "Morality and Germanness in *Die Zauberflöte*," in *Morality and Viennese Opera in the Age of Mozart and Beethoven* (London: Routledge, 2017), 84–122.

14. For the alternative melody, see NMA, II/5/19 (hereinafter just NMA), xii and 377, No. 5a$_1$. I am indebted to Jessica Waldoff for this observation.

15. Erik Smith, "The Music," in COH, 116, from which subsequent page references in the text are taken.

16. That the prevailing iambic tetrameter is partially interrupted in these four lines for Papageno may not be insignificant; similarly, the *tutti* at "O so eine Flöte" (mm. 111–32) is marked by another, more emphatic textual metrical shift.

17. Here I follow the 1791 libretto for the Vienna premiere, which attributes the words "Entweiht ist die heilige Schwelle" (mm. 151ff.) to the "Priester." Mozart's autograph assigns these parts to "die Eingeweihten von innen," entering them on the staves previously allotted to Tamino and Papageno; see FACS, II:257 and III:[85]. The NMA (see *supra*, n. 14) assigns these parts to tenor and bass "coro."

18. In the 1791 libretto, No. 11 is headed merely "Duetto," but followed by the direction "(Beyde Priester ab.)"; the autograph assigns the vocal parts to "1:^{b}" and "2:^{t} Priester," while the NMA gives "Zweiter Priester" and "Sprecher"; see FACS, II:235 and III:[84].

19. The 1791 libretto directs that "Papageno fällt vor Schrecken zu Boden; singt, da schon alle Musik stille ist"; Mozart's autograph, however, gives only the direction "fällt zu Boden," placed above this first cry; see FACS, II:257 and III: [85].

20. Smith, in COH, 117. Subsequent references in the text are to the same page.

21. I am indebted to Stephane Crayton for the preparation of Examples 7.1 and 7.2 for this chapter.

22. Christoph Wolff, "Musicological Introduction," in FACS, III:[27].

23. See Larry Laskowski, "Voice Leading and Meter: An Unusual Mozart Autograph," in *Trends in Schenkerian Research*, ed. Allen Cadwallader (New

York: Schirmer, 1990), 41–50. Smith, in COH, 122, argues that the original barring ("Bei Männern . . .") is the "correct" one; Wolff, "Musicological Introduction," [23–24], makes an interpretative case for the revised barring as "the improved reading."

24. Smith, in COH, 121, is happy to accept that *"Die Zauberflöte* is full of wrong stresses, permitted by Mozart because he regarded the character of the music as more important."

25. FACS, III:[83], [90]; II:227 ("Priester"), 297 ("Priestern").

26. FACS, III:[96]; II:424. The earlier appearance of the SATB chorus in the Act 2 finale is identified as "Chor" in both libretto and autograph; see FACS, III:[94]; II:71.

8 | Musical Topics, Quotations, and References

MARK FERRAGUTO

Compared to Mozart's three Da Ponte operas and to the coronation opera with which it is exactly contemporaneous (*La clemenza di Tito*), *The Magic Flute* stands out for its eclectic blend of musical styles. Composed for the Theater auf der Wieden, *The Magic Flute* reflects the popular orientation of this suburban Viennese theater, incorporating musical characteristics from such diverse genres as magic opera, fairy-tale opera, *Singspiel*, and low comedy (especially the Hanswurst tradition), alongside stylistic elements from *opera buffa* and *opera seria*. While the work's referential character results in part from Mozart's kaleidoscopic use of musical topics ("styles or genres taken out of their proper context and used in another one," according to Danuta Mirka[1]), many individual moments seem to draw their inspiration from earlier works. At least one scene – the duet of the Armored Men in Act 2 – includes a musical quotation that has been the subject of much speculation and debate, but this quotation seems to be the exception rather than the rule. Some scholars, however, have posited that the opera contains a vast network of musical borrowings and allusions. This chapter explores these claims in the broader context of *The Magic Flute*'s extraordinary array of musical styles and genres and offers a detailed critical examination of its possible references to specific works.

Topics

Any consideration of musical references in *The Magic Flute* should begin by addressing topics (*topoi*). In the eighteenth century, topics were a lingua franca through which recognizable situations and emotions could be wordlessly communicated without relying on a listener's familiarity with specific compositions. In *The Magic Flute*, topics work in tandem with key associations and orchestration to perform a variety of functions: (1) to orient the listener, (2) to aid in characterization, and (3) to connect individual moments with the opera's larger themes.

The opening scene, Tamino's encounter with the serpent and rescue by the Three Ladies, illustrates how Mozart deploys topics to orient and engage the listener. Following the overture, the opera begins *in medias res*. String tremolos, rapid arpeggios, scalar descents, and the key of C minor – all hallmarks of the *tempesta* or *Sturm und Drang* style – conjure a "stormy" atmosphere that eighteenth-century audiences would have instantly recognized.[2] Without yet knowing who Tamino is or why he is being pursued, the listener knows that he is in danger, well before he cries for help in measure 18. When the Three Ladies arrive to vanquish the serpent, there is an accompanying change of topic: wind-band orchestration and dotted rhythms indicate a march. This new topic, which precedes the Three Ladies' cries of "Triumph!" is reinforced by the modulation to E-flat major, a key that was associated with the classically heroic ideal of *Tugend* (virtue) in many theatrical works.[3] This association is made explicit in Mozart's Act 1 finale, in which Tamino sings – in E-flat major – that he has come to the temple to seek "that which belongs to love and virtue" ("Der Lieb' und Tugend Eigentum"). Mozart hence uses topics – together with keys and scoring – to ground the listener's experience of the scene, while also forecasting tonalities that will gain significance as the opera unfolds.

Mozart also uses topics to introduce and animate his characters. The folk-like style of Papageno's strophic "Vogelfänger" aria, for instance, marks him as an everyman, in contrast to Tamino, whose noble upbringing and loftier purpose are reflected in the more elevated style of his through-composed "portrait" aria. The Queen of the Night's recitative and aria in Act 1, meanwhile, are conspicuously grandiose, recalling *opera seria*. A full-scale orchestral introduction marks her spectacular entrance; accompanied recitative allows the Queen to introduce herself; and an impressive two-tempo aria displays her emotional range, moving from a sentimental G minor (as she laments the loss of her daughter) to a coloratura-laden B-flat major (as she entrusts Tamino with Pamina's rescue). In "Der Hölle Rache," Mozart combines the "rage" aria type with the strict contrapuntal style, infusing the Queen's ire with a particular sense of authority.[4] Sarastro's music, by contrast, tends toward the *feierlich* (a solemn, hymn-like style) and is suggestive of Masonic ritual, while the music of his servant Monostatos invokes the popular *alla Turca* style through its circular melodic figures, limited harmonic vocabulary, and repetitive phrases. Rooted in exoticizing Western European depictions of Turks and Turkishness, this style could also signify cultural and racial Otherness more generally.[5] Pamina's G-minor aria "Ach ich fühl's," meanwhile, exemplifies an aria type associated with sentimental heroines in distress; however, she also shares a folk-like duet with Papageno, imbuing her character with a greater emotional breadth than that of her counterpart, Tamino.

Two topics, the "strict" style (variously called the *strenge, gebundene,* or *fugenartige Schreibart* by the music theorist Heinrich Christoph Koch) and the *feierlich,* relate individual moments to the opera's overarching themes. Standing in stark contrast to the *galant* idiom that more typically characterizes Mozart's writing, these two styles help to depict the opera's elements of ritual and mysticism. On the one hand, they create distinctive musical atmospheres that help dramatize the libretto's fantastical invocation of distant or mysterious cultures (ancient Egypt, Freemasonry). On the other hand, they recall contemporary sacred genres, reinforcing the religious tone of the temple scenes. In the case of the strict style, which appears most prominently in the overture and the duet of the Armored Men (on which more later), the "law" of counterpoint analogizes the "law" of the temple: by alluding to the strict style, Mozart musically illustrates the notion that Tamino must follow the law in order to reach Enlightenment. However, as Keith Chapin has noted, "the rules of the Temple are malleable": Tamino, despite being a prince, is allowed to become an initiate (Act 2, scene 1); similarly, as Pamina proves her worth, the interdiction on the initiation of women is rescinded (Act 2, scene 28). Chapin views the strict style as a more flexible signifier, arguing that it stands for the progressive rationalism of the Enlightenment era. The blending of *galant* themes with contrapuntal procedures in the overture, he argues, "symbolizes the process of modernization that the subsequent action represents."[6]

Musical Sources and Affinities

Another category of musical references involves allusions to specific works, whether by Mozart or by other composers. Writing in 1913, Théodore de Wyzewa suggested that "the score of *Die Zauberflöte* practically presents us with a 'pot-pourri,'" calling for scholars to assemble "an inventory of those 'sources' from which [Mozart] drew the varied materials for his last opera."[7] Although Wyzewa himself never attempted such an inventory, A. Hyatt King took up the call in a 1950 article, republished in 1955 as part of his book *Mozart in Retrospect: Studies in Criticism and Bibliography.* Uncovering the "sources" for *The Magic Flute* has remained an area of interest into the twenty-first century.[8]

King's study is a tour de force, offering approximately one hundred precursors for the opera's themes (see Table 8.1). Many of these derive from Otto Jahn's Mozart biography (as well as its revisions by Hermann

Table 8.1 Melodic sources and affinities of *The Magic Flute*, according to A. Hyatt King (1955)

Idea in *The Magic Flute*	Melodic source/affinity	Previous mentions noted by King
Overture		
Threefold chord	Mozart, *König Thamos*, no. 2, opening	
	Holzbauer, *Günther von Schwarzburg*, opening	
Fugal subject	Clementi, Sonata in B-flat Major, Op. 24, no. 2, opening	*Caecilia* 1829
	Piccini, *Il Barone di Torreforte*, Act I, scene 3, quartet	Della Corte
	Mozart, *Idomeneo*, no. 5, violin part	
	Mozart, Symphony No. 38 ("Prague"), K. 504, I: 37–42 *et passim*	
	Mozart, Sonata in B-flat Major, K. 498a, I: 81	
	Mozart, Sonata in B-flat Major, K. 570, I: 45, 46	
	Rolle, *Lazarus oder die Feyer der Auferstehung*, overture	*Caecilia* 1843
	Haydn, *Il mondo della luna*, Act I finale	
	Cimarosa, *Il matrimonio segreto* (1792), Act I, "Io ti lascio"	
No. 1		
Last part of trio	Mozart, *Le nozze di Figaro*, no. 13	
No. 3		
"Dies Bildnis"	Mozart, Violin Sonata in F Major, K. 377, I, opening	
	Mozart, String Quintet in G Minor, K. 516, III: 18–21	
	Mozart, Sonata in C Major, K. 279, I: 22	
	Gluck, "Die frühen Gräber"	Einstein
	Haydn, Sonata in B-flat Major, Hob. XVI:41, I, opening	
"Ich fühl' es"	Mozart, *Idomeneo*, no. 11	
	Mozart, String Quartet in E-flat Major, K. 171, I: 1, 2	
	Mozart, Symphony No. 40 in G Minor, K. 550, II: 77–79	
	Gassmann, *I Viaggiatori ridicoli*	Haas
	works by C. P. E. Bach, Grétry, Paisiello	Abert
	Haydn, Sonata in G Major, Hob. XVI:27, II: 18–20	
Postlude	Mozart, *Zaide*, no. 4, ending	
	Mozart, String Quartet in B-flat Major ("Hunt"), K. 458, III, ending	
No. 4		
Introduction	G. Benda, *Ariadne*	*Caecilia* 1843
"Ihr ängstliches Beben"	Mozart, *Idomeneo*, no. 11, "L'angoscie, gl'affanni …"	
"Auf ewig dein"	Mozart, *Die Entführung aus dem Serail*, no. 6, ending	
Coloratura section	P. Wranitzky, *Oberon*, no. 6 ("Dies ist des edlen Huons Sprache")	"a common-place of Mozart criticism"

Table 8.1 (cont.)

Idea in *The Magic Flute*	Melodic source/affinity	Previous mentions noted by King
No. 5		
Orchestral motive	Mozart, *Idomeneo*, no. 23	
	Mozart, Flute Concerto in D Major, K. 314, I	
	Mozart, *La clemenza di Tito*, no. 22	
	Gluck, *Alceste*, Act 1, no. 4	
"Hm! Hm! Hm!"	Philidor, *Bucheron*, septet	
No. 6		
"Du feines Täubchen"	Mozart, String Quintet in E-flat Major, K. 614, IV: 27 −30, 205–12	
	Mozart, German Dances, K. 602, no. 4, opening	
	Mozart, Keyboard Concerto in F Major, K. 413, II, opening	
No. 7		
Duet	Mozart, Symphony No. 36 in C Major ("Linz"), K. 425, III, opening	
No. 8		
"Zum Ziele führt dich diese Bahn"	"Die Katze lässt das Mausen nicht" (folksong found in *Augsburger Tafelkonfekt* 1737; Bach, "Coffee Cantata," final chorus; Mozart, Divertimento in E-flat Major, K. 252, IV, main theme; Mozart, Concerto for Two Keyboards, K. 365, III, main theme: *passim*; Beethoven, Piano Concerto No. 1 [1795], III)	Wyzewa
Tamino's recitative	Gluck, *Iphigénie en Aulide*, Agamemmnon's soliloquy	
"Sobald dich führt der Freundschaft Hand"	Mozart, Sonata in A Minor, K. 310, I: 129–32	
Tamino's flute solo and "Wie stark ist nicht dein Zauberton"	Mozart, Andante for Flute and Orchestra in C Major, K. 315, flute entry	
"Schnelle Füße, rascher Mut"	Mozart, *La finta semplice*, no. 17	
"He, ihr Sklaven, kommt herbei!"	Mozart, *Die Entführung*, no. 7, "Marsch fort, fort, fort …"	
	Mozart, *Don Giovanni*, no. 1, "Notte e giorno faticar …"	
"Es lebe Sarastro, Sarastro lebe!"	Mozart, *König Thamos*, no. 1, "Erhöre die Wünsche …"	
	Mozart, Sonata for Two Keyboards in F Major, K. 497, I: 125	
"O wär' ich eine Maus" (Papageno)	Mozart, Concerto for Two Keyboards in E-flat Major, K. 365, I: 269, 270	
"Mir klingt der Muttername süße"	Mozart, Serenade for Wind Octet in E-flat Major, K. 375, III: 26–32	
	Mozart, "Als Luise," K. 520	
	Mozart, Violin Sonata in E-flat Major, K. 481, II: 19–21	
	Mozart, *Idomeneo*, no. 21, "M'avrai compagna al duolo"	

Table 8.1 (cont.)

Idea in *The Magic Flute*	Melodic source/affinity	Previous mentions noted by King
No. 9		
March of the Priests	Gluck, *Iphigénie en Tauride*, marches	
	Wranitzky, *Oberon*, march	
	Mozart, *Così fan tutte*, no. 29, "pietoso il ciglio"	
	Mozart, *Sinfonia Concertante* in E-flat Major, K. 297b, III	
	Mozart, *Idomeneo*, no. 25	
	Mozart, sketch from 1784	
	Mozart, Divertimenti in F Major, K. 247, IV and K. 253, I	
	Corelli, Op. 5, no. 6, opening	"surely . . . musical coincidence"
No. 10		
"Stärkt mit Geduld sie in Gefahr"	Haydn, Symphony No. 85 in B-flat Major ("La Reine"), I: 93–95	
No. 12		
"Wie? Wie? Wie?"	Mozart, String Quartet in G Major, K. 387, IV: 108–10	
No. 13		
Opening	Mozart, Keyboard Concerto in E-flat Major, K. 271, III: 35–39	
	Mysliveček, Overture to *Demofoonte*, opening	Quoted in letter to Mozart from his father
"Alles fühlt"	Grétry, *Amitié à l'épreuve*, "Grande, grande réjouissance"	Abert
No. 15		
Opening	Mozart, *Idomeneo*, no. 31	
No. 16		
Violin figure	Mozart, Violin Concerto in A Major, K. 219, III, ending	
	Mozart, String Trio in E-flat Major, K. 563, II, ending	
	Mozart, Sonata in E-flat Major, K. 281, III: 18–21	
No. 17		
"Nimmer kommt ihr, Wonnestunden"	Mozart, *Le nozze di Figaro*, no. 28, "finché non splende . . . "	
"Meinem Herzen mehr züruck" repetition	Gluck, *Orfeo*, Orpheus's first aria, ending	
No. 19		
"Der Götter Wille mag geschehen"	Mozart, Clarinet Quintet in A Major, K. 581, I: 42–44	
	Mozart, Concerto for Three Keyboards in F Major, K. 242, I: 74, 75	
	Mozart, Keyboard Concerto in B-flat Major, K. 450, I: 33–35	
	Mozart, Keyboard Concerto in F Major, K. 459, III: 151–3	
	Mozart, Sonata in G Major, K. 283, II: 10	

Table 8.1 (cont.)

Idea in *The Magic Flute*	Melodic source/affinity	Previous mentions noted by King
	Mozart, Sonata in C Major, K. 309, II: 67, 68	
	Mozart, Keyboard Rondo in F Major, K. 494: 70, 71	
	Mozart, Serenade in D Major ("Haffner"), K. 250, VIII: 1, 2	
"Ach, gold'ne Ruhe"	Mozart, *Idomeneo*, no. 21, "Peggio è di morte"	István Barna
No. 20		
Melody	Scandello, chorale "Nun lob mein Seel den Herrn" (lines 7 and 8)	C. F. Becker, *Neue Zeitschrift für Musik* 1839; Jahn
	Haydn, *Il mondo della luna*, "Wollt' die Dreistigkeit entschulden"	Chantavoine
No. 21		
"Führt mich hin, ich möcht' ihn seh'n"	Mozart, *Le nozze di Figaro*, no. 29, "Che smania, che furor"	Chantavoine
	Mozart, *Die Maurerfreude*, "wie dem Starren Forscherauge"	Chantavoine
Fugal subject (duet of the Armored Men)	H. Biber, Mass of 1701, Kyrie	Abert
Chorale melody	Luther, "Ach Gott, von Himmel sieh' darein"	"generally recognized"
	Kirnberger, setting of "Es wollt uns Gott gnädig sein"	
Tamino's flute-playing; chords on trumpets and drums	Mozart, Divertimento in C Major, K. 188	
	Mozart, *Les petits riens*, no. 3	
Flute music	Mozart, *Così fan tutte* ("nearly a dozen appearances")	
	Mozart, String Trio in E-flat Major, K. 563, II: 54	
	Mozart, String Quartet in B-flat Major, K. 589, III: 7, 36, &c.	
	Mozart, String Quartet in A Major, K. 464, I: 234	
	Mozart, Minuets, K. 585, no. 5, trio	
	Mozart, Armonica Quintet in C Minor, K. 617, rondo: 16, &c.	
Papageno and Papagena's duet	Mozart, Keyboard Concerto in F Major, K. 459, finale	
	Mozart, Keyboard Concerto in G Major, K. 453, finale	
"Heil sie euch Geweihten"	Mozart, *König Thamos*, no. 7, "Höchste Gottheit"	
	Mozart, *Le nozze di Figaro*, no. 29, "Contessa, perdono"	
	Mozart, *Idomeneo*, no. 31, "Scenda Imeneo"	
"die Schönheit und Weisheit"	Mozart, Divertimento in F Major, K. 253, I: variation 3	
	Mozart, *Idomeneo*, no. 16, "Del ciel la clemenza"	

Abert and Hermann Deiters); others stem from the work of Wyzewa and Georges de Saint-Foix; still others from Jean Chantavoine's *Mozart dans Mozart*, King's own observations, and a handful of other sources. A few cases, such as the claim that the overture's fugal subject is based on the opening theme of Clementi's Sonata in B-flat, Op. 24, No. 2, date back to the early nineteenth century. According to his pupil Ludwig Berger, Clementi played this sonata during his piano duel with Mozart in the presence of the emperor in December 1781.[9]

King credits the pastiche-like quality of *The Magic Flute* in part to Mozart's incredible memory and in part to the haste and difficult conditions in which he composed the opera. He concludes that "*Die Zauberflöte* presents a paradox virtually without parallel in music history – an opera universally admitted to be a work of genius, and seemingly one of striking originality, which is in part a synthesis of material drawn from a variety of sources."[10] However, the emergence of a work of "striking originality" from a "synthesis of material" would not have been thought paradoxical in the eighteenth century, nor was it without parallel (one thinks of the "recycling" practices of Handel and Bach). Moreover, many of the melodies that King proposes seem to be related to *The Magic Flute* by virtue of what Jan LaRue has termed "family resemblance" rather than actual reminiscence.[11] Despite its inclusion of many intriguing and plausible connections, King's inventory of sources raises perhaps more questions than it answers.

Ironically, King did not locate any sources for *The Magic Flute* in the handful of works that most closely resemble it: the fairy-tale *Singspiele* produced by Schikaneder at the Theater auf der Wieden. These works – *Oberon, König der Elfen* (November 7, 1789), *Die schöne Isländerin, oder Der Muffti von Samarkanda* (April 22, 1790), *Der Stein der Weisen, oder Die Zauberinsel* (September 9, 1790), and *Der wohltätige Derwisch, oder Die Schellenkappe* (early 1791) – contain many parallels with *The Magic Flute*.[12] Perhaps the most significant of these are found in *Der Stein der Weisen* (The Philosopher's Stone), a collaborative opera to which Mozart contributed music. As David J. Buch has observed, in addition to offering a "romantic mixture of solemn, comic, magic, and love scenes," both works feature "a similar two-act structure with an *introduzione*, large-scale episodic finales, and similar arias and ensembles," "musical segments for the working of the mechanical stage and for magic episodes," and "traditional supernatural devices" such as "enchanted march music, magical wind ensembles, and the use of descending octave leaps for magic invocations."[13] Astromonte's entrance music, attributed to Johann Baptist Henneberg, may have provided a model for the Queen of the

Night's: in both cases, a syncopated prelude designed to accompany stage machinery gives way to an accompanied recitative and two-part aria ending with a coloratura section in B-flat major.[14] Astromonte's proclamation "Zittert nicht" (Tremble not) even anticipates the Queen's opening line, "O zittre nicht." Of course, there are also important differences between these two numbers: while the Queen's aria is in a closed bipartite form, for instance, Astromonte's initiates a through-composed complex involving the chorus; the Queen's aria also includes a poignant slow section in the minor mode that is unlike anything sung by Astromonte. Thus, if Mozart modeled the Queen of the Night's entrance on Astromonte's, he felt free to adapt Henneberg's concept to suit his dramatic needs.

Henneberg may also have inspired another musical idea in *The Magic Flute*. As Alan Tyson noted, his children's song "Das Veilchen und der Dornstrauch" (The Violet and the Thornbush), published in a collection to which Mozart also contributed three numbers (*Liedersammlung für Kinder und Kinderfreunde*; Vienna, 1791), contains a brief passage reminiscent of the closing idea in the first quintet for the Three Ladies, Tamino, and Papageno (No. 5, mm. 230–33 or 234–37).[15] Henneberg was the *Kapellmeister* at the Theater auf der Wieden and participated in the earliest rehearsals and performances of *The Magic Flute*. Hence, it is plausible, as Tyson suggests, that Mozart referenced the song as a tip of the hat to his younger colleague. That said, the passage in question is so short (and, arguably, musically commonplace) that a definitive conclusion is difficult to reach.

Papageno's "Ein Mädchen oder Weibchen" and the Duet of the Armored Men

Of course, in situations involving music by other composers, Mozart's documented knowledge of the work in question may enhance the plausibility of the musical relationship. Here, the complex case of Papageno's aria "Ein Mädchen oder Weibchen" comes to the fore. In a note published in the *Neue Zeitschrift für Musik* in 1840, Carl Ferdinand Becker drew attention to the melodic similarity between the opening of Papageno's aria and the seventh and eighth lines of the popular Lutheran chorale "Nun lob, mein Seel, den Herren" (see Examples 8.1a and 8.1b). Noting that Mozart quotes a different Lutheran chorale in the duet of the Armored Men, Becker found it unsurprising that "Nun lob" should appear in *The Magic Flute*, even if the reference was an "innocent and, for the composer himself,

Example 8.1 Some melodic antecedents of Papageno's aria "Ein Mädchen oder Weibchen" (No. 20).

(a) Mozart, "Ein Mädchen oder Weibchen" (1791)

(b) Bach, "Nun lob, mein Seel, den Herren" (BWV 225), lines 7 & 8 (1727)

(c) "Es war ein wilder Wassermann" (folksong)

(d) Kunzen, "Au bord d'une fontaine" (1786)

(e) Kunzen, "Der Landmann" (1788)

unconscious mystification."[16] Becker never attempted to answer the question of how precisely Mozart knew the chorale, nor did his suggestion of an "unconscious" reminiscence require him to demonstrate that the reference was of any particular significance.

There, the matter seemingly rested until Max Friedländer's 1902 study *Das deutsche Lied im 18. Jahrhundert*, in which he derived the tune of Papageno's aria from an altogether different source, the folksong "Es war ein wilder Wassermann" (see Example 8.1c). Friedländer mentioned the folksong as a source for Friederich Kunzen's 1786 lied "Au bord d'une fontaine" (see Example 8.1d), noting that Mozart too used the melody for Papageno's aria. However, he provided no evidence that Mozart (or Kunzen) knew it. Nevertheless, Hermann Abert (1919–21) reiterated and amplified Friedländer's notion, mentioning operatic melodies by Galuppi (1771), Grétry (1778), and Paisiello (1784) that have a similar design and folklike character (and that Mozart was perhaps more likely to have known). Chantavoine (1948) suggested yet another piece with a related melody, Bonafede's Act 1 aria from Haydn's *Il mondo della luna* (1777).

But in a 1963 article, Frederick W. Sternfeld, without explicitly rejecting Friedländer's claim, reopened the possibility that Mozart based Papageno's aria not on the folksong but on "Nun lob," providing ample evidence that Mozart encountered this chorale in the 1780s through settings by J. S. Bach.[17]

In terms of melodic provenance, Sternfeld's case is the stronger of the two. But which is the more plausible model? On the one hand, Mozart certainly knew "Nun lob," but from a generic, stylistic, and textual point of view, the chorale has little to do with the drama at hand. Furthermore, although the melodic resemblance is striking, the tune in question comes rather incongruously from the seventh and eighth phrases of the chorale (themselves appearing, with antiphonal passages interspersed, in the middle section of Bach's motet *Singet dem Herrn ein neues Lied*, BWV225 – a work Mozart both heard and studied in 1789). On the other hand, while we cannot be certain that Mozart ever encountered the folksong suggested by Friedländer, here the genre, tone, and text resonate with Papageno's character. In addition, the first two measures of the folksong align neatly with the beginning of Papageno's melody (although the next two measures are less closely related to it than the eighth phrase of "Nun lob"). Which domains should one privilege in asserting a musical borrowing?

In the operatic context, one might pose another question: Assuming Mozart was aware of what he was doing, what dramatic purpose does the musical borrowing serve? A subtle allusion to a Lutheran chorale seems to be above Papageno's pay grade. Indeed, it seems more likely that Papageno's aria was designed to bring out the artless naiveté – "der schein der Bekannt" – that J. A. P. Schulz and his circle (including Kunzen) sought in composing lieder in a folklike style.[18] Songs like Kunzen's "Au bord d'une fontaine" and "Der Landmann" (Example 8.1e) – both related to "Es war ein wilder Wassermann," but published in Mozart's day – in this respect represent a contemporary "type" of which Papageno's aria is an example. Though it is impossible to prove or disprove Mozart's indebtedness to "Nun lob," I would argue that his engagement with contemporary folksongs – and their artful adaptations on the operatic stage – is ultimately of greater significance for understanding "Ein Mädchen."

The strong desire among scholars to link Mozart and J. S. Bach has also led to curious conclusions regarding the provenance of the chorale in the duet of the Armored Men, the only indisputable musical quotation in the opera. The source, Martin Luther's "Ach Gott, vom Himmel sieh darein" (1524) was identified as early as 1798 by Friedrich Rochlitz.[19] (Mozart slightly alters Luther's melody, omitting the repetition of the *Aufgesang*

Example 8.2 Precursors of the duet of the two Armored Men by Kirnberger (1771) and
Mozart (1782).
Example 8.2a Kirnberger, trio on "Ach Gott, vom Himmel sieh darein," mm. 1–9, *Die
Kunst des reinen Satzes in der Musik* (Berlin and Königsberg: G. J. Decker and
G. L. Hartung, 1774; first published 1771), vol. 1, 238–39 (clefs modernized for ease of
comparison).

and adding a newly composed final phrase to the *Abgesang* to allow for
a tonic cadence.) Abert maintained that Mozart discovered this melody in
the first volume of Johann Philipp Kirnberger's treatise *Die Kunst des
reinen Satzes in der Musik* (1771–79), where it is used as a cantus firmus
in no fewer than twelve separate examples.[20] One of these, a trio in
B minor, not only relates to the duet of the Armored Men, but also closely
resembles Mozart's cantus firmus sketch of 1782 based on the same chorale
melody and written in the same key of B minor (see Example 8.2).[21]

In a 1956 article, however, Reinhold Hammerstein argued that Mozart
was unlikely to have found the melody in Kirnberger's book. His reasoning
hinged on two claims: first, Mozart does not appear to have known the
treatise (nor was it in his *Nachlass*), and second, Kirnberger reproduced the
chorale without its text, an element that for Hammerstein was a crucial
impetus for the musical quotation.[22] Hammerstein instead suggested that
Mozart may have either found the chorale in a Protestant hymnbook or
heard it in the Masonic lodges, arguing that its treatment in the duet of the
Armored Men owed more to Bach's motet *Jesu, meine Freude*, BWV227.

Example 8.2b Mozart, cantus firmus sketch on "Ach Gott, vom Himmel sieh darein," mm. 1–8, KV Anh. 78/K. 620b (1782), *Neue Mozart Ausgabe* II/5/19 (Kassel: Bärenreiter, 1970; digital version, Internationale Stiftung Mozarteum, 2006), 377.

To be sure, Mozart's encounter with Bach's music was transformative and may well have influenced his approach in this scene; however, the scene's relationship with Kirnberger's examples – especially in light of Mozart's sketches – is too strong to ignore. Recently, Markus Rathey has provided compelling evidence that Mozart knew and engaged with Kirnberger's treatise, detailing the musical similarities among Kirnberger's examples, the sketches, and the scene.[23]

Whether or not Luther's text, a paraphrase of Psalm 12, motivated Mozart to select "Ach Gott" for the duet of the Armored Men remains a matter for speculation. As Hammerstein and others have noted, Luther's fifth stanza – with its images of fire, trial, and purification – relates strongly to Schikaneder's text for the scene.[24] Of course, Mozart may well have come into contact with the chorale in multiple forms; one need not dismiss the significance of the chorale text simply because Kirnberger did not include it in his examples. Ultimately, however, the intertextual reference to Psalm 12 is less significant than the presence and setting of the tune itself. By alluding to the baroque genre of the chorale prelude in a *Singspiel*, Mozart blends the sacred and the secular, the "ancient" and the "modern," as well as the unfamiliar and the familiar. In so doing, he lends an oracle-like authority to the proclamation read by the two Armored Men, impressing upon both Tamino and the listener that the path to Enlightenment will be full of great hardships ("voll Beschwerden") and still greater mysteries.

A Musical Panorama

Beethoven is said to have admired *The Magic Flute* because it employs "almost every genre, from the lied to the chorale and the fugue," and because of the way Mozart used different keys "according to their specific psychical qualities."[25] As in the case of tonalities with their characteristic – if not always agreed-upon – emotional associations, the opera's musical references add psychological depth to its characters and situations while illuminating the libretto's most important themes. No theatergoer, then or now, could claim to have a comprehensive picture of these references. Indeed, some of the melodic borrowings that modern scholars have heard in *The Magic Flute* would probably have surprised Mozart, who was, after all, using a common vocabulary and engaging intuitively, as well as intentionally, with his musical environment. Nonetheless, *The Magic Flute* presents a musical panorama unlike that of perhaps any other contemporary opera. Much more than the result of a patchwork approach to composition, the work's stylistic allusions and juxtapositions are an essential element of its dramatic conception. Mozart's wide-ranging referentiality both elaborates and elevates Schikaneder's libretto, bringing its singular combination of comedic, heroic, magical, romantic, allegorical, and fairy-tale elements to life.

Notes

1. Danuta Mirka, "Introduction," in *The Oxford Handbook of Topic Theory*, ed. Danuta Mirka (New York: Oxford University Press, 2014), 1–60, 2.
2. See Clive McClelland, "Ombra and Tempesta," in ibid., 279–300.
3. John David Wilson, "Of Hunting, Horns, and Heroes: A Brief History of E♭ Major before the *Eroica*," *Journal of Musicological Research* 32/2–3 (2013): 163–82.

4. Some have interpreted the Queen's forays into high baroque style as evidence of her "artificiality." See Carolyn Abbate, *In Search of Opera* (Princeton: Princeton University Press, 2001), 68.

5. Matthew Head has argued that both Monostatos and Osmin (*Die Entführung aus dem Serail*) are characterized "in terms of excessive emotion, an absence of self-control, as much as, if not more than, any specific musical signs of Turkish or African 'race,' respectively." Matthew Head, *Orientalism, Masquerade and Mozart's Turkish Music* (London: Royal Musical Association, 2000), 57.

6. Keith Chapin, "Strict and Free Reversed: The Law of Counterpoint in Koch's *Musikalisches Lexikon* and Mozart's *Zauberflöte*," *Eighteenth-Century Music* 3/1 (2006): 91–107.

7. Quoted in A. Hyatt King, *Mozart in Retrospect: Studies in Criticism and Bibliography* (London: Oxford University Press, 1955), 141–63, 141–42.

8. See, for instance, Judith A. Eckelmeyer, "Two Complexes of Recurrent Melodies Related to *Die Zauberflöte*," *Music Review* 41 (1980): 11–25; Guy Shaked, "Mozart's Competition with Antonio Salieri and *The Magic Flute*," *Opera Journal* 48/2 (2015): 3–20.

9. See Hermann Abert, *W. A. Mozart*, trans. Stewart Spencer, ed. Cliff Eisen (New Haven, CT: Yale University Press, 2007), 624–25.

10. King, *Mozart in Retrospect*, 158.

11. Jan LaRue, "Significant and Coincidental Resemblance between Classical Themes," *Journal of the American Musicological Society* 14/2 (1961): 224–34, 224.

12. See David J. Buch, *Magic Flutes & Enchanted Forests: The Supernatural in Eighteenth-Century Musical Theater* (Chicago: University of Chicago Press, 2008), 335ff.

13. Ibid., 342–43. See also the table comparing the two works' structures in *Der Stein der Weisen*, ed. David J. Buch (Middleton, WI: A-R Editions, Inc., 2007), xiv.

14. Buch, *Magic Flutes & Enchanted Forests*, 343, 349.

15. Alan Tyson, "Two Mozart Puzzles: Can Anyone Solve Them?" *Musical Times* 129/1741 (1988): 126–27.

16. C. F. Becker, "Mozart und Scandelli," *Neue Zeitschrift für Musik* 12/28 (April 3, 1840): 112.

17. Frederick W. Sternfeld, "The Melodic Sources of Mozart's Most Popular *Lied*," in *The Creative World of Mozart*, ed. Paul Henry Lang (New York: W. W. Norton, 1963), 127–36.

18. See the preface to Friederich Ludewig Aemilius Kunzen, *Weisen und Lyrische Gesänge* (Flensburg: Korten, 1788).

19. See the "Anmerkung" in Friedrich Rochlitz, "Anekdoten aus Mozarts Leben (Fortsetzung)," *Allgemeine musikalische Zeitung* 1/10 (December 5, 1798): cols. 145–52. Rochlitz misidentified the chorale as "Aus tiefer Noth schrei' ich zu dir" but corrected himself in the twelfth issue.

20. Abert, *W. A. Mozart*, 1290.

21. Abbé Maximilian Stadler, who owned Mozart's sketch (KV Anh. 78/K. 620b), was the first to connect the scene to Kirnberger's treatise in his *Nachtrag zur Vertheidigung der Echtheit des Mozartischen Requiem* (Vienna: Tendler und von Manstein, 1827), 12–13. However, he mistakenly related the scene to Kirnberger's setting of "Es wollt uns Gott gnädig sein," the example immediately following "Ach Gott, vom Himmel sieh darein." It is easy to see how Stadler could have confused the two examples – the chromatic sighs in "Es wollt uns" look suspiciously like those in the duet of the Armored Men. As I am not the first to suggest, Mozart might have engaged with both examples in thinking about the scene.

22. Reinhold Hammerstein, "Der Gesang der geharnischten Männer: Eine Studie zu Mozarts Bachbild," *Archiv für Musikwissenschaft* 13/1 (1956): 1–24, 9.

23. Markus Rathey, "Mozart, Kirnberger and the Idea of Musical Purity: Revisiting Two Sketches from 1782," *Eighteenth-Century Music* 13/2 (2016): 235–52.

24. For a side-by-side comparison, see ibid., 241.

25. Anton Felix Schindler, *Beethoven As I Knew Him*, ed. Donald W. MacArdle, trans. Constance S. Jolly (Mineola, NY: Dover, 1996), 367 (translation emended). "Stellte Beethoven unter andern Mozarts *Zauberflöte* aus dem Grunde am höchsten, weil darin fast jede Gattung, vom Liede bis zum Choral und der Fuge, zum Ausdruck kommt, so bestand ein zweiter Grund dafür noch in der darin angewandten Psyche verschiedener Tonarten." Anton Schindler, *Biographie von Ludwig van Beethoven*, vol. 1 (Münster: Aschendorff, 1871), 164–65.

9 | Instrumentation, Magical and Mundane

EMILY I. DOLAN AND HAYLEY FENN

No art, and music least of all, suffers pedantry, and a certain latitude of mind is sometimes precisely what makes a great genius ... What Kirnberger would have said about Mozart's harmony! Not to mention his orchestration. Tamino passes through fire and water to the sounds of flute and kettledrum, with gentle accompaniment from *pianissimo* trombones! We know that the ordeal by fire and water of good taste now requires an entire arsenal of wood and brass weaponry, which is being daily augmented by strange inventions such as keyed bugles, flugelhorns, etc. cleverly made conspicuous by their dissonance. We know that every wind player, since he is no longer allowed to rest, wishes he had the lungs of Rameau's nephew, or the bewitched fellow who with his breath set in motion six windmills eight miles away. We know that the pages of many scores now appear so black that a cheeky flea can relieve itself on them with impunity, since nobody notices it. And why? For effect – effect!

Thus wrote E. T. A. Hoffmann, somewhat world-weary, in 1820.[1] Hoffmann sketched out the inevitable development of style: music marches in the direction of increasing loudness and strangeness, in the direction of militarization. Hoffmann went on to comment that the death of Gluck – whose orchestration was widely admired – was well timed, as it prevented him from completing his opera *Der Hermannschlact*, for which he imagined creating new brass instruments. Gluck's demise spared the world his descent into excessive orchestration. In this context, Hoffmann's invocation of *The Magic Flute* is noteworthy: Janus-faced, it simultaneously represents the kind of modern music that would have shocked earlier eighteenth-century theorists, while also serving as a model of moderation in comparison with the music that followed it.

Hoffmann's chosen scene – the trial of fire and water – has attracted its fair share of musicological attention. Igor Stravinsky heard it as morbid; Carolyn Abbate heard it, in its literal repetition, as mechanical, like a *Flötenuhr*: perfect and dead.[2] Jean Starobinski heard the flute in this passage as a form of "lenient, non-violent power" that ultimately represents the "power of music and musicians."[3] Marianne Tettlebaum has stressed the static nature of the music and the strange lack of any sense of real threat.[4] Hoffmann, however, alights on this example, not for its morbidity or strangeness but for its restraint. Tamino plays a graceful, adagio melody on his flute, accompanied by subdued brass and timpani; it is a march, but the gentlest of marches. In its subversion of a military topic, it represents the inverse of music's militaristic progression that Hoffmann so decried. For Hoffmann, it embodied Mozart's good taste.

As one of the few scenes in which the titular magic flute actually performs, it is hardly surprising that this scene has invited repeated analysis. Indeed, one might expect an opera named for an enchanted instrument to brim with unusual or immediately striking orchestration, or at least for the magic flute itself to have more strikingly powerful music. But in this scene there is no bombast, rather a kind of musical effortlessness. The effortlessness of Tamino's trials is in keeping with the larger sound-world of the entire opera, in which light textures and ethereal sonorities dominate. At the same time, such apparent effortlessness bespeaks the work done by instruments and orchestration within the opera: instruments function both as (magical) agents, indicators of characters, and as stage props. This chapter attempts to bring these two aspects of the opera into productive dialog, considering both Mozart's approach to his orchestra and the opera's dominant instrumental textures while also thinking about the complicated forms of instrumental agency that play out on the stage.

The Orchestral Basics

From the perspective of orchestration, *The Magic Flute* represents a fascinating historical moment. It draws on, and plays with, ideas of instrumental character – that is, the notion that individual instruments have particular, well-defined dispositions that govern their dramatic deployment. This was intimately tied to the late eighteenth-century consolidation of the orchestra as a musical body. As Dolan has written elsewhere, this transformation went hand in hand with the notion that the orchestra functioned as an instrumental society, bringing together a diverse group of instruments, whose contrasting meanings were strengthened and reinforced by that diversity.[5] This created a semiotic paradox: this generative power required composers to respect the nature of individual instruments, and yet the idea of instrumental character found its strongest articulation at precisely the moment composers began to use instruments in ways that challenged or subverted their characters. Carl Zelter complained in 1798 about the ways in which composers had stopped respecting the basic character of musical instruments: for example, the flute, the "sweetest of all instruments," was made to "shriek."[6] For him, contemporary composers had ruined special effects – such as using trumpets and drums in an adagio movement – through sheer overuse.[7] C. F. Michaelis, in 1805, likewise wrote about the misuse of wind instruments, reminding his reader that each instrument had its own emotional range: "One [wind instrument] is more suitable for gentle complaints, the other better able to express deep melancholy, gloomy seriousness. One is better suited to cheerful and light effusions, the other more to tenderness and the comfort of the familiar; one is more suitable for feminine gentleness and indulgence, another better able to express masculine strength, courage, and defiance."[8] For Michaelis, these instruments were characters that were both natural and under threat. Mozart's orchestration by and large respects the qualities of the individual instruments: we encounter no shrieking flutes. When he does subvert an instrument's expected behavior – such as in the trial scene – it is typically to use instruments in ways that are gentler and more understated than would be typical.

The basic instrumental forces of *The Magic Flute* are in keeping with late eighteenth-century orchestral norms: the score calls for two flutes (one doubling on piccolo), two oboes, two clarinets (doubling on basset horns), two bassoons, two horns, two trumpets, three trombones, timpani, strings, plus Papageno's magic bells, which are identified in the autograph as *istromento d'acciaio* and understood to be a keyed glockenspiel.[9] Most numbers use a relatively small subset of the full orchestral complement, though that subset varies continuously from number to number. Trumpets, drums, and trombones are used – as one would expect – at special moments of heightened drama; the basset horns likewise serve to signal the solemnity of Sarastro's realm and are heard only at the end of the first act finale and at the beginning of the second act. The piccolo is called for in just one number in the score: Monostatos's second act aria.

Erik Smith has noted that the orchestration of *The Magic Flute* is more restricted than that of Mozart's contemporary operas (*Così fan tutte* and *La clemenza di Tito*), something he attributed to the "markedly inferior" orchestra of the Theater auf der Wieden in comparison to that of the Nationaltheater.[10] More recently, however, David J. Buch has argued against the popular notion that performances at the Theater auf der Wieden were shoddy: plenty of reports circulated praising the high level of musicianship at the theatre.[11] Indeed, we might note that neither *Così fan tutte* nor *La clemenza di Tito* call for trombones or basset horns, and, while Mozart favors lighter orchestral textures, the *range* of color in this opera is greater than in his other operas. Indeed, as Rose Rosengard Subotnik has stressed, Mozart's approach to the sound-world of *The Magic Flute* is one that emphasizes not just sonic diversity but an ecosystem of instrumental sound that ranges from the "civilized violins" to the "earthy panpipes."[12] Furthermore, the less soloistic writing for the orchestra is also a dramatic necessity: in order for the magic flute's (relatively limited) solo moments to carry dramatic power, they must stand in relief against the orchestral palette, never overshadowed by other moments of solo writing for other (nonmagical) instruments.

Instrumental Characters

Mozart uses orchestration to help shape the characters on stage, in ways both subtle and bold. In the Act 1 quintet, for example, when Papageno's mouth has been padlocked by the Three Ladies as a punishment for lying, his repeated "hm"s are doubled at pitch by the bassoon. The doubling of Papageno's vocal noise with the sound of the double-reed produces a form of orchestrational synthesis. At this moment, the sound production of Papageno's voice is distributed between his body and the orchestra. We might understand this either as Papageno becoming an instrument or, perhaps, as the bassoon becoming part of Papageno. Abbate has drawn attention to the strangeness of how Papageno sings (and does not sing) with his magic bells and to the unusual timbral effects of the blending of voice and bells.[13] But Papageno's instrumentally enhanced humming shows how chimerical, "man-instrument" timbres can arise under less magical conditions. Bassoons can create musical cyborgs, too.

At other moments, instruments help to shape characters in a more complementary manner. The piccolo that makes its sole appearance in Monostatos's troubling aria is a striking example.[14] Richard Wigmore has suggested that this instrument makes the aria all the more sinister, presumably because of its exotic connotations.[15] Certainly, the piccolo was used in "Turkish" contexts to invoke the sound of a forceful Janissary band: recall the overture to *The Abduction from the Seraglio*, where the piccolo is deployed in all of its militaristic shrillness. In this sense, one might understand how the piccolo could be heard as menacing. And yet here the flittering, scintillating melody, which is to be played *piano* throughout to give it the effect of distance, sounds more skittish than threatening. The piccolo, even as it provides a sonic marker of Otherness, also serves to lighten the overall texture. We might hear it sympathetically as conveying Monostatos's nervousness. As with the trial scene, Mozart's setting softens and tempers the tension.

The Three Spirits are arguably the "lightest" of *Die Zauberflöte*'s characters: not only are they performed by ethereal boy sopranos but they can fly. (We do not discover this until the second act, when the Spirits return the confiscated musical instruments to Tamino and Papageno – and deliver to them much-needed sustenance – with the help of a flying machine.) In line with Masonic symbolism, the Spirits might be identified, Anthony Besch observes, with "the element of air."[16] Translated into music, this means that lower-register instruments are used sparingly, as are sustained notes and legato lines in the melodies, thus imbuing them with a breathy, buoyant quality. Even the mere mention of the Three Spirits is enough to invoke this texture: we hear a sonic preview when, in the Act 1 quintet, the Three Ladies reassure Tamino and Papageno that the Three Spirits will be on hand to provide counsel during their quest ("Drei Knäbchen, jung, schön, hold und weise/ Umschweben euch auf eurer Reise"). Here, the tempo slows to an andante and warm clarinets enter for the first time over pizzicato strings. The first two measures of the Ladies' *sotto voce* melodic line alternates eighth notes with rests, before yielding to a gently lilting figure. Anticipating the arrival of the Spirits, this passage includes many of their musical attributes.

At the beginning of the first act finale, when the Spirits lead Tamino to the temples of Wisdom, Reason, and Nature, muted trumpets, *piano* trombones, and muted timpani provide some rhythmic articulation for a hymnlike melody in the violins and a harmonic cushion in the flutes, clarinets, violas, and celli. What Erik Smith describes as "a suitably airborne effect" is achieved when the brass and timpani drop out as the Boys themselves take up the melody.[17] And arguably the lightest orchestration underscores the first appearance of the flying machine in Act 2, scene 16, when they come to the aid of Tamino and Papageno. Their trio opens with an unaccompanied violin melody of rising pairs of thirty-second notes, which are answered by sighing bassoons, second violins, and violas. As the melodic peak is reached and the violin hiccups tumble earthwards into trills, they are joined by the flute and bassoon. The violin quips continue to fill rests between vocal phrases, which are supported by the remainder of the strings.

The Three Spirits are from the genus of the *deus ex machina*, the theatrical conceit where a divine being intervenes to bring about a happy ending. That the Spirits in some way "govern" the opera was not lost on the director of the 2019 production of *The Magic Flute* for the Staatsoper Unter den Linden. Yuval Sharon cast the entire opera as a puppet show, complete with the singers on strings. Instead of travelling in a flying machine, the Three Spirits are contained within what appear to be gas canisters, floating on a cloud. As the opera progresses, their activity expands – cutting Pamina's strings and playing the bells *for* Papageno as he summons Papagena – until their true identity is revealed. For the final chorus, the backdrop rises to reveal a puppet theatre, of miniature proportions, presided over by the Three Spirits, who now appear as boys at play, in casual clothes, jumping up and down excitedly with some friends. The Spirits turn out to be puppeteers par excellence: they keep everything light, while remaining in total control. We might say that they are in charge of both the drama and, it would seem, the orchestration.

Instruments as Characters

Three instruments feature in the opera's diegesis: the magic flute, the magic bells, and Papageno's pipes. These onstage instruments are by no means unique to opera. Think of Orpheus's lyre, Radamès's triumphal procession, or Beckmesser's lute. Indeed, certain instruments frequently migrate to the stage in opera – aurally, if not necessarily visibly, so distinctive is their timbre – to accompany drinking songs, serenades, and ballads or to signal royal or military company. In other words, the onstage presence of musical instruments makes explicit moments of self-conscious music-making.

In *The Magic Flute*, though, we find a somewhat different situation, one that goes beyond the demarcation of narrative worlds and performance modes to open up questions of musical agency, materiality, and meaning. For a start, neither Tamino's flute nor Papageno's bells function as straightforward accompaniment. Tamino's flute cannot, of course: he must either sing or (pretend to) play. Benedict Schack, the tenor who premiered the role of Tamino, was also known to play wind instruments, and so for a long time – persisting into the *Grove Music* entry on *The Magic Flute* today – many have assumed that Schack both sang the role of Tamino and played the flute. Theodore Albrecht, however, has convincingly discredited this assumption, which seems to have been based on overgenerous readings of Schack's musical abilities, as well as on a misunderstanding of what was meant by the fact that, according to contemporary reports, he "sang and played" the role of Tamino.[18] So, Schack and his descendants usually mime – and sometimes there is no pretense even of that.

While Tamino's flute must function always as a solo instrument, Papageno's bells could, in theory, be pressed into service as an accompaniment instrument, since the performer can sing and play at the same time. At first, however, there is some ambiguity around the bells' playing mechanism – more specifically, around whether or not they required a player. As with Tamino's flute, Papageno receives the magic bells from the Three Ladies in preparation for their quest to save Pamina; but unlike the flute, the bells are something of an organological enigma. The autograph identifies the instrument as an *istromento d'acciaio*; the libretto specifies "eine Maschine wie ein hölzernes Gelächter" (a machine like wooden laughter). Confusing matters further, when the Three Ladies present Papageno with the bells in Act 1, Papageno asks what is inside, suggesting that he is handling some kind of a box. The Ladies respond accordingly by explaining that the bells are inside, but Papageno remains perplexed about their musical nature. For it is not immediately apparent to him what he needs to do with the bells – indeed, whether the bells need him to do anything at all. "Will I also be able to play them?" he asks the Three Ladies. "Yes, of course!" comes the answer.

Despite this quashing of Papageno's initial uncertainty, the pragmatics, the pitfalls, and the pranks of performance can sustain the instrument's ambiguity. Mozart himself was fully cognizant of – and, arguably, excited by – the potential to manipulate the grey space between the narrative world of the drama and the realities of performance. In an oft-quoted letter to his wife, Constanze, Mozart delights in his interference during Papageno's Act 2 aria:

> I went backstage during Papageno's aria with the Glockenspiel as I felt such an urge to play it myself today. – As a joke I played an arpeggio at a point where Schikaneder has a rest – he was startled – he looked into the wings and saw me – the 2nd time round I didn't play anything – this time he stopped as well and refused to go on – I guessed what he was thinking and again played a chord – he then hit the Glockenspiel and said *shut up* – everyone laughed then – it was because of this joke, I think, that many people discovered for the first time that he wasn't playing the instrument himself.[19]

The instrument responsible for the onstage prop's acoustic presence is understood to be a keyboard instrument not dissimilar to a celeste. Onstage, the bells are represented by all sorts of contraptions, from magical-looking machines to tambourine-like instruments. Rarely do modern productions aim to conjure the illusion that these props actually produce the music we hear: the quirky boxes and twinkling rattles are obviously incapable of producing the florid runs and quick arpeggiations of the bells' music.

Such music, furthermore, far exceeds the role of accompaniment. As Abbate observes, while the alteration of the bells and Papageno's voice is born of an "acoustic fact of life" (i.e., the original instrument would not have been able to carry over Schikaneder's singing and so had to play in the gaps between the voice), this compositional necessity has taken on a symbolic dimension, entangling Papageno in an aesthetic of automation and mechanization.[20]

There is, of course, an instrument that Papageno does play: his panpipes. At the opposite end of the aesthetic spectrum to the bells, panpipes connote nature and earthliness, and therefore might seem an obvious extension of Papageno's status as *Naturmensch*. Indeed, the five-note panpipe call functions as a metonym for Papageno and is one of the most characteristic keynotes of the opera. As a consequence, perhaps, the agency behind Papageno's *Waldflötchen* or *Faunen-Flötchen*, as they are identified in the libretto and score, respectively, have hardly received much scrutiny in the literature. Since it is notated as part of Papageno's vocal line, it seems likely that Schikaneder did indeed play the pipes himself. What precise type of instrument he played is more ambiguous, since the iconic image of Schikaneder as Papageno does not include the pipes (later images do often show Papageno with a five-pipe set). Furthermore, panpipes are relatively ephemeral instruments, so precious few examples of panpipes survive from the eighteenth century. Interestingly, however, starting in the years after the first performances of *The Magic Flute* and stretching across the nineteenth century, panpipes began to be referred to in German as "Papagenopfeife" or "Papagenoflöten."[21] Today, Papageno might play or he might mime. A few instrument makers specialize in special five-note sets of pipes, specifically made for productions of *The Magic Flute*. These are often not true panpipes, but a set of fippled whistles, which are easier to play.[22]

Today, directors and performers of *Die Zauberflöte* are confronted with the question of how instruments should behave dramatically onstage. In the recent revival of Simon McBurney's 2013 production for the English National Opera, Papageno (Thomas Oliemans) carries around a tabletop celeste in a briefcase, enlisting the assistance of a player from the pit for the Act 1 finale. In his Act 2 aria, in the hope of summoning his mate Papagena, he plays the instrument himself on stage. Thematizing the question of agency, McBurney makes sure that we all know exactly who and what is making the music. And the flute receives equally special treatment. When Pamina is confirmed alive by the Priests in the Act 1 finale, Tamino is moved to express his thanks through music. And so, McBurney's Tamino, played by Rupert Charlesworth in 2019, descends the steps into the pit and offers his flute, glinting in the spotlight, to the principal flautist. The ensuing musical offering is delivered onstage, in full view of the audience. When Tamino/Charlesworth joins in and his vocal lines begin to dovetail with those of the flute, the gestural language of the performance is expanded from that of a solo to that of a duet: singer and flautist enact their musical partnership through movement as well as sound.

These visuals foreground the chain of labor relations involved in this particular act of music-making and, in so doing, flatten out the hierarchy of voice and instrument, singer and musician – and even of the music itself. Echoing the readings of the flute's music proffered by Tettlebaum and Abbate as detached and mechanical, respectively, McBurney's magic flute is neither Tamino's prop nor his appendage, but a fully agential character, capable of asserting its will, albeit with the help of a player. By putting his flute, quite literally, in the hands of a flautist, Tamino/Charlesworth separates his musical persona from that of the flute, making explicit the distinction between each source of musical power. In doing so, he also highlights something else – namely, that when the on-stage actors make no serious attempt to mime their performances, the music can appear all the more magical, as the sound so clearly exceeds its apparent materiality.

It might seem as though we have strayed a long way from the issue of orchestration and instrumentation. But these more overt ways in which the opera plays with instruments and agency should attune us to the subtler ways in which Mozart uses instrumentation to define the various characters' personalities. The light touch that pervades the opera – from the understated brass and timpani that support the flute through the trials to the celestial pizzicati of the Three Spirits' lofty music – likewise tells us something about instrumental labor in this opera. We might say that the magic of *The Magic Flute* is its ability to create a world in which humans and instruments work together so smoothly and naturally and where they so easily complement each other's agency.[23]

Notes

The authors extend their gratitude to David J. Buch, Charlie Hind, John Koster, Albert Rice, and Neal Zaslaw for their help and insights.

1. E. T. A. Hoffmann, "Zufällige Gedanken bei dem Erscheinen dieser Blätter," *Allgemeine Zeitung für Musik und Musikliteratur* (October 9 and 16, 1820), repr. in *Cäcilia* 3/9 (1825): 8–9; trans. by Martyn Clark in David Charlton,

E.T.A. Hoffmann's Musical Writings: Kreisleriana, The Poet and the Composer, Music Criticism (Cambridge: Cambridge University Press, 1989), 427–28.

2. Carolyn Abbate, *In Search of Opera* (Princeton: Princeton University Press, 2001), 102.
3. Jean Starobinski, "A Reading of *The Magic Flute*," *Hudson Review* 31/3 (1978): 409–24, 418.
4. Marianne Tettlebaum, "Whose Magic Flute?" *Representations* 102 (2008): 76–93, 84. Kerman went so far as to declare: "This still climax, with flute and drums and quiet brass, is surely the most extraordinary in all opera." Joseph Kerman, *Opera as Drama* (New York: Alfred A. Knopf, 1956), 127.
5. See Emily I. Dolan, *The Orchestral Revolution: Haydn and the Technologies of Timbre* (Cambridge: Cambridge University Press, 2013), 148ff.
6. Carl Zelter, "Bescheidene Anfragen an die modernsten Komponisten und Virtuosen," *Allgemeine musikalische Zeitung* 1/9 (November 28, 1798): cols. 141–44, at col. 142.
7. Ibid., cols. 152–55, at col. 152.
8. Christian Friedrich Michaelis, "Einige Bemerkungen über den Missbrauch der Blasinstrumente in der neuern Musik," *Allgemeine musikalische Zeitung* 8/7 (November 13, 1805): cols. 97–102, at cols. 99–100.
9. On the constitution of Mozart's orchestras, see Dexter Edge, "Mozart's Viennese Orchestras," *Early Music* 20/1 (1992): 63–88.
10. Erik Smith, "The Music," in COH, 131.
11. See David. J. Buch, "Die Hauskomponisten am Theater auf der Wieden in der Zeit Mozarts (1789–1791)," in *Acta Mozartiana* 48, no. 1/4 (2001): 75–81.
12. Rose Rosengard Subotnik, "Whose 'Magic Flute': Intimations of Reality at the Gates of the Enlightenment," *19th-Century Music* 15/2 (1991): 132–50, at 145–47.
13. See Abbate, *In Search of Opera*, 83.
14. Even though this is the only number in which the piccolo is called for, it is often used to substitute acoustically for Papageno's panpipes in productions where Papageno mimes.
15. Richard Wigmore, "Human Enlightenment and Redemption," ENO Programme Booklet (2019).
16. Anthony Besch, "A Director's Approach," in COH, 184.
17. Smith, "The Music," 136.
18. Theodore Albrecht, "Anton Dreyssig (c. 1753/4–1820): Mozart's and Beethoven's *Zauberflötist*," in *Words about Mozart: Essays in Honor of Stanley Sadie*, ed. Dorothea Link and Judith Nagley (Woodbridge: Boydell Press, 2005), 179–92.
19. Letter of October 8–9, 1791 (authors' translation). MBA, IV:159–61.
20. Abbate, *In Search of Opera*, 83.
21. As one of many such examples: in the 1807 edition of Johann Georg Krünitz, *Oekonomische Encyklopädie oder allgemeines System der Staats- Stadt- Haus- u.*

Landwirthschaft, ed. Heinrich Gustav Flörke, vol. 106 (Berlin: Joachim Pauli, 1807), one finds the following entry: "Papagenopfeife, f. Panpfeife. Panpfeife, oder Hirtenpfeife, ein Instrument, welches aus 7 in einer Reihe an einander gefügten Pfeifen von zunehmender Größe besteht. S. im Art. Pan, oben, S. 3331. Jetzt verfertigt man die Panpfeife aus blechernen Röhren, und die vor einigen Jahren so allgemeine Papagenopfeife, worauf Papageno in der Zauberflöte, einem Singespiele von Schikaneder, bläset, ist eine Abart derselben" (355). Notable here is that the term "Papagenopfeife" is being used to describe a seven-tube panpipe.

22. For examples of these instruments, see the instruments advertised on the following websites: http://hindocarina.com/ocarinas/index.php?l=product_detail&p=623 (accessed April 19, 2023), https://earlymusicshop.com/products/kobliczek-papageno-flute (accessed April 19, 2023). These specially made sets of pipes for *The Magic Flute* have a long history: the 1991 exhibition at the Kunsthistorische Museum in Vienna, *Die Klangwelt Mozarts*, featured a five-note set of "pipes" (actually a set of five one-note recorders) for use in the opera. Gerhard Stradner et al., *Die Klangwelt Mozarts: 28 April bis 27 Oktober 1991: Wien, Neue Burg, Sammlung Alter Instrumente* (Vienna: Das Museum, [1991]), 315–16.

23. On the clarinet and Tamino's agency, see Tettlebaum, "Whose Magic Flute?," 82–83.

10 | The Dialogue as Indispensable

CATHERINE COPPOLA

Complaints about the libretto have long shadowed *The Magic Flute*. The spoken dialogue especially has been disparaged, both for its contribution to a purportedly incomprehensible plot and because of traditions that exalt music and devalue speech in an operatic context. Criticisms of this type were immediate. Berlin's *Musikalishen Wochenblatt* reported in 1791 that "*Die Zauberflöte* . . . fails to have the hoped-for success, the content and the dialogue [*Sprache*] of the work were just too terrible."[1] Count Zinzendorf wrote in his diary that "the music and the decorations are pretty; the rest an unbelievable farce."[2] A review of a French adaptation of 1865 also targeted the spoken word, expressing the wish that "everything in Schikaneder's dialogue that is unnecessary or makes no sense" had been cut, leaving only "the sung part, which has the delicate and ideal meaning that Mozart's genius adds to the hollow words."[3] By 1913, Edward J. Dent could famously conclude: "The libretto of *Die Zauberflöte* has generally been considered to be one of the most absurd specimens of that form of literature in which absurdity is only too often a matter of course."[4]

While this unfortunate reception history has often been used to justify broad cuts in the dialogue in modern productions, not everyone subscribes to this view. Conductor René Jacobs has championed the dialogue: "No opera loses so much as *Die Zauberflöte* if one strips it of its drama, and that means also and *above all* the spoken dialogue."[5] Even if it is accepted that the spoken text is important, there is, however, an additional consideration for modern scholars and audiences. Recent criticism of the text has been focused less on the supposed absurdity of the plot and more on issues of gender and race. And even though the sung portions of the libretto contain much of what is deemed offensive, the dialogue remains an easy target for excision. Of course, the spoken word in opera has always been more controversial than what is sung, hence the disparity between the level of censorship of plays and their transformations as operatic texts.

The critic Walter Bernhart asks, "What is the significance or the benefit of the absence of music in the spoken sections?" He concludes that "it is only in spoken dialogue that wit and intellectual brilliance can find comprehensible expression, and . . . that a rational argument which tries to explain and interpret the dramatic situation can meaningfully be developed; whenever such reflections are done in singing they are bound to fail."[6] Wit is essential to *Singspiel*, and the dialogues in *The Magic Flute* provide a range from slapstick humor to more sophisticated wordplay. While the spoken words may not always aim for "intellectual brilliance," they do "interpret the dramatic situation" with nuanced treatment of controversial issues that are essential to understanding the opera as a whole and also to evaluating modern claims of moral superiority. To put this another way, close reading of many passages demonstrates that words and phrases cannot be cut without consequence.

The dialogue provides a wealth of detail with respect to character and plot that needs to be understood as essential to the whole dramatic action. To illustrate, let me begin at the end of Act 1, scene 1. When, according to the stage directions, Tamino "awakens and looks timidly about," the audience has already watched the Three Ladies kill the serpent.[7] In the ensuing exchange, Tamino unwittingly feeds Papageno the language with which to claim credit for the women's action: "So you strangled [*erdrosselt*] it?" Papageno confirms, "Erdrosselt!" and delivers a comic aside to the audience: "I've never been as strong in my life as I am today."[8] When Tamino says of the Three Ladies, "I suppose they're very beautiful," Papageno insults them, alluding to their veils: "I don't think so, because if they were beautiful they wouldn't cover their faces." The Ladies return in scene 3, and he makes an about-face: "You ask if they're beautiful, and I can only reply that I never saw anything more charming in my life"; then aside, "There, that should soon calm them down," reinforcing his duplicity. He is punished as the Ladies deliver a maxim about the importance of truth. While the women are demeaned, it is clearly men who have failed: Tamino arrived with a bow but no arrows (explicit in stage directions) and Papageno lied. Thus, within this vaudevillian context, perhaps we are meant to question male superiority even before we meet the Queen. The dialogue reframes our view of a singularly misogynistic text.

In this scene and others, comedy appears to make palatable the more progressive, as well as the more problematic, aspects of the text. This chapter offers a number of close readings, centering on Monostatos, the Queen, and Sarastro. Each of these characters is given important dialogue that conveys in speech a desire to be understood as more than a stereotype, and each takes grave action when their words are disregarded. By letting them speak, we allow them to transcend their prevailing two-dimensional characterizations to appear as fully formed (and flawed) characters.

Monostatos: "Because I Am the Same Color As a Black Ghost?"

The power of comedic dialogue to engage serious issues lies at the heart of the brief but crucial interaction in Act 1, scene 14, just after we, along with Papageno, meet Monostatos for the first time. The presumptions based on appearance expressed there have a corollary in the spoken exchange of scene 2 when Tamino asks Papageno's identity and he replies: "A man, like you!" When Papageno asks the same question, Tamino identifies himself by rank: "Then I would answer that I am of princely lineage." Papageno underscores their class divide: "That's too high-flown for me." Tamino presses, "I'm not sure whether you are human." Papageno's feathered garb is a visible reason for Tamino's query ("To judge from those feathers that cover you"); yet it may also signal the folly inherent in judging humans by class and appearance.

That folly is first explicit in song when Papageno and Monostatos are equally startled by each other's difference and they sing in short comic bursts: "That is the devil there's no doubt!" (scene 12). The presumption of danger in the Other is treated as ridiculous. In that light, the ensuing spoken words – often cut in modern performances – can be understood as a critique of racist assumptions. Papageno reflects, "Am I not a fool to take fright like that? After all, there are black birds in the world, why shouldn't there be black men too?" Before judging that line, note that he admits ignorance (confirmed in scene 2, he was unaware of lands and people beyond his own) and realizes that humans can have black skin. While these and other lines have seemed too problematic to stage in contemporary productions, in this case it is not just an analogy to the animal world – which in isolation would certainly be problematic – but a matter-of-fact blackness that suggests the problem is in the perceiver, Papageno, and in white members of the audience, then and now.

The hypocrisy of such censorship could not be more starkly revealed than when compared to US officials in Los Angeles, California, who originated the abhorrent abbreviation NHI – no humans involved – in cases concerning young Black men of low economic status.[9] The title of Ava DuVernay's 2019 film, *When They See Us,* captures a similar perspective: before the trial of the later exonerated teens who were falsely accused and convicted for a brutal 1989 rape, they were dubbed a "wolf pack," a characterization with roots in the centuries-old branding of non-Europeans as savage.[10] In 2020, while global police brutality was protested at unprecedented levels, American news host Tucker Carlson asked, "Why doesn't anybody stand up for the rest of us, for civilization?"[11] and the French far right embraced the word *ensauvagement* to stoke fears that immigration would remake France as an uncivilized place.[12]

Relegating racism and misogyny to an uncomfortable past ignores both their persistence today and their resistance in Mozart's time. In 1772, Diderot called out the cognitive dissonance of claiming Enlightenment while enslaving fellow human beings.[13] This context informs Monostatos's speech preceding his strophic aria (Act 2, scene 7). However, his reflections are tainted with sexism – "here I find the cold beauty" – as though because Pamina is beautiful she has no right to her indifference.[14] In 1792, Mary Wollstonecraft pinpointed this trap: "I lament that women are systematically degraded by receiving the trivial attentions, which men think it manly to pay to the sex, when, in fact, they are insultingly supporting their own superiority."[15] Monostatos then asks, "But really, what was my crime? . . . And what man . . . could remain cold and unfeeling at such a sight?" He seeks the same entitlement as white men regarding nonconsensual acts. The hypocrisy of excising those words is exposed by Tatyana Fazlalizadeh's "stop telling women to smile" campaign: "Women have talked to me about how things can jump from a seemingly nice comment to instantly becoming an insult and becoming an assault if the woman doesn't respond the way the man wants her to."[16]

Monostatos verbalizes that escalation: "That girl will make me lose my senses yet. The fire that smoulders within me can still consume me. If I knew . . . that I was completely alone and unobserved . . . I'd risk trying it again." Blaming the victim for his physical response, the Black overseer is a convenient stand-in for white Europeans such as George Booth, who wrote in a pamphlet of 1739: "If Nature . . . has given the Fair-Sex stronger Inclinations; it has also given them a natural Modesty and Check upon them, which we [men] have not."[17] Not only do women censor their desires, but, according to John Burton in 1793, they have a sensor for impropriety: "Modesty is a female Virtue; . . . Nature herself gives the alarm at any improper conversation or behaviour."[18] Quaint in retrospect, fallacies concerning female physiology have consequences. And this is still true. Here is US representative Todd Akin (Republican – Missouri) in 2012: "If it's a legitimate rape, the female body has ways to try to shut that whole thing down," preventing pregnancy; and in 2016, a judge asked whether the victim had attempted to prevent her assault by "closing her legs."[19] This book goes to press in the wake of the US Supreme Court decision overturning *Roe* v. *Wade*, for which Justice Samuel Alito repeatedly cites seventeenth-century British jurist Matthew Hale to claim an "unbroken tradition of prohibiting abortion on pain of criminal punishment." Positioning him as one of the "eminent common-law authorities," Alito omits Hale's view of marital rape as exempt from criminal prosecution, of rape in general as "an accusation easily to be made and hard to be proved, and harder to be defended by the party accused, tho never so innocent," and his decisions that were used as precedent for the Salem witch trials. Historian Lauren MacGivor Thompson notes that even for his time Hale "was particularly misogynistic. For a Supreme Court Justice to be [citing him] in 2022 is really astonishing."[20]

Parallels between Mozart's time and ours do not cancel the misogyny of Monostatos's speech, but cutting his spoken lines worsens matters, as it isolates the racial content of his ensuing aria: "White is beautiful! I must kiss her." He has just expressed in dialogue the sexist attitude that was spelled out by Booth and Burton, and yet if that gendered justification – with which white males would identify – is cut, then we are left only with the sung text that racializes desire. Without the dialogue, then, it is understandable that many modern productions choose to cut or sanitize the aria, but that reaction may also stem from the extremes with which his character has traditionally been painted.

Monostatos has appeared to be the leering Black male caricatured as "the evil principle, a real monster with splendid white teeth."[21] Exaggeration is not the fault of the opera – in which we have noted Papageno's lesson about white misperceptions of blackness – but of white reactions to the onstage accosting of a white woman by a Black man: "U.S. history is rife with the consequences of widespread White complicity in the propagation of racist stereotypes portraying Black men as beast-like sexual predators, lying in wait to violate White women."[22] The discomfiting persistence of this "danger" narrative underpins whitewashing the character. Thomas Rothschild recognized "an enlightening twist in the libretto when Monostatos complains elsewhere that he should avoid love 'because a black man is ugly!' And Papageno argues: 'There are black birds in the world, why not black people too?'" But Rothschild complicates matters when he continues: "If one does not want to delete these passages of text at the expense of the dramaturgical logic, they fail to completely conceal the black skin of Monostatos. At least in the metaphorical sense, the blackness must be indicated."[23]

This raises an important question: How should Monostatos be represented on stage? Perhaps the perspective gained by a revaluation of the dialogue can inform directorial decisions. One thing is certain: if Monostatos is portrayed true to text, Black singers need to be represented in other roles too.[24] Censorship in the name of color blindness is no solution to this problem; I submit that whites are actually color mute. For philosopher Kate Manne, "those who are included in ... our 'common humanity' are also capable of reducing us to shame when we wrong them. ... No wonder then that avoidance – a deliberate attempt to 'miss' the other ... – is subsequently so common."[25] Shameful performance traditions include blackface and the monkey-like costumes in 2001 for the Paris Opéra. In 2019, for Berlin Opera's first new production of *The Magic Flute* in twenty-five years, Yuval Sharon's characters are marionettes with wide-open whites of the eyes, creating an unintended minstrel effect against Monostatos's brown skin. Sharon added dialogue that signals present-day virtue around presumably extinguished racism: "There are these critical moments ... where they ... say ... 'This doesn't seem right, you don't tell stories like this today ... this must be a very, very old text.'"[26] We might see these words as a trope on the work's moralistic statements; as Martin Nedbal reminds us, "Even from the earliest operatic works ... characters turn to the audience to deliver instructional reflections drawn out of onstage occurrences."[27] But Sharon contorts this tradition to distance the present, concluding: "So then it just becomes part of the play, but it's not a comfortable part of the play."[28]

That swerve ignores the role of the dialogue in questioning racist ideas. After the Queen's climactic revenge aria, the dialogue of Act 2, scene 9, gives Pamina space to reflect: "Must I commit murder? Ye gods, that I cannot do. I cannot! (*She remains sunk in thought.*)" Monostatos reappears: "Put your trust in me! (*He takes the dagger from her. Pamina cries out in fright.*)" He does not yet threaten; continuing the racial remonstrance from his aria, he asks, "Why do you tremble? At my black colour, or at the murder that is planned?" Unlike the accusers documented by Ava DuVernay, Pamina does not buy into the danger narrative. To his either/or question – Is it race or your guilty conscience? – she chooses the latter, saying "Then you know?" expressing fear only of what he might disclose. He will reveal the plan to Sarastro unless she "loves" him. Faced with defiance, he returns to race: "No? And why not? Because I am the same color as a black ghost? Is it not so? Ha, then die!"

Without this very uncomfortable dialogue, we miss nuance. While Monostatos condemns rejection based on race, he resorts to physical threat that justifies fear regardless of race. And while Sarastro interrupts the threat to Pamina, he does so with a puzzling reaction to Monostatos: "I understand only too well. I would have you know that your soul is as black as your face. And I would have punished you with the utmost severity for this black crime had not a wicked woman ... forged the dagger for it. You may thank the evil behaviour of that woman if you now escape unpunished." Sarastro creates an intersectional hierarchy: he *would have* punished the man he has just insulted, but does not; however, without having witnessed the woman's order, he *does* judge her harshly enough to exonerate Monostatos, even though he saw Monostatos threaten to kill Pamina. In context, Sarastro's words to Monostatos are not as harsh as they have sometimes been thought to be.

As he is fleshed out in the dialogue, then, Sarastro is not a benevolent caricature, but just as flawed as the Queen. In fact, the plot device of using speech to interrupt a threat to Pamina is just one point of similarity that connects these two authority figures.

The Queen: "With Your Father's Death My Power Too Went to the Grave."

The dialogue preceding the Queen's iconic aria "Der Hölle Rache" offers an explanation – not an exoneration – of her murderous order and her threat to disown Pamina. Without it, the operagoer might conclude either that the Queen is thoroughly evil or that she inexplicably transforms into a caricature of malevolence after the intermission. Yet her Act 2, scene 8, appearance actually begins as a rescue: according to the stage directions, just as Monostatos "creeps slowly and softly" up to Pamina, the Queen physically shields her daughter by emerging "from the central trap door amid thunder, so that she is standing right in front of Pamina." While the Queen easily dispatches Monostatos, the ensuing dialogue shows that she is no match for Sarastro's power.

One word is especially significant in this dialogue: *entreißen*, which denotes a violent tearing away, but its secondary meaning is to rescue, complicating the way in which both Sarastro and the Queen deal with Pamina. Here is the passage:

QUEEN ... Unhappy daughter, now you are torn [*entrissen*] from me forever.
PAMINA Torn from you? Oh, let us flee, dear mother! Under your protection I will brave any danger.
QUEEN Protection? Dear child, your mother cannot protect you any longer. With your father's death my power too went to its grave.
PAMINA My father ...
QUEEN ... of his own free will gave the sevenfold circle of the sun to the initiates; Sarastro now wears that potent sign on his breast. When I spoke of it with

your father, he said with furrowed brow: "Woman! My last hour has come. All the treasures I alone possessed are yours and your daughter's." – "What of the all-consuming circle of the sun?", I hurriedly interrupted. – "It is destined for the Initiates," he replied. "Sarastro will wield it as manfully as I did until now. And now, not a word more. Do not delve into mysteries that are unfathomable to a woman's mind. Your duty, and that of your daughter, is to submit to the guidance of wise men."

Unpacking these words, we see that the transfer of power is complete – Sarastro wears its symbol. The Queen flouts expectations, growing impatient at the offer of treasure, asking instead about the conveyance of power.[29] Her request is denied due to a presumed inability to lead; her husband's negation of female speech ("not a word more") resonates with John Fordyce's 1766 claim that only a despicable woman "talks loud[ly], contradicts bluntly, looks sullen . . . and instead of yielding, challenges submission."[30]

This dialogue is not a relic. The speech of today's female Supreme Court justices is so devalued that they are interrupted three times more frequently than their male counterparts.[31] When 2016 US presidential candidate Kirsten Gillibrand questioned Fox News reports on reproductive rights, anchor Chris Wallace scolded, "I'm not sure it's frankly very polite [of you] when we've invited you here."[32] Journalist Yamiche Alcindor probed President Trump's response to the pandemic in 2020 and he admonished, "Be nice. Don't be threatening."[33]

This dialogue also clarifies that it is only after learning that Pamina is aligned with those who would destroy her that the Queen calls for Sarastro's murder. The elements of rescue and the wish to protect Pamina presented in Act 2 are thus consistent with the Second Lady's dialogue in which she describes the "motherly heart" of the Queen in Act 1 (scene 5). These dialogues challenge a trope of inconsistency so influential that some modern directors present the sympathetic Queen of Act 1 as a skillful deception. For example, in Barrie Kosky's production she is animated as a spider from the get-go. Perhaps that notion is inspired by Sarastro's drawing an analogy between prejudice against his men and a spider's web in the dialogue at the beginning of Act 2, to which we now turn.

Sarastro and the Priests: "That Woman Thinks Herself Great."

The Queen's dual loss – her daughter and her claim to power – puts into perspective Sarastro's words to the Priests at the start of Act 2: "The gods intend the gentle, virtuous maiden Pamina for the gracious youth; that is the main reason why I snatched [*entriß*] her from her arrogant mother. That woman thinks herself great; she hopes to beguile the people by means of deception and superstition and destroy the firm foundations of our temple. But she must not succeed." While the rescue aspect of *entreißen* serves the view that Sarastro saved Pamina from her mother, his dialogue clarifies that he abducted her for Tamino and that the Queen's ambition is offensive to him. But there is no evidence for the accusation that she is deceptive.[34] The refusal to accept a nuanced Queen is linked to today's "ethical pedestal": "If voters even perceive that a woman has been dishonest or acted unethically, regardless of her actual actions, the cost is high."[35] The words of a perpetrator of the 2020 plot to kidnap Michigan's governor Gretchen Whitmer are a profanity-laced version of Sarastro's statements: "This tyrant [expletive] loves the power she has right now."[36] During the 2020 US vice presidential debate, then Senator Kamala Harris was characterized by commentator Harlan Hill as "an insufferable power-hungry smug [expletive]."[37] It is important to remember Sarastro's reductive view of the Queen as an "arrogant" woman who "must not succeed," when, in Act 2, scene 12, Pamina begs him not to punish her mother. He replies, "You will see how I am revenged on your mother." Without this revelatory dialogue, we might believe the message of his beautiful ensuing aria, "Within these halls we know no vengeance … we forgive our enemies."

The spoken words provide necessary context for the pageantry of Act 2, scene 1, which is emphasized by its placement at the start of the second act. Mozart himself called this the "solemn scene" in a letter of October 8, 1791, in which he reported that he was so offended by his companion's laughter at this moment that he "called him a Papageno and cleared out."[38] The Viennese audience often took the work's moral lessons seriously.[39] Yet, could Mozart's companion have been the only spectator to find humor here? Might it have been provoked by words that seemed pompous and hypocritical? Perhaps we, too, can simultaneously question Sarastro's judgment against female ambition and admire his humility as a conveyor of a higher power, charging the Speaker to "teach both men by your wisdom what the duty of humanity is; teach them to acknowledge the power of the gods." He is not a clichéd dominant male, yet his dialogue still begs the question: On what basis does he, like the Queen's husband, declare that she could not wield power as well as he could?[40] Tinged with the same arrogance of which he accuses the Queen, Sarastro's words reveal a flawed human, complicating the serious intent alluded to by Mozart in his letter and for which he wrote such effective music.

The Queen's explanatory dialogue is often cut, leaving the impression that she is driven solely by a need for control; while, paradoxically, Sarastro's words are left intact, even though they reveal his controlling nature. In Act 1, scene 5, the First Lady tells Tamino that the Queen "has heard each word" before she asks him to rescue Pamina. But in scene 18 Sarastro presumes to divine Pamina's thoughts: "For without needing to press you I know more of your heart." When she does speak, he interrupts to demonstrate his disrespect for her mother (and by extension all women):

PAMINA My mother's name sounds sweet to me; she is . . .
SARASTRO . . . a proud woman. A man must guide your hearts, for without one every woman tends to step out of her natural sphere.

This dictum foreshadows the Queen's rescue dialogue, where her husband insists that she "submit to the guidance of wise men."

It may be more than coincidence that Sarastro's words follow the moment where significant text about the hypocrisy of those in power had been penned for Papageno and Pamina at the conclusion of scene 17 (but were cut): "The truth is not always good, Because it harms the great ones." Nedbal attributes Mozart's omission of these lines to his wish to support Enlightenment ideals.[41] Conversely, perhaps it was safe to let the Three Ladies question the "falsehoods of these Priests" (Act 2, scene 5) since, as females, they would not be believed. Just before that claim, another outsider, the lower-class Papageno says, "Hey, let's have lights here! . . . It's really strange: every time one of these gentlemen leaves us, however wide you open your eyes, you can't see a thing." In the context of the Three Ladies' speech, we might consider Papageno's joking style as a comedic literalism that also hints at institutional hypocrisy.

When, in Act 2, scene 3, Tamino confirms that he seeks "friendship and love," he is asked, "Are you prepared to fight for them with your life?" His affirmation might give us pause, given both his capitulation in the opening scene and his use of Papageno as a surrogate in the first attempt to find Pamina. Those scenes reveal that physical confrontation does not come easily to Tamino. Still, in language reminiscent of the Queen's husband, Sarastro feeds the masculine power narrative in his culminating scene 21 dialogue: "Prince, your conduct thus far has been manly and calm; now you still have two dangerous paths to tread. If your heart still beats as ardently for Pamina, and if you wish one day to reign as a wise prince, the gods must accompany you further. . . . Let Pamina be brought in!" Thus, Tamino is twice rewarded: he gets Pamina and the power to govern that was denied the women, although Pamina actually leads him through the final trials.

Undervaluing the abilities and contributions of women remains relevant to this day: for example, the gender gap in the sciences is due partly to "women systematically receiving less credit for their work."[42]

What I hope to have shown here is that we must let the dialogue speak to us and, just as important, we must speak back – not to judge the eighteenth century but to learn from its contradictions as we continue to learn from our own. As this reading has shown, despite differences in gender, race, and class among the characters of the Queen, Monostatos, and Sarastro, they have in common the wish to be understood. And each conveys that wish most clearly in spoken words. Each also resorts in speech to a grave action when their words are ignored: the Queen orders a murder; Monostatos threatens one; and Sarastro, while keeping his own hands clean, banishes the Queen and excludes her from the benevolence afforded to the rest of humanity.

Conversations around gender, race, and class are essential for musicology to remain relevant, as we will long reckon with the societal tipping point of 2020. For *The Magic Flute*, a revaluation of the dialogues is a good place to start.

Notes

I am deeply grateful to Jessica Waldoff for guiding this essay into its final form with consummate wisdom and warmth.

1. *Musikalisches Wochenblatt*, December 10, 1791. MDL, 358; MDB, 409.
2. Viennese diarist Count Zinzendorf, November 6, 1791. MDL, 360; MDB, 412.
3. William Gibbons, "(De)Translating Mozart: *The Magic Flute* in 1909 Paris," *Opera Quarterly* 28/1–2 (2012): 47.
4. Edward J. Dent, *Mozart's Operas: A Critical Study* (London: Chatto, 1913): 327.
5. Liner notes for *Mozart: Die Zauberflöte*, Akademie für alte Musik Berlin, René Jacobs, Harmonia mundi, 2010, 3 compact discs (emphasis added).
6. Walter Bernhart, "Absence of Words and Absence of Music in Opera," in *Meaningful Absence across Arts and Media: The Significance of Missing Signifiers* ed. Werner Wolf, Nassim Balestrini, and Walter Bernhart (Leiden: Brill, 2019), 180.
7. Into the 1780s, female Masons declare faithfulness "while they also ritually and triumphantly slay the serpent." Janet M. Burke and Margaret C. Jacob, "French Freemasonry, Women, and Feminist Scholarship," *Journal of Modern History* 68/3 (1996): 527.
8. Translations follow Charles Johnston, included in the liner notes cited *supra* n. 5.

9. Sylvia Wynter, "No Humans Involved: An Open Letter to My Colleagues," *Knowledge on Trial* 1/1 (1994): 42–71. See also Taja-Nia Y. Henderson and Jamila Jefferson-Jones, "#LivingWhileBlack: Blackness as Nuisance," *American University Law Review* 69/3 (2020): 863–914.

10. This case is the subject of Anthony Davis's Pulitzer Prize-winning opera *The Central Park Five* (2019).

11. Michael M. Grynbaum, "Floyd Case Presents Ideological Challenge for Law-and-Order Conservatives," *New York Times*, May 30, 2020.

12. Norimitsu Onishi and Constance Méheut, "A Coded Word from the Far Right Roils France's Political Mainstream," *New York Times*, September 4, 2020.

13. Denis Diderot, *Histoire*, bk. XIX, chap. 15, in Abbe Guillaume-Thomas Raynal's *Histoire des Deux Indes* (1780), cited in Sankar Muthu, *Enlightenment against Empire* (Princeton: Princeton University Press, 2003). Still, many abolitionists believed Black people were intellectually inferior. Rana Hogarth, "Of Black Skin and Biopower: Lessons from the Eighteenth Century," *American Quarterly* 71/3 (2019): 837–47.

14. For "die spröde Schöne," I depart from Johnston's "coy beauty," which implies a flirtatious complicity not justified in the text. In a structural parallel, we saw Tamino question Papageno's humanity after the latter's strophic aria.

15. Mary Wollstonecraft, *A Vindication of the Rights of Woman* (London: Johnson, 1792), chap. 4.

16. www.theguardian.com/world/2013/oct/03/stop-telling-women-to-smile-tatyana-fazlalizadeh.

17. George Booth [2nd Earl of Warrington], *Considerations upon the Institution of Marriage* (London: John Whiston, 1739).

18. John Burton, *Lectures on Female Education and Manners* (London: Johnson, 1793), I:212.

19. Marie Cramer, "Judge Who Asked Woman if She Closed Her Legs to Prevent Assault Is Removed," *New York Times*, May 28, 2020.

20. Deanna Pan, "Who Was Matthew Hale, the 17th-Century Jurist Alito Invokes in His Draft Overturning Roe?" *Boston Globe*, May 6, 2022. Pan cites Jill Hasday, constitutional law professor at the University of Minnesota Law School: "There are many themes running through America's legal traditions that have deep injustices embedded within them. We have to decide how we're bound by the past. And nothing is forcing us to carry the consequences of women's legal subordination forward in time."

21. Günter Meinhold, *"Zauberflöte" und Zauberflöten-Rezeption: Studien zu Emanuel Schikaneders Libretto "Die Zauberflöte" und seiner literarischen Rezeption* (Frankfurt am Main: Lang, 2001), 121.

22. Ashley C. Rondini, "White Supremacist Danger Narratives," *Contexts* 17/3 (2018): 60–62.

23. Thomas Rothschild, "'Das ist der Teufel sicherlich.' Papageno trifft Monostatos: Ein Vergleich," in *'Regietheater': Konzeption und Praxis am*

Beispiel der Bühnenwerke Mozarts ed. Jürgen Kühnel, Ulrich Müller, and Oswald Panagl (Salzburg: Mueller-Speiser, 2007), 337.

24. Inclusion will require systemic change: "The real issues involve altering the systems of education and access so that anyone in the United States can feel entitled to work hard, recognize if they have an exceptional talent, and expect a fair chance of having a career in the arts." Naomi André, *Black Opera: History, Power, Engagement* (Urbana: University of Illinois Press, 2018), 14.

25. Kate Manne, "Melancholy Whiteness (or, Shame-Faced in Shadows)," *Philosophy and Phenomenological Research* 96/1 (2018): 238.

26. Ben Miller, "New Magic for a Classic Opera in Berlin," *New York Times*, February 17, 2019.

27. Martin Nedbal, *Morality and Viennese Opera in the Age of Mozart and Beethoven* (London: Routledge, 2017), 1.

28. I do not presume to speak for underrepresented people. According to Charisma Lucario, a Black student in my class, "If I were to have watched this version it would have made me uncomfortable knowing that they highlighted the dialogue by stating the views about black people were not their own but did nothing to change it. If you didn't want to change it then just leave it be and have the audience deal with the dialogue in their own way. Adding extra dialogue puts an unnecessary spotlight on it."

29. Rejecting treasure is a feminist act. William Alexander, in 1779, praised women for their charity and then charged "the same women with 'levity, dissipation, and extravagance.'" Barbara Taylor, "Enlightenment and the Uses of Women," *History Workshop Journal* 74 (2012): 81.

30. James Fordyce, *The Character and Conduct of the Female Sex* (London: T. Caddell, 1776): 83, cited in Rosalind Carr, *Gender and Enlightenment Culture in Eighteenth-Century Scotland* (Edinburgh: Edinburgh University Press, 2014), 14.

31. Tonja Jacobi and Dylan Schweers, "Justice, Interrupted: The Effect of Gender, Ideology, and Seniority at Supreme Court Oral Arguments," *Virginia Law Review* 103 (2017): 1494.

32. www.mediaite.com/election-2020/foxs-chris-wallace-interrupts-kirsten-gillibrand-to-defend-his-network-thats-not-very-polite/.

33. www.businessinsider.com/coronavirus-trump-snaps-at-yamiche-alcindor-be-nice-2020-3.

34. Using unfounded accusations to attack female ambition eliminated women from the 2020 US Democratic presidential field. Maggie Astor, "'A Woman, Just Not That Woman': How Sexism Plays Out on the Trail," *New York Times*, February 12, 2019.

35. "What is the 'ethical pedestal'?" Women and Politics Institute, School of Public Affairs, American University, October 3, 2019. www.genderontheballot.org/what-is-the-ethical-pedestal/.

36. October 9, 2020 www.vox.com/2020/10/9/21509239/gretchen-whitmer-kidnapping-plot-wolverine-michigan-governor.

37. www.nbcnews.com/think/opinion/trump-calls-kamala-harris-monster-will-gop-misogyny-win-2020-ncna1242748.

38. See Jessica Waldoff, *Recognition in Mozart's Operas* (New York: Oxford University Press, 2006), 309.

39. Nedbal, *Morality and Viennese Opera*, 90.

40. Women writers have defended female fitness to govern since 1405, with Christine de Pizan's *The Book of the City of Ladies*.

41. Nedbal, *Morality and Viennese Opera*, 89.

42. Marc J. Lerchenmueller and Olav Sorenson, "Junior Female Scientists Aren't Getting the Credit They Deserve," *Harvard Business Review*, March 22, 2017.

11 | Music, Drama, and Spectacle in the Finales

JOHN PLATOFF

When Mozart sat down to write the finales to *The Magic Flute*, how did he know what to do?

The question may seem absurd, since we are talking about someone now widely regarded as the greatest opera composer of the eighteenth century, and one of the greatest of all time. Yet, Mozart's operatic compositions for the previous nine years – since the completion of *Die Entführung aus dem Serail* in 1782 – had been almost entirely Italian, including, most importantly, the three *opere buffe* he wrote with Lorenzo Da Ponte: *Le nozze di Figaro, Don Giovanni,* and *Così fan tutte*. And *Die Entführung*, though one of Mozart's greatest successes, was typical of the *Singspiel* of its day in lacking the extended, multisectional finales that the composer created for *The Magic Flute*. His one-act *Der Schauspieldirektor* of 1786, written to represent German opera in a special competition between the Italian and German companies, was more of a play with music and contained a relatively brief finale in a single movement.

Mozart was not the only one focused on Italian opera since 1782. With the abandoning of Emperor Joseph's National Singspiel project and the reinstallation of an *opera buffa* company in 1783, the court theaters in Vienna had been producing Italian comic opera almost exclusively for most of the decade. Even after the brief restoration of the German troupe in 1785 and despite the great success of two German works by Dittersdorf, *Der Apotheker und der Doktor* (1786) and *Die Liebe im Narrenhause* (1787), opera in German generally took a back seat to *opera buffa* in Vienna, at least at the imperial theaters (the Burgtheater and the Kärntnertortheater).[1]

It was chiefly at commercial suburban theaters in the later 1780s that a popular *Singspiel* repertory began to develop. In particular, the Theater auf der Wieden, where Emanuel Schikaneder became director in 1789, presented two series of *Singspiele* with enormous success. One was a set of farces about the "two Antons," starting in July 1789 with *Der dumme Gärtner aus dem Gebürge oder Die zween Anton,* and continuing with six more operas about the Antons in the next six years.

Schikaneder's other series was a succession of fairy-tale operas. It began with Paul Wranitzky's *Oberon* in September 1789; continued with a group of collaboratively composed operas, including, most importantly, *Der Stein der Weisen oder Die Zauberinsel* (September 1790); and led to Schikaneder and Mozart's *The Magic Flute* in September 1791 and beyond.[2] As David Buch and others have shown, Mozart – already a longtime friend of Schikaneder's – was well acquainted with the operatic activity at the Theater auf der Wieden and in fact composed portions of *Der Stein der Weisen*, including parts of one of the finales.[3]

Some, though not all, of the operas in these two series contained the lengthy, multisectional finales that were the hallmark of *opera buffa* – and that Mozart created for *The Magic Flute*. And while *The Magic Flute* finales owe much to the standard model that Mozart drew upon in creating the finales of his Da Ponte operas, they also show features that do not stem from the typical practices of finales in the *opera buffa* repertory. As we shall see, many of these features can be clearly seen in the finales of Schikaneder's earlier *Singspiele* at the Theater auf der Wieden.

In his discussion of *The Magic Flute*, Hermann Abert claimed that its finales have "absolutely nothing in common with a typical Italian *opera buffa* finale."[4] Yet, in several respects, the two finales of *The Magic Flute* are not so different from those that Mozart composed for the three Da Ponte operas, which are in turn representative of the finales written for Italian *opere buffe* in Vienna in the 1780s. On the contrary, the similarities are hard to miss.

To begin with, the finales of *The Magic Flute* are "chain finales," meaning that they comprise a succession of ensemble (or, occasionally, solo) sections in a series of tempos, meters, and keys. Mozart's finales in the Da Ponte operas contain between eight and twelve musical sections and run between 521 and 939 measures, with an average of about 725. In performance they last between sixteen and twenty-four minutes. *The Magic Flute* finales fit this pattern (they are 586 and 920 measures long, respectively), although the longer Act 2 finale has fifteen musical sections and typically takes twenty-nine or thirty minutes to perform, making it the longest finale Mozart ever composed (see Table 11.1).[5]

Like the Da Ponte opera finales, those of *The Magic Flute* are musically continuous, never interrupted by passages of simple recitative, and the home keys of their successive sections move away from the initial tonic key of the finale, only to return to the tonic at the end.[6] Moreover, and again like the finales of *opera buffa*, the individual movements rely both on

Table 11.1 *The Magic Flute*, overview of the Act 2 finale

Section	Measures	Key	Meter	Tempo	Stage set	Scene number	Characters
1	1–44	E-flat	2/2	Andante	A short garden	Scene 26	Three Boys
	45–93					Scene 27	Three Boys; Pamina
2	94–189	E-flat	3/4	Allegro			Three Boys; Pamina
3	190–248	C minor	2/2	Adagio	Two great mountains, one with a waterfall, the other with fire	Scene 28	Two Armored Men; Tamino (then Pamina offstage)
4	249–77	[A-flat]	2/2	Allegretto			Two Armored Men; Tamino
5	278–361	F	3/4	Andante			Two Armored Men; Tamino; Pamina
6	362–89	C	C	March: Adagio			Tamino; Pamina
7	390–412	C	C	Allegro			Tamino; Pamina; Chorus, offstage
8	413–533	G	6/8	Allegro	A short garden	Scene 29	Papageno
9	534–42	[G minor]	6/8	Andante			Papageno
10	543–75	C	2/2	Allegretto			Papageno; Three Boys
11	576–615	C	2/2	Allegro			Papageno; Three Boys
12	616–744	G	2/2	Allegro			Papageno; Papagena
13	745–823	C minor	2/2	Più moderato	"The entire theater transforms into a sun"	Scene 30	Queen of the Night; Monostatos; Three Ladies
	824–27	E-flat		Recitative			Queen of the Night; Monostatos; Three Ladies; Sarastro; Tamino; Pamina; Three Boys; Chorus
14	828–45	E-flat	C	Andante			Sarastro; Tamino; Pamina; Three Boys; Chorus
15	846–920	E-flat	2/4	Allegro			Sarastro; Tamino; Pamina; Three Boys; Chorus

passages in which the dramatic action moves forward – typically involving dialogue among the characters onstage – and on expressive passages, in which, for the most part, all characters sing together.[7] These expressive passages slow the pace of the drama, allowing the characters to reflect on, or express their feelings about, what has just taken place. And they tend to be the moments of greatest musical richness in each section, as multiple voices take over from preceding passages sung mostly in dialogue. A clear example in the Act 2 finale of *The Magic Flute* is the passage sung by Pamina and the Three Boys in measures 146–82: after they have prevented her suicide and promised to lead her to Tamino, all sing together in praise of "two hearts that burn with love for one another."

If the structural similarities between *The Magic Flute* finales and the finales of *opera buffa* are readily apparent, though, the differences are also highly significant. And nearly all of them can be connected to the new, distinctly different traditions reflected in the German operas being produced by Schikaneder at the Theater auf der Wieden.

In characterizing *Der Stein der Weisen* as an important model for *The Magic Flute* and the fairy-tale operas that followed, David Buch listed a number of the work's stylistic features, the most relevant here being his characterization of its finales. In his words, they were "conceived as a series of contrasting episodes with magic scenes, comic episodes, and tableaus with solemn, ceremonial (*feierlich*) expression; this structure necessitated a quickly changing mixture of ensembles, solos, recitatives, instrumental music, and choruses."[8]

To a great extent – and not surprisingly – Buch's description of the finales of *Der Stein der Weisen* fits the finales of *The Magic Flute* as well. We may trace three differences of special interest between Mozart's finales for *The Magic Flute* and those for his Da Ponte operas. The differences arise for various reasons, but each connects directly to Buch's account of the finales of *Der Stein der Weisen*. One difference is the need for ceremonial, quasi-religious or magical scenes, which are central to the story of *The Magic Flute* (and others in Schikaneder's series of fairy-tale operas) but play no part in the more human comedy of *opere buffe*.[9] Another is the greater attention to sets and set changes in Schikaneder's scenically lavish productions. A third is a looser, more episodic approach to the construction of a finale, which corresponds to the more episodic structure of Schikaneder's libretto for *The Magic Flute*. In what follows I consider each of these differences in turn.

1. The *feierlich* (solemn or ceremonial) style was a hallmark of the fairy-tale opera at the Theater auf der Wieden, beginning with Wranitzky's highly successful *Oberon*. As in *The Magic Flute*, it was not limited to finales but employed for formal and ceremonial scenes throughout the operas.[10]

Strikingly, many of the *feierlich* numbers, both in *The Magic Flute* and in the other fairy-tale operas, are marches. The March of the Priests that opens Act 2 of *The Magic Flute* is one such example, as are the two marchlike numbers for the Three Boys that begin each of *The Magic Flute*'s finales. These three pieces share a cut-time time signature, a tempo of andante or larghetto, a reliance on dotted rhythms (a bit less so in the March of the Priests), and a sense of nobility and gravity. While they are otherwise scored quite differently, two of the three pieces employ trombones – as does another conspicuously *feierlich* piece, Sarastro's aria "O Isis und Osiris."[11]

Beyond the two marches that begin *The Magic Flute*'s finales, there are also other references to the *feierlich* style in each finale. In the Act 1 finale, three short passages occur at the end of the lengthy scene between Tamino and the Priest (mm. 137–39, 143–45, and 149–51). As Tamino asks three questions about when Enlightenment will reach him and whether Pamina is still alive, he is answered – first by the Priest, and in the second and third passages by an offstage chorus of Priests – by the same grave, solemn, marchlike phrase in A minor, in an andante tempo with dotted rhythms. (Here, as in so many other places in the opera, the use of a three-fold repetition is symbolic rather than incidental.)[12]

The *feierlich* style is even more prominent in the Act 2 finale. In addition to the opening march for the Three Boys, there is the impressive passage in which the two Armored Men sing a chorale melody (this passage is discussed further below); there are the two flute solos with which Tamino and Pamina brave the trials of fire and water – though perhaps a bit more cheerful and lively than some of the other *feierlich* scenes, these passages still rely on the same dotted rhythms and march topos – and the closing chorus of the opera, which begins with a grand Andante march of praise (mm. 828–45) before giving way to the final celebratory Allegro.

2. Schikaneder's operatic productions of German opera at the Theater auf der Wieden, as John Rice and others have noted, were considerably more lavish than productions at the Burgtheater, where "scenery was not a high priority for Emperor Joseph II and his theater director Rosenberg."[13] For example, Rice showed that Da Ponte's libretto for *Don Giovanni* calls for

nine sets during the work's two acts, two of them reused in each act, so that seven different sets in all would have been needed. (While *Don Giovanni* was originally conceived for the Nostitz Theater in Prague, the settings remained the same for the 1788 production at the Burgtheater.) By contrast, *The Magic Flute* libretto calls for thirteen sets, no fewer than nine of them in the second act alone (with only one of those reused, so that eight different sets – one more than in *Don Giovanni* – would have been employed in the act).[14] More generally, Buch notes that "Schikaneder's librettos for the theater [auf der Wieden] specify a mechanical stage with three trap doors, movable flats and backdrops, and devices to accommodate flying machines, storms, sea battles, and similar effects."[15]

The relative economy of set changes in the Da Ponte operas is notable in their finales, all but one of which use a single set throughout. Only in the Act 1 finale of *Don Giovanni* is there a change, from the garden outside Don Giovanni's palace to a great hall within. But while the first finale of *The Magic Flute* occurs entirely in a single location – the grove with three temples in which Tamino first learns of Sarastro's brotherhood – the second finale uses four distinct scenes (see Table 11.1). The first and third of these are the same "short garden" – that is, a garden scene that uses only the front portion of the stage, so that stagehands can work behind a cloth backdrop to prepare the full-stage set that will be used next.[16] In the first garden scene, the Three Boys confront and comfort Pamina; in the later one, Papageno contemplates suicide, is reminded by the Boys to use his magic bells to summon Papagena, and is blissfully reunited with her. The same set remains for the subsequent section in which the Queen of the Night and her retinue reappear, bent on revenge. (While some modern scores indicate, and some productions employ, a change of scene for the Queen's entrance, it is quite clear in the original libretto that no change of scene occurs.)

These two short-set episodes permitted the preparation of the two impressive full-stage sets. The first contains "two great mountains," one with a waterfall, the other with a fire burning; this is of course the setting for the two trials that Tamino and Pamina must endure. In the second full-stage scene, which appears only for the final moments of the opera, "the entire theater is transformed into a sun," as the Queen and her entourage sink down into the floor, and Sarastro and his followers celebrate the courage and virtue of Tamino and Pamina.

3. It is in their episodic nature that Mozart's *Magic Flute* finales most clearly diverge from the model of the *opera buffa* finale, one of whose

hallmarks is dramatic continuity. In an *opera buffa*, a finale follows a set of characters through a single sequence of connected plot events. A clear example is the Act 1 finale of *Così fan tutte*, in which the pretended suicide attempt by the two male lovers sets up the series of comic scenes that follows, with all six characters involved. Dramatic continuity is maintained in all of the Da Ponte opera finales by the presence throughout of some of the central characters, while others may come and go.

The sense of an episodic finale, on the other hand – what Abert described as "a lively array of scenes . . . loosely held together by the thread of the plot"[17] – arises from points at which all the characters on stage exit, to be replaced by others involved in another aspect of the story, giving a sense of "meanwhile . . ." It can be heightened by a set change, which strengthens the separation between two successive scenes.

Only once does either of these devices occur in any of the Da Ponte opera finales. Both instances take place in the Act 1 finale of *Don Giovanni*, whose main focus is Giovanni's attempt to seduce Zerlina during the festivities to which he has invited her wedding party. As mentioned above, the finale begins in Don Giovanni's garden. After Giovanni leads his guests inside (i.e., offstage), the trio of Donna Anna, Donna Elvira, and Don Ottavio appear in the garden, bent on confronting him. At Don Giovanni's order, Leporello calls to them from the window to invite them inside. As the scene changes to the "illuminated room" in the palace, they join the rest of the characters for the remainder of the finale.

The moment of the three maskers' entrance does create the feeling of a separate episode (which, as I have said, is atypical of an *opera buffa* finale). However, the end of the scene has the opposite effect: when the set changes to the interior of Don Giovanni's palace and the three masked figures join Don Giovanni's party, they converge back into the main dramatic flow of the finale. The set change does not further contribute to an episodic feeling; on the contrary, it emphasizes the convergence.

A similar succession of events – a complete change of characters, followed by a convergence – occurs once in the Act 1 finale of *The Magic Flute*: Tamino, aided by the Three Boys, searches for Pamina. After his lengthy conversation with the Priest – seen by many scholars as the central "conversion moment" of the opera – he plays his flute, leading to a musical exchange between the flute and Papageno's pipes. Tamino rushes off to find Papageno, hoping to find Pamina as well, just as they enter in search of him. After the subsequent scene with Monostatos and his Slaves, Pamina and Papageno are discovered by Sarastro and his brotherhood; they are then joined by Monostatos, who brings with him the captured Tamino, thus uniting all the characters for the closing portion of the finale.

It is in the Act 2 finale of *The Magic Flute* that the episodic, "meanwhile ..." nature of the *Singspiel* finale described by Buch and Abert can be seen most clearly: there are no fewer than five phases of action with different groups of characters onstage – that is, when one entire group of characters exits and another enters. (Again, and as we have seen, such a wholesale change occurs only once in any of Mozart's Da Ponte opera finales.) And the use of multiple stage sets heightens the sense of separation between these parts of the finale.

As mentioned above, finale 2 opens in a "short garden" in which the Three Boys discuss Pamina's plight and then comfort her, promising to guide her to Tamino (see sections 1–2 in Table 11.1). What follows is something never found in any of Mozart's *opera buffa* finales: a complete change of scene, characters, and mood. As Pamina and the Three Boys exit, the set changes to the two mountains. The new episode begins with an utterly different feeling: the two Armored Men escort Tamino and sing a solemn prophecy about his path to Enlightenment – a brilliant, *feierlich* evocation of a Bachian chorale prelude and one of the most stunning musical moments in the finale, if not the entire opera.[18] Tamino is soon joined by Pamina, and he plays the flute as the couple brave the trials of fire and water; at the conclusion of the trials, their triumph is confirmed by an offstage chorus (sections 3–7).

What follows is the most clearly self-contained episode of the finale, marked by a set change back to the garden: Papageno's scene in which his attempt at suicide is prevented by the Three Boys, leading to his reunion with Papagena (sections 8–12). The story arc of the bird-couple concludes there, and they have no further role in the events of the opera; there is no reunion of master and sidekick as one might have expected for Tamino and Papageno. A number of stage directors address this absence by putting Papageno and his bride onstage for the final scene, even though the libretto does not mention them and Mozart gives them no music to sing.

Yet another complete change of characters follows, but no change of scene (despite, as mentioned earlier, what one sees in a number of modern productions): as the happy Papageno and Papagena exit, Monostatos and the Queen of the Night, with her Three Ladies, enter the same garden, planning to attack Sarastro's brotherhood (section 13). And finally, as the plotters are overthrown and sink into the earth, a last set change "transforms the entire theater into a sun" and reveals Sarastro and the Chorus, who hail the gods Isis and Osiris and the triumph of courage and wisdom (sections 13–15).

Interestingly, the original libretto suggests that Schikaneder and Mozart wanted to *minimize* the sense of episodic separation at this moment, and visibly juxtapose the downfall of the Queen with the triumph of Enlightenment. The libretto's stage directions clearly indicate that the transformation scene, which must have been spectacular, occurs *before* the final lines for Monostatos and the Queen, "Zerschmettert, zernichtet ist unsere Macht, / Wir alle gestürzet in ewige Nacht" (Our power is broken and destroyed, / We are plunged into eternal night). These lines would thus have been sung as a despairing, defeated response to the blazing light of the sun; and Sarastro, Tamino, and Pamina would have witnessed the disappearance of the plotters.[19]

Perhaps the most striking feature contributing to the episodic nature of *The Magic Flute* finales is the sharp changes in musical style that heighten the sense of separation from one section to the next. Examples of such stark changes are many, and we may point to just a few as examples. In the Act 1 finale, the conclusion of Tamino's scene with the Priest leads to his playing his flute and hearing Papageno's pipes in reply. In the final brief Presto of the scene (mm. 212–25) he sings excitedly of the possibility of finding Pamina, yet his vocal line is elegant and noble, shaped around expressive high notes. Moments later, with Pamina and Papageno's "Schnelle Füße, rascher Mut," the music changes to a playful, patter-driven style with a completely different character.

In the Act 2 finale, we have already seen several dramatic changes in style and mood, such as the C-minor music of the two Armored Men (beginning in m. 190) that follows Pamina's happy, lyrical quartet with the Three Boys. Another is the entrance – also in C minor – of the Queen of the Night and her plotters, hard on the heels of the silly and delightful music of Papageno and Papagena's reunion (mm. 745ff.).

But even within what is ostensibly a single musical section, Mozart often creates a sharply varied series of musical styles. The opening ninety-three measures of the Act 2 finale vividly illustrate the composer's flexibility, and the sense of separate episodes that results.

As already noted, the finale opens in *feierlich* style, with the Three Boys foretelling an end to superstition and the return of a glorious day of wisdom; they sing homophonically to a noble andante march (mm. 1–28). Yet as soon as they see Pamina, the style changes to a livelier feeling, animated by an "oom-pah" string accompaniment (beginning in m. 30). This *agitato* accompaniment and the rapid dialogue among the Boys might almost make the passage sound comical, were it not for the turn to C minor and the chromatic stepwise lines of measures 36–37 and 43. As the Boys' confrontation with Pamina continues, Mozart freely shifts among styles: the pulsating accompaniment and chattering dialogue; several moments of elevated tragedy for Pamina, culminating in the moment of her suicide attempt at measures 84–91; and serene, *feierlich* beauty, as when the Boys call out to Pamina at measures 63–66. The effect within this one short scene is almost kaleidoscopic, as Mozart emphasizes an instant responsiveness to every momentary phase of the drama over stylistic consistency and continuity. And it is surely this degree of stylistic variety within a section, as well as the even starker stylistic changes between sections described above, that accounts for the perception of Mozart's *Magic Flute* finales as episodic.

In the end, of course, it is no surprise that Mozart's finales for *The Magic Flute* reflect the influences both of the *opera buffa*, of which he was such a master, and of the fairy-tale German operas his friend and collaborator Schikaneder was producing with great success at the Theater auf der Wieden. At the level of overall structure, the model of the *opera buffa* finale prevailed – as, indeed, it did in the finales of the other Viennese German operas of the decade, from Dittersdorf's *Der Doktor* to Wranitzky's *Oberon* and the collaborative *Der Stein der Weisen*. There is no reason to doubt, in fact, that the chain-finale model was simply borrowed from *opera buffa* by composers of German opera, a familiar set of procedures easily adaptable to their own, somewhat different, needs. As to character and style, on the other hand, we can recognize in *The Magic Flute* finales the same episodic feeling and the same mixture of widely differing elements that pervade the opera as a whole: the *feierlich* and the farcical, the grandeur of Sarastro's prayer to Isis and Osiris and the captivating silliness of the bird-couple's stuttering happiness in "Pa-Pa-Pa."

By comparison with the finales of *The Magic Flute*, those of *Der Stein der Weisen* and the other German operas performed in Vienna during Mozart's last few years seem a bit ordinary. Or, to put it the other way around, in comparison to the finales of these works, those of *The Magic Flute* sparkle with life. Yet, this difference lies not in a different approach or a different set of procedures but in the fact that Mozart's ability to animate each character and characterize each moment is unmatched. When Pamina laments, for instance – whether at length in her devastating Act 2 aria, "Ach ich fühl's," or more briefly in her contemplation of suicide in the finale to Act 2 – her sadness is gripping to a degree that the grief of the lovers Nadir and Nadine in *Der Stein der Weisen* cannot reach. Similarly, the humorous scenes for Lubano (the Papageno character) in the same opera are charming, but they are never as funny or as touching as those for Papageno himself. As in so many other musical genres, Mozart outdistanced his contemporaries not by the uniqueness of his approach but by the brilliance of his dramatic instincts and musical invention.

Notes

1. Ian Woodfield, *Cabals and Satires: Mozart's Comic Operas in Vienna* (New York: Oxford University Press, 2019), presents a detailed and insightful picture of the relationships and rivalries in Vienna between the *opera buffa* and *Singspiel* companies and their singers, composers, and supporters.

2. For a fuller picture of the German opera in Vienna during Mozart's decade there, see Estelle Joubert's chapter in the present volume.

3. Emanuel Schikaneder et al., *Der Stein der Weisen*, ed. David J. Buch, Recent Researches in Music of the Classical Era 76 (Middleton, WI: A-R Editions, 2007), ix–xii. See also David J. Buch, "Mozart and the Theater auf der Wieden: New Attributions and Perspectives," *Cambridge Opera Journal* 9/3 (1997): 195–232.

4. Hermann Abert, *W. A. Mozart* (1923–24), ed. Cliff Eisen, trans. Stewart Spencer (New Haven, CT: Yale University Press, 2007), 1273.

5. My estimates of performance times are based on an informal survey of recent recordings of the operas.

6. The keys of Mozart's finales are invariably C, D, or E-flat, as these keys made possible the use of trumpets and timpani. This was the practice as well for other contemporary composers of *opera buffa*. See Daniel Heartz, "Constructing *Le nozze di Figaro*," *Journal of the Royal Musical Association* 112 (1987): 77–98.

7. Many of the standard procedures of the *opera buffa* finale are discussed in John Platoff, "Musical and Dramatic Structure in the Opera Buffa Finale," *Journal of Musicology* 7 (1989): 191–230.

8. David J. Buch, *Magic Flutes & Enchanted Forests: The Supernatural in Eighteenth-Century Musical Theater* (Chicago: University of Chicago Press, 2008), 336.

9. I except here the supernatural elements of *Don Giovanni*, which are nearly unique in the Viennese *opera buffa* repertory. The only other Viennese opera of the period I am aware of that features magical elements is Casti and Salieri's *La grotta di Trofonio* (1785).

10. For a discussion of particular *feierlich* numbers in *Oberon, Der Stein der Weisen,* and *Der wohltätige Derwisch*, some of them with similarities to numbers in *The Magic Flute*, see Buch, *Magic Flutes & Enchanted Forests*, 293–94, 301–02, 307.

11. Buch, *Magic Flutes & Enchanted Forests*, 307, points out that Franz Gerl, who
    sang the role of Sarastro, also sang the dervish role in *Der wohltätige Derwisch*,
    and that his music in that opera probably influenced Mozart's for Sarastro.
    A duet in that opera "actually contains a melodic phrase that Mozart quotes in
    the first finale of *Die Zauberflöte.*"

12. Among others, see Jessica Waldoff, *Recognition in Mozart's Operas* (New York:
    Oxford University Press, 2006), 22–35.

13. John A. Rice, *Mozart on the Stage*, Composers on the Stage (Cambridge:
    Cambridge University Press, 2009), 176.

14. Ibid., 186–91.

15. Schikaneder et al., *Der Stein Der Weisen*, ix.

16. Rice, *Mozart on the Stage*, 161–94, discusses long and short sets in some detail
    in his chapter on theaters and stage design.

17. Abert, *W.A. Mozart*, 1273, is here referring to the Act 1 finale, but his words
    apply equally well to the finale of Act 2.

18. Buch, *Magic Flutes & Enchanted Forests*, 294, mentions the Chorus of
    Dervishes in D minor for unison basses in Wranitzky's *Oberon* that may have
    inspired Mozart's scene. While Wranitzky's chorus lacks imitative
    counterpoint, its walking bass (employing both legato and staccato
    articulation), and unison, chorale-like melody for the chorus create a feeling
    startlingly like that of Mozart's Armored Men. See Paul Wranitzky and Johann
    Georg Carl Ludwig Gieseke, *Oberon, König Der Elfen: Singspiel in Drei Akten*,
    ed. Joachim Veit and Christoph-Hellmut Mahling, Die Oper: Kritische
    Ausgabe von Hauptwerken der Operngeschichte 2 (Munich: G. Henle, 1993),
    105–08.

19. For what reason I do not know, the NMA score of the opera both abridges
    these crucial stage directions and changes their location, so that the
    transformation occurs *after* the plotters have sunk into the earth (see NMA II/
    5/19, 351–53).

PART III

Approaches and Perspectives

12 | Seeking Enlightenment in Mozart's *Magic Flute*

RICHARD KRAMER

Was ist Aufklärung? What is Enlightenment? This seemingly innocuous question, tucked away in a footnote to an essay by an obscure theologian, Johann Friedrich Zöllner, writing in the *Berlinische Monatsschrift* for December 1783, managed to stimulate the interest of such luminaries as Moses Mendelssohn, Johann Georg Hamann, Christoph Martin Wieland, and Immanuel Kant. It was Kant's "An Answer to the Question: What is Enlightenment?" that remains the most widely known and vigorously debated response to Zöllner's question. Kant initiates the discussion with this bold challenge: "*Sapere aude!* [dare to know] Have the courage to use your *own* understanding!" This, he adds, "is thus the motto of enlightenment."[1]

What *Is* Enlightenment?

In a certain sense, *The Magic Flute* may be understood as a playing-out of Kant's motto, a challenge that is at the core of Tamino's perilous journey. But the idea of Enlightenment and the complexity of original thought encompassed under its banner demands of us that we examine the deeper questions that it asks: What view of Enlightenment is conveyed in Mozart's music and Schikaneder's libretto, and how does this view accord with those strains of thought and expression, of wit and sensibility, that we take to constitute the defining aura of the Enlightenment?

That Zöllner even deemed his innocent question worthy of public debate is in itself instructive, suggesting that an answer was no more evident to its contemporaries than, say, an answer to the question "What is post-modern?" might be to a generation closer in time to our own. *Enlightenment*: the term itself has, over time, inspired a formidable list of commentary and critique.[2] There is in the first instance a distinction to be made between the condition of thought that goes by that name and, with the definite article in front of it (*The* Enlightenment), the historical period that it encompasses. When does it begin, this historical period? When does it end? Isaiah Berlin, with broad brush, writes of the "noble, optimistic, rational doctrine and ideal of the great tradition of the Enlightenment from the Renaissance until the French Revolution, and indeed beyond it, until our own day." With enviable clarity, Berlin argues for the commonly held notion of the Enlightenment as a new age governed by rational thought, defined as "a logically connected structure of laws and generalizations susceptible of demonstration or verification."[3]

And yet, in the midst of the German Enlightenment in the 1770s and 1780s there is manifest, notably in literature and the arts, a grain of thought and expression, of feeling – of sensibility – touching a core of human behavior, that could not be explained in purely rational terms. For Berlin, the authors whose works express and indeed ennoble this aspect of human behavior – such major figures as Herder, Lessing, J. G. Hamann, Goethe – are even perceived as figures of an "anti-Enlightenment," their formidable contributions to the history of ideas yet recognized without the slightest demur.

To take this narrow view of the Enlightenment as exclusively the domain of reason and scientific enterprise is to misread the vibrancy of a creative imagination, in its spontaneity and wit, born in tension with the alleged certainties of rational thought. To think of the Enlightenment in purely aesthetic terms is to conjure in the mind such iconic literary works as Diderot's *Rameau's Nephew*, Laurence Sterne's *Sentimental Journey through France and Italy*, Rousseau's *Confessions* and Goethe's *The Sorrows of Young Werther*, or the three Da Ponte librettos set by Mozart, to cite only the most widely known, in which the rigors of convention and the rule of reason are challenged in the disposition to know the world as felt experience. In all these works, the irreconcilable conflict between a rational world and the inscrutable fantasy of human creativity is understood as a function of the human condition. It is precisely this ironic view of the world that the historian Hayden White identifies in the writings of Kant, who "apprehended the historical process less as a development from one stage to another in the life of humanity than as merely a conflict, an *unresolvable* conflict, between *eternally opposed* principles of human nature: rational on the one hand, irrational on the other."[4]

Irony, if not in the high-minded sense that White attributes to Kant's view of the world, is a trope that infiltrates a reading of *The Magic Flute* in diverse modes. The events, the dramatic unfoldings, the apparent contradictions of its plot are well known, and so too are the seemingly endless interpretations of the symbols, real and imagined, that embellish the opera.[5] The essence of Enlightenment, however, is to be sought and found less in the staging of those rituals and ceremonies that inspire so much of the music in the opera than in the play of its all-too-human personae – Pamina and Tamino, chiefly – over against these inert, monolithic structures in which they dwell.

A striking instance of this play comes early in the finale to Act 2. The theater is transformed, displaying two massive mountains, a waterfall seen or heard in the one, volcanic flame spewing from the other, an augury of the trials of fire and water about to be undertaken. An iron door is closed at either wing of the stage. Tamino, barefoot, is led onto the stage by two men in black armor. Antiphonal music, strings and trombones answered by the winds, announces their arrival, in C minor. The strings now take up a fugato in a *stile antico* associated with Bach, against which the Men in Armor intone, cantus-like in octaves (and doubled in the winds and the three trombones), the inscription engraved on the pyramid located above them at center stage. Their tune is a parody of the Lutheran hymn "Ach Gott von Himmel sieh darein." Significantly, Mozart composes a final phrase that brings tonal closure, even introducing a Neapolitan sixth with its obligatory D-flat into a "phrygian" tune that to eighteenth-century ears would otherwise have seemed to end on the dominant. The chorale tune, it turns out, is one that Mozart encountered as early as 1782, for he employed it as a cantus firmus in an exercise in B minor for string quartet, very likely inspired by its extensive treatment, also in B minor, in Kirnberger's magisterial theoretical treatise *Die Kunst des reinen Satzes in der Musik.*[6]

More than one critic has been led to wonder why Mozart, composing for an audience of Viennese Catholics, chose to appropriate a Lutheran chorale, and indeed one whose text, pleading God's pity for wretched humanity, would only contradict the enlightened Masonic themes of the opera – though it is doubtful that Mozart, having come upon the tune among the textless examples in Kirnberger, would have had Luther's verses in mind.[7] Perhaps it was an aura that Mozart was after: an ethos, a distance of time and place that this austere music would have invoked.

"Mich schreckt kein Tod" (Death does not frighten me), Tamino bursts out, finding a D-flat, now a dissonant ninth above a dominant, that dismisses the severe tone of the chorale. And it finds Pamina's ear, offstage. A few bars of music, three simple phrases in the upper strings that modulate to the dominant of F major, choreograph the opening of the massive door that separates them and the silent moment in which Pamina and Tamino finally embrace. A fermata prolongs the moment. Measured time resumes in a less anxious Andante. The two now sing to one another, exchanging a deeply affecting expression of love, their music redolent of

another touching moment of reconciliation, the Count's "Contessa, per-
dono" in the fourth act finale of *Figaro*; here, too, its Andante following
from a fermata silent with anticipation. In both scenes, the moment is
savored, joined in *Figaro* by all nine characters, in *Flute* by the two Men in
Armor, who sing in a rich quartet with the lovers to "des Tones Macht" (the
power of tone).

What follows is indeed a crux of the opera, in more than one sense:
a final rite of initiation in the trials by fire and water that will lead Tamino
and Pamina to their purification. In the run-up to the moment, Pamina
urges Tamino to put in play the magic flute, crafted by her father at
a witching hour "from the deepest roots of a thousand-year oak" (anticipating Sieglinde's narrative in Act 1 of Wagner's *Die Walküre*). Tellingly, it
is the instrument itself, rich with symbolic and mystical allure, that is given
pride of place at this critical juncture, its occult powers attending our
protagonists through their trials. Yet, if this ordeal were to have any real
meaning as a test of character, as evidence of a maturation of thought, if the
true experience of *Aufklärung* is in the recognition of a process of mind no
longer dependent upon mythic superstition, upon unquestioned authority,
then it would appear that, at this decisive moment in the opera, an
opportunity to embody the genuine experience of a truly enlightened
coming of age has been sacrificed in favor of theatrical display. The
moment is further tinged with irony, for this instrument, a gift from the
Queen of the Night, will now serve to ensure entry into Sarastro's realm.
Here again, the opera traffics in the devices of ritual and ceremony, its
principal players manipulated more as puppets than as independent,
thinking beings.

What is this music that the flute plays? Whose music? Are we meant to
hear in it an improvisation signifying the spontaneity of original thought,
of Tamino's mind in action, or rather a set piece programmed through
some coded device penetrating player and instrument? The latter, I should
think, to judge from the stiff formality of the thing and its literal repetition
during the second trial. It is a drab piece, and yet it is hard to imagine how
the circumstance of its performance might have led Mozart to some bolder
solution – though perhaps that was precisely his intent: to display the
aridity of a music deprived of true imagination. For Edward Dent, the
music "has something of the solemnity of the Dead March in [Handel's]
Saul," an observation that only underscores the dour effect.[8] The libretto
actually calls for an accompaniment of "gedämpfte Pauken" (muffled
timpani) and Mozart has the timpanist play only in the silences between
the flute's phrases. No less telling is the accompaniment on the beats: three

trombones, two horns, and two clarini. "Otherworldly" is the word that comes to mind, the trombone choir taking its customary role as the voice of the supernatural.

As the initiates emerge, the warmth of the strings embraces them, setting in bold relief that glimpse of the stark, inhospitable world that they, with their flute, have endured. "Ihr Götter, welch ein Augenblick!" (You gods, what a moment!), they calmly sing, more out of relief than in ecstasy. They have, by these lights, achieved Enlightenment.

Monostatos and Blackness

But Enlightenment, in its more human dimension, inhabits the psyches of even the lesser figures of the opera. One character easily misunderstood is the much-maligned Monostatos. Hermann Abert sees through the misunderstanding to a more complex hearing of the aria "Alles fühlt der Liebe Freuden": "one of [Mozart's] most original dramatic character pieces," writes Abert, in which Monostatos "elevates himself to a character of the first order," a man, it would follow, whom we must now take seriously. "The aria," writes Abert, "unfolds with a sensual flickering and tingling that causes the listener's blood to race through his veins and makes his nerves tingle." Indeed! But then Abert must evidently convince himself that the lowly Moor is incapable of such eloquence. The opening dotted quarter-note is "brutally ejaculated," and "the whole shaping of the melody has something disorderly, even chaotic about it. It writhes around the note c' with dogged savagery, touching on the other degrees of the scale in a fairly primitive order."[9] To the contrary: our blood races, our nerves tingle precisely because the edginess of the music captures the anxious thrill at the brink of this moment of forbidden desire. No savagery here, no disorderly chaos.

Before the aria, Monostatos is overcome by the sight of Pamina asleep. "Und welcher Mensch ... würde bey so einem Anblick kalt und unempfindlich bleiben? Das Feuer, das in mir glimmt, wird mich noch verzehren." (What man would remain cold and unfeeling at such a vision? The fire that smolders within me will yet consume me.) His words convey a feeling no less genuine than those expressed in Tamino's *Bildnis* aria in Act 1: "dies Etwas kann ich zwar nicht nennen, doch fühl ich's hier wie Feuer brennen; soll die Empfindung Liebe sein?" (This something I can't quite name, but I feel it here like fire burning. Could this feeling be love?) But, of course, circumstances do not allow us to equate the two. Monostatos, as he himself is all too aware, is black and on that ground alone is disqualified in this society from a relationship with Pamina. "Ist mir denn kein Herz gegeben," he sings; "bin ich nicht von Fleisch und Blut?" (Was I not given a heart? Am I not of flesh and blood?). We are put in mind of Shylock, and perhaps the allusion is not coincidental.[10] To suggest that Schikaneder and Mozart intended to hint at deeper issues of racial inequity would be to speculate beyond the limits of the evidence. This, too, is an Enlightenment moment, full of contradiction: the genuine human impulse up against the grain of conventional morality. His aria is "to be played and sung as softly as if the music were a great way off," the libretto instructs, so as not to disturb the slumbering Pamina, even while his cunning music hints at a clandestine intent. In the end, the Queen of the Night rudely interrupts this little fantasy, and we are left only with the memory of a fleeting moment that touches something in us – not unlike Barbarina's affecting search for that lost pin (*Figaro*, Act 4, scene 1) and any of those other lesser figures who come to life in Mozart's music.

The Languages of Enlightenment

Enlightenment: *Aufklärung*. While the equivalence of the two terms as designators of a generalized concept is beyond dispute, it is yet worth contemplating whether the two words signify cultural domains that are not perfectly synonymous. This is more than a splitting of linguistic hairs. "Language," as Berlin paraphrases J. G. Hamann's notion, "is what we think with, not translate into."[11] When Mozart composes with his native German in mind, the music will convey not merely the syntax and prosody of the language but the memes deep-wired in native language and culture.

A telling display of this phenomenon comes in Tamino's great *Bildnis* aria. Purged of the conventional trappings of aria – the grand ritornello, the formal repetitions, the virtuosic exploitation of voice and singer all forfeited for an immediacy of expression – the music plays more for the intimacies of cavatina. Setting aside the implausibility of his having, in a matter of moments, fallen madly in love with this miniature portrait of a woman whom he has never seen, the naïvety of Tamino's response is trumped by a music that fires an unknown yearning, mapping his gradual recognition of a feeling – an *Empfindung* – that can only be love. But then comes the most remarkable passage. The music, having settled in the key of the dominant, now initiates its return toward the tonic. A pedal tone on the dominant extends for ten bars before resolution, and it is during these ten bars (mm. 34–43) that Tamino probes what are perhaps his first libidinal urges. Schikaneder's text is worth reading as it is given in the original libretto, here showing the concluding sestet of a poem modeled on the Petrarchan sonnet (though in iambic tetrameter):

O wenn ich sie nur finden könnte!	Oh, if only I could find her!
O wenn sie doch schon vor mir stünde!	If only she now stood before me!
Ich würde – würde – warm und rein –	I would – would – warm and pure –
Was würde ich! – Sie voll Entzücken	What would I? Enraptured I'd
An diesen heißen Busen drücken	Press her to this fervid breast,
Und ewig wäre sie dann mein.[12]	And she'd be mine forever.

That second couplet captures the moment: Tamino wondering what he would do, what he should be expected to do, were she to materialize before him. "Warm and pure"; the fantasy of the erotic touch comes to him in mid-sentence, an intrusion that breaks the syntax as it interrupts the effort to finish the thought. "What *would* I do," he can only ask himself. The fit of Mozart's music, the diction of these stammered thoughts, is so natural that one is tempted to imagine poet and composer working through the prosody together. But it is Mozart's exquisite translation of Schikaneder's paratactic construction, and especially at measures 38–44, that deserves close scrutiny:[13] the heart-stopping harmonic rhythm over the pedal tone at "ich würde – würde," the poignant D-flat appoggiatura in the first violins at the downbeat of measure 40, and C-flat at measure 41; the eros of the phrase at "warm und rein," the G-flat giving the voice its warmth; the uptick in harmonic rhythm in the following bar, the bass moving finally from its pedal tone, capturing the climactic outburst at "was würde ich!"

The details of voicing in the orchestra are subtle and complex – and the autograph score displays not a single blemish nor evidence of a second thought. Two moments in particular capture a sense of Mozart's keen ear for the telling signs of the inner drama. At measure 40 the horns are given a bar of silence, interrupting their offbeat pedal tones. A glance at the autograph score will confirm that this is no oversight.[14] Perhaps Mozart wants Tamino's heart to miss a beat: he has begun to formulate an answer to this vision of Pamina. And then, when the question is finally asked, there is a full measure (44) of silence. Here again, Mozart is imagining Tamino onstage, not quite ready to answer his own question. He needs a moment – and so do we. The timing is perfect. In what follows Mozart takes a necessary liberty with Schikaneder's poem, in which "sie voll Entzücken" actually completes the broken sentence, as though it read: "Ich würde [– warm und rein – was würde ich?] sie voll Entzücken an diesen heißen Busen drücken … ." Mozart, however, must make a fresh beginning after the cadential pause at "Was würde ich?" and so the new musical paragraph begins "Ich würde sie voll Entzücken." The convoluted construction of the poem is altered by Mozart in deference to a stage business that wants a coherent sense of formal closure: Tamino, finally bringing to mind what it would mean to press Pamina to his overheated breast.

Returning to Hamann's notion of language as the "organ of thought" – "Not only is the entire faculty of thought founded on language … but language is *also the center of reason's misunderstanding with itself*"[15] – and recalling Herder's foundational *Essay on the Origin of Language* – "*Man, placed in the state of reflection which is peculiar to him, with this reflection for the first time given full freedom of action, did invent language*"[16] – as defining statements of an Enlightenment ethos, it seems all the more apposite to recognize in Tamino's *Bildnis* aria its moving and subtle play with the syntactical nuances of language, poem and music locked in linguistic embrace.

The point is driven home to me by Joseph Kerman's essay "Translating *The Magic Flute*," a donnish critique of a well-known translation of the opera by W. H. Auden and Chester Kallman. In the Addendum to the essay, the task of putting Tamino's aria into English is explored. "Mozart's poem is wretched (in case you hadn't known)," Kerman avers. "As poetry Auden's is immensely better."[17] Here is Auden's translation of these lines that we've been studying:

Ich würde – würde – warm und rein –   O tell me, image, grant a sign –
Was würde ich?   Am I her choice?

For Kerman, Auden's poem fails to meet the declamatory implications of the music. He offers an alternative:

Ich würde – würde – warm und rein –   I'll seek her, seek her, far and near –
Was würde ich?   But how, indeed?

Putting aside the central thesis of Kerman's essay (written in the 1950s at a time when the translating of opera was a topic of heated debate), it is difficult today to read these translations without feeling that Mozart's music, as a rehearing of Schikaneder's language, has been traduced. And we might begin with Kerman's notion of the "wretchedness" of the poem. Schikaneder's poem is, pointedly, not a stand-alone sonnet and cannot be judged as though it were. Rather, Schikaneder has in view a dramatic situation: a love-struck Tamino, driven to stammered phrases at the first sight of an image of Pamina. His poem must serve to heighten the moment and afford Mozart the words that will inspire Tamino to sing. The music that he does inspire makes sense only as an expression of *these* words, in *this* language. It is the inflection of "würde" in the conditional mood, and the sonorous depth of the word as it is sung, that cannot be translated. In the service of a more elegant poetry, these reformulations by Auden and Kerman lose the isolation of "warm und rein" as a touching disturbance of thought and syntax and only point up the perfect fit of Mozart's music to Schikaneder's language.[18]

It is precisely this fluent play with syntax that, to my mind, is at the core of Enlightenment thought. There is reason behind it, of course, but language and music give the impression of spontaneous wit, of a mind in motion.

When, in the forlorn sigh at the opening of her aria late in Act 2, Pamina sings "Ach ich fühl's," it is as though she were echoing Tamino's "Ich fühl es, wie dies Götterbild mein Herz mit neuer Regung füllt." What they are feeling is another matter: for Tamino, rapture in the first stirrings of something he will come to recognize as love; for Pamina, uncomprehending despair that her feelings for him seem to be unrequited.[19] To hear the two as though singing to one another across the contrivances of plot in the opera is to apprehend their music as an expression of something greater. When Pamina sings "Sieh Tamino! diese Tränen [fließen Trauter dir allein]," she actually appropriates the intervallic contour and very nearly the pitches of Tamino's "Ich fühl es." And there is the quality of the music to contend with. No other music in the opera touches us in quite the same way. And yet the two arias are very different. I am reminded here of the remarkable coupling in the String Quintet in G minor, K. 516, where the profound Adagio ma non troppo in E-flat (played *con sordino*) – what Abert aptly calls "one of Mozart's most profoundly heartfelt [*innerlichsten*] pieces" – is followed directly by another Adagio, now in the key of G minor, its pulsating inner parts and pizzicato bass suggesting an arioso for solo violin, saturated in the gestures of pathos (a foil, as it turns out, for a spirited *lieto fine* in G major).[20]

If her aria suggests a similar play with the conventions of pathos, Pamina forces them to extreme ends in the final couplet: "Fühlst du nicht der Liebe Sehnen, so wird Ruh' im Tode sein!" (If you don't feel the yearning of love, there will be peace in death!) The chromaticism is intense, the intervallic leaps extreme. But perhaps most striking of all is an epilogue in the orchestra that seems to issue from the troubled mind of the disconsolate Pamina. The incessantly throbbing 6/8 accompaniment is abandoned, and the first violins take up a chromatic variant of the "Sieh Tamino" motive, now driven in a descent across two octaves in a complex run of hemiolas against the meter. The texture is further complicated by the staggered entry of the flute and then the bassoon, both doubling the first violins, joined finally by a new counterpoint in the oboe and second violins. This is not the usual patterning of Mozartean orchestration. The effect is dizzying. What we learn from her final phrases is that Pamina is sufficiently distraught to consider suicide. The increasing complexity of music in the epilogue, its distortion of rhythm, its bending of the Tamino motive, and the gradual amplification of texture all suggest an almost neurotic focus on a Tamino whose silence will drive her to madness.[21] Indeed, when she appears to the Three Boys at the beginning of the finale, Pamina carries the dagger that she intends to employ in her own death: "halb wahnwitzig" (half mad), she is described in the libretto.

The trials that Pamina must endure, in an ignorance imposed by a powerful and misogynistic social order, arouse our sympathy precisely because they emanate from a well of human feeling. The trials by fire and water, for all the pompous ceremony that frames them, enact a ritual of Enlightenment. Pamina's ordeal, her decision to use the dagger not in the service of her mother's command to murder Sarastro but in her own death as an extreme act of despair at what she believes to be the loss of Tamino, is about something else.

The Two Plots

To accept the contradictions, the apparitions, the occult, and Schikaneder's fabulous *mise en scène* as the apparatus of fairy-tale – following the lead of others who have written about the opera[22] – is to free ourselves of the burden of having to justify the drama as a display of Enlightenment theory, strictly defined. And this allows us to come to terms with those moments in Mozart's music where the *esprit* of Enlightenment can be felt: where the music touches a human (and humane) chord in its principal players, as though to contravene the immutable structure of ritual authority and mythic morality.

Indeed, it makes a certain sense to speak of two Enlightenment plots in *The Magic Flute*. The master plot is the familiar one, a superstructure of hierarchies, of empires pitched in darkness and light, evoking evil and good, a mapping of the journey from the one to the other as a moral and ethical coming of age, an entering into the temple of wisdom. It espouses a program for the achieving of Enlightenment and describes a world governed by its ideas. The other plot, resistant to reductive archetypes, engages the expression of inner feeling, of *Empfindung*. Here, dramatic action is driven not by an a priori application of extrinsic ideas but by the interplay of human beings in all their imperfections, their misprisions on display, in counterpoint against the grain of the master plot.

Was ist Auflärung? Herr Zöllner's not-so-innocent question remains. If *The Magic Flute*, in its master plot, may appear to provide an answer, the wonder of Mozart's music, its way of getting into the psyche of its singers, throws the question back at us. If there is some merit in apprehending the opera as a playing out of two plots, then perhaps one fragment of the idea of Enlightenment is to be located in a paradoxical reciprocity of the two. Returning finally to Hayden White's formulation of Kant's view of an Enlightenment world apprehended as "a conflict, an *unresolvable* conflict, between *eternally opposed* principles of human nature," it is tempting to hear in *The Magic Flute* a similar opposition of principles. If, in its conclusion, the opera must appear to resolve its conflicts, it is into the deeper currents that underlie those conflicts that Mozart's seductive music draws us. It is here, in these deeper currents, that a theater for the Enlightenment makes itself felt.

Notes

1. A translation of Kant's essay is given in *What Is Enlightenment? Eighteenth-Century Answers and Twentieth-Century Questions*, ed. James Schmidt (Berkeley: University of California Press, 1996), 58–64.
2. For a glimpse of its extent, see the formidable "Select Bibliography" in ibid., 537–53. In a chapter titled "Operatic Enlightenment in *Die Zauberflöte*," Jessica Waldoff sets the term, and its exposition in the opera, in a rich context. See her *Recognition in Mozart's Operas* (Oxford: Oxford University Press, 2006), 17–43, esp. 17–22.
3. Isaiah Berlin, *The Magus of the North: J. G. Hamann and the Origins of Modern Irrationalism*, ed. Henry Hardy (New York: Farrar, Straus and Giroux, 1994), 28–29.
4. Hayden White, *Metahistory: The Historical Imagination in Nineteenth-Century Europe* (Baltimore: Johns Hopkins University Press, 1973), 58.
5. For a probing account of the intellectual and cultural background of the opera, see Nicholas Till, *Mozart and the Enlightenment: Truth, Virtue and Beauty in Mozart's Operas* (New York: W. W. Norton, 1992), 270–319.
6. Johann Philipp Kirnberger, *Die Kunst des reinen Satzes in der Musik* (Berlin: Decker, 1776–79; repr. Hildesheim: Georg Olms, 1968), I:161–67, 181–89. For more on this matter, see my review of the Mozart *Skizzen* (NMA X/30/3) in *Notes: Quarterly Journal of the Music Library Association* 57/1 (2000): 188–93.

7. See, for one, Edward J. Dent, *Mozart's Operas: A Critical Study*, 2nd ed. (London: Oxford University Press, 1947), 248–49. Of significance here is a page of sketches that reveal Mozart drafting an original tune for the Men in Armor before entering the Lutheran hymn tune directly beneath it, both in C minor. See NMA, X/30/3, *Skizzen*, ed. Ulrich Konrad (Kassel: Bärenreiter-Verlag Karl Vötterle, 1998) Skb 1791b, fol. 9v; and, for a slightly different transcription, the appendix to the score of the opera, NMA, II/5/19, *Die Zauberflöte*, ed. Gernot Gruber and Alfred Orel (Kassel: Bärenreiter-Verlag, 1970), 377, where the earlier string quartet fragment in B minor is misleadingly given as a sketch for the opera.

8. Dent, *Mozart's Operas*, 250. One is reminded of Mozart's harsh words for the instrument, in a letter from Paris of February 14, 1778, when writing about a commission for several works from Ferdinand Dejean, an amateur flautist: "dann bin ich auch, wie sie wissen, gleich stuff wenn ich immer für ein instrument das ich nicht leiden kann schreiben soll." MBA, II:281. ("Moreover, you know that I become quite powerless whenever I am obliged to write for an instrument which I cannot bear." LMF, 481.)

9. Hermann Abert, *W. A. Mozart* (Leipzig: Breitkopf & Härtel, 1956), II:664; in English as *W. A. Mozart*, trans. Stewart Spencer, ed. Cliff Eisen (New Haven, CT: Yale University Press, 2007), 1281.

10. On the point, see also Anthony Arblaster, *Viva la Libertà: Politics in Opera* (London: Verso, 1992), 42. For Anthony Besch, Monostatos is "a subtly conceived portrait of a man coerced by circumstances, colour and creed into resentful isolation and neurotic repression." See his chapter in COH, 178–204, esp. 198.

11. Berlin, *Magus of the North*, 76.

12. The original libretto (Vienna: Ignaz Alberti, 1791) is given in full facsimile in FACS, III:67–96.

13. On parataxis, I have in mind the brilliant essay "Parataxis: On Hölderlin's Late Poetry," in Theodor W. Adorno, *Notes to Literature*, II, trans. Shierry Weber Nicholsen (New York: Columbia University Press, 1992), esp. 132–33.

14. These bars can now be studied in the splendid facsimile edition of the manuscript; see FACS, I:67–75.

15. This comes from Hamann's "Metacritique on the Purism of Reason," taken here from *What is Enlightenment?*, ed. Schmidt, 154–67, esp. 156. For the original, see Johann Georg Hamann, *Briefe*, ed. Arthur Henkel (Frankfurt am Main: Insel Verlag, 1988), 121. The emphasis is Hamann's.

16. Johann Gottfried Herder, *Abhandlung über den Ursprung der Sprache* (Berlin: Christian Friedrich Voß, 1772); in Johann Gottfried Herder, *Sämtliche Werke*, V, ed. Bernhard Suphan (Berlin, 1891; repr. Hildesheim: Georg Olms, 1967), 34. The translation is from *On the Origin of Language* (Jean-Jacques Rousseau, *Essay on the Origin of Languages*; Johann Gottfried Herder, *Essay on the Origin*

of Language), trans. John H. Moran and Alexander Gode (Chicago: University of Chicago Press, 1966), 115. The emphasis is Herder's.

17. Joseph Kerman, *Write All These Down: Essays on Music* (Berkeley: University of California Press, 1994), 241–56, esp. 251–53. For the full Auden/Kallman text, see W. H. Auden and Chester Kallman, *The Magic Flute: An Opera in Two Acts; Music by W. A. Mozart; English Version after the Libretto of Schikaneder and Giesecke* (London: Faber and Faber, 1957).

18. I leave unexamined the speculation that the author of some, if not all, of the libretto is by Carl Ludwig Giesecke, a speculation argued in detail by Edward Dent (*Mozart's Operas*, 234–43) and taken up in part by Wolfgang Hildesheimer, who writes of "Giesecke's decisive participation in the libretto" on the basis of a copy of it that was in his possession. See Hildesheimer, *Mozart*, trans. Marion Faber (New York: Farrar, Straus and Giroux, 1982), 324. For compelling arguments against Giesecke's collaboration, see COH, esp. 92–98.

19. In a thoughtful study of these two arias, Thomas Bauman is led to the insight that Tamino and Pamina "each [act] as a silent partner in the single aria granted to the other." See his "At the North Gate: Instrumental Music in *Die Zauberflöte*," in *Mozart's Operas*, ed. Daniel Heartz (Berkeley: University of California Press, 1990), 285.

20. Abert, *W. A. Mozart*, II:364.

21. Bauman ("At the North Gate," 286) writes: "As in the closing ritornello of Tamino's aria . . . reflection now succeeds fervor, thought masters feeling." But it seems to me that the opposite is the case: reflection, of which there is very little in Pamina's aria, is now driven off in irrational obsession.

22. Jessica Waldoff (*Recognition in Mozart's Operas*, 17), for one, writes of "the fairy-tale logic that governs this opera," citing David J. Buch, "Fairy-Tale Literature and *Die Zauberflöte*," *Acta Musicologica* 64 (1992): 30–49

Birdsong and Hieroglyphs: Exoticism
and Enlightened Orientalism in *The Magic Flute*

MATTHEW HEAD

When it comes to exoticism – "the evocation of a place, people or social
milieu that is (or is perceived or imagined to be) profoundly different
from accepted local norms in its attitudes, customs and morals" – *The
Magic Flute* is possibly the most baffling of all repertory operas.[1] How to
make sense of the outlandish coexistence of a Japanese hunting costume
(Act 1, scene 1), a Turkish table, gondola, palm forest, and canal (Act 1,
scene 9, dialogue), the vaults of a pyramid (Act 2, scene 20), six lions,
three probably white male slaves, a man named after a Persian prophet
(Sarastro/Zoroaster), another (in feathers) whose name sounds like
"parrot" (Papageno), and a villainous black-faced Moor?[2] Intensifying
this mélange, the opera elides exoticism and magic – something far from
inevitable in eighteenth-century opera – and it unfolds in a place of the
imagination resisting the worldly concreteness of geography and historical time. In an older literature, the eclectic exoticism of the opera was
tidied away through a selective emphasis upon Egyptian-Masonic allegory (on which more below). The situation is now quite different thanks
to the research of David J. Buch, which reinstates the genre of "fairy-tale"
opera as a historical category.[3] This does much to anchor the opera in its
own time and place. However, there is still foundational work to be
done. Buch's subject was the supernatural, not exoticism; understand-
ably, then, he groups together European fairy tales and those of Middle
Eastern origin. The latter shape *The Magic Flute* in specific ways that can
be usefully teased out.

   In trying to make sense of this opera, we might turn to Ralph Locke's
handsome two-volume survey of exoticism.[4] This landmark study offers
not only historical perspective but a framework for appraising how music
contributes to the characterization "of a remote or alien milieu" –
whether or not the music is exoticized.[5] However, Locke only touches
on *The Magic Flute*. This may be because it speaks less clearly to issues of
cross-cultural representation than Mozart's *The Abduction from the
Seraglio* (K. 384; 1782), which he explores in detail. Indeed, *The Magic
Flute* is a problem case if exoticism is taken to involve the representation

of actual places, remote in place or time. Arguably, the opera unfolds in a place of the imagination, though one not without some specific historical and cultural points of reference. If it can be located at all, it might be thought of as a picturesque parkland – these were fashionable at the time and often adorned with the rocks, temples, grottos, and even pyramids that appear in the opera – or the make-believe, exotic landscape of an oriental fairy tale. Like those spaces, it is constituted by existing fictions and fantasies, its intertextual web encompassing an ever-expanding range of allusion and debt. (There is always *another* source for the libretto of *The Magic Flute*.) For these reasons, the worldly reality of the characters is attenuated. Powerfully archetypical, but not realistic in novelistic terms, they exist primarily as figures of the theater and of theatrical performance. Identification with them is of course possible, and degrees of alterity harden in the course of the story, but the fairy-tale world of the opera, eliding magic and the exotic, differs from the culturally specific setting of Mozart's earlier "Seraglio" operas – *The Abduction* and *Zaide* (K. 344; 1780) – and from the Da Ponte operas, in which critics often celebrate realism and psychological depth.

The sense of free-floating location is enhanced by our never knowing where the characters are from. Tamino, a traveler, first appears in a "Japanese hunting costume."[6] No clear model for this garment has been identified. Possibly, Schikaneder was alluding to a seventeenth-century Dutch men's fashion, inspired by the kimono.[7] Even if this were true, however, it would not tell us where Tamino himself was from. As for Papageno, he is unable to name the region in which he lives even when asked point-blank by Tamino.

Indeed, Tamino's urbane questioning initially baffles Papageno. In the first spoken dialogue of the opera, he comes across as an unworldly indigene, unaware of rank, of other lands, and of the strange practice of giving places a name:

TAMINO *(taking Papageno's hand)* Hi there!

PAPAGENO Huh?

TAMINO Tell me, merry friend, who are you?

PAPAGENO Who am I? *(to himself)* Stupid question! *(aloud)* A man, like you. And if I ask you, who you are?

TAMINO I'd answer that I am of noble birth.

PAPAGENO That's over my head. You'll have to put it more simply, if I'm going to understand you!

TAMINO My father is a Lord, who rules over many lands and peoples; so I'm called a Prince.

PAPAGENO Lands? Peoples? Prince?

TAMINO That's why I ask you –

PAPAGENO Slow down! Let me ask [the questions]! Are you telling me there are *other* lands and peoples beyond these mountains?

Act 1, scene 2, dialogue[8]

Papageno also claims to know nothing of his family and ancestry, a hint that his origins are not entirely human, but also playing into his construction as existing in a state before or outside of civilization:

TAMINO Tell me, then, what region are we in?

PAPAGENO In what region? *(looks around)* Between valleys and mountains.

TAMINO True enough! But what is this region called? Who rules over it?

PAPAGENO I can answer that about as well as I can tell you how I came into the world.

TAMINO *(laughs)* What? You don't know where you were born, or who your parents were?

PAPAGENO Nothing! I know no more nor less than I was raised and fed by an old but very jolly man.

In this dialogue, Papageno borders on a "noble savage" – a figure of the European imagination long employed to relativize, and to critique, European social norms – here, concerning rank and territorial ownership. As Dorinda Outram observes, the exotic in the eighteenth century could even be home, viewed through the eyes of a foreign visitor.[9]

Locating Exoticism in *The Magic Flute*

At least three major literary-theatrical traditions of exoticism feed into the libretto of *The Magic Flute*. Any one of them might have served as the basis of an opera. Taken together, they help create a sense of narrative abundance. The first is "abduction" or "seraglio" opera that shapes Act 1, in which Tamino sets off to rescue Pamina from captivity. The second, which until recently received the lion's share of scholarly attention, is the initiation of a prince (here, Tamino) into the secret wisdom of Isis and Osiris, a scenario involving ancient Egyptian motifs. The third centers on the magical-exotic adventures of a stock comic character, involving magic wishes and Genii (the Three Boys) – this is Papageno's adventure, taking place largely in Act 2.

The ingenious combination of these traditions helps account for the twists and turns of the story, the relative independence of its subplots, as well as inconsistencies about the time and place of the fictional world. I begin by tugging at these three strands. In doing so, I highlight the subtle, pervasive influence of *The Tales of One Thousand and One Nights* (also known as *The Arabian Nights*) on the opera, a collection of Middle Eastern stories that became wildly popular in Europe after their translation into French by Antoine Galland between 1704 and 1712.[10] In a final section, I explore what might connect the opera's dual concerns with the religion of ancient Egypt and with nature, the realms of Sarastro and Papageno, or, to write things small, with hieroglyphs and birdsong. I suggest these dual realms offer the audience a potentially transformative encounter with the archaic, the "original," and the divinely revealed. Adapting a rubric from Srinivas Aravamudan, I call this type of encounter "enlightened Orientalism," a utopian mode linking the moral ideals of the late eighteenth century to an exemplary, imaginary "Orient."[11]

Abduction Opera

The first act of *The Magic Flute* is shaped by the "abduction" plot. This had developed in the court theater of the *Ancien Régime*, in part because France then enjoyed close diplomatic ties with the Islamic Ottoman Empire.[12] It appeared fully formed as early as Rameau's *entrée* "The Generous Turk" in the Parisian opera ballet *Les Indes galantes* of 1735.[13] Abduction opera was particularly favored, from the middle of the century, in the predominantly Catholic Habsburg Empire, where it spoke to a history of territorial and religious conflict – but also diplomacy and trade – with the Ottoman Empire. Typically, the plot involved a Christian woman held captive in a sultan's polyamorous harem.[14] In an act of gallant heroism, her European sweetheart comes to rescue her, but their escape is foiled. Facing death, they take leave of each other, only to receive unexpected pardon and freedom from the wise and beneficent sultan.

Undoubtedly, the image of the Turk occasioned anxious fantasies of political despotism, sexual excess, and violence, at one level offering an antithesis to the rhetorical ideals of the European Enlightenment. These thrillingly transgressive associations form a background of expectation for abduction operas. They also attach to Ottoman characters of low social status – such as Mozart's most enduring pantomime villain Osmin in *The Abduction*. In the (un)expected denouement, however, these negative associations are banished by the sultan's largesse, which provides a morally didactic *coup de théâtre*. The sense of looking beyond cultural and religious differences to discover a transcendent or universal morality is part of the enlightened orientalism of such works (and was epitomized by Voltaire's *Treatise on Tolerance* [1763] and Gotthold Ephraim Lessing's five-act drama *Nathan the Wise* [1779]). In the arts, at least, displays of religious hatred were out of fashion. There were other expedients, too. It was not wise, in court-sponsored opera, to present unflattering images of rulers, whatever their background.

The conventions of abduction opera are summoned, but also transformed, near the beginning of Act 1 of *The Magic Flute* as Tamino sets off heroically to rescue Pamina from her captivity at the hands of an Eastern-sounding patriarch and presumed villain, Sarastro. The Queen of the Night sets him on this mistaken course when – in one of many acts of nested storytelling in the opera – she relays through the Three Ladies the tale of Pamina's "abduction by a powerful, evil demon":

> FIRST LADY She sat all alone on a lovely May morning in a refreshing cypress grove, always her favorite place to visit. The villain crept in unobserved.
> SECOND LADY She heard, and –
> THIRD LADY Besides his evil heart, he can metamorphose into every imaginable form; in this way, he got Pamina too.
> FIRST LADY This is the name of the royal daughter, so you may worship [her].

> Act 1, scene 5, dialogue

In this scene, both the technique of telling a story within the story and the reference to an "evil demon" show the influence of the *Thousand and One Nights* (henceforth *Nights*), a "household title" of the eighteenth century, whose influence on German-language theater is only now coming to light.[15] Locke, emphasizing its importance as a repository of motifs, notes the prominence of "sultans, harems, harem guards, slaves from sub-Saharan Africa, [and] summary executions."[16] Pushing Locke's observation a bit further, the *Nights* brokered the enduring marriage of the supernatural and the exotic.

Tamino, who seems already to know about operatic abduction plots, falls instantly in love. He indulges in an ardent aria of erotic sensibility (Act 1, scene 4, "Dies Bildnis ist bezaubernd schön"), in which – recalling Belmonte's parallel aria ("O wie ängstlich") in *The Abduction* (Act 1, scene 5) – he reports forensically on the sensations of love and imagines an ecstatic union with his beloved. He sets off to rescue Pamina, arriving like a valiant knight at the boundary of Sarastro's realm. There, he is rebuffed by the voice of a guard (Act 1, scene 15), just as Belmonte was barred entry to Pasha Selim's estate by Osmin (*The Abduction*, Act 1, scene 2).

It turns out that an escape attempt is already in progress – Papageno has beaten him to it. As Papageno and Pamina take flight, Sarastro arrives to the sound of a triumphal chorus with trumpets and drums (Act 1, scene 18) – "Long live Sarastro!" This follows abduction conventions – Pasha Selim is also celebrated as a ruler by a stage chorus at a parallel moment of *The Abduction* (Act 1, scene 6). From this point, principal motifs of abduction opera are much compressed, but faithfully reproduced. Pamina and Tamino are brought before Sarastro; Monostatos gleefully anticipates his reward and their punishment (cf. *The Abduction*, Act 3, scene 5), but instead he is reprimanded for his viciousness (cf. *The Abduction*, Act 3, scene 6). Sarastro hints that he had hoped to receive Pamina's love, but grants her freedom to love Tamino (cf. *The Abduction*, Act 3, scene 9).

While abduction operas typically conclude at this point, *The Magic Flute* uses Sarastro's beneficence as a starting point for the rest of the drama, acting as a doorway into his Egyptian realm of sacred wisdom. At this point, Sarastro sheds his association with the Ottoman sultan of abduction opera. The implied confrontation of Christianity and Islam gives way to the discovery of a more ancient, spiritual system hidden behind the curtain of Act 2. A stage direction evokes the startling change of scenery as the curtain rises:

The theater is a palm forest, all the trees are silvery, the leaves are gold. [There are] 18 seats of [woven palm] leaves, on each seat is a pyramid and a big black horn set with gold. In the middle is the largest pyramid, and the largest trees. Sarastro along with other Priests come in solemn steps, each holding a branch of palm. The procession is accompanied by a march played by wind and brass instruments.

Abduction motifs do not completely disappear in Act 2, however. Instead, they are displaced onto Monostatos, through whom they are also given considerable complexity. The fact that Sarastro keeps slaves and uses Monostatos – a *Mohr* – to oversee them (and to keep tabs on the captured Pamina) is consistent with the harem fictions of the *Nights*, though admittedly not with Mozart's *The Abduction*. Correspondingly, and perhaps in the absence of any established musical codes for characters of specifically African identity, Mozart employed a subtle version of his *alla turca* style for Monostatos's notorious aria "Alles fühlt der Liebe Freuden." He does not employ Janissary percussion (the bass drum, triangle, and cymbals used in *The Abduction*), but retains the piccolo – also used in *The Abduction* for

"Turkish music" – and melodic fingerprints, including the arabesques that turn in semiquavers around the tonic and dominant pitches.

However, Schikaneder complicated Monostatos's characterization with some antiracist, and even antislavery, motifs. Already, back in Act 1, scene 12, a relativistic perspective is introduced. When Papageno and Monostatos first catch sight of each other's strange appearance they simultaneously beg for mercy, in a stuttering duet, each believing the other to be the devil incarnate. In the following dialogue, however, Papageno begins to reflect: "Aren't I foolish, to get so frightened? There are black birds in the world, so why not black people." In the first strophe of his aria "Alles fühlt der Liebe Freuden" (Act 2, scene 7), Monostatos takes this further, questioning prejudice against his complexion, asserting the universality of his desire for love, and – implicitly – milking the audience for sympathy:

Everyone feels the joy of love, / bills and coos, fusses, hugs and kisses, / but I must go without love / because a black man is ugly! / Is there no sweetheart for me?

This sentiment, if not the actual words, recalls the then famous slogan of the British and American campaigns for the abolition of slavery – "Am I not a man and a brother" – an epithet that Josiah Wedgewood incorporated in his antislavery medallion of 1787. Mozart's choice of a neutral, C major march rhythm in this aria avoids lending Monostatos the radical alterity that the dramatic situation imparts to him as Pamina's potential rapist. He is kept safely at a distance by *pianissimo* and *lontano* performance directions. Messages about Monostatos are thus extremely mixed.

Racism and misogyny collide. Immediately before this aria, Monostatos's rues that, as a black man, he is not allowed to love a white woman. However, this moment of enlightened critical reflection (it sounds like a soundbite from Voltaire or Lessing) is undercut by the fact that Pamina detests his unsolicited attentions and that Monostatos is justifying a crime he has not yet successfully committed. In a nocturnal garden, signifying folly and desire, he spies on Pamina, who sleeps in a bower of flowers:

Ah, so there's the elusive beauty! And so they wanted to beat the soles of my feet just on account of this precious plant? So, I'm to thank my lucky stars that I'm still here with my skin intact. Hm! What was my crime exactly? That I was infatuated with a flower that grew on foreign soil? And what man, even if he hailed from a gentler clime, would remain cold and unmoved by such a sight. By heavens! The girl will rob me of my reason yet. The fire that glows within me will yet consume me.

Monostatos's reference to a "fire" within him parallels Tamino's love-struck reaction to Pamina's portrait (Act 1, scene 4). Both men experience "fire" as they gaze at Pamina, who is rendered passive by portraiture and by sleep. Adding further complexity, this type of romantic desire overtakes both men involuntarily. In binding them to Pamina, it resembles the bonds of servitude, on the one hand, and Papageno's magic music, on the other – this, too, acts invisibly and at a distance. In these ways, slavery is elaborated metaphorically, becoming part of the poetics of the opera, rather than a subject of critique.

The Mysteries of Isis and Osiris

A second major strand of exoticism involves Prince Tamino's journey of spiritual development, culminating in his initiation into the Mysteries of Isis and Osiris within an ancient Egyptian pyramid. This venerable literary topos preceded the rise in the nineteenth century of an archaeological, forensically documentary Egyptology. That mode was spurred by the Napoleonic invasion of Egypt and Syria (1798–1801), the rediscovery of the Rosetta stone in 1799, and deciphering of hieroglyphs in 1822, and involved the accumulation of positivistic knowledge – facts – but also an increasing sense of alienation. Paradoxically, ancient Egypt became more "remote and alien" as more was discovered about it. Edward Said detected this imperialist objectification in the stage sets of Verdi's *Aida*, but saw in Mozart's *The Magic Flute* an earlier, enlightened mode of sympathetic and cosmopolitan identification.[17] Only a detailed history of staging and iconography could speak to the influence of the pharaonic turn on later stagings of Mozart's opera, but Karl Friedrich Schinkel's designs from 1815, drawing on the *Description of Egypt* (1809–21) produced by Napoleon's large contingent of scholars, are generally regarded as landmarks in this process.[18]

In Vienna in 1791, ideas about, feelings for, and uses of ancient Egypt were based on Classical sources, Biblical narratives, and literary fiction. References to Egyptian wise men and magicians in the Old Testament (e.g., Exodus 7:11) suggested that the Egyptians received divine wisdom through direct revelation. According to Acts 7:22, this knowledge was transmitted to the Israelites: "Moses was learned in all the wisdom of the Egyptians and was mighty in words and in deeds." This wisdom was bound up with the practice of magic (in a way that now seems counterintuitive). When pharaonic priests test Moses and Aaron, they transform Egyptian staffs into snakes (Exodus 5:7) – an ambivalent image that resonates with the opening of *The Magic Flute.*

There were several major Classical sources for the Mysteries of Isis available to an educated elite in Vienna in 1791. Audiences did not need to read the classics, however, to get the gist because these canonical sources were widely diffused through historical writing, fiction, and household encyclopedias. In the genealogy of *The Magic Flute,* the most important of these was book 11 of Apuleius's *Metamorphoses,* written in Latin in the second century AD, also known, in English, as *The Golden Ass.* It was a landmark because it was the first novel to fictionalize initiation into the Mysteries of Isis as part of a hero's story of adventure and development. Lucius has dabbled with magic and inadvertently turned himself into an ass. He is eventually released from that humbling state when Isis appears to him in a dream, declaring:

I am the progenitor of nature, mistress of all elements, first-born of generations . . . the peoples on whom the rising sun shines its rays, both Aethiopians and the Aegyptians, who gain strength by ancient doctrine, worship me with the appropriate ceremonies, [and] call me by my right name, Queen Isis.[19]

As in *The Magic Flute,* the actual wisdom of Isis is never disclosed, emphasis falling instead upon an initiatory ritual (in Lucius's words) "performed as a rite of voluntary death and salvation attained by prayer" – a direct corollary of Tamino and Pamina's trial in Act 2, scene 28, in which courage, love, and music substitute for prayer.[20] Like Tamino, Lucius does not eat or drink during his initiation (a motif of self-abnegation comically ignored by Papageno). Students of *The Magic Flute* will notice Apuleius's reference to a palm tree with golden leaves and to a procession in which the initiated carry insignia (cf. the stage direction at the beginning of Act 2). Also bearing directly on the opera are Isis's references (in the quotation from Apuleius above) to ceremony, ancient doctrine, the sun, and the elements. The fact that Isis appears to Lucius in a dream is evocative of the second act of the opera, which is unveiled like an alternative reality and involves an almost hypnogogic slowing of time during the Procession of the Priests and Sarastro's aria "O Isis und Osiris."

Apuleius's *Metamorphoses* shaped two texts often mentioned as sources for *The Magic Flute*: Jean Terrasson's novel *Sethos,* published in French in 1731 – ostensibly as the translation of an ancient Greek manuscript – and Ignaz von Born's essay "Über die Mysterien der Ägypter" (On the Mysteries of the Ancient Egyptians), published in Vienna in the Freemasons' periodical *Journal für Freymaurer* in 1784. Peter Branscombe highlights "numerous similarities" between *Sethos* and Schikaneder's libretto, via the German translation of the novel by Matthiaus Claudius (1777–78). Among them are the words of the two men in black armor in Act 2, scene 28, which are drawn directly from *Sethos*, and the Priests' singing of hymns to Isis and Osiris. He also shows that in describing Tamino's trials, Schikaneder probably drew vocabulary directly from Born's essay: "'Verschwiegenheit' ('discretion'), the phrase 'rein und lauter' ('clean and pure') ... and 'Heiligthum' ('sanctuary') and 'Fremdling' ('stranger')."[21]

In publishing his essay, Born employed a sleight of hand. By the middle of the eighteenth century, a branch of German-speaking Masonry had taken *Sethos* to heart as an authentic representation of the Egyptian cult of Isis and used it as a template to develop its own rituals of initiation.[22] Perhaps these Masons even half-believed Terrasson's claim to be translating an ancient manuscript. In an act of *faux naïveté*, Born used *Sethos* and Classical sources – including Apuleius – to suggest a continuous tradition between the ancient Egyptian mysteries and Freemasonry. This was entirely circular logic in the service of the prestige and imaginary lineage of a beleaguered, secret fraternity.

Born's argument subsequently fostered a reading of *The Magic Flute* as a secret handshake. This involved a fine leap of logic: if Schikaneder could be shown to have drawn on Born's essay, then the opera could be shown to be both "about" Freemasonry and a celebration of it. An alternative, more cautious perspective is that the self-mythologizing and theatrical rituals recently developed in Viennese Freemasonry helped give Schikaneder the idea for some scenes in Act 2 – without those scenes necessarily being "about" Freemasonry. That is, Freemasonry offered source materials, inspiration, even a mediating step for Schikaneder's staging of initiation into the Wisdom of Isis, but it did not "own" that subject. To read the entire opera as Masonic allegory involves tidying away many inconvenient questions: Are the opera's high-moral ideals not eighteenth-century commonplaces ("Wisdom," "Nature," and "Reason")? Why does Sarastro keep slaves? Why does a hereditary prince end up on top? Why write Pamina into the story?

The sound-world Mozart created for Sarastro's realm also frustrates the essentialism of Masonic readings. Sarastro's aria (No. 10) is a prayer offered to Isis and Osiris for the protection of Pamina and Tamino. As an adagio bass aria with chorus, it is an extremely unusual type of piece. This alone is sufficient to impute a sense of difference to the music, without the need for any quasi-ethnomusicological evocation of ancient Egyptian (or Masonic) music specifically. The inclusion of three trombones – instruments strongly associated with the operatic underworld and the voices of spirits – situates Sarastro's voice between the human and divine, life and death. The low vocal register, the omission of violins, flutes, and oboes, the quiet dynamic, and the richness of divided legato violas convey subterranean sensations. When the all-male choir enters in measure 25, the melody finds itself in the higher of the two bass parts (bass 2), covered by repeated notes in the two tenor parts above – an eerie, sepulchral effect. The character is mysterious, hovering between light and dark. Sarastro's initially poised, diatonic melody is disturbed by a chromatic turn as he refers to "danger" (mm. 21–22), even though at this point the music is modulating, optimistically, to the dominant. Then the tone darkens with modulations to minor keys – including a pictorial plunge in unisons to the tonic minor for a reference to the "grave" (m. 35). In these ways, Mozart conveys the danger of Tamino's impending trial (described below).

Papageno's Wishes

A third theatrical tradition of exoticism that shaped *The Magic Flute* concerns Papageno. It involved the exotic-magical adventures of a stock comic character, loveably idiotic and sometimes mischievous. Buch's survey of operatic supernaturalism suggests this scenario developed early in the eighteenth century, in improvised Italian comedy, the *commedia dell'arte,* and from there entered French comic opera (*opéra comique).* The trigger, again, was Galland's French edition of the *Nights.*[23] Though the chronology and transmission are not entirely clear – much comic theater was semi-improvised, by traveling troupes, and the music rarely survives – this tradition was apparently adapted in Vienna, under the headings of *Zauberkomödie, Zauberlustspiel,* and *Mährchen.* This is the repertoire that incurred Leopold Mozart's disapproval during the family's sojourn in Vienna in 1767–68 as (implicitly) unenlightened, fostering superstition, and failing to instruct: "the Viennese, generally speaking, do not care to see serious and sensible performances, have little or no idea of them, and only want to see foolish stuff, dances, devils, ghosts, magic, clowns … witches and apparitions."[24]

Papageno's adventure takes a specific form, however, one not observed to date and drawn from the *Nights*: it unfolds as a series of wishes granted by Genii (here "the Three Boys," who, though named as such within the libretto, are listed as "drei Genien" in the dramatis personae). A well-known example of this type of adventure is "Aladdin and the Wonderful

Lamp." Aladdin's wishes are for safety and freedom (he finds himself imprisoned underground by a sorcerer), for food (he and his mother are poor and hungry), and for a bride (specifically the sultan's daughter). He gains these through magic objects (a ring and a lamp) that contain genii, released when the object is rubbed. They present themselves to Aladdin as "slaves" and exist only to do his bidding. He is not particularly deserving of his good fortune – destiny thrusts it upon him.

Without suggesting dependence on this story specifically, it is notable that Papageno is also a somewhat unlikely recipient of good fortune, magically arranged. When we first meet him, he sings of his happiness, but reveals his desire for a wife. He is given a box of magic bells by the Three Ladies – supernatural beings – which he uses to make this wish and others come true. During his attempt to escape with Pamina from Sarastro's palace (Act 1, scene 17), he uses the bells to make venomous Monostatos dance offstage – in this way (like Aladdin) he ensures his safety. Later, in Act 2, scene 16, when he and Tamino find themselves alone in Sarastro's palace, the Three Genii bring Papageno not only his bells but a table laid with food and drink ("ein schöner gedeckter Tisch"). Rather unheroically, he tucks in, praising the cook and the wine cellar. In Act 2, scene 22, he finds himself frightened and alone, when a voice ("the Speaker") informs him that he has failed the trial – but that he can grant him a wish:

SPEAKER [You failed the trials.] Therefore, you will never feel the heavenly joy of the initiate.

PAPAGENO Not to worry, there are many people like me. A good glass of wine would be my biggest pleasure right now.

SPEAKER Do you not have anything else you wish for?

PAPAGENO Not so far.

SPEAKER Your wish is my command! – *(He leaves.) – (A large cup, filled with red wine, appears out of the ground.)*

PAPAGENO Hurray! That's great! – *(drinks)* Wonderful! – Heavenly! – Divine! – Ha! I'm so happy that, if I had wings, I'd fly to the sun. – Ha! – This does my heart good! – I'd like – I wish – yes, what then [do I wish]?

This dialogue leads directly into Papageno's aria "Ein Mädchen oder Weibchen" (Act 2, scene 22), which, in context, conveys his wish for a sweetheart or wife. (Clearly, it took a glass of wine for this wish to come out.) In this aria he plays his magic bells with increasing virtuosity on each strophic repetition. That form, involving three stanzas, is apt to convey the classic threefold repetition of wishes in fairy tales. Meanwhile, the two-tempo structure – which sees Papageno lurch repeatedly from a relatively sedate Andante in 2/4 meter into an Allegro in 6/8 – suggests his mounting, if intoxicated, desire. As soon as the song is over, his sweetheart appears as if by magic, albeit in disguise as an amorous aged woman. Less than enthusiastic, he promises to be faithful – at least (he whispers) until someone prettier comes along.

His trials are not yet over. In adapting the formula of the wish from the *Nights,* Schikaneder introduced an enlightened element of moral development – Papageno must prove himself worthy of his wishes coming true, or at least pay for his weaknesses. When we next meet up with him, he is suicidal (Act 2, scene 29). His potential bride was whisked away by the forces of magic because his promise to her was not truly meant. Theatrically, he threatens to hang himself – by now perhaps anticipating the Genii will come to his aid. Just in time, they do, reminding him to use his magic bells. He does, uttering a wish between virtuosic bursts on his glockenspiel:

Ring, little bells, ring! / Bring my sweetheart here! / Ring, little bells, ring! / Bring my little wife here!

With the literalness that characterizes the magic wish of the *Nights,* the Three Boys bring Papagena from the sky. Implicitly, Papageno has learned his lesson.

Birdsong and Hieroglyphs

From this outline of three main strands of exoticism in *The Magic Flute,* it is evident that the opera, like the *Nights,* contains many stories.[25] There are more that might be drawn out. Sometimes they are miniatures, told in the strophic lyrics of arias – as when Papageno fantasizes about catching young women in cages and trading them for sugar; sometimes they are fleeting moments of narrative, as when Pamina discloses that her father carved the flute in a "magic hour" from a thousand-year oak, or when Monostatos secures from the Queen of the Night a promise that Pamina will be his when they bring down the realm of Sarastro. Sometimes (again, as in the *Nights)* they are abandoned mid-course, like Tamino's plan to rescue Pamina from Sarastro and return her to the Queen of the Night. Amid this exuberance, or narrative excess, two realms stand in perplexing disconnect: the spiritual wisdom of ancient Egyptian mysteries and Papageno's habitus – the realm of nature. However, they are united, conceptually, as archaic, ancestral places – realms of hieroglyphs and birdsong.

Hieroglyphs appeared in the frontispiece to the published libretto of the opera and are strongly implied in its description of Tamino's purifying trial (Act 2, scene 28). (See Figure 4.9 earlier in this volume.) This trial is undertaken as a condition of his initiation but also, in another sense, as part of it. The libretto describes a rocky landscape with two mountains, stage left and right. One, shrouded in dark mist, contains a noisy waterfall; the other, back-lit with hell-red fire, houses spitting flames. Sombre, archaic music is heard, evoking an atmosphere of labyrinthine grief. Two men in black suits of armor – I imagine them like medieval knights in princely coats of arms – lead Tamino to a towering pyramid center stage. It is inscribed with an illuminated script which is "read" aloud to Tamino by the Armored Men but is surely what they sing: "Whoever wanders this path of woes, is purified by fire, water, air, and earth."[26] Their melody, a Lutheran chorale tune, is from another time and place – an exotic relic that Mozart dug out from a treatise on counterpoint published twenty years before by the Bach student Johann Kirnberger. The script on the pyramid is presumably in hieroglyphs. A German inscription on the pyramid would be rather incongruous, and Prince Tamino would hardly need that to be read aloud by knights from a bygone age.

Declaring that this vale of tears holds no fear for him, Tamino is rewarded by reunion with Pamina. They will wander the dark path together. (The libretto is of little help here, and with the original costumes and sets lost, we have to imagine how this would have been staged.) The royal couple are shored up by their virtuous love and by Tamino's piping of his magic flute, carved (Pamina discloses) from "a thousand-year oak." For this oldfangled instrument, worthy of Methuselah, Mozart provided a generic march tune: a venerable type of piece that Johann Friedrich Sulzer (writing in the early 1770s) related back to the earliest uses of "measured tones ... to support the body's strength in physical ordeals."[27] As they emerge from darkness into blinding light, Tamino and Pamina exclaim, "You Gods, what a moment! We are granted the happiness of Isis." This sublime moment of illumination suggests the revelation of transcendental spiritual knowledge, the cult of Isis and Osiris melding with the biblical narrative of creation in one of the Enlightenment's favorite motifs: *fiat lux* ("Let there be light!").

This mind's-eye reconstruction suggests that ancient Egypt in *The Magic Flute* is not (only) a place marked by alterity but (also) belongs to a fantasy of origins, continuity, and rebirth. Initiated into an archaic – but ongoing – legacy, Tamino is spiritually reborn. His future path, and the social order he will rule over, are transformed by the experience of this remote time and place. Within the fictional world at least, *this* exotic locale has a transfiguring effect, catalyzing historical progress and social transformation.

This encounter writes into the opera, or inscribes, a theory of art that possessed broad period currency. As David Wellbery puts it brilliantly, if elliptically, in a study of Lessing's *Laocoon* (1767), "the Enlightenment attributes to art the capacity to renew the life of culture by reactivating its most archaic mechanisms."[28] While Lessing's archaic was Greek antiquity, *The Magic Flute* displaces classicism with fantasies of ancient Egypt and (semiwild) nature. These are twinned, and subtly but differently exoticized, within the fiction. They are captured in my title's allusion to birdsong and hieroglyphs, which are styled, within the opera, as divine, original, and possessing (re)generative power.

Though excluded from the Mysteries of Isis, Papageno is also a figure about origins – especially musical ones.[29] He both is and is not exotic. We know what he looked like, because Schikaneder included a picture of himself playing the part in the libretto sold at the earliest performances in the Theater auf der Wieden (Figure 4.2 earlier in this volume). And quite a look it is! With a headdress of feathers and a bird whistle that looks like a panpipe, he has a remote resemblance to older iconography of North American first peoples. In another early illustration he is shown playing a hammered dulcimer slung from his neck in the manner of a "Hungarian-Gypsy" (Romany) musician.[30] However, living alone on the edge of a forest – in a straw hut, he tells the inquisitive Tamino – he belongs more to a type of hypothetical savage imagined by Enlightenment theorists in their library-bound explorations of mankind in the state of nature. Such a figure existed at the vanishing point of the rustic, the exotic, and the antique, providing a way of imagining human nature before it was shaped by diverse local customs and manners. As Dorinda Outram notes, for most of the eighteenth century, the opposite of culture was not another culture but nature.[31]

It is in this context that we can hear his bird whistle and his own chirpy singing as allusions to the origins of music. Just as hieroglyphs were often regarded as "holy writing," even as a divine gift containing original spiritual wisdom, so divinely created birdsong had long been cited as the origin of music – not least by the same Jesuit priest, Anthansius Kircher, who wrote prolifically (if erroneously) about ancient Egypt.

There were newer theories, too, but the idea that mankind learned music from the birds was just too alluring to put aside entirely. Papageno, himself named after and resembling a tropical bird, reactivates or alludes to this theory. He is clearly the opera's natural musician. The libretto and music occasionally suggest he is not only a bird-catcher but a birdman. When Tamino first encounters Papageno, he doubts he is fully human:

PAPAGENO Why are you looking at me so suspiciously and mischievously?

TAMINO Because – because I have my doubts if you are human.

PAPAGENO Why's that?

TAMINO Judging by your feathers, which cover you, I think you're –
(*goes towards him*)

PAPAGENO [Surely] not a bird? Stay back, I say . . .

Much later, in his love duet with Papagena (Act 2, scene 29, finale, "Pa-Pa-Pa"), Papageno regresses from words to a single syllable, and from melody to beating, repeated notes. His melody comes to resemble that of a bird breaking into song. Comically mimetic, and probably accompanied by a feathery mating dance, this extraordinary number, coming close to the end of the opera, intensifies covertly avian features of Papageno's earlier music (magical and otherwise). Rhythmically mechanical, involving melodic gestures of outrageous simplicity, intensely repetitive – and yet utterly magical – the parrots' duet unlocks a theory of musical origins that spills out from this number into the opera as a whole. Arguably, even the Queen of the Night is touched by this stylized birdsong in the repeated notes and arpeggios of her coloratura in "Der Hölle Rache."[32]

In his two solo arias ("Der Vogelfänger bin ich ja" and "Ein Mädchen oder Weibchen") Papageno's idiom is an ingenious, Mozartian fantasy of aboriginal music. Both numbers are strophic lieder, an aria type that was common for socially lowly characters in comic opera, and which (like that Lutheran chorale melody in Tamino's trial) was said to suit the musically untutored. Both of Papageno's arias belong to established types of lied – the first is a working song (which tells us his occupation and is sung as he goes about it); the second is a drinking song (which he sings with a large cup of wine in his hand, and it keeps spilling over from an Andante in duple meter to a rushing – specifically hunting – 6/8).[33] Both lieder are based on the rhythmic and melodic profile of the contredanse – a rustic, stamping, line dance – employ pastoral keys (G major and F major, respectively), and employ prominent open, perfect fifths between bass and melody. In "Der Vogelfänger bin ich ja" these extend into another pastoral fingerprint, the horn-fifth figure (m. 4), highlighted by a pair of orchestral horns. Extremely catchy and distinctive, these songs also possess that "impression of the familiar" that the composer-critic Schulz, inspired by Herder's celebration of old vernacular poetry, equated with the German *Volkslied* (literally, people's song).[34] Both of Papageno's lieder can be heard as stage songs – as if he were singing them to himself – even though the libretto does not make this completely explicit. Heard in this way, they tap into a period idealization of orality, which came to the fore in Herder's preface to his *Volkslieder* of 1779. The fact that Papageno's magic music appears improvised – in "Ein Mädchen oder Weibchen" each strophic repetition occasions ever more fantastical variations of the same material – also ties in with the aesthetic premium placed upon natural spontaneity.

As an art of strophic repetition, and variation, Papageno's magic music reaches back to birdsong. Activating or, more cautiously, alluding to "archaic" beliefs about music and natural magic (music's power to influence people and things), this stage music offers a (fictional) glimpse of the art before its scientific and aesthetic rationalization. The "renewal" (in Wellbery's sense) this offers is the re-enchantment of music – an art that had officially shed much of its metaphysical and magical power in the course of the seventeenth and eighteenth centuries in the intellectual contexts of scientific rationalism and the aesthetic doctrine of mimesis (according to which music could imitate or represent the magical but not be it). Similarities between the magic music of the opera and the rest of the score – highlighted by Buch in an incisive analysis – can be explained in many ways, but potentially they re-enchant the music of the opera as a whole. The timing, in 1791, is tantalizing, as music was soon to be returned to metaphysics (a sort of philosophical supernatural) by German romantic aesthetics. Wilhelm Heinrich Wackenroder's landmark *Outpourings of an Art-Loving Friar* was published only six years later.

Conclusion

Why *The Magic Flute* drew upon, but also overthrew, the abduction plot is intriguing, but unknowable. In terms of dramatic effect, it adds surprise and wonder to the encounter with ancient Egyptian motifs in Act 2. Those motifs, far from serving the putatively liberal philosophy of Freemasonry, end up reaffirming the rights of a hereditary prince to a position of leadership – implicitly to the sovereignty for which he was destined by birth. While it is too easy to draw direct links between operatic plots and political contexts, it is difficult not to recognize a counterrevolutionary element in the Egyptian turn of *The Magic Flute*. In 1791, Austria was winding up to war against the forces of an expansionist French Republic in defense of the *Ancien Régime*. Though Austria did not officially declare war on the French Republic until 1792, it had already acted militarily in January 1791 to reinstate the rule of the hereditary bishops of Liege, ousted by the Revolution of 1789. Then, in July of 1791, Austria committed to join Prussia in defending the monarchic government of Louis XVI in the so-called Declaration of Pillnitz. By September 30, 1791, when the opera premiered, Louis XVI and his family, foiled in their attempted flight, were under arrest and France had a new Republican constitution. As an argument in favor of enlightened but absolute monarchy, as a celebration of sovereignty, *The Magic Flute* was of this moment.

The abandonment of the abduction plot, at least in Tamino's story, may also reflect the opera's political-military context. The image of a beneficent sultan was probably untimely in 1791 when Austria was once more at war with the Ottoman Empire (the Austro-Turkish war ran from 1788 to 1791). Mozart, who from the end of 1787 was employed as royal chamber composer, supplied a bellicose and patriotic song, the "Lied beim Auszug in das Feld" (K. 552; August 11, 1788), intending to whip up support for this unpopular conflict.[35] In this context, perhaps, the opera was dragged by the seat of its Turkish trousers into another, less politically sensitive, pre-Islamic realm. These observations about the opera's military contexts are not central to this chapter, but they are important to understanding the immediate context in which it was conceived, performed, and understood.

To conclude, in this chapter I have offered an archaeology of the opera's diverse exoticism in a study of its poetics, not its politics. In doing so, I have come to realize that the exoticism of *The Magic Flute* – which, by standard definition, constructs an "alien" world, "remote" in time, place, and cultural norms from Vienna in 1791 – is itself rendered all the more exotic by the passage of time. *The Magic Flute* constructs the remote and alien in ways that are remote from (admittedly unstable) twenty-first-century cultural norms. For this reason, exoticism is not contained within the opera's fictional world, but informs all encounters with *The Magic Flute* today. The canonization of this opera, its status as a monument and masterwork, fosters the falsely proprietorial sensation that it belongs to us and is about us.

In its original form, however, it is lost to us. We must bring it forth through research, acts of the imagination, and – possibly revisionist – performance. Not only are the original sets and costumes lost; it was produced for a stage quite unlike that of modern opera houses. Narrow and deep, the stage was capable of near instantaneous transformations of scene via a rope-and-pulley technology that sent backdrops scuttling back and forth. One scene, with all its furniture, could be prepared behind another, and then revealed, in seconds. The effect was integral to the opera's fairy-tale and exotic character. With trap doors and aerial machinery, characters could appear and vanish, as if by magic. On modern stages, these sensational effects are impossible, creating a mismatch between the theatrical fiction and its mode of representation. Anglophone and other non-German-speaking students of the opera face additional losses. The German dialogue, which reveals so much about the characters' identities, is often abbreviated in performance; nor is it readily available, in full, in translation. Engaging historically with *The Magic Flute* involves a conjuring act or, to use an orientalist metaphor, a magic lamp through which the opera is constituted, in the mind's eye and ear, as at once familiar and strange, an exotic experience of something that is not simply there.

Notes

1. Ralph Locke, "Exoticism," in *Oxford Music Online* (accessed May 28, 2019).
2. I infer that the Three Slaves are white because slave three refers disparagingly to Monostatos as "der schwarze Monostatos" and as "der Mohr."
3. *Magic Flutes & Enchanted Forests: The Supernatural in Eighteenth-Century Musical Theater* (Chicago: University of Chicago Press, 2008), chap. 6.
4. Ralph Locke, *Music and the Exotic from the Renaissance to Mozart* (Cambridge: Cambridge University Press, 2015); *Musical Exoticism: Images and Reflections* (Cambridge: Cambridge University Press, 2009, corr. pb. 2011).
5. The slightly chilling phrase is not from Locke but from Carl Dahlhaus, *Nineteenth-Century Music*, trans. J. Bradford Robinson (Berkeley: University of California Press, 1989), 302.
6. Tamino wears a Japanese hunting costume in Act 1, scene 1. Older literature reported that a printing error in the first edition of the libretto (Vienna: Alberti, 1791) created an ambiguity – the costume could be read as Japanese or Javanese. However, Irmen reports that the libretto shows a broken "p" not "v." See Hans-Josef Irmen, *Mozart's Masonry and The Magic Flute*, trans. Ruth Ohm and Chantel Spenke (Zülpich: Prisca, 1996), 223.
7. For example, Nicolaes Maes's painting of Cornelis Munter (1679) shows a wraparound silk garment with central waist band, then known as a "Japanese jacket." See Charlotte Higgins, "The Old Black," *The Guardian* (June 22, 2007), www.theguardian.com/artanddesign/2007/jun/22/art.fashion.
8. All translations from *The Magic Flute* are my own.
9. Dorinda Outram, *The Enlightenment* (Cambridge: Cambridge University Press, 1995), 65.
10. See Ulrich Marzolph and Richard van Leeuwen, *The Arabian Nights Encyclopedia*, 2 vols. (Santa Barbara: ABC-Clio, 2004).

11. Srinivas Aravamudan, *Enlightenment Orientalism: Resisting the Rise of the Novel* (Chicago: University of Chicago Press, 2012).

12. Thomas Betzwieser, *Exotismus und "Türkenoper" in der französischen Musik des Ancien Régime* (Laaber: Laaber-Verlag, 1993). See also Matthew Head, *Orientalism, Masquerade and Mozart's Turkish Music* (London: Royal Musical Association, 2000), 40–49.

13. Noted in Larry Wolff, *The Singing Turk: Ottoman Power and Operatic Emotions on the European Stage from the Siege of Vienna to the Age of Napoleon* (Stanford, CA: Stanford University Press, 2016), 4.

14. Not always, however. See Matthew Head, "Interpreting 'Abduction' Opera: Haydn's *L'incontro improvviso*, Sovereignty and the Esterház Festival of 1775," *TheMA* 1/1 (2012): 1–18.

15. The phrase "household title" is from Aravamudan, *Enlightenment Orientalism*, 12.

16. Locke, *Music and the Exotic*, 74–75.

17. Edward W. Said, *Culture and Imperialism* (New York: Vintage, 1993), 133–58; *Orientalism* (1978; London: Penguin Books, 1995), 118.

18. See the lavishly illustrated discussion by Annette Frese, "'Das Theater verwandelt sich . . .': Bühnenbilder, Figurinen und Illustrationen zur Zauberflöte," in *Theater um Mozart*, ed. Bärbel Pelker (Heidelberg: Universitätsverlag Winter, 2006), 143–208.

19. Apuleius, *The Golden Ass,* bk. 11, sec. 5, cited from an original, parallel translation by Sarolta A. Takács in her "Initiations and Mysteries in Apuleius' *Metamorphoses*," *Electronic Antiquity* 12/1 (2008): 73–87, at 84.

20. Apuleius, *The Golden Ass,* bk. 11, sec. 21, cited from Takács, "Initiations and Mysteries," 85. Takács emphasizes that in withholding the wisdom of Isis, the text preserves the boundary between the un/initiated.

21. COH, 10–18, 21.

22. Florian Ebeling, "Ägyptische Freimaurerei zwischen Aufklärung und Romantik," in *O Isis und Osiris: Ägyptens Mysterien und die Freimauerei*, ed. Florian Ebeling and Christian E. Loeben (Rahden: Marie Leidorf, 2017), 29–124, at 44.

23. Buch, *Magic Flutes & Enchanted Forests*, 207–24, 245–63, and *passim*.

24. Leopold Mozart to Lorenz Hagenauer, Vienna, January 30–February 3, 1768. LMF, 80; MBA, I:254.

25. Marina Warner, *Stranger Magic: Charmed States & The Arabian Nights* (Cambridge, MA: Harvard University Press, 2011) also emphasizes narrative exuberance.

26. In a brilliant account of *The Magic Flute*, Abbate takes this further: "because the armored men also *sing* what they read, the scene suggests that music itself – pitches and rhythm – is encoded in the Egyptian ideograms on the pyramid." See Carolyn Abbate, *In Search of Opera* (Princeton, NJ: Princeton University Press, 2001), 95.

27. Cited from Andrew Haringer, "Hunt, Military, and Pastoral Topics," in *The Oxford Handbook of Topic Theory*, ed. Danuta Mirka (Oxford: Oxford University Press, 2014), chap. 6, at 200.

28. David E. Wellbery, *Lessing's Laocoon: Semiotics and Aesthetics in the Age of Reason* (Cambridge: Cambridge University Press, 1984), 6–7. Regeneration through antiquity is a broader topos of the period. See Downing A. Thomas, *Music and the Origins of Language: Theories from the French Enlightenment* (Cambridge: Cambridge University Press, 1995), 174–75.

29. This phase of my argument depends somewhat upon my study of eighteenth-century theories of music's origins. See "Birdsong and the Origins of Music," *Journal of the Royal Musical Association* 122/1 (1997): 1–23.

30. See COH, 99.

31. Outram, *Enlightenment*, 78.

32. See Abbate, *In Search of Opera*, chap. 2.

33. Heinrich C. Koch, *Kurzgefaßtes Handwörterbuch der Musik für praktische Tonkünstler und für Dilettanten* (1807; Hildesheim: Georg Olms, 1981), s.v. "Lied," 213–14.

34. Preface to Johann Abraham Peter Schulz, *Lieder im Volkston, bei dem Claviere zu singen*, 2nd edn., vol. 1 (Berlin: G. J. Decker, 1785). See also Matthew Head, *Sovereign Feminine: Music and Gender in Eighteenth-Century Germany* (Berkeley: California University Press, 2013), 138.

35. For discussion of this song and bibliography, see Head, *Orientalism*, 36–39.

14 | Partial Derivatives: Sources, Types, and Tropes in *The Magic Flute*

THOMAS BAUMAN

Fans of detective stories will remember that in both Agatha Christie's *Murder on the Orient Express* and A. Conan Doyle's "The Five Orange Pips" the difficulty confronting Poirot and Holmes is not one of too few suspects or too few clues, but too many. *The Magic Flute* has for much of its history posed a similar problem to those who have investigated the possible sources of its plot, characters, and meaning.

Several contributing factors spring immediately to mind. Information about the origins and gestation of the project remains unusually murky. Further, unlike the court-sanctioned operas that preceded it in Mozart's career, *The Magic Flute* made its initial home in a theatrical environment to which historians of opera have devoted relatively little attention. The collaboration with Schikaneder was also an unusual one for Mozart in that he was working with not just a librettist but also the commissioner of the work, the director of the theater where it was to be performed, and a principal in its first cast. But most of all, the text that Mozart's music brought to life grew out of no single, identifiable source.

Although our training has historically equipped musicologists to deal with musical sources rather than literary texts and their sources, we of course know that operas begin not as musical scores but as literary narratives, and that where those narratives come from and how they are shaped and reshaped for the musical stage is as much a part of an opera's pedigree as its musical genesis. This should be especially apparent for a work like *The Magic Flute*, destined as it was for a particular kind of musical stage, one on which words are not *poesia fatta per musica* but a combination of the spoken and sung delivered by actor-singers trained and practiced in, theatrically speaking, a bilingual tradition.

From the very beginning, efforts to identify the sources of *The Magic Flute* found themselves entangled in problems of interpretation, more often than not instigated by the well-nigh irresistible urge to uncover some hidden meaning beneath its motley, child-friendly surface. Ideally, historians of any art form should try to distinguish work-to-interpretation issues from source-to-work problems. In reality, however, they are always intermingling. For Mozart's earlier operas (*Così fan tutte* appears to be a notable exception) the presence of a single, clearly identifiable model helps regulate inquiry into both how a work came to be and what it has come to mean. The absence of a single-source model for *The Magic Flute*, however, opened to a tribe of hunter-gatherers a potentially limitless store of possible antecedents. Interest at first centered on fairy tales and other magic operas, but later, as the opera grew in stature, the stockpile expanded to include plays by Shakespeare and Calderón, the *Bildungsroman*, and legends from Classical antiquity.

How, then, does one go about assessing the wide array of candidates that over time have been scattered across the literature on *The Magic Flute* as models, or influences, or in some degree consanguine ancestors? It may prove useful to take as a point of departure the work of two writers, in fact both Germanists rather than musicologists by training, who have attempted a more or less systematic inventory while keeping at bay the legacy of legends and misinformation concerning the opera's genesis and authorship. Peter Branscombe's inaugural chapter in his Cambridge Opera Handbook, "The Sources," singles out seven literary antecedents drawn from a variety of genres: epic, novel, play, essay, and opera (both heroic and comic).[1] These he orders not by weight but by date, from the twelfth-century French romance *Yvain*, to *Kasper der Fagottist*, an exact Viennese contemporary of Mozart's opera. Egon Komorzynski chose a different path in his biography of Schikaneder, whom he spent half a century defending from calumny and disparagement.[2] He orders his sources following what he imagines to have been the creative stages that led to the finished opera.

Choosing his words carefully, Branscombe strives for an evenhanded, impartial evaluation. The relevance of the Arthurian *Yvain*, previously absent from the literature on *The Magic Flute*, he limits to the opera's opening scene, for whose origins "no satisfactory explanation has so far been offered."[3] He lavishes greatest attention on the French novel *Sethos* (1731), identifying both parallels and outright borrowings. Branscombe notes some "resemblances" in Tobias von Gebler's tragedy *Thamos, König in Ägypten* (1773, itself much indebted to *Sethos*), but after only a single paragraph on the play he turns his attention to Mozart's incidental music as the more significant link. Next, he notes a few "verbal echoes" in Schikaneder's text from Ignaz von Born's essay on the mysteries of the Egyptians (1784), but he reserves discussion of Freemasonry as an influence for a separate chapter on the opera's "intellectual background." In 1856 Otto Jahn had declared that Schikaneder's play began life as in essence a dramatization of "Lulu, oder Die Zauberflöte," a *Märchen* from Wieland's three-volume collection *Dschinnistan* (1787–89). Although

Jahn's assertion maintained uncritical currency for the next century, Branscombe finds the story's importance exaggerated and, moreover, has little to say about the significance of the other tales in the collection, which many have found an important fund of motifs and features. He puts more stock in Carl Ludwig Giesecke's (unacknowledged) adaptation of Sophie Seyler's *Hüon und Amande* for Paul Wranitzky as *Oberon*, given its premiere under Schikaneder's direction in 1789. Branscombe not only hears "literary echoes" of this work in *The Magic Flute* but also finds common dramatic situations. (Edward Dent, too, had singled it out as an "obvious" model.[4]) Another contemporary Viennese magic opera, however, Perinet's farrago *Kaspar der Fagottist*, produced by Schikaneder's rival Marinelli while he and Mozart labored on their own opera, and which gave rise to the notorious "plot reversal" thesis, Branscombe dismisses curtly as "probably not a material influence."

Earlier, Komorzynski had also canvassed many of these antecedents, but his analysis bristles with the biases and distortions that Branscombe had been at pains to avoid. First, the fifty years separating the two editions of his biography of Schikaneder had only deepened Komorzynski's atrabilious exasperation and disgust with Otto Jahn's many "falsehoods" disparaging Schikaneder and promoting Giesecke as the true author of *The Magic Flute*. Second, he rejected out of hand Jahn's warm advocacy of "Lulu" as model and instead declared, with even greater enthusiasm and considerably less evidence, that Gebler's *Thamos* was the opera's "main foundation." Komorzynski seems to have been seduced by the loftier dramatic pedigree of Gebler's heroic plot, coupled with a more general urge to restore Schikaneder's literary credentials, which Jahn and Dent had denied him and invested instead in "Professor" Giesecke. But in pairing up successive scenes in *The Magic Flute* with this "main foundation," Komorzynski can adduce little beyond the priestly scenes in Act 2 and the similarity of the names Thamos and Tamino to support his leading candidate.

Both Branscombe and Komorzynski confine their source surveys to literary works and treat separately other social and cultural influences on the opera. The most familiar and most discussed of these is of course Freemasonry. Outside Vienna a few forays proposing or suggesting Masonic associations had already appeared in the 1790s, but it was again Jahn who gave Freemasonry property rights to a decisive share in the opera's character and meaning. Serious study of Freemasonry as a hidden allegory, however, began only with Paul Nettl in 1932, ratified in Jacques Chailley's elaborate scene-by-scene exegesis in 1968.[5]

The Masonic allegory enjoyed steady, if not exclusive, hermeneutic favor until 2004, when David Buch mounted a spirited attack on Masonic and other esoteric and cryptic readings of the opera, which in his view had eclipsed or obscured its indebtedness to popular traditions.[6] Having studied in detail European fairy-tale literature, Schikaneder's earlier stage works, and the repertoires of Vienna's suburban theaters, Buch concludes that a great many of the purportedly Masonic elements in *The Magic Flute*, as well as other striking features of the libretto, could as readily have been found by Schikaneder in these contemporaneous sources (plot reversal, rejection of Monostatos, the trial scene, misogyny, the Three Genii, and thwarted suicides). Buch's larger aim, however, was not simply to debunk the excesses of Masonic readings but to sketch, in both its literary and musical dimensions, the lineaments of a new Viennese genre, the eighteenth-century "fairy-tale opera."

Earlier, Stefan Kunze had rejected this designation: "[The opera's] world of images is related to the fairy tale," he wrote in 1982, "but the work itself is no 'fairy-tale opera.'"[7] Kunze called it instead "a drama of education" ("*ein Erziehungsdrama*"). Instruction as a tenet of theatrical representation is of course as old as theater itself, but the trials and spiritual growth Tamino and Pamina undergo had no precedent in Mozart's earlier operas – nor in Schikaneder's, for that matter. Their trials also bear only fleeting resemblance to those found in eighteenth-century literary antecedents like Rousseau's *Émile* or Goethe's *Wilhelm Meister*.

What kind of an opera did Schikaneder and Mozart themselves think they were writing? Mozart's personal catalogue called *The Magic Flute* simply "a German opera" ("*eine teutsche Oper*"), and Schikaneder's published libretto carried the designation "eine große Oper" (a grand opera) – a term neither man had used before and which most probably was prompted by the production's lavish visual effects and considerable musical ambitions. Something on this order was apparently what struck Salieri and the singer Cavalieri when they attended a performance as Mozart's guests: "You cannot believe," Mozart wrote to Constanze, "how agreeable they both were, – how greatly not only my music but the libretto and everything taken together pleased them. They both said it was an opera worthy to be performed at the grandest festivity before the grandest monarch."[8]

Beyond being told to expect something grand, those at the premiere who carried a copy of Schikaneder's published text into the theater would have found little additional help in its cast list. From top to bottom, the characters are listed by name and nothing else – no descriptor to suggest role type, occupation, or relationship to each other. Kunze's strained attempt to subsume the seven principals under the traditional eighteenth-century system of role types only serves to highlight how little *The Magic Flute* relies on familiar theatrical conventions. One could argue, and with more than a little justification, that many of the most memorable characters in Mozart's earlier Viennese operas also defy categorization as mere role types (Osmin, the Countess, Don Giovanni, and Fiordiligi come immediately to mind). But even here the associations and parallels occasionally proposed by commentators between the cast of *The Magic Flute* and figures from other Mozart operas (Monostatos – Osmin, Sarastro – Don Alfonso, Pamina – Ilia) fail to capture any real continuity with the past.

Still and all, if the characters do not conform to traditional role types, their actions may yet conform to a familiar plot type. But here, too, the opera frustrates expectations. Of Northrop Frye's four narrative categories (Comedy, Romance, Tragedy, and Satire), Romance is the only one that comes close to the opera's unusual plotline.[9] According to Frye, a Romance narrative, typically chivalric, is most fully realized in "the successful quest," which has three stages: perilous journey (*agon*), crucial struggle (*pathos*), and exaltation of the hero (*anagnorisis*). A good deal of torsion is needed to twist the plot of *The Magic Flute* and its protagonist into conformity with this scheme. Its crypto-Egyptian setting, unlike the one traversed by Giesecke's knight-errant in *Oberon*, is anything but medieval, and a protagonist whose first line is "Help!" and whose first onstage act is to faint is anything but chivalric. Similarly, Frye's description of the hero of a Romance as "a central character who never develops" works for Hüon in *Oberon* but not for Tamino. Though, in the literal sense, the opera's protagonist[10] Tamino as hero emerges only slowly. In fact, once the Queen has sent him on his quest to rescue her daughter, we lose track of his adventures for a while and involve ourselves instead with the perils besetting Pamina and Papageno. Tamino's "crucial struggle" in his confrontation with the Priest in the Act 1 finale pits him against not the dark antagonist Frye prescribes but his benighted self, and the exaltation he receives at the end of the opera is not for him alone as its hero but for the couple ("euch Geweihten") of which he forms a part.

Taken together, the poor fit in *The Magic Flute* of traditional plot types and role types, as well as its marked deviations from Mozart's earlier operas and from the fare in its own day at Vienna's suburban theaters, together with the slow but spectacular growth in enthusiasm for the new work, all reinforce the perception of the opera as something new and unexpected. To see Mozart's last opera as not a culminating but an exploratory work should also put to rest much of the accumulated nonsense about the opera's conception and creation: that Schikaneder tapped Mozart for a popular work to save him from bankruptcy, for instance, or that its plot was changed in desperation over its similarity to a rival work, or that it was a defensive action to "save the Craft."[11]

Mozarteans have in fact shown little inclination to celebrate *The Magic Flute* as the culminating masterpiece of his operatic career, but prefer to see it instead as the dawn of what would have been a new chapter in that career. Some Austro-German writers go even further in proclaiming it the gateway work that inaugurated and inspired nineteenth-century German Romantic opera. Kunze, who declares it "a manifesto of a new, higher, and elevated humanity," draws comparisons throughout his chapter on the opera not with other Viennese magic operas, about which he seems to have known little, but with the music of Beethoven and Wagner.[12]

While the atypicality of *The Magic Flute* opened a wide field for its exegetes, what seems puzzling is the need felt by many of them to stake a claim to sole proprietorship of the work's meaning and to put down other claimants. It may be worth considering whether their different readings are necessarily at odds with each other. For example, to acknowledge the currency of some of the opera's features in popular sources does not invalidate their Masonic associations, and initiation into esoteric rituals ought to enrich rather than obscure connections to the idea of a drama of education.

In his book *The Genesis of Secrecy* Frank Kermode explored the implications for literary divination of works that invite both popular and esoteric interpretations.[13] He pointed in particular to a passage in the Gospel of Mark where Jesus tells his disciples why he preaches in parables. Somewhat surprisingly, Jesus tells them that he does so not to reveal spiritual truths but instead to hide them from "those on the outside . . . so that they may indeed see but not perceive, and may hear but not understand." Only to his disciples, to the initiates, are such mysteries to be disclosed.

Kermode labeled the different interpretations made available to outsiders and insiders as, respectively, "carnal" and "spiritual." As one of the high priests of academia, he naturally favored the latter and saw a direct parallel to them in the dissection, divination, and deconstruction of narrative texts that goes on in university seminar rooms. An even greater authority had much earlier voiced a similar distinction between popular and esoteric readings and applied it specifically to Schikaneder's libretto. Toward the end of his long life, Goethe, talking to Eckermann about his forthcoming *Faust II*, speculated that the "unwashed" will no doubt be content to take pleasure in what they see, whereas "the higher meaning will not escape the initiate, as is the case with *The Magic Flute* and other things."[14]

Practically from its inception, the special nature of *The Magic Flute* has inspired a steady stream of deep dives into a seemingly bottomless pool of hidden meanings. In addition to the perennial Masonic explorations, an assortment of allegorical, metaphorical, symbolic, mystical, numerological, and archetypal constructions continue to bear out Jocelyn Godwin's twin observations that all great symbolic works of art engender a variety of interpretations and that, in the case of *The Magic Flute* in particular, its exegetes "all find the libretto sensible, consistent, and full of meaning."[15] Franz Grasberger goes even further: for him the opera is every inch a *Symbolstück* whose plot simply cannot be taken at face value.[16]

For those who view *The Magic Flute* as a kind of parable enshrouded in esoteric lore, it follows almost of necessity that insiders' interpretations based on such lore will be deeper, higher, and more spiritual than ones discerned by "those on the outside." Gernot Gruber has suggested a different analytic division, one that avoids the bias that the insider-outsider model enjoins.[17] Interpretations in one group, which he labels causal-historical, ground themselves in the opera's cultural-political world; those in a second, metahistorical group dispense with this limitation in favor of the abstract, the mythic, or the universally human.

The first thing we might notice is that hidden meanings can fall into the first as readily as the second of Gruber's categories. In the opera's early years, for example, writers in the Francophile Rhineland took the Queen of the Night as a cipher for the *Ancien Régime*, while those in conservative Austria saw her realm as a coded depiction of the Revolution's Jacobin rabble. The second thing to notice is that for much of the opera's reception history these and similar causal-historical readings predominated. In 1923 Emil Blümml inventoried a spate of such "*Ausdeutungen*," many of them political allegories and all of them fitting comfortably in Gruber's causal-historical track.[18] Metahistorical in(ter)ventions, on the other hand, have grown ascendant in our postmodern age. This shift brought with it a turn from interpretations that favor allegory to explorations that rely on the symbol and the archetype.

Archetypes differ from causal-historical categories like role types and plot types precisely in their metahistorical character. One sees this immediately in the case of Papageno. Jahn's biography had labeled him causal-historically as a "Hanswurst," a clown figure indispensable to Viennese popular theater, an ascription repeated in 1920 by Hermann Abert in his revision of Jahn's work. Some recent writers see Papageno instead as an instance of the "wild man" archetype, familiar in German folklore but, as Ehrhard Bahr has noticed, almost entirely absent from eighteenth-century German literature.[19] Godwin has applied the concept of the archetype developed by Carl Jung with enthusiasm to the other principal roles in *The Magic Flute* (Tamino–anima, Pamina–animus, Monostatos–shadow, Sarastro–sage, Queen of the Night–devouring mother). He concedes that, unlike allegorical interpretations, Jungian archetypes "cannot have been in the creators' minds," but they nonetheless find their justification in Jung's collective unconscious. Further, he implies that the opera's second act inevitably demands of its interpreters some such hermeneutic tool. "The historical-allegorical interpretations may explain the characters and the basic plot, but if that were all, the opera might as well end as soon as Tamino's loyalties are transferred to Sarastro at the end of Act 1."[20]

Archetypes, while they may liberate the interpreter from the constraints of history (and of whatever may have been in the authorial mind), remain types, and pretty rigid ones at that. Other interpreters have preferred to approach the opera armed with the more flexible arsenal furnished by the symbol. Here, *The Magic Flute* offers no end of low-hanging fruit. In harvesting this bounty, one master trope has outdone all others – the conflict between day and night, light and darkness, and between their personification in Sarastro and the Queen of the Night. The danger in deployments of this trope has lain in construing its oppositions in extreme or even absolute terms. Grasberger, for example, describes Sarastro as "the completely spiritualized man, in his way as unreal as the Queen of the Night is uncanny."[21] For Chailley, theirs is an irreconcilable conflict between two worlds, masculine and feminine. Alfons Rosenberg does Chailley one better: for him, they are locked in the mother of all wars, "the primeval battle between the powers of light and darkness," which he traces back to Babylonian and biblical creation myths.[22]

Night and day, light and darkness, are what cultural anthropologists like to call complementary opposites: together, they comprise a whole, but not a higher-order one. That achievement is left to the new initiates, Pamina and Tamino. As the embodiment of "Schönheit und Weisheit" (in the words of the final chorus), they hold out at the opera's end a utopian promise. The opera, however, leaves identifying what this might be to its exegetes.

In the theater, of course, utopianism is bad for business, and both Goethe's attempted sequel and Schikaneder's own "Part Two," *Das*

Labyrinth, paint a dark future for the young couple, in which the Queen
and her minions return to resume the "primeval battle." Several recent
writers have turned instead to the original engagement and to calling into
question its tropological self-evidence. This has required some creative
engineering. Jessica Waldoff, for example, amalgamates the opera's master
trope with the quest archetype. Sarastro and the Queen necessarily recede
into the background as the opera's "dominant metaphor" transmutes from
a standoff to a journey, from the intractable opposition of Night and Day to
"the move from darkness to light."[23] That this is Tamino's journey she
emphasizes with a liberty she takes in translating his cry at the very heart of
the drama:

> O ewige Nacht! Wann wirst du schwinden?
> Wann wird das Licht mein Auge finden?

Word order suggests that the second verse of this couplet should read in
English: "When will the light find my eye?" Waldoff, however, does greater
justice to Tamino's quest by translating it poetically as "When will my eyes
find the light?" She also stresses that, although the "high-minded theme" of
The Magic Flute is a quest for knowledge (rather than for a damsel in
distress), historically and ideologically the opera is a post-Enlightenment
work in which the enlightenment Tamino seeks is to be spelled with
a lower-case "e." By this orthographic change, Waldoff effectively relocates
the concept of enlightenment from its eighteenth-century cultural-
historical acceptation to Gruber's metahistorical category and its orientation toward the universally human.

Another strand of recent scholarship dealing with the opera and its
symbols revisits Sarastro, and especially the Queen, in order to wrest
them from their traditional roles as simple hypostatizations of the two
poles of its master trope and to explore each of them instead as complex
and, indeed, contradictory individuals.

Petra Fischer, in her essay "The Rehabilitation of Sensual Nature," warns
that the night–day dichotomy is insufficient as an interpretation of either
the opera itself or the Queen and Sarastro.[24] As a topos, darkness-and-light
is not as simple as black-and-white. Like Kunze, she rejects the
Märchenoper designation, under which the opera's master trope reduces
to the unnuanced good–evil antinomy of fairy tales. The stories in
Dschinnistan, to look no further, ask us to accept without explanation the
assignment of good and evil to their characters. In *The Magic Flute*,
however, the Queen is not immediately and existentially evil. She has
a back story. Her earlier marriage suggests that the opera's two opposing

spheres were once united but have since degenerated and reached a point of imbalance that she and Sarastro are incapable of righting. The eponymous magic flute itself becomes of interest in Fischer's interpretation: unlike Oberon's horn and similar magic instruments in other operas, it has an origin separate from its donor, in the prelapsarian world of Pamina's father. Pamina, in fact, is for Fischer the key to the "rehabilitation" in the title of her essay, for it is she who tells Tamino the story of the flute's origin, and who must undergo her own trials (more severe than Tamino's, because more real) before the world she remembers can emerge once more. The joint initiation of Tamino and Pamina, then, suggests not so much a restoration of an old order, which few in 1791 would have thought feasible, as something akin to Miranda's "brave new world."

If commentators have often idealized Pamina as a child of nature, they have just as often cast her mother as the embodiment of *Unnatur*, as a being so consumed by her power struggle with Sarastro that she is willing to suborn even that most natural of bonds, between mother and child, to bring about his destruction. In her revisionist portrait of the Queen, Kristi Brown-Montesano has argued against taking Sarastro and the Queen as simple avatars of the opera's master trope, for where there is no real parity of power there can be no real dualism. Despite the advance publicity of Papageno and the Three Ladies, the Queen gives only the appearance of a powerful absolute potentate. Beneath this exterior roils an inner mother-ruler conflict.[25] Mozart's memorable music for her, in consequence, amounts to little more than a sham display of power, masking her inability to take matters into her own hands. Brown-Montesano pleads for the restoration in Act 2 of the full spoken dialogue between mother and daughter preceding "Der Hölle Rache," routinely cut or even eliminated from performances and recordings and the only instance where the Queen admits her powerlessness: "Dear child," she tells Pamina, "your mother can no longer protect you. All my power was buried with your father."

Alfred Einstein once wrote: "Never did Mozart write 'for eternity,' and it is precisely for that reason that much of what he wrote is for eternity."[26] As a proposition this makes little sense, a point we can demonstrate easily enough by simply substituting another composer of the day for Mozart. ("Never did Dittersdorf write 'for eternity,' and it is precisely for that reason that much of what he wrote is for eternity.") In terms of our present discussion, though, what Einstein seems to have done is to draw a metahistorical conclusion from a causal-historical premise. This conflating of Gruber's two categories invites us to consider whether they may, like the many interpretations they subsume, complement rather than compete with each other. The trick is to expand and integrate rather than reduce and eliminate. That may not be an especially welcome prospect for those who must decide how to stage the opera. Like Poirot and Holmes, they will face not too few options but too many. Happily, those who write about this provocative work need contend with no similar perplexity. For, as a member in particularly good standing of Godwin's "great symbolic works of art," *The Magic Flute* will no doubt continue to attract mutually enriching, multidimensional readings of its plot, characters, and meaning.

Notes

1. COH, 4–34.
2. Egon Komorzynski *Emanuel Schikaneder: Ein Beitrag zur Geschichte des deutschen Theaters*, 2nd edn. (Vienna: Ludwig Doblinger, 1951; orig. pub. Berlin: B. Behr's Verlag, 1901).
3. COH, 7.
4. Edward J. Dent, *Mozart's Operas: A Critical Study*, 2nd edn. (London: Oxford University Press, 1947; orig. pub. London: Chatto & Windus, 1913). Dent, however, is talking about Wranitzky's music as a model for Mozart, who "was not a practised hand at writing the kind of opera that Schikaneder wanted" (ibid., 243). Dent's own research into the sources of Schikaneder's play centers on *Sethos*.
5. As the title of his study indicates, Chailley took Schikaneder's contribution as seriously as Mozart's: Jacques Chailley *La Flûte enchantée, opéra maçonnique: Essai d'explication du livret et de la musique* (Paris: R. Laffont, 1968).
6. David J. Buch, "*Die Zauberflöte*, Masonic Opera, and Other Fairy Tales," *Acta Musicologica* 76/2 (2004): 193–219; "Fairy-Tale Literature and *Die Zauberflöte*," *Acta Musicologica* 64/1 (1992): 30–49.
7. "Ihre Bildwelt ist dem Märchen verwandt, das Werk aber kein 'Märchenoper.'" Stefan Kunze, "*Die Zauberflöte*: Theater als Sinnbild," in *Mozarts Opern* (Stuttgart: Philipp Reclam jun., 1984), 554–646, at 584.
8. Letter of October 14, 1791. MBA, IV:161–62.
9. Northrop Frye, *Anatomy of Criticism: Four Essays* (Princeton: Princeton University Press, 1957), 186–206.
10. "The Greek *protagonistes* means the actor who takes the chief part in a play. . . . Pro- in *protagonist* is not the opposite of *anti-*; *-agonist* is not the same as in *antagonist*." H. W. Fowler, *A Dictionary of Modern English Usage* (Oxford: Clarendon Press, 1926), 471.

11. This hare-brained notion, which scarcely deserves a moment's serious consideration, features in H. C. Robbins Landon. *1791: Mozart's Last Year* (London: Thames and Hudson, 1988), 127–37.

12. Kunze, *Mozarts Opern*, 554.

13. Frank Kermode, *The Genesis of Secrecy: On the Interpretation of Narrative* (Cambridge, MA: Harvard University Press, 1979).

14. "Wenn es nur so ist, daß die Menge der Zuschauer Freude an der *Erscheinung* hat; dem Eingeweihten wird zugleich der höhere Sinn nicht entgehen, wie es ja auch bei der 'Zauberflöte' und anderen Dingen der Fall ist" (January 29, 1827). Johann Peter Eckermann, *Gespräche mit Goethe in den letzten Jahren seines Lebens*, ed. Ludwig Geiger (Leipzig: Max Hesse, [1902]), 174. The joy of the spectator alluded to here must be distinguished from the deception practiced in the name of secrecy that Kermode describes (see *supra*, n. 13). It suggests rather the well-known distinction Mozart himself drew between *Liebhaber* and *Kenner* when writing to his father about the Viennese reception of his keyboard concertos in his letter of December 28, 1782. LMF, 833; MBA III: 245–46.

15. Jocelyn Godwin, "Layers of Meaning in *The Magic Flute*," *Musical Quarterly* 65/4 (1979): 471–92, at 472–73.

16. Franz Grasberger, "Zur Symbolik der *Zauberflöte*," in *Bericht über den internationalen musikwissenschaftlichen Kongreß Wien Mozartjahr 1956*, ed. Erich Schenk (Graz: H. Böhlaus Nachf., 1958), 249–52, at 250.

17. Gernot Gruber, "Bedeutung und Spontaneität in Mozarts *Zauberflöte*," in *Festschrift Walter Senn zum 70. Geburtstag*, ed. Ewald Fässler (Munich: E. Katzbichler, 1975), 118–30, at 118.

18. Emil Blümml, "Ausdeutungen der *Zauberflöte*," *Mozart-Jahrbuch* 1923, 109–46.

19. Ehrhard Bahr, "Papageno: The Unenlightened Wild Man in Eighteenth-Century Germany," in *The Wild Man Within: An Image in Western Thought from the Renaissance to Romanticism*, ed. Edward Dudley and Maximillian E. Novak (Pittsburgh: University of Pittsburgh Press, 1972), 249–57.

20. Godwin, "Layers of Meaning," 484.

21. Grasberger, "Zur Symbolik," 251.

22. ". . . den Urkampf zwischen den Mächten des Lichtes und der Finsternis." Alfons Rosenberg, "Die Symbolik von Mozart's *Zauberflöte*," *Symbolon: Jahrbuch für Symbolforschung* 3 (1962): 64–76, at 68.

23. Jessica Waldoff, "Operatic Enlightenment in *Die Zauberflöte*," in *Recognition in Mozart's Operas* (Oxford: Oxford University Press, 2006), 17–43, at 19 (orig. pub. as "The Music of Recognition: Operatic Enlightenment in *The Magic Flute*," *Music & Letters* 75/2 [May 1994]: 214–35).

24. Petra Fischer, "Die Rehabilitierung der Sinnlichkeit: Philosophische Implikationen der Figurenkonstellation der *Zauberflöte*," *Archiv für Musikwissenschaft* 50/1 (1993): 1–25.

25. Kristi Brown-Montesano, "Feminine Vengeance II: (Over)Powered Politics: The Queen of the Night," in *Understanding the Women of Mozart's Operas* (Berkeley: University of California Press, 2007), 81–106. Her monograph also includes chapters on Pamina and the Three Ladies.

26. Alfred Einstein, *Mozart: His Character, His Work*, trans. Arthur Mendel and Nathan Broder (New York: Oxford University Press, 1945), 109.

Pamina, the Queen, and the Representation
of Women

JESSICA WALDOFF

For most of *The Magic Flute*'s history, its representation of women went unquestioned. Now, however, this aspect of the work is widely regarded as problematic. With its foregrounding of Sarastro's temple and his order, the worldview represented on the stage is largely that of a brotherhood of men who espouse highly objectionable views of women. At the temple gates a Priest instructs Tamino: "So a woman has beguiled you? A woman does little, talks much" (Act 1, scene 15).[1] As the trial of silence commences, Tamino and Papageno are warned by the Priests in their duet (No. 11): "Beware of women's tricks; this is the first duty of the Brotherhood" (Act 2, scene 3). Tamino learns quickly from his new mentors, instructing Papageno in the Act 2 quintet: "She [the Queen] is a woman, and has a woman's mind." Meanwhile, Sarastro advises Pamina: "A man must lead your hearts, for without his guidance every woman tends to step out of her natural sphere" (Act 1, scene 18). These and other statements are framed in general terms, but they complicate the opera's portrayal of its female characters, especially Pamina and the Queen of the Night.

Often in modern productions these and other misogynistic lines are altered, mistranslated in the supertitles, or left out. The opera's representation of women, however, is not created by the sung and spoken text alone. To the contrary, it also depends on the events of the plot and the way the conflict at the heart of it is dramatized and resolved. The opera sets the rule of men, led by Sarastro, against the rights of a woman, the Queen. The forces of light vs. dark, truth vs. falsehood, and knowledge vs. ignorance are all aligned in the opera as male vs. female. By the end of the opera, a powerful woman and her entourage – consisting of her Three Ladies and the Moor, Monostatos – have joined forces to fight an established order of "wise" men. The opera's "happy" ending is thus achieved (at least in part) by the exclusion of "others" who threaten the temple.

These basic elements of character and plot are difficult to alter or reconceive in performance. Directors have nonetheless tried to do so. Ingmar Bergman, for example, in his 1975 film *The Magic Flute*, transformed Sarastro into the Queen's estranged husband and Pamina's father, thus creating a personal reason for the Queen's resentment. He thereby reduced a clash of worlds to a family conflict. Increasingly in modern productions, the Queen is made to look less human and more otherworldly or cartoonish. Julie Taymor created a truly extraordinary Queen for the Metropolitan Opera House (2004): she appears larger than life through the use of multiple wing-like extensions to her costume operated by puppeteers. Barrie Kosky's Queen for the Komische Oper Berlin (2012) is conceived as a giant animated spider who appears, literally, to trap Tamino and Pamina in her web. It is not uncommon to see the Queen in a costume inspired – at least in part – by one of Disney's evil queens, making her appear more two-dimensional. But do such changes to the text or the costumes change the role misogyny plays in the story? Does a more cardboard or cartoonish characterization of the Queen – or Monostatos, for that matter   make it easier to accept the opera's celebratory ending from which they are excluded?

How, then, should we understand the opera's representation of women? Attempting to answer this question may help us to better understand and appreciate both Pamina and the Queen. It may also allow us to reconcile the opera's problematic attitudes toward gender with its dramatization of Enlightenment themes. To begin, we might compare the opera's representation of women to its assumptions about how they behave.

Gender as Perspective

It has become a commonplace in recent decades that "gender" is a cultural concept rather than a "natural" or biological one. In an essay that explores the role of gender in literary and cultural analysis, Myra Jehlen writes:

In this sense, gender may be opposed to sex as culture is to nature so that its relation to sexual nature is unknown and probably unknowable: how, after all, do we speak of human beings outside of culture? From the perspective of gender, identity is a role, character traits are not autonomous qualities but functions and ways of relating. Actions define actors rather than vice versa. Connoting history and not nature, gender is *not* a category of human nature.[2]

The representation of women in *The Magic Flute* depends on both a text and a context in which "character traits are not autonomous qualities but functions and ways of relating." Gender is performed on stage within a clearly established context and frame of reference, one that has changed dramatically in the wider world since the opera was first conceived and produced. For this reason, gender is an aspect of the work that complicates modern readings and performances of the opera.

Lest it be thought that gender is a subject more important to us moderns than it was to those in the eighteenth century, it is worth noting how concerned contemporary writers were with shaping the education, behavior, inclinations, habits, morals – the very identity – of young persons of both sexes. Take, for example, Rousseau's *Émile*, which addresses the education and development of both his hero (a natural man brought up away from the corruption of society) and his intended wife, Sophie. "The man," he writes, "should be strong and active; the woman should be weak and passive; the one must have both the power and the will; it is enough that the other should offer little resistance."[3] Book V is devoted to Sophie, who "must possess all those characters of her sex which are required to enable her to play her part in the physical and moral order."[4] The influence of Rousseau's *Émile* can hardly be overstated. In her *Vindication of the Rights of Woman*, published in 1792, Mary Wollstonecraft challenges *Émile* and its author repeatedly. "The private or public virtue of woman is very problematical," she writes, "for Rousseau, and a numerous list of male writers, insist that she should all her life be subjected to a severe restraint."[5]

The differences between the sexes, though not a new topic, were now widely studied in the eighteenth century, and a growing body of medical and other writings attempted to establish these differences as biological and observable. In *The Enlightenment*, Dorinda Outram explains: "Women were increasingly defined as closer to 'nature' than were men, as well as being more determined by 'nature', meaning anatomy and physiology. . . . Equally the notion that women are closer to nature than men included . . . the claim that because of their physical 'nature' they were emotional, credulous, and incapable of objective reasoning."[6] Central to this view, as G. J. Barker-Benfield explains, was a gendered understanding of the nerves: "not only were women's nerves interpreted as more delicate and more susceptible than men's, but women's ability to operate their nerves by acts of will . . . was seriously questioned."[7] Kant, in his *Observations on the Feeling of the Beautiful and Sublime*, makes exactly this point: "The content of woman's great science, rather, is humankind . . . . Her philosophy is not to reason, but to sense."[8] In his final chapter he associates the terms of his title with the natural qualities of the two genders: "one expects that a person of either sex brings both [the beautiful and the noble] together, in such a way that all the other merits of a woman should unite solely to enhance the character of the beautiful, which is the proper reference point; and . . .

among the masculine qualities the sublime clearly stands out as the criterion of his kind."[9]

The cultural context for understanding gender roles is not merely one in which the opera was conceived, it is located *in* the opera itself. The opera's statements on gendered behavior may be understood as part of the moral didacticism that Martin Nedbal associates with the goals of German national theater.[10] Just as the opera lays out its tenets concerning the behavior of women, it lays out clear guidelines for the behavior of men. As the Three Boys lead Tamino to the temple gates, they instruct him: "Be steadfast, patient, and discreet – be mindful of this, in short, be a man" (Act 1, scene 15). Tamino tells Papageno: "A wise man considers and does not heed what the common rabble says" (Act 2, scene 5). In the Act 2 quintet, all moralize together: "A man is strong in spirit; he thinks before he speaks." At one point, when Papageno is told "Be a man!" he replies, "I wish I were a girl!" (Act 2, scene 2).

To understand the opera's representation of gender, we do not need to be fully versed in contemporary views of the subject. The opera constructs gender roles as it unfolds through its use of situations and language. To use Jehlen's phrase, "actions define actors." Women, the opera tells us, require the guidance of wise men: with it, they have great potential for virtue and love; without this guidance, they are likely to gossip, beguile, and mislead. Nevertheless, Schikaneder and Mozart's strikingly vivid characterizations of Pamina and the Queen complicate many of the opera's patriarchal assumptions and raise important questions about gender and power.

Pamina as an Idealized Image

As a heroine of the sentimental genres, Pamina is characterized by her virtue, her capacity for feeling, and her ability to arouse pathos in others. Her goodness and courage prove not only that she is destined for Tamino but that she is his match in both temperament and character. In Act 2, Tamino, Pamina, and the two Armored Men sing, "A woman who does not fear night and death is worthy and will be initiated" (scene 28). The implication is clear: Pamina, who has already faced "night" (despair) and "death" (suicide), is such a woman. She is transformed from a maiden in need of rescue into a seeker of Enlightenment. While she achieves an extraordinary destiny, she does so without contravening period expectations. For this reason, Pamina's virtue is ultimately rewarded with the man of her heart and initiation into the temple.

Pamina's first appearance in Act 1 is not in person, but as a portrait that the Three Ladies present to Tamino. The stage directions describe what happens next: "Tamino, from the moment he received the portrait, has been absorbed in it; his love increases, as if he were deaf to all these exchanges." Tamino does not notice the exit of the Three Ladies, nor that Papageno remains behind. He then sings his aria "Dies Bildnis," during which the portrait's effect continues to take hold. The key is arguably significant – E-flat, the key of the overture, the upcoming duet about the power of love, "Bei Männern," and "Heiligtum." Schikaneder and Mozart deliberately focus attention on the male gaze rather than on its object. We are invited to see the loveliness that transfixes Tamino through his eyes.

Mozart creates a sense of affective immediacy by having Tamino begin without any preamble from the orchestra. His melody opens with a leap of a sixth ("This image is enchantingly fair"), an interval often used to characterize statements of love, which here suggests the sudden blossoming of affection. The interval is repeated in the second line a step lower and again on the repetition of "mein Herz" (my heart) in line 4. His growing affection is confirmed in line 3 – "Ich fühl' es" (I feel it) – emphasized by an appoggiatura on the key word "fühl'," and then repeated. Tamino is not merely gazing at the portrait but is deeply affected by it. In the second verse, he describes the sensation he feels ("burning like fire") and asks if it can be love. Mozart poses the question with a pregnant pause on the dominant of the new key (m. 25). Tamino then answers "Ja, ja, die Liebe ist's allein" (Yes, yes, it can only be love) and confirms the arrival in B-flat. The effect could hardly be more convincing if he had actually met Pamina.

This portrait (an image) is one of the opera's most important representations. Its transformative effect on Tamino is not merely a necessary plot spring; it leads to a second representation (the aria), an unfolding of the first, that reveals the naturalness and spontaneity of emotional life. In creating this scene, Schikaneder and Mozart depicted a conception of the relationship of beholder and artwork that was new in the eighteenth century. Tamino's rapt attention is a version of the "absorption" Michael Fried discusses in his *Absorption and Theatricality: Painting and Theatricality in the Age of Diderot*.[11] Tamino's ability to *see* Pamina – to imagine he is with her, to develop strong feelings for her, to envision their future life together – only from gazing at her portrait illustrates something the French critic Denis Diderot claimed was true about the paintings of Greuze and others: that they could inspire sensation and feeling in the beholder, blurring the distinction between the world of the canvas and the real world. Such portraits and other paintings were valued for their ability to *absorb* the beholder (stopping the beholder motionless before a painting and inspiring a profound sense of connection with the painting's subject) and to *represent* absorption (creating the illusion of a world in the painting in which its subjects are completely overwhelmed by feeling and separated from the beholder's gaze). Tamino's aria demonstrates both qualities of absorption: he is consumed by the portrait, which inspires in him an attachment to a woman he has never met; at the same time, his aria offers a representation of absorption as it unfolds for us on stage as if we (and Papageno) were not there to witness it.

Through her portrait, Pamina embodies the ideals of womanhood that the culture of sensibility has ascribed to the sentimental heroine: beauty, virtue, immediacy of feeling, and the ability to inspire and ennoble those around her. Later in Act 1, Papageno, who uses the portrait to identify Pamina, refers to her more than once as "Fräuleinbild," not letting us forget that she is both maiden and image. "Fräuleinbild" is a clever wordplay on the term "Frauenbild," which indicated in the eighteenth century both woman and the image of woman (potentially an idealized image).[12]

Pamina as "Virtue in Distress"

When the Three Ladies return after Tamino's reverie with the portrait, they tell him that Pamina has been abducted. The First Lady reassures Tamino, however, on the point of her virtue: "In spite of all pain innocence suffers, she remains true to herself." One of the most familiar representations in the literature of sensibility, G. J. Barker-Benfield tells us, "is the figure of 'virtue in distress,' the virtue a woman's, her distress caused by a man."[13] Pamina's abduction, which merges elements from the sentimental genres with various other sources, had many precedents in literature and opera by 1791. The most important of these was the vogue for "exotic" operas, including Mozart's own *Die Entführung aus dem Serail* (1782). In such stories, a young girl of European origin has been abducted or is being held against her will in a distant land where she is threatened by unwanted male attention. At a time when patriarchal power could not be challenged directly, the suffering heroine – "virtue in distress" – inspired sympathy and admiration in others. Both in literature and on the operatic stage, she asserted a certain moral power – to lead by example.

The details of Pamina's abduction and her attempts to preserve her virtue are essential to Schikaneder's and Mozart's development of her character. We learn from the Three Slaves (Act 1, scene 9) that Pamina has escaped from Monostatos – "just at the moment when he thought himself the victor." They root for Pamina, describe Monostatos as their tormentor, and anticipate with delight how events will lead to his being punished by Sarastro. In the next scene, however, Monostatos (from offstage) orders the Slaves to bring chains. They respond with dismay:

FIRST SLAVE *(läuft zur Seitentür)*   *(runs to the side door)*
Doch nicht für Pamina? O ihr Götter!   But not for Pamina? Oh, ye gods!
da seht, Brüder, das Mädchen ist gefangen.   Look, brothers, the girl is caught.

SECOND AND THIRD SLAVES
Pamina? – Schrecklicher Anblick!   Pamina? – What a terrible sight!

FIRST SLAVE
Seht, wie der unbarmherzige Teufel   Look how the merciless devil is
sie bei ihren zarten Händchen faßt. –   seizing her by her delicate little
   hands. –
Das halt' ich nicht aus.   I can't bear it.
(geht auf die andere Seite ab)   *(exit on the opposite side of the stage)*

SECOND SLAVE
Ich noch weniger. –   Nor can I. –
(auch dort ab)   *(exit there also)*

THIRD SLAVE
So was sehen zu müssen,   To have to see something like this
ist Höllenmarter.   is hell-torture.
(ab)   *(exit)*

Act 1, scene 10, dialogue

The Slaves demonstrate how the sentimental heroine inspires pity and sympathy in others, and this sets the scene for Pamina's entrance as "virtue in distress," newly recaptured by Monostatos. Her first words in the ensuing trio (No. 6) are "Oh, what torment! What pain!" Threatened by Monostatos, she asks to die. In chains, Pamina faints at the end of the ensemble.

In Act 2, a similar episode occurs in scene 7. Monostatos discovers Pamina sleeping in a garden. Alone and unobserved, he describes his passion for her as a fire that smolders within him. He longs to kiss her, and in his aria "Alles fühlt der Liebe Freuden" he resolves to steal the kiss. As it happens, Monostatos is prevented by the arrival of the Queen. After the Queen's exit, he threatens Pamina again: she must submit to him or die. Pamina refuses and asks for mercy: "No! . . . spare me . . . I have given my heart to the youth." She is saved this time by the arrival of Sarastro (scene 11).

These events are salacious. The entire plot strand is titillating, and the authors know it will succeed from *Die Entführung* and other "exotic" operas of the period. Leaving aside important questions – why Sarastro would expose Pamina to Monostatos's unwanted attention and threats, and why Schikaneder and Mozart chose to make their aggressor a dark-skinned Moor – it is clear that Monostatos's attempts to violate Pamina place her virtue at risk, test her fidelity and courage, and allow us to observe her suffering and distress.

Onto this abduction narrative, however, Schikaneder and Mozart have grafted another type of sentimental plot – that of abandonment. In Act 2, scene 8, Pamina is told that she must kill Sarastro and take the all-powerful sevenfold circle of the sun (*Sonnenkreis*), or she will be abandoned by her mother. The Queen does not mince words: "Be cast off and abandoned forever." This places Pamina in the situation of many sentimental heroines who either have no family to protect them (Richardson's Pamela) or have been treated badly by family members (Richardson's Clarissa). Later, in Act 2, scene 18, when Tamino will not speak to her, Pamina believes that he, too, has abandoned her.

In musical terms, there is surely no more affecting moment in the opera than Pamina's devastating G-minor lament "Ach ich fühl's." Hearing Tamino's flute, Pamina discovers Tamino and Papageno in a hall where they are undergoing the trials of silence, but her beloved, remembering the Speaker's instructions, refuses to speak to her. Believing herself forsaken, Pamina exclaims, "Oh, this is worse than injury – worse than death!"

Pamina's aria unfolds in 6/8 over a consistent rhythmic accompaniment in the strings that alludes to the siciliano. Her melody has sometimes been called songlike, presumably because it tends toward the "natural" and avoids operatic display, but it should be noted that it does not follow any regular structure or form, allowing her a very expressive style of singing. Both text and music depict Pamina's sense of loss. Her first antecedent phrase outlines two descents: a fifth ("Ach ich fühl's") and a fourth ("es ist vershwunden"). Extended use of dissonant suspensions and appoggiaturas create anguish and the impression of profound despair and weeping. Love's longing ("der Liebe Sehnen"), the central image of the second verse, permeates the chromatic writing there, ushering in a chain of diminished seventh sonorities to problematize the phrase "then I will find rest [*Ruh*] in death" (mm. 24–26). On repeating these words at measure 30, Mozart recasts in the minor a melody associated with the words "meinem Herzen" (my heart) in the first verse, effectively bringing the abandoned heart to a darker place. Pamina's grief is intensified by other chromatic strategies as well: the presence of the Neapolitan at measure 32 on the word "Ruh," and leaps of a diminished seventh depicting "love's longing" at measures 24, 27, and 29. In measure 34, Pamina leaps an octave and a diminished fifth from g″ to c-sharp′ – it is the largest leap in the aria and appropriately articulates the leap she makes in her thoughts: to find rest in death.

Tamino's presence – in silence – is essential to the visual and scenic tableau. At the crucial moment when Pamina addresses Tamino directly – "Sieh, Tamino" – he turns away from her. At the aria's end, he allows her to leave the stage, heartbroken, without attempting to stop her. Pamina, not knowing the reason for his silence, experiences it as rejection. This effect is crucial to the opera's representation of abandonment.

The opera's exploration of "virtue in distress" reaches its culmination when Pamina attempts to take her own life in a climactic scene in the Act 2 finale. She enters the garden "half out of her wits," holding the dagger the Queen intended for Sarastro. Text and music offer a vivid demonstration of how the sentimental heroine could lose herself – mind and body – to despair. As Janet Todd explains, "a susceptible organism could easily become erratic and deranged."[14] The heightened sensibility cherished in the period was also a mark of vulnerability to nervous disorders, hysteria, and madness. A shock of passion or disappointment could quickly over-whelm a sensitive constitution. At the same time, such madness could be cured if the cause of the despair is removed. (Lorenzi and Paisiello's *Nina*, which reached Vienna in 1790, engaged the sympathy of audiences across Europe with this exact narrative.)[15]

When Pamina enters at measure 45, the signs of despair and disorder are obvious in the music: the minor mode (C minor, which then modulates quickly to F minor and then to G minor), the pervading use of chromati-cism, the offbeat *agitato* figure in the strings, the presence of the lament figure, and the emphasis on diminished seventh sonorities and awkward leaps in the vocal line. When the Three Boys attempt to intervene in A-flat (m. 63), Pamina responds with her reason for despair – that she has been abandoned. At the crucial moment, just before she attempts suicide, she addresses Tamino: "False youth, farewell! See, Pamina dies for you." Her exclamation is marked here by a rising chromatic line (as she reverses the lament figure), now powerfully supported by the low strings and winds. The textual reference attempts to collapse past and present. Pamina recalls the moment in her aria when she addressed Tamino but he did not respond to her – the moment that first confirmed her feelings of abandonment and set her on her present course. (To some, it may even appear that her vocal line expands the interjection of the flute and oboe in the aria.) We are reminded of her words at the end of her aria that she would find peace in death.[16]

Pamina can be restored to her senses only by reassurance that things are not as they seem. As she raises the dagger, the Three Boys take action. Mozart dramatizes the conflicting realities of his characters with a harmonic juxtaposition: Pamina's attempt to stab herself cadences in G minor (see the vocal line in mm. 92–93); the Boys interrupt her ("stopping her arm"), deflecting her intended cadence to E-flat (a key already associated with Tamino and love in this opera). In what follows, they restore Pamina to her right mind by reassuring her that Tamino loves her ("for he loves you alone").

Schikaneder and Mozart have marked their heroine with a highly sensitive body, on which the spontaneous signs of emotional life may readily be observed. Pamina's abduction, abandonment, and even her thoughts of suicide allow her to emerge as the quintessential sentimental heroine who overcomes danger and despair to be united with her beloved Tamino. Their triumph together in the trials offers a compelling representation of female empowerment.

The Queen as Mother

Like Pamina, the Queen is represented with deliberate reference to behaviors and ways of being associated with her gender. But while Pamina embraces the roles of loving daughter and future wife, the Queen is clearly unwilling to be defined by the socially constructed roles of mother and widow. She vividly recalls her husband's dying instruction – that she "submit to the guidance of wise men" (Act 2, scene 8) – and rejects it. She will not give up her ambition to rule in her husband's place. When the Queen threatens her daughter, it becomes clear that she places ambition above any sense of maternal duty or affection. The Queen is, in fact, the only dark and vengeful mother ever to appear in Mozart's operas.

To put the Queen in context, it is important to note that the figure of the mother on the eighteenth-century operatic stage is relatively rare. Only three other mothers appear in Mozart's operas and all play sympathetic roles: Venus assures the happy marriage of her son Ascanio in *Ascanio in Alba*; Paneta, believed dead, returns to unite her daughter Celidora with her beloved in the unfinished *L'oca del Cairo*; Marcellina is happily reunited with her son Figaro (and his father Bartolo) in *The Marriage of Figaro*. Mary Hunter concludes in her important study *The Culture of*

Opera Buffa in Mozart's Vienna that "mothers are almost entirely absent" from the repertory she surveyed, finding only four in a group of 450–500 characters.[17] Families and households are headed up onstage by fathers, uncles, or guardians. From the perspective of social hierarchy, mothers were unnecessary to these stories since both lineage and property were passed through the male line. But the real reasons for their absence are probably more complex, as Hunter suggests: "The characteristic absence of a female figure with any real claim to authority also allows the image of an 'ideal' male-headed hierarchy to appear unimpeded."[18] Operas follow tendencies observable elsewhere in the period. In eighteenth-century novels, for example, mothers are largely absent. As Ruth Perry explains in her *Novel Relations*, "maternal absence was more poignant for heroines for they were more vulnerable to the designs of libertine men or the avarice of relatives."[19] The absent mother was virtually a precondition of the gothic novel. In the best-known fairy tales, too, the natal mother is generally absent, often replaced by a wicked stepmother. Monstrous mothers (including substitute mothers), Marilyn Farcus suggests, "locate the challenges and obstacles to 'good' motherhood that society and culture refuse to acknowledge."[20]

The representation of the Queen as a mother is vital to her character. She is not merely a woman seeking power or vengeance, like Electra in *Idomeneo* or Vitellia in *La clemenza di Tito*. She is something far more inconceivable to the eighteenth-century mind: a natal mother willing to betray her daughter to achieve power. In many stories, it is precisely the substitution of a wicked stepmother or other female figure for the birth mother that makes this manipulation of the child possible. In *The Magic Flute*, however, the natural mother is herself the monstrous mother. This contradiction, which lies at the heart of the story, is an important aspect of her character that has not been fully appreciated and explored.

Even before the Queen appears in Act 1, heralded by thunder and illuminated by the stars in the night sky, motherhood is already essential. The Three Ladies have informed Tamino that she is the mother of the "royal daughter" he adores. In her recitative and aria "O zittre nicht . . . Zum Leiden" the Queen addresses Tamino as her son and speaks of his ability to console her mother's heart. In the aria's Andante she describes her situation in sentimental terms, emphasizing her grief: "I am destined to suffer, for I miss my daughter, because of her all my happiness was lost . . . ." The music reflects her distress compellingly with its turn to G minor and use of chromaticism, and, as it continues, with agitated figures in the orchestra and the lament figure in the vocal line to underscore her detailed account of Pamina's abduction. In the

Allegro moderato she addresses Tamino as a mother: "You will be my daughter's savior." The emotions associated with motherhood were increasingly celebrated as "naturally feminine" during the eighteenth century. John Brown, in his *On the Female Character and Education* (1765), claimed that a woman's affection for her husband and children was "the first Duty of her Life, the very Purpose of her Being."[21] Beth Tobin has shown how the celebration of women as mothers and wives in magazines such as the *Lady's Magazine* (which was enormously popular from the mid-1780s to the end of the century) helped to develop the concept of an idealized domesticity that pervaded the late eighteenth century.[22]

Tamino has no reason to doubt the Queen's representation of herself. He tells the Priest in the Act 1 finale that Sarastro is a "fiend" and a "tyrant." When asked to explain his statements, he says they have been "proven by an unhappy woman, oppressed by grief and misery." Significantly, it is in this context that the Priest says "So a woman has beguiled you? A woman does little, talks much. Young man, do you believe in wagging tongues?" We may well ask why this statement – so clearly aimed at one particular woman and the threat she poses to Sarastro's temple – is framed in general terms. The Queen's title – *Königin der Nacht* – may also have indicated to contemporary audiences that she was not what she seemed. Jane K. Brown makes this point, citing the Grimms' *Deutsches Wörterbuch*, which defines "Nachtkönig/in" as someone who cleans latrines. Relevant instances of the term occur in eighteenth-century Viennese theater, one involving the clown Hanswurst.[23]

It is not until later in the opera that we have the opportunity to observe the Queen interacting with her daughter. In her dialogue with Pamina in Act 2, scene 8, the Queen recounts the tale of how her husband, before his death, had insisted that the sevenfold circle of the sun was destined for the initiates: "Sarastro will manage it in a manly way, as I have until now. And now, not another word; do not attempt to inquire into matters that are incomprehensible to the female mind. Your duty and that of your daughter is to submit to the guidance of wise men." Focused on her desire for power and vengeance, the Queen offers no maternal support or affection. She is deaf to her daughter's entreaties of "Dear Mother," deaf to her request for protection, deaf to her affection for Tamino. In her second aria, "Der Hölle Rache," the Queen wields motherhood as a weapon; Pamina must either murder Sarastro or be abandoned by her own mother. The Queen is revealed here not merely as a "bad" mother but as a danger to the social and moral order. The exact danger she poses is unwittingly confirmed by a textual echo, for it is she who embodies the danger of which the Priests warned. Her words "Death and despair [*Tod und Verzweiflung*] flame all around me!" appear to breathe life into the warning the Priests gave Tamino and Papageno in Act 2, scene 3: "Many a wise man let himself be taken in ... death and despair [*Tod und Verzweiflung*] were his reward."

Spectacularly difficult coloratura passages in both of the Queen's arias have become emblematic of her role. It is necessary therefore to consider exactly how the nature of her operatic speech affects or shades what she says and how that speech participates in the construction of her character. No other character in the opera sings in the same bravura style, demonstrating extraordinary range (up to the f''' above high c'''), agility, and power.[24] The most striking coloratura passage of Act 1 appears near the end of her aria as the Queen promises Tamino: "And when I see you victorious, then will she be yours forever." Thirteen measures of vocalise elaborate the word "then" (*dann*) and two measures – including a leap up to high f''' – highlight the word "forever" (*ewig*). There can be no question about the power of this musical speech, which is astonishing, magical, and transcendent. It is also persuasive. The Queen deploys her vocal power with particular attention to the sense of the words: her vocalise suspends the flow of words precisely on *dann* and *ewig* to illustrate the magical forever that will be achieved only at the point when Tamino is rewarded. Tamino's reaction confirms both that he is astonished ("Was it real, what I saw? Or do my senses beguile me?") and persuaded ("Protect my arm, steel my courage").

In her second aria, the Queen employs many musical devices associated with revenge, including extraordinary passages of coloratura, in an effort to persuade her daughter to murder Sarastro. Lengthy melismatic vocalises occur on two words (indicated in italics) to emphasize the crucial warnings of each verse. "If Sarastro does not feel death's pain by your hand, then you are my daughter *nevermore* [*nimmermehr*]"; "Be abandoned forever, let be destroyed all the *bonds* [*Bande*] of nature." The Queen's menacing passagework powerfully hints at the duration of *nimmermehr* with two long vocalises that suspend normal operatic speech. In the second verse, an even longer melismatic passage quite literally illustrates the promised destruction of family ties by splitting the word and severing the larger phrase "bonds of nature." The effect is terrifying. But, in the end, apparently, it is not persuasive. Pamina, to whom this aria is addressed, will not murder Sarastro. At the level of the plot, the Queen's vocal power fails.

Is there, however, a level on which the Queen's vocal power succeeds? Writing about the Queen, Carolyn Abbate asks whether we hear the

character or the singer at moments of vocal astonishment, suggesting that
her Act 2 aria be read "as oscillating between drama – the angry tirade by
the character – and voice-object that comes to the fore *precisely* in the
melismatic vocalises."[25] For Abbate, the Queen as a character ceases to
exist: "the locus of voice is now not a character, not human, and
somehow not present." Not all who hear the Queen's vocal feats will
respond in the same way, of course, but the sheer vocal power and
brilliance of the singer in performance may break the fourth wall to
have an effect that lies outside the circumference of the drama. This
possibility, in turn, has complicated the way commentators and audiences have understood her role within the drama. Some commentators
have returned to her first aria to find evidence of deception. Some have
viewed her coloratura as evidence of hysteria. Many have complained
that the Queen's appearance as ostensibly good in Act 1 is an inconsistency in the plot. Whether acknowledged or not, the Queen's coloratura has played a vital role in these debates. In the first aria, it is
a rhetorical strategy that perfectly aligns with Tamino's feelings and
the goals of the plot. In the second aria, however, the Queen's spectacular melismatic passages stand in direct opposition to Pamina's
innermost feelings and the goals of the plot. Abbate's observation
that we may dissociate the character in the story from the singer on
the stage explains the special thrill audiences experience on hearing the
Queen sing, especially in Act 2. The Queen's vocal power overwhelms
and dominates, whether or not it succeeds as a rhetorical strategy.

In 1979 Catherine Clément offered what is perhaps still the most
radical feminist reading of this opera when she described it as "women's
undoing."[26] "The winning world," she writes, is not the world of the
Queen; it is "the other one, the father's, the men's world." Clément's
strident view follows Bergman's version of the story rather than
Schikaneder and Mozart's, but her larger point – that the Queen reflects
the culture's oppressive attitude toward women – influenced
a generation of scholars. The Queen, she insists, "does not make
sense." She is a "madwoman, cut off from everyone else"; her coloratura,
a "babbling language" of rage and tenderness, a "losing song." Abbate, as
we have seen, focuses on the Queen's singing to challenge traditional
ways of understanding her role. In her important chapter "Magic Flute,
Nocturnal Sun," she considers a variety of precedents for understanding
the Queen as a "female king" whose masculine aspirations "reflect deep
cultural anxieties about female rule." The Queen's voice, Abbate argues,
"becomes an object of intense desire, and her arias an occasion for

celebration: the winning song."[27] Kristi Brown-Montesano suggests that the Queen's command of the night sky associates her with the sublime (as it was understood in the period), but that her gender posed a problem. As a result, the Queen might be thought an embodiment of the "Female Sublime" or "Bad Sublime." The Queen threatens the brotherhood because she "manifests both the beautiful and the sublime, upsetting the sexual assumptions that informed these categories for Enlightenment thinkers."[28] These and other feminist readings context-ualize, reinterpret, and even vindicate the Queen.

For my part, I am happy to let the Queen be the villain. It is enough for me that she is a glorious villain. With just over twelve minutes on stage, she steals the show. And it is clear that her dark, starry kingdom is a necessary counterpart to Sarastro's temples of Wisdom, Reason, and Nature. Of what value would the pursuit of Enlightenment be if it were not contrasted and clarified by an imposing, mysterious veil of darkness? For many, the Queen is the most memorable role in the opera. She is an archetypal character who represents the potential darkness, chaos, and unpredictability of human behavior. She overwhelms all in her presence with the forceful persua-sion of visual and vocal spectacle. She is not merely aloft in the night sky; she is able to roam freely in the underground passages beneath the temple. She is a formidable danger, difficult to defeat. She represents the threat of disorder, vengeance, deception, and hypocrisy. Even when she has disappeared from view, she might return at any moment – and she does, in two sequels.[29]

Focusing on the role gender identity plays in the characterization of the Queen makes it possible for us to better understand the role misogyny plays in the opera as a whole. On the one hand, misogyny is not required to condemn the Queen. As a "bad" mother, her behavior is neither natural to, nor typical of, women; it contradicts the deepest instincts of human nature. On the other hand, misogyny is pervasive and fundamental. To sense its magnitude, we must look beyond the Priests' generalizing com-ments to the structure of the plot and the representation of its characters. While the mother chooses power and position over the "natural" affection of the domestic sphere, the daughter is entirely motivated by an innate affection for others that furthers the domestic goals of eighteenth-century society. Women like the Queen, who refused to embrace their socially constructed gender roles, were dangerous. They threatened the very social, moral, and ethical beliefs upon which society was built and functioned.

Conclusion

To return to my earlier question: How, then, should we understand the opera's representation of women? Both mother and daughter are defined by their actions. Pamina, a sentimental heroine whose exemplary behavior is appropriate to the period, is rewarded by the events of the plot. Her mother is not. The reasons for this are many, as I have tried to suggest. The Queen has a role to play by resisting the status quo. She is unhappy with the opera's social and moral worldview; she refuses to align herself with its objectives and goals. She clearly articulates her reasons for doing so. As a result, the opera's final scene excludes her. It also excludes others – the Three Ladies, Monostatos, Papageno, and Papagena. For modern audiences, this can be disturbing.

Concentrating on what disturbs us, however, may help us to reconcile the opera's representation of women with its dramatization of Enlightenment themes. Like all artworks that have been thought to reflect a universal human experience, *The Magic Flute* is limited by the circumstances of its creation and first performance. And yet, there is a "we" in the opera that attempts to capture a sense of the universal that many still cherish. It is the "we" of the opera's maxims: a testament to the potential of humankind from which, arguably, no one is excluded – at least in theory. This is analogous to the "We the people" at the start of the U.S. Constitution, which in 1787 embraced only some men and no women at all, and remains aspirational even today. This Enlightenment vision has persisted with the opera and drives attempts to resolve "problems" such as the opera's misogyny. Often these matters have been understood as inconsistences. But Enlightenment thinkers were more comfortable with inconsistency and unresolved difficulties than we are. This is fundamental to the concept of enlightenment. "If it is asked," Kant writes in 1784, "'Do we now live in an *enlightened* age?' the answer is 'No, but we do live in an age of *enlightenment*.'"[30]

I would suggest that these inconsistencies and contradictions are central to understanding *The Magic Flute* both in Mozart's day and in ours. Perhaps the opera's comments about women and men, and about its Black man and its birdman, are best understood as part of its engagement of a broader question – what it means to be human – in an age of enlightenment. Many characters in the opera are given opportunities, including Tamino, Pamina, the Queen, Papageno, and Monostatos. But are they given equal opportunity and a level playing field? In the age of

#MeToo and Black Lives Matter, we understand the failings of the Enlightenment period so well partly because we are still dealing with them, just as we are still struggling to live in a more perfect world. In my view, this makes the dramatic contradictions and complexities of *The Magic Flute* more relevant on a modern stage.

Notes

1. This and subsequent translations from the libretto are my own.
2. Myra Jehlen, "Gender," in *Critical Terms for Literary Study*, ed. Frank Lentricchia and Thomas McLaughlin, 2nd edn. (Chicago: University of Chicago Press, 1995), 265.
3. Jean-Jacques Rousseau, *Émile*, trans. Barbara Foxley (London: Everyman, 1997), 385.
4. Ibid., 384.
5. Mary Wollstonecraft, *A Vindication of the Rights of Woman* (Oxford: Oxford University Press, 1993), 225.
6. Dorinda Outram, *The Enlightenment* (Cambridge: Cambridge University Press, 1995), 83.
7. G. J. Barker-Benfield, *The Culture of Sensibility: Sex and Society in Eighteenth-Century Britain* (Chicago: University of Chicago Press, 1996), xvii–xviii.
8. Immanuel Kant, *Observations on the Feeling of the Beautiful and Sublime*, trans. John T. Goldthwait (Berkeley: University of California Press, 1991), 79.
9. Ibid., 76–77.
10. Martin Nedbal, *Morality and Viennese Opera in the Age of Mozart and Beethoven* (London: Routledge, 2017), esp. 1–11, and 84–91.
11. Michael Fried *Absorption and Theatricality* (Chicago: University of Chicago Press, 1988).
12. For different readings, see Jane K. Brown, "The Queen of the Night and the Crisis of Allegory in *The Magic Flute*," *Goethe Yearbook* 8 (1996): 151; Kate Bartel, "Pamina, Portraits, and the Feminine in Mozart and Schikaneder's *Die Zauberflöte*," *Musicology Australia* 22 (2018): 34.
13. Barker-Benfield, *Culture of Sensibility*, xvii.
14. Janet Todd, *Sensibility: An Introduction* (London: Methuen, 1986), 19. See also John Mullan, *Sentiment and Sociability: The Language of Feeling in the Eighteenth Century* (Oxford: Clarendon Press, 2002), esp. chap. 5, "Hypochondria and Hysteria," 201–40.
15. For a discussion of Paisiello's *Nina*, its influence, and the French work upon which it was based, see Stefano Castelvecchi, *Sentimental Opera: Questions of Genre in the Age of Bourgeois Drama* (Cambridge: Cambridge University Press, 2013), chap. 5, 125–60.

16. For a discussion of this moment in her earlier aria, see Thomas Bauman, "At the North Gate: Instrumental Music in *Die Zauberflöte*," in Daniel Heartz, *Mozart's Operas* (Berkeley: University of California Press, 1990), 283–86; for a longer discussion of this scene in the Act 2 finale, see Jessica Waldoff, *Recognition in Mozart's Operas* (New York: Oxford University Press, 2006), 70–75.

17. Mary Hunter, *The Culture of Opera Buffa in Mozart's Vienna: A Poetics of Entertainment* (Princeton: Princeton University Press, 1999), 62–3, esp. n. 29. For the *seria* context, see Martha Feldman, "The Absent Mother in Opera Seria," in *Siren Songs: Representations of Gender and Sexuality in Opera*, ed. Mary Ann Smart (Princeton: Princeton University Press, 2000), 29–46.

18. Hunter, *Culture of Opera Buffa*, 62.

19. Ruth Perry, *Novel Relations: The Transformation of Kinship in English Literature and Culture 1748–1818* (Cambridge: Cambridge University Press, 2004), 337.

20. Marilyn Francus, *Monstrous Mothers: Eighteenth-Century Culture and the Ideology of Domesticity* (Baltimore: John Hopkins University Press, 2012), 170.

21. Cited in Perry, *Novel Relations*, 341.

22. Beth Fawkes Tobin, "'The Tender Mother': The Social Construction of Motherhood and the *Lady's Magazine*," *Women's Studies* 18 (1990): 205–21.

23. Brown, "Queen of the Night," 144–45.

24. Paul Corneilson, "Josepha Hofer: First Queen of the Night," in *Mozart Studien* 25 (2018): 477–500.

25. Carolyn Abbate, *Unsung Voices: Opera and Musical Narrative in the Nineteenth Century* (Princeton: Princeton University Press, 1991) 10–11, at 11; see also Michel Poizat, *The Angel's Cry: Beyond the Pleasure Principle in Opera*, trans. Arthur Denner (Ithaca: Cornell University Press, 1992), 65–67, and 99–104.

26. Catherine Clément, *Opera, or the Undoing of Women*, trans Betsy Wing, fwd. Susan McClary (Minneapolis: University of Minnesota Press, 1988), 70–76, at 73–74. Originally published as *L'opéra ou la défaite des femmes* (1979).

27. Carolyn Abbate, *In Search of Opera* (Princeton: Princeton University Press, 2001), chap. 2, 55–106, at 86, 87.

28. For a consideration of the "Bad Sublime," see Kristi Brown-Montesano, *Understanding the Women of Mozart's Operas* (Berkeley: University of California Press, 2007), 98–101, at 98.

29. J. W. Goethe's *The Magic Flute, Part II*, begun in 1795, which he hoped to have set by Paul Wranitzky but never completed; and Schikaneder and Peter von Winter's *Das Labyrinth*, which premiered on the same stage in 1798. Josepha Hofer reprised her role as the Queen.

30. Immanuel Kant, "An Answer to the Question: What Is Enlightenment?" trans. James Schmidt, in *What Is Enlightenment? Eighteenth-Century Answers and Twentieth-Century Questions*, ed. James Schmidt (Berkeley: University of California Press, 1996), 58–64. Originally published as "Beantwortung der Frage: Was ist Aufklärung?" *Berlinische Monatsschrift* (1784).

16 | Blackness and Whiteness in *The Magic Flute*: Reflections from Shakespeare Studies

ADELINE MUELLER

They called him "the Shakespeare of music." For some early critics, it was because of Mozart's grasp of the "magnificent" and "terrifying."[1] For others, it was his deft mixture of tragedy and comedy in the operas, particularly *Don Giovanni*.[2] One defended Mozart's "*Bizarrerien*" by claiming that, like Shakespeare, Mozart had "a certain indifference to the old rules of art. ... Shakespeare drew criticism for his astonishing situations, Mozart for his astonishing modulations."[3] And, perhaps most famously, E. T. A. Hoffmann wrote of Mozart in 1821: "Fiery imagination, deeply felt humour, and extravagant abundance of ideas pointed this Shakespeare of music in the direction he had to follow."[4]

The connections between Mozart and Shakespeare were biographical as well as critical, particularly when it came to *The Magic Flute*. While in London on their European tour, Leopold copied into his travel diary – in careful English – Lorenzo's famous speech on Orpheus and the power of music from *The Merchant of Venice*, prefiguring Tamino's taming of the wild animals in Act 1, scene 15.[5] *The Magic Flute*'s librettist Schikaneder was a renowned Shakespearean actor, whose productions Mozart may well have seen during his troupe's Salzburg sojourns.[6] And Christoph Martin Wieland, the German poet who published *Dschinnistan* (1786–89), the fairy-tale collection from which Mozart and Schikaneder drew many elements of *The Magic Flute*, was also among the first to translate Shakespeare's plays into German. Wieland's own 1780 poem based on *A Midsummer Night's Dream*, *Oberon, König der Elfen* (a copy of which was in Mozart's library at his death), had been a huge success at the Theater auf der Wieden in 1789, in a *Singspiel* adaptation starring many of the same singers who would later create the leading roles in *The Magic Flute*.[7]

Beyond the biographical and intertextual connections between the two artists, Mozart and Shakespeare each stand as a colossus of art, a one-man canon. Through them and in invoking them, many of us long to see ourselves at our most transcendent, our most timeless, our most brilliant, and our most humane. Yet they each cast a long shadow, particularly in an age increasingly wary of heroes and universals. The dissonances – and, perhaps more uncomfortably, the enduring similarities – between the racial and other norms and stereotypes enshrined in Shakespeare's and Mozart's works, and the structural racism and other civil rights indignities and injustices of our own time, are becoming increasingly tangible in the wake of the social justice turn in the humanities and performing arts.

Monostatos is the most blatantly racialized of the outcasts populating what is often claimed as Mozart's most universal, and universally appealing, opera. According to Operabase, *The Magic Flute* was the most frequently performed opera worldwide in the 2020/2021, 2021/2022, and 2022/2023 seasons, and since 2004/2005 it has never dipped below the top five.[8] Furthermore, for at least the last fifty years or so, it has been commonly used to introduce English- and German-speaking children to both Mozart and opera as a genre, whether in television programs, children's books, or family-friendly productions. To judge from publicity materials for the longstanding productions at the Vienna and Salzburg Marionette Theaters and *Die Zauberflöte für Kinder* at the Vienna State Opera (which sees some 7,000 schoolchildren attend each year), entire generations of Austrians are being raised to take the character Monostatos – and his portrayal by white tenors in blackface – for granted.[9]

In 2005, Malcolm Cole offered the first study of Monostatos in terms of the racial ideologies of Mozart's day. Cole argued that the character, whose name translates to "standing alone," is "a composite of that host of negative traits – physical, mental, emotional, moral, and spiritual – commonly associated with the Black 'Other' (and not only in the eighteenth century)."[10] Other commentaries have followed from scholars and theater practitioners such as Derek Scott, Nasser Al-Taee, Steffen Lösel, and Kira Thurman.[11] Historians including Uta Sadji, Peter Martin, Barbara Riesche, and Wendy Sutherland have surveyed the long tradition of African characters and stereotypes in eighteenth-century German literature, theater, and visual culture.[12] And yet, discourses of race are still largely absent from Mozart scholarship.[13]

In performance, however, the anti-Black racism of Monostatos has long been painfully familiar to Black singers. American tenor Charles Holland, who had left the United States for Europe in 1949, reluctantly agreed to sing Monostatos for the Paris Opéra in 1954 in exchange for the role of Nadir in *The Pearl Fishers* at the Opéra Comique (Holland was the first Black singer to appear on that stage). Holland had initially refused to sing Monostatos, his colleague George Shirley later recalled, because it was "a role he considered an embarrassment to the race."[14] In 1959, Austrian critics scoffed at Leontyne Price's casting as Pamina in her Vienna State Opera debut, dismissing a "dark-skinned Pamina" as unrealistic (conveniently ignoring the far less "realistic" nature of Monostatos in blackface).[15] Such debates about race and opera casting are by no means resolved over half a century later, as the controversies over the 2015 Metropolitan Opera's decision to end blackface in *Otello* productions and Anna Netrebko's defiant use of blackface in *Aida* make plain.[16] Even as predominantly white companies have begun to cast across and beyond "the color line," it is not only Monostatos that has caused harm for Black singers. Bass Kenneth Kellogg, who has sung Sarastro in several *Magic Flute* productions, has recalled the way he cringes whenever he utters Sarastro's line from Act 2, scene 11 sizing up Monostatos: "I know your soul is as black as your face." Kellogg wonders whether it need be an integral part of *The Magic Flute* for Monostatos to be a person of color, contrasting it with Verdi's *Otello*, where "the dramatic tension of the entire opera" is racial tension.[17] Yet, as Black Shakespearean actors in the *Othello* tradition have commented for generations, the dramaturgical centrality of race is nevertheless embodied in a dehumanized protagonist.[18]

Kellogg's comparison to Verdi's Shakespeare adaptation suggests one model for grappling with the troubling history of a *Singspiel* like *The Magic Flute*: Shakespeare studies. Scholars working at the intersections of premodern critical race theory, postcolonial studies, Shakespeare studies, and performance studies have for decades considered how what Kim Hall calls "race thinking" permeates Shakespeare's texts, contexts, and audiences, as well as productions and interpretations in our own time.[19] Already in 1996, Margo Hendricks described the "shaping fantasy" of race in *A Midsummer Night's Dream*, training her critical-historicist lens on the nameless, voiceless "Indian boy" of the play and directorial interventions on his "culturally predetermined orientalism."[20] Ronald Takaki has shown how Shakespeare's audience would have understood *The Tempest* in terms of contemporary English invasions of Ireland and incursions into the New World, with Caliban's "racialized savagery" serving to prop up the dispossession of land and enslavement of bodies in settler-colonialist scenarios remarkably similar to Prospero's.[21] Examinations of race and race thinking in Shakespeare extend beyond the so-called "race plays": as Hall has argued, "Any discussion of race must deconstruct whiteness and not focus just on minoritized people."[22] What is now often abbreviated (and circulated in social media) under the hashtag #ShakeRace works to make the often obscured power structures undergirded by whiteness in Shakespeare visible.[23] Similar power structures bind Monostatos to the non-Black characters with whom he interacts – Papageno, Pamina, Tamino, the Queen, and

Sarastro – and to the fundamental whiteness of Enlightenment itself that the *Singspiel* apotheosizes. Monostatos's blackness, whether framed as threatening, laughable, or pitiful, contains traces of Othello, Caliban, Shylock, and Aaron (who in *Titus Andronicus* speaks a line remarkably similar to Sarastro's: "Aaron will have his soul black like his face").

In this essay, I consider how we might address the legacies of race and racism in *The Magic Flute*, and what opportunities there might be to re-envision the *Singspiel* if we consider parallels in the Shakespeare repertory and #ShakeRace studies. What kind of freedom or flexibility might we have to adapt, translate, appropriate, and "unsettle" *The Magic Flute* in scholarship, performance, and pedagogy by taking our cue from experimental approaches to Shakespeare?[24] Mozart, like Shakespeare, is a towering icon of the "universal" in Western art with global reach, yet one whose meanings are constantly being made and remade in specific places. As we revisit Monostatos's meanings in his own time, and in several key moments in *The Magic Flute*'s performance history, we might ask, with the global Shakespeare scholar Alexa Alice Joubin, "What values and ideas does [Mozart's] cultural work sustain or undermine?"[25]

Monostatos and *The Magic Flute*'s Race Problem

Constructed out of a range of orientalist and anti-Black tropes, Monostatos has among his closest literary antecedents a number of so-called "Moors" and enslaved characters in Wieland's *Dschinnistan*.[26] He was written for Joseph Nouseul, a member of Schikaneder's troupe known for his comic grotesques and villains.[27] A 1783 guide to actors of the day criticized Nouseul as artificial and overwrought, his performances "a perpetual grimace."[28] If this was still true in 1791, Schikaneder may well have written to Nouseul's type. As with Osmin's relationship to Bassa Selim in Mozart's other "exotic" *Singspiel, Die Entführung aus dem Serail*, Monostatos is middle management in Sarastro's slave economy, an overseer yet with little power of his own. Osmin and Monostatos may even represent the outsourcing and disavowal of Enlightenment colonial violence: as Ritchie Robertson writes, "In *Die Entführung* Bassa Selim proves to be noble and generous, and sends the captives home, while all the threats of torture are blamed on his servant Osmin (anticipating the division of responsibility between Sarastro and Monostatos in *The Magic Flute*)."[29]

Monostatos is a foil to all of the *Singspiel*'s main characters: he is made foolish in his encounters with Papageno, attempts to capture Tamino,

Figure 16.1 Image of Pamina from *Die Rheinische Musen* (Mannheim, 1795). Courtesy of Österreichische Nationalbibliothek.

serves and plots against Sarastro, and ends up a would-be co-conspirator with the Queen of the Night. Above all, however, he represents a persistent sexual threat to Pamina, and the contrast in their skin color is fetishized. Papageno describes Pamina as "whiter than chalk," just before remarking of Monostatos, "There are black birds in the world, why not black men too? (an ostensibly neutral observation that is later undercut by Sarastro's aforementioned line in Act 2, scene 11, "I know your soul is as black as your face")."[30]

The gender, racial, and moral binaries between Pamina and Monostatos were reinforced in a volume of *Die Rheinische Musen* (Mannheim, 1795), where they were the only figures from the *Singspiel* to be shown in sequential theater costume engravings (Figures 16.1 and 16.2). When viewed in succession, these two images create a composite scene that could well have recalled for readers the Act 5, scene 2 murder of Desdemona from Shakespeare's *Othello*. The murder scene was a popular

Figure 16.2 Image of Monostatos from *Die Rheinische Musen* (Mannheim, 1795). Courtesy of Österreichische Nationalbibliothek.

one for illustrations of eighteenth- and nineteenth-century editions of *Othello*, "keeping alive the image of a besieged, white femininity so crucial to the production of the black man as a 'savage.'"[31] Like Othello, Monostatos is repeatedly referred to as "the Moor" – he even claims the label himself. But his characterization also overlaps with that of Caliban in Shakespeare's *Tempest*, a popular text for German translation and adaptation in the 1790s.[32] Both the Prospero-Miranda-Caliban triangle and the Sarastro-Pamina-Monostatos triangle stage a confrontation between a racialized character and a white supremacy that is split into male power and female vulnerability. Like Caliban, but also Shylock and even Malvolio in *Twelfth Night*, Monostatos is at once a threat and an object of mockery and scorn, a figure of alterity at first exploited, then punished or shunned, by the protagonists. The audience is meant to fear Monostatos, to laugh at his folly and punishment, and to rejoice at his defeat and expulsion. In this way, Monostatos falls somewhere between Shakespeare's comic antagonists and his tragic hero Othello.

In Schikaneder's original libretto, Monostatos has the most lines of spoken dialogue save only for Papageno. Yet in most modern productions of *The Magic Flute*, much of Monostatos's spoken dialogue is omitted or drastically reduced – especially Act 1, scene 9, in which three *Sklaven* discuss him in his absence. While these characters' racial-ethnic identity is not named, they describe Monostatos as "schwarzer Monostatos" and "der Mohr," suggesting that they do not share his racialization.[33] They cheer the fact that Pamina has briefly escaped Monostatos's attempted assault, so that when she enters in Act 1, scene 11, the audience will already have judged Monostatos – a judgment confirmed when Pamina calls him *Barbar*.

The dehumanization of Monostatos and those he oversees is thematized in the use of the *Singspiel*'s magic instruments. First, Tamino enchants the wild animals of the realm with his flute (in Act 1, scene 15), and then immediately thereafter Papageno enchants Monostatos and his *Sklaven* with his glockenspiel (in Act 1, scene 17). Mozart's audience was surely meant to notice the parallels between these two scenes; indeed, both the animals and the *Sklaven* might well have been (and frequently continue to be) portrayed by the same rank-and-file company members. This familiar elision of blackness and animality finds visual representation in a colored engraving from the ca. 1794 series by artist Joseph Schaffer, sold as individual prints and later published in the Brno *Allgemeines europäisches Journal* in 1795 (see Figure 4.4 earlier in this volume).[34] The obscure, ape-like figures (though the description accompanying the image identifies them as "animals of various kinds") typify a process of "bestialization and thingification" that Zakiyyah Iman Jackson describes as "imagining black people as an empty vessel, a nonbeing, a nothing, an ontological zero."[35] The presence of these faceless dark beings surrounding Tamino as he plays at the gates of Reason, Wisdom, and Nature acts as a foil in every way: in their physicality and their anonymity, they are the antithesis of the Enlightenment prince.

Whether based on an actual production or on a fanciful interpretation of the published libretto, Schaffer's costumed men are literally "things of darkness," the phrase with which Prospero describes Caliban in Act 5, scene 1 of *The Tempest*. As Kim Hall writes in her pathbreaking book, *Things of Darkness: Economies of Race and Gender in Early Modern England*, "Caliban functions as a 'thing of darkness' against which a European social order is tested and proved."[36] *The Magic Flute* is a similar proving ground for European whiteness, with Monostatos and the wild animals equally subdued by Papageno, Tamino, and their instruments of control.

Monostatos's lone aria, the Act 2, scene 7 "Alles fühlt der Liebe Freuden" (Everyone feels the joys of love), is the crux of his racialized, gendered, and sexualized outsider status. In Schikaneder's printed libretto it is preceded by an extended monologue (frequently cut in modern productions) in which Monostatos rationalizes his actions and gives voice to his desire for Pamina. While his passion continues to dominate the text once Monostatos breaks into song, Mozart undercuts any noble sentiment with nervously pattering sixteenth notes at a galloping allegro tempo. *Alla turca* gestures cement Monostatos's difference from any other singing character in the *Singspiel* – while also suggesting an affinity with *Die Entführung*'s Osmin and his Act 1, scene 3 litany of violent fantasies, "Erst geköpft, dann gehangen" (First beheaded, then hanged).[37] In fact, Monostatos's lines frequently unfold as breathless, Osmin-like lists ("schnäbelt, tändelt, herzet, küßt"). In a final denial of sentiment, "Alles fühlt" unfolds at a *sempre pianissimo* dynamic, reinforced in the score and libretto with the highly specific stage direction "Everything is sung and played as quietly as if the music were a long way away." Even the music, in other words, is distanced, Monostatos's voice furtive.

In "Alles fühlt" Monostatos comments candidly on the double standard he experiences because of his race. "I must forego love, / Because a black man is ugly," he observes ruefully, repeating the second line; later he avows "A white one has conquered me!" Some have read the aria as Monostatos's plea for common humanity: his repeated line in verse 1 "Am I not made of flesh and blood?" is a kind of counterpart, as Derek Scott has noted, to Shylock's line from *The Merchant of Venice* "If you prick us, do we not bleed? ... And if you wrong us, shall we not revenge?"[38] But while Monostatos is marginally more sympathetic than a character like Osmin, as Al-Taee points out, his status as a racialized scapegoat cannot be explained away by reading "Alles fühlt" as racial critique.[39] Nor do I hear in Mozart's music what Cole describes as "a breath of understanding and sympathy" imparted to the character.[40] Rather, Monostatos's spoken and sung lines convey mainly deviousness, lust, and cowardice, and at the *Singspiel*'s end he is consigned to eternal night together with his co-conspirators, thwarted in their efforts to unseat Sarastro (in another echo of Caliban's fate at the end of *The Tempest*).

Interventions, Reclamations, and Refusals in Performance

As a character rooted in blackface and racism, Monostatos has been all too easy to appropriate for explicitly racist productions, as in 1941 at the "Salzburg War Festival," which was rebranded by the Nazis as a morale booster for wounded soldiers on the 150th anniversary of both Mozart's death and the premiere of *The Magic Flute*.[41] In a puff piece on this "model staging" in the *Salzburger Volksblatt*, Otto Kunz declared that *The Magic Flute*, "the loveliest of all musical fairy tales, is today the common property of mankind."[42] The sole image chosen to accompany the article, however, was the scene where Monostatos looms over the sleeping Pamina during "Alles fühlt der Liebe Freuden." The familiar racist trope of the Black man as sexual aggressor, already cemented in *The Magic Flute*'s visual tradition over a century earlier, was here weaponized as an instrument of Nazi propaganda. The *Volksblatt* saw no contradiction in juxtaposing such racist fearmongering alongside the article's claim that *The Magic Flute* represented Mozart's "highest hymn to humanity."[43] Similarly, the *Neues Wiener Tagblatt* rhapsodized over this production: "Is it not this eternality [*Ewigkeit*] behind whose banner we have rallied in this war: the eternality of the nation and of the nobility it claims as its own: its genius?" Lauding the wounded soldiers who filled the seats at the Felsenreitschule, the critic went so far as to posit Mozart as their standard-bearer, fantasizing that the soldiers "listen to the genius for whom they are fighting."[44]

Other productions, however, have contested the racial legacy of *The Magic Flute*. In the following two examples – one an early nineteenth-century parody, the other an early twenty-first-century intercultural adaptation – lines of influence with Shakespeare suggest ways to understand theatrical negotiations between universality and particularity, between the specifics of the time and place in which a play or opera was originally created and performed, and the new meanings and values to which that piece can be put.

A number of parodies and sequels emerged in the years immediately following *The Magic Flute*'s premiere.[45] In 1818 a new one was produced at the Theater in der Leopoldstadt, a suburban theater in competition with the Theater an der Wien, which had just opened its own revival of Mozart's *Singspiel*. *Die travestirte Zauberflöte* (The Magic Flute Travestied) was written by Leopoldstadt playwright Karl Meisl, with new music by Wenzel Müller, the troupe's resident composer (the score appears to be lost).[46] It was one of a number of satirical *Lokalstücke* that reimagined

Shakespeare, myths, and popular *Singspiele* in the world of contemporary Vienna.[47] The Queen of the Night is now a procuress, the widow of a waste-removal contractor ("Frau von Putzweg" translates to "Mrs. Clean-Way").[48] Sarastro is a gambler and glutton; Papageno is a farmhand named Wastl; and the action takes place against the backdrop of the bustling streets, coffee houses, and taverns of the Wieden district and Prater.[49]

Surrounded by all these burlesques on the original characters, Monostatos is sympathetic, if reduced; he is now nameless, just "Ein Mohr," and is identified only as Sarastro's valet. His solo "Alles fühlt der Liebe Freuden" has all but disappeared; the first few lines are absorbed into a quodlibet sung not by him but by Wastl. No longer is he an overseer or sexual predator; and his racialization, far from being presented as "proof" of his villainy, is rather a plight that seems designed to elicit audience empathy. In his first scene, Pamina enters shouting at him, ordering him to leave her alone. His reply is far gentler than any of his dialogue in Schikaneder's original *Magic Flute* libretto: "Do not be so cruel, gracious maiden," he says. "If only you could see into my heart, how tenderly it beats for you."[50] In response, Pamina doubles down on the insults, threatening to order another beating from Sarastro if, in her cruel words, "such a black Moor dares to come near a dazzling white skin like mine! If you come near me, it's just like a fly falling into a cup of milk." To these slurs, Monostatos replies not with threats but with a rueful account of his own efforts to "wash out" his blackness. For three months, he says, he had soaked himself in bleach, only to find – and to be reminded by the washerfolk – that "one cannot wash a Moor white."[51] The Moor gives up on wooing Pamina and exits, after which she ponders aloud that she cannot be angry that a Moor adores her, for "the more colorful [*bunter*] the crowd of lovers, the more it honors a girl."

On one level, making Monostatos into a nonthreatening, even endearing, figure is just another way for Meisl and Müller to turn the original *Magic Flute* on its head. But it is more than just an inversion played for laughs. "The Moor" gives voice to his suffering, he is not cast out of the Prater society, and at the end of the *Singspiel* it is he who introduces the closing chorus, a cynical indictment of "modern marriage" that compares it to a ride on a merry-go-round. This suggests that Meisl had confidence that audiences would welcome a sympathetic Moor. This might have been due to the actor – we do not know who played the Moor, but it may well have been Johann Sartory, who had starred in another popular *Singspiel* that had already been in the repertoire of the Theater in der Leopoldstadt for years: *Othello, der Mohr in Wien* (Othello, the Moor in Vienna). This parody, with text by Ferdinand Kringsteiner and music by Ignaz Schuster, premiered in 1806 and was a favorite at the Theater in der Leopoldstadt, revived every year through 1814 and 1819–1823.[52] *Othello, der Mohr in Wien*, in turn, was a parody of the popular *Othello, der Mohr von Venedig*, a traditional adaptation of Shakespeare's play from Wieland's translation, which had premiered at the Burgtheater in 1785 and was revived in 1787 and 1790, and thereafter each year from 1800 through 1806.[53] If Sartory had played the Moor in *Die travestirte Zauberflöte*, it would have heightened the intertextual associations with his star turn in *Othello, der Mohr in Wien*. Like *Die travestirte Zauberflöte*, Kringsteiner's *Othello* transposes the action of Shakespeare's original play to contemporary Vienna, and while it too ends happily, it includes several explicit racist epithets. Desdemona's father, bewailing her upcoming marriage to Othello, complains, "If only the Moor were not so black!" to which Desdemona replies, "Dear father – he will bleach himself yet."[54] The father replies with a slur speculating about the skin color of his future grandchildren. These references to skin whitening – already a major cosmetics industry since the seventeenth century – echo the moral connotations long imputed by Europeans to dark and fair skin, as well as accounts of multiracial populations in the colonies and colorism in discourses of scientific racism.[55]

More recent productions of *The Magic Flute*, particularly by directors from predominantly English-speaking countries, have confronted the troubling implications of Monostatos and his casting in new ways. Some attempt to minimize the racism of the original libretto by substituting Monostatos's racialization with another visual signifier of monstrosity. The "flabby, fake pot belly," leather straps, and heels of Julie Taymor's popular Metropolitan Opera production (the 2007 revival) arguably trade one category of stereotypes for another; and while Australian director Barrie Kosky and the UK-based performance group 1927's silent-film staging for the Komische Oper Berlin (2012) reimagined Monostatos as F. W. Murnau's 1922 Nosferatu, they retained the problematic visual signifier of black hands on a white body for "Alles fühlt."[56] Yet, these and other interventions are themselves often subject to backlash from critics who see them as either taking the easy way out or threatening the integrity of the piece.[57] Revisionist approaches, particularly those that take more liberties with Schikaneder's text and even Mozart's music, can achieve new kinds of integrity, as Sheila Boniface Davies and J. Q. Davies write of Isango Portobello's multilingual and musically eclectic *Magic Flute, Impempe Yomlingo* (2007). The Cape Town company's act of translation and transposition, they argue, "underscores the transformative elements of the story on one hand, while enacting a politics of cultural and aesthetic reform on the other."[58]

Another such production is by Madeline Sayet, an American director who works in both opera and Shakespeare. Sayet is a member of the Mohegan Tribe, founder of the Native Shakespeare Ensemble at Amerinda, and executive director of the Yale Indigenous Performing Arts Program. Her production of *The Magic Flute* was for the Glimmerglass Festival's fortieth anniversary season in 2015. She and her librettist Kelley Rourke set out to re-envision Schikaneder and Mozart's tale by incorporating elements of Mohegan and other Native storytelling traditions – what Shakespeare scholars would call "intercultural" or "diasporic" Mozart.[59] Sayet was particularly concerned with how to represent Monostatos because of her experiences with Indigenous stereotyping in theater. As she puts it, "Whether it's blackface, yellowface, or redface, we are not costumes for you to put on."[60] Her solution was to construe Monostatos as a trapper, an outsider figure who represents white encroachment, exploitation, and interference. Sayet's Monostatos is also a policer of boundaries: when he presents Tamino to Sarastro in the Act 1 finale, he proclaims, "You see how I protect the order. / A trespasser has breached your borders. / Good thing you have a guard like me."[61] Sarastro's response echoes the threat in Schikaneder's original, while stopping short of carrying out the original punishment: "Oh yes, I know you very well. / Be grateful I don't have you flogged." As mentioned before of other productions, most of Monostatos's lines are omitted or replaced, from his monologue before "Alles fühlt" to his closing bargain with the Queen for Pamina. Rourke and Sayet also omit Sarastro's line about Monostatos's soul. Finally, the Glimmerglass production demonstrates that recuperative casting does not exist in a vacuum, nor does it apply only to the minoritized characters. While Monostatos was portrayed by a white singer, tenor Nicholas Nestorak, the casting of nonwhite singers in the roles of Tamino, Pamina, the Queen of the Night, and Sarastro made it easier for Monostatos's presence to avoid reinscribing a racist ideology.[62] As Sayet commented on the production, "I saw a world that reflected the one we live in, and the one I will continue to grow in: not the past, but the future."[63]

Sayet recently participated in a virtual seminar series hosted by New York's Red Bull Theater, *Exploring Othello in 2020*, in which a cohort of actors, directors, playwrights, and scholars offered a four-part table-read of *Othello*, wrestling with the play and its legacies as artists of color. She affirmed the fact that Shakespeare's play is "not neutral," observing that Shakespeare has often been used "as a weapon of white supremacy."[64] Sayet's deep ambivalence about canonicity and white supremacy have found expression in other interventions, such as her production of *The Tempest*, which, in her words, considers "what would happen if Caliban could get his language back."[65] Inverting the character hierarchy is another strategy of Shakespeare appropriation that has found a place in literary and theatrical works such as Aimé Césaire's *Une Tempête* (1969), Susan Gayle Todd's *Sycorax* (2010), and Toni Morrison's *Desdemonda* (2011). Sayet confessed an impulse toward this approach when first developing the Glimmerglass *Magic Flute*: "In my guts I wished I could scrap *Magic Flute* and make a show just about Monostatos."[66]

Perhaps the most extreme strategy of resistance would be the refusal of performance altogether. Whether temporary or permanent, individual or collective, such a move immediately prompts questions about canonicity and the obligations of performance as opposed to scholarship. It can seem blasphemous to suggest that we retire such a beloved work from our contemporary operatic museum – although canons are dynamic, and there are plenty of other un- and underperformed operas by Mozart and his contemporaries. At the very least, opera companies, directors, conductors, and audiences must be prepared to ask what the next *Magic Flute* production will offer besides cozy familiarity and guaranteed ticket sales.

Here again, we may look to Shakespeare studies for a model. At that same *Exploring Othello* seminar series, moderator Ayanna Thompson – author of the introduction to the new Arden edition of the play and a founding member of the ShakeRace and RaceB4Race networks – suggested it might be time for a "performance hiatus" on *Othello*.[67] She hastened to add, and has said elsewhere, that plays like *Othello* should still be read, taught, and discussed, but that it is irresponsible to stage them "until we get to a different place in our society about what we can talk about, what we can face."[68] If leading figures in Shakespeare studies can advocate for a temporary performance hiatus for *Othello*, alongside radical reimaginings of its text, surely we can at least contemplate the same for *The Magic Flute*. Ultimately, as with so many other enduring works, the mirror that *The Magic Flute* holds up to us reflects that which we aspire to be, and also that which we are reluctant to admit we are – the violence embedded in the ideal. As Mozart scholars at the intersection of past history and present performance, we would do well to consider, in the words of Hall, how we might "undo and redo the scripts that we have inherited."[69]

Notes

1. "Prachtvoll": Friedrich Rochlitz, "Anekdoten aus Mozarts Leben," *Allgemeine musikalische Zeitung* 1/10 (December 5, 1798): col. 152; "schauerlich": Christian Friedrich Daniel Schubart, "Frankfurter Theater," *Dramaturgische Blätter* (May 21, 1789): 116. Both quoted in Gernot Gruber, *Mozart and Posterity*, trans. R. S. Furness (Boston: Northeastern University Press, 1991 [1985]), 87–88. See also John Daverio, "Mozart in the Nineteenth Century," in *The Cambridge Companion to Mozart*, ed. Simon Keefe (Cambridge: Cambridge University Press, 2003), 177.

2. Franz Horn, "Musikalische Fragmente," *Allgemeine musikalische Zeitung* 4/26 (March 24, 1802): col. 421. Quoted in Abigail Chantler, *E. T. A. Hoffmann's Musical Aesthetics* (Abingdon: Routledge, 2006), 130. See also Gruber, *Mozart and Posterity*, 89–91.

3. Johann Karl Friedrich Triest, "Bemerkungen über die Ausbildung der Tonkunst in Deutschland im achtzehnten Jahrhundert," *Allgemeine musikalische Zeitung* 3/23 (March 4, 1801): col. 391n.

4. Hoffmann, "Further Observations on Spontini's Opera *Olimpia*" (1821), in *E. T. A. Hoffmann's Musical Writings:* Kreisleriana, The Poet and the Composer, *Music Criticism*, trans. Martyn Clarke, ed. David Charlton (Cambridge: Cambridge University Press, 1989), 440. Quoted in Daverio, "Mozart in the Nineteenth Century," 177.

5. Leopold Mozart's travel diary, no date [London, 1765]. MBA, I:200.

6. See Kurt Honolka, *Papageno: Emanuel Schikaneder, Man of the Theater in Mozart's Time*, trans. Jane Mary Wilde (Portland, OR: Amadeus, 1990 [1984]), 40–42.

7. David J. Buch, *Magic Flutes & Enchanted Forests: The Supernatural in Eighteenth-Century Musical Theater* (Chicago: University of Chicago Press, 2008), 293–95.

8. *Operabase*, www.operabase.com/statistics/en (accessed May 3, 2023).

9. On the annual performances for schoolchildren, see *Wiener Staatsoper*, www .wiener-staatsoper.at/spielplan-kartenkauf/detail/event/969262397-die-zauberfloete-fuer-kinder/ (accessed May 3, 2023). The 2003 DVD is broadcast around Austria annually, conducted by Seiji Ozawa, with tenor Herwig Pecoraro in blackface as Monostatos.

10. Malcolm S. Cole, "Monostatos and His 'Sister': Racial Stereotype in *Die Zauberflöte* and Its Sequel," *Opera Quarterly* 21/1 (2005): 18.

11. Derek Scott, "A Problem of Race in Directing *Die Zauberflöte*," in "*Regietheater*": *Konzeption und Praxis am Beispiel der Bühnenwerke Mozarts*, ed. Jürgen Künel, Ulrich Müller, and Oswald Panagl (Anif: Müller-Speiser, 2007); Nasser Al-Taee, *Representations of the Orient in Western Music: Violence and Sensuality* (Farnham: Ashgate, 2010); Steffen Lösel, "Monostatos:

Racism in *Die Zauberflöte*," *Soundings* 102/4 (2019): 275–324; Kira Thurman, "The Character, Monostatos, in Mozart's Opera, *The Magic Flute* (1791)," *Black Central Europe*, https://blackcentraleurope.com/sources/1750-1850/the-character-monostatos-in-mozarts-opera-the-magic-flute-1791/ (accessed May 3, 2023).

12. Uta Sadji, *Der Mohr auf der deutschen Bühne des 18. Jahrhunderts* (Anif: Müller-Speiser, 1992); Peter Martin, *Schwarze Teufel, edle Mohren: Afrikaner in Geschichte und Bewußtsein der Deutschen* (Hamburg: Hamburger Edition, 2001); Barbara Riesche, "Schöne Mohrinnen, Edle Sklaven, Schwarze Rächer: Schwarzendarstellung und Sklavereithematik im Deutschen Unterhaltungstheater (1770–1814)" (PhD thesis, Ludwig-Maximilians-Universität Munich, 2007); Wendy Sutherland, *Staging Blackness and Performing Whiteness in Eighteenth-Century Drama* (Abingdon: Routledge, 2016).

13. Among the welcome exceptions signaling new musicological attention to these issues are the papers presented at "Talking About Race and Gender in *The Magic Flute*," Mozart Society of America Study Session, virtual, November 2020; Lily Kass, "*The Magic Flute*, Sung in English," paper presented at the Annual Meeting of the American Society for Eighteenth-Century Studies, St. Louis, MO, March 2023; and John M. Cowan, "Monostatos: Ethnoracial Representation and Cultural Politics in *Die Zauberflöte*" (MM thesis, University of Miami, 2023).

14. George Shirley, "Il Rodolfo Nero, or The Masque of Blackness," in *Blackness in Opera*, ed. Naomi André, Karen M. Bryan, and Eric Saylor (Urbana: University of Illinois Press, 2012), 266–67.

15. Kira Thurman, *Singing Like Germans: Black Musicians in the Land of Bach, Beethoven, and Brahms* (Ithaca: Cornell University Press, 2021), 234–38, esp. 235–36.

16. See Michael Cooper, "An 'Otello' without Blackface Highlights an Enduring Tradition in Opera," *New York Times* (September 17, 2015); Olivia Giovetti, "Color Blind: Anna Netrebko and Blackface," *VAN Magazine* (June 13, 2019), https://van-magazine.com/mag/anna-netrebko-blackface/.

17. Quoted in Anne Midgette, "Talking Race and 'Blackface' in Opera: The Long Version," *Washington Post* (October 16, 2015).

18. See, for instance, Keith Hamilton Cobb, remarks at "Exploring Othello in 2020: Seminar 1 of 4," *Red Bull Theater* (October 7, 2020), https://youtu.be/K9yDHFfKPps (time stamp 13:10).

19. William Shakespeare, *Othello: Texts and Contexts*, ed. Kim F. Hall (Boston: Bedford/St. Martin's, 2007), esp. intro.

20. Margo Hendricks, "'Obscured by Dreams': Race, Empire, and Shakespeare's *A Midsummer Night's Dream*," *Shakespeare Quarterly* 47/1 (1996): 60.

21. Ronald Takaki, "*The Tempest* in the Wilderness: The Racialization of Savagery," *Journal of American History* 79/3 (1992): 892–912.

22. Kim F. Hall, "Beauty and the Beast of Whiteness: Teaching Race and Gender," *Shakespeare Quarterly* 47/1 (1996): 461.

23. See, for instance, Ian Smith, *Black Shakespeare: Reading and Misreading Race* (Cambridge: Cambridge University Press, 2022); *Anti-Racist Shakespeare*, ed. Ambereen Dadabhoy and Nedda Mehdizadeh (Cambridge: Cambridge University Press, 2023); Farah Karim-Cooper, *The Great White Bard: How to Love Shakespeare While Talking about Race* (New York: Viking, 2023).

24. David Levin, *Unsettling Opera: Staging Mozart, Verdi, Wagner, and Zemlinsky* (Chicago: University of Chicago Press, 2007).

25. Alexa Alice Joubin, "Global Shakespeares as Methodology," *Shakespeare* 9/3 (2013): 274.

26. Buch, *Magic Flutes & Enchanted Forests*, esp. 296–97, 333–35. See also Malcolm Cole, "Mozart and Two Theaters in Josephinian Vienna," in *Opera in Context: Essays on Historical Staging from the Late Renaissance to the Time of Puccini*, ed. Mark A. Radice (Portland, OR: Amadeus Press, 1998), 119; Egon Komorzynski, "'Die Zauberflöte' und 'Dschinnistan,'" *Mozart-Jahrbuch* 1954, 177–94.

27. See COH, 150–51; David J. Buch, "Introduction," in *Der Stein der Weisen*, ed. Buch (Middleton, WI: A-R Editions, 2007), x, xviin6.

28. "Herr Nouseul," in [Johann Jost Anton von Hagen], *Gallerie von Teutschen Schauspielern und Schauspielerinnen der ältern und neuern Zeit* (Vienna: Edeln von Epheu, 1783), 169.

29. Ritchie Robertson, *Mock-Epic Poetry from Pope to Heine* (Oxford: Oxford University Press, 2009), 194.

30. Act 1, scene 12, and Act 1, scene 14, respectively. This and subsequent translations are my own.

31. Jyotsna Singh, "Othello's Identity, Postcolonial Theory, and Contemporary African Rewritings of *Othello*," in *Women, "Race," and Writing in the Early Modern Period*, ed. Margo Hendricks and Patricia Parker (London: Routledge, 1994), 290. See also Nancy Rose Marshall, "The Many Shades of Shakespeare: Representations of Othello and Desdemona in Victorian Visual Culture," in *Transculturation in British Art, 1770–1930*, ed. Julie F. Codell (Farnham: Ashgate, 2012), 73–92.

32. See Paul Abdullah, "Shakespeare Storms in German Opera: *The Tempest* in 1798"; Adeline Mueller, "Caliban Hero" (unpublished papers presented at Annual Meeting of the American Musicological Society, 2017).

33. See Walter Brauneis, "Wolfgang Amadé Mozarts 'Zauberflöte' und Innsbruck: Neue Quellen zum Erstaufführungsdatum im National-Hoftheater gegenüber der Innsbrucker Hofburg und zu den sechs Szenenbildern des Innsbrucker Zeichners und Kupferstechers Joseph Schaffer," *Wissenschaftliches Jahrbuch der Tiroler Landesmuseen* 2 (2009): 58. Brauneis reproduces a 1793 Prague carnival ball ticket with an engraving of the "Es klinget so herrlich" scene (Act

1, scene 17) in which the *Sklaven* are depicted with a similar skin tone to Pamina and Papageno, far paler than Monostatos.

34. Karl Hain's company staged *The Magic Flute* in Brno in 1793. See Daniel Heartz, *Mozart, Haydn and Early Beethoven, 1781–1802* (New York: W. W. Norton, 2009), 283.

35. "Theaterkostums," *Allgemeines europäisches Journal* (Brünn: Joseph Georg Traßler, 1795), II:206. Zakiyyah Iman Jackson, *Becoming Human: Matter and Meaning in an Antiblack World* (New York: New York University Press, 2020), 1. See also Brauneis, "Mozarts 'Zauberflöte' und Innsbruck," 56–57, which cites evidence that the "wilde Thiere" were most often apes and big cats in early productions. Eighteenth-century manifestations of the anti-Black racist "simianizing" trope are discussed in Silvia Sebastiani, "Challenging Boundaries: Apes and Savages in Enlightenment," in *Simianization: Apes, Gender, Class, and Race*, ed. Wulf D. Hund, Charles W. Mills, and Silvia Sebastiani (Zurich: Lit, 2015), 105–38.

36. Kim F. Hall, *Things of Darkness: Economies of Race and Gender in Early Modern England* (Ithaca: Cornell University Press, 1995), 142.

37. On *alla turca* and exoticism in Mozart's music, see Matthew Head, *Orientalism, Masquerade and Mozart's Turkish Music* (London: Royal Musical Association, 2000) (and Head's contribution to the present volume); Al-Taee, *Representations of the Orient*, esp. 146–48; Mary Hunter, "The *Alla Turca* Style in the Late Eighteenth Century: Race and Gender in the Symphony and Seraglio," in *The Exotic in Western Music*, ed. Jonathan Bellman (Boston, MA: Northeastern University Press, 1998).

38. "Bin ich nicht von Fleisch und Blut?" Act 2, scene 7. Curiously, in the original printed libretto this line reads "Ich bin auch den Mädchen gut?" Scott, "A Problem of Race," 341.

39. Al-Taee, *Representations of the Orient*, 147.

40. Cole, "Monostatos and His 'Sister'," 20.

41. Erik Levi, *Mozart and the Nazis: How the Third Reich Abused a Cultural Icon* (New Haven, CT: Yale University Press, 2010), esp. 157–59.

42. Otto Kunz, "Salzburger Kriegsfestspiele 1941," *Salzburger Volksblatt* (August 4, 1941), 3.

43. Ibid.

44. Siegfried Melckinger, "Kulturbericht: Salzburger Kriegsfestspiele – Eröffnung mit 'Zauberflöte'," *Neues Wiener Tagblatt* (August 4, 1941), 3.

45. See Hayoung Heidi Lee, "Papageno Redux: Repetition and the Rewriting of Character in Sequels to *Die Zauberflöte*," *Opera Quarterly* 28/1–2 (2012): 72–87; *Mozarts Zauberflöte und ihre Dichter: Schikaneder, Vulpius, Goethe, Zuccalmaglio*, ed. Werner Wunderlich, Doris Ueberschlag, and Ulrich Müller (Anif: Mueller-Speiser, 2007); Donald G. Henderson, "The 'Magic Flute' of Peter Winter," *Music & Letters* 64/3–4 (1983): 193–205; Peter Branscombe,

"An Old Viennese Opera Parody and a New Nestroy Manuscript," *German Life and Letters* 28/3 (1975): 210–17.

46. Franz Hadamowsky, *Das Theater in der Wiener Leopoldstadt 1781–1860* (Vienna: Generaldirektion der Nationalbibliothek, 1934), 291.

47. See *Ein Jahrhundert Alt-Wiener Parodie*, ed. Otto Rommel (Vienna: Österreichischer Bundesverlag für Unterricht, Wissenschaft und Kunst, 1930); W. E. Yates, *Theatre in Vienna: A Critical History, 1776–1995* (Cambridge: Cambridge University Press, 1996), 92, 93.

48. Jane K. Brown, "The Queen of the Night and the Crisis of Allegory in *The Magic Flute*," *Goethe Yearbook* 8 (1996): 142–56, esp. 144–45.

49. Otto Rommel, *Die Alt-Wiener Volkskomödie: Ihre Geschichte vom Barocken Welt-Theater bis zum Tode Nestroys* (Vienna: Anton Schroll, 1952), 866.

50. Karl Meisl, *Theatralisches Quodlibet oder Sämmtliche dramatische Beyträge für die Leopoldstädter Bühne*, vol. 4: *Die travestirte Zauberflöte* (Pest: Hartleben, 1820), Act 1, scene 8, 21.

51. This is a spin on the popular Renaissance proverb "wash an Ethiope white" expressing the futility of going against nature. See "Aethiopem lavare," in Geoffrey Whitney, *A Choice of Emblems* (1586), 57. Discussed in *Othello*, ed. Hall, 185; Karen Newman, *Essaying Shakespeare* (Minneapolis: University of Minnesota Press, 2009), 38–58.

52. There were several connections between the cast of *Die travestirte Zauberflöte* and the original 1791 *Magic Flute* cast: the 1818 Sarastro was played by Karl Schikaneder, Emanuel's brother; and the 1818 "Nachtkönigin" was played by Elisabeth Schack, who had played one of the Three Ladies in the original 1791 production and whose husband Benedikt originated the role of Tamino. See Hadamowsky, *Das Theater in der Wiener Leopoldstadt*, 222, for performance details.

53. The lead role was portrayed by Joseph Lange, the husband of Aloysia (Weber) Lange, who created the role of the Queen of the Night in *The Magic Flute*. See Renata Häublein, *Die Entdeckung Shakespeares auf der deutschen Bühne des 18. Jahrhunderts: Adaptation und Wirkung der Vemittlung auf dem Theater* (Tübingen: Max Niemeyer, 2005), 148–65; for performance details, see Franz Hadamowsky, *Die Wiener Hoftheater (Staatstheater) 1776–1966: Verzeichnis der Aufgeführten Stücke mit Bestandsnachweis und Täglichem Spielplan, Teil 1: 1776–1810* (Vienna: Georg Prachner, 1966), 95.

54. Ferdinand Kringsteiner, *Othello, der Mohr in Wien, Eine Posse mit Gesang* (Vienna: Wallishausser, 1806); Act 1, scene 10.

55. See, for instance, Patricia Akhimie, *Shakespeare and the Cultivation of Difference: Race and Conduct in the Early Modern World* (New York: Routledge, 2018).

56. On Monostatos in Taymor's *Flute*, see Anthony Tommasini, "An Opera at the Met That's Real and 'Loud,'" *New York Times* (January 1, 2007); Betty Leigh Hutcheson, "Twenty-First Century Exoticism: Taymor Does the Magic Flute," *Brooklyn Rail* (February 2007), https://brooklynrail.org/2007/02/music/magic-flute. On Monostatos in Kosky and 1927's *Flute*, see Zachary Woolfe, "The Happy Results of a Speedy Shift," *New York Times* (November 26, 2013); Mark Swed, "Review: Brilliant Transformation of 'The Magic Flute,'" *Los Angeles Times* (November 25, 2013).

57. See, for instance, Tim Ashley, "Whitewashed or Just Plain Colourless?," *The Guardian* (July 9, 2008); Rupert Christiansen, "Why *The Magic Flute* Has Driven Directors to Despair," *The Telegraph* (February 23, 2019).

58. Sheila Boniface Davies and J. Q. Davies, "'So Take This Magic Flute and Blow. It Will Protect Us As We Go': *Impempe Yomlingo* (2007–11) and South Africa's Ongoing Transition," *Opera Quarterly* 28/1–2 (2012): 56.

59. On intercultural Shakespeare, see, for instance, Yong Li Lan, "Ong Keng Sen's 'Desdemona', Ugliness, and the Intercultural Performative," *Theatre Journal* 56/2 (2004): 251–73. On diasporic Shakespeare, see Alexa Alice Joubin, "Global Shakespeare Criticism beyond the Nation State," in *The Oxford Handbook of Shakespeare and Performance*, ed. James C. Bulman (Oxford: Oxford University Press, 2017), 423–40.

60. Quoted in Alison Kinney, "Blackface, Diversity, and Getting Opera Right in 2015," *Good* (September 25, 2015), www.good.is/articles/otello-blackface-glimmerglass-mohegan-magic-flute-opera.

61. Kelley Rourke, *The Magic Flute* [libretto] (unpublished, 2015, quoted with permission of author).

62. Nestorak studied with George Shirley, referenced earlier in the anecdote about Charles Holland's aversion to Monostatos. See Kevin Doubleday, "Quick Q&A: Young Artist Nicholas Nestorak," Glimmerglass Festival (August 1, 2015), https://glimmerglass.org/2015/08/quick-qa-young-artist-nicholas-nestorak/.

63. Quoted in Kinney, "Blackface."

64. Madeline Sayet, remarks at "Exploring Othello in 2020: Seminar 1 of 4" (time stamp 33:42).

65. Quoted in "Madeline Sayet on Where We Belong," *Folger Shakespeare Library* (June 1, 2021), www.folger.edu/shakespeare-unlimited/where-we-belong-sayet.

66. Quoted in Kinney, "Blackface."

67. Ayanna Thompson, remarks at "Exploring Othello in 2020: Seminar 2 of 4," *Red Bull Theater* (October 14, 2020, https://youtu.be/8Zd5jOV8XLg (time stamp 1:10:47). See William Shakespeare, *Othello*, ed. E. A. J. Honigmann, with a new introduction by Thompson (London: Bloomsbury, 2016).

68. Thompson, in "Free Shakespeare on the Radio: *Richard II*: Episode 4," *WNYC Studios* (July 16, 2020), www.wnycstudios.org/podcasts/free-shakespeare-

podcast-richard-ii/episodes/free-shakespeare-public-richard-ii-episode-4
(time stamp 1:38).

69. Kim F. Hall, "Introduction," in Keith Hamilton Cobb, *American Moor*
(London: Methuen Drama, 2020), xi.

PART IV

Reception, Interpretation, and Influence

17 | *Zauberflöte*: A Cultural Phenomenon in an Age of Revolution

IAN WOODFIELD

In August 1794, the *Journal des Luxus und der Moden*, a beautifully illustrated fashion magazine, alerted its readership to a cultural phenomenon: *Die Zauberflöte*.[1] Mozart's opera had swept through German-speaking Europe on an irresistible tide of enthusiasm, its progress coming to a temporary halt only at the linguistic border.[2] Already there were many different stage versions, but this represented only part of the opera's triumph. As one sold-out production followed another, *Die Zauberflöte* began to permeate the fabric of daily life, generating an extensive material legacy of its own. Merchandise on offer ranged from cheap trinkets, mementos of productions, to expensive gifts, based not just on the appeal of the music but on the colorful characters and the eye-catching visual imagery. Yet even as the world flocked to see this beguiling fairy tale and purchase its brand, it faced a revolutionary war that would demolish nations, destroy alliances, and displace millions. The opera was not immune to the effects of this chaos, and darker threads run through the tapestry of its early reception.[3]

The year during which *Die Zauberflöte* established its position as an icon of Viennese culture was a turbulent one for the Austrian monarchy. The early death of Leopold II in March 1792, just two years into his reign, left his inexperienced son Franz facing a war with France. Vienna celebrated his accession with a public illumination, accompanied by firework displays, wind-band music, and Turkish ensembles. On the name day of the new emperor, an installation in the Augarten featured an artificial mountain with miners at work, accompanied by "beautiful" music.[4] The commemoration of the revered empress Maria Theresia, still a significant event a decade after her death, began with a banquet in the Schönbrunn Orangerie. The imperial party then visited a Venetian fair to drink coffee in a boutique, where incidental music was provided by a clock that played an opera air from a well-known work every minute.[5] Later, there was a ballet in a magnificently lit Chinese garden house, and the day's entertainment came to an end with a Papageno-like figure, a Jewish lad clad as a bird-catcher, who performed more than fifty birdcalls before revealing that his cage was in fact empty.[6] A light approach to entertainment, favoring mixed-genre variety programmes, was now in vogue; it was an environment tailor-made for *Die Zauberflöte*.

It is not known when Franz and Marie Therese first saw the opera in the theater, but they soon got to know its music. A score featured in the décor of their Haus der Laune (house of caprice), a folly constructed in 1798 in the English landscape park at Laxenburg: "On the frescoed walls are real title pages and pieces of music by famous composers ... entire volumes attached to the wall can be leafed through."[7] Imperial soirées began to feature its music in an undemanding genre: the quodlibet. Marie Therese commissioned several medleys featuring opera arias. John Rice makes the intriguing suggestion that Ignaz von Seyfried's offering, based on a repertoire list supplied by the empress herself, was intended to represent her husband. If so, "Dies Bildnis ist bezaubernd schön" salutes him as a high-minded hero who receives a gentle reminder of his wife's physical attractions!

In view of the enthusiasm for Mozart's Italian comedies along the cultural axis linking Bohemia with Saxony, it is not surprising that Prague, Dresden, and Leipzig were quick to stage *Die Zauberflöte*. As soon became the pattern everywhere, success on the stage inspired a range of merchandise. In Prague, sets of invitation cards were produced, featuring scenes from the opera; two pairs survive from 1793 and 1794.[8] When Joseph Seconda's production opened in Leipzig in January 1793, twelve colored engravings were put on sale, depicting characters in costume.[9] Each figure is accompanied by a phrase of text, in most cases the first line of its character's aria.[10] Aspects of the iconography of these illustrations may well derive from the Leipzig production. Another set of pictures was published in Trier in 1797, also displaying vivid imagery. The Queen is shown wearing an ordinary black ball gown, brilliantly emblazoned with stars; one of her three assistants appears to offer Tamino a recorder; and fearsome men in black stand before portcullises that bar the way to the testing ground. The captions feature snippets of text, by no means restricted to aria first lines; Monostatos, seen from behind as he gazes upon the sleeping Pamina, exclaims: "Weiss ist schön." This set also has a narrative element, focusing on happy endings: Tamino and Pamina ("Tamino mein"); and Papageno and Papagena ("Nun bin ich dir ganz gegeben").[11]

As a keen card player himself, Mozart would doubtless have been chuffed to learn that a memento on offer in Leipzig was a board game, a variant of the ancient *gioco dell'oca* (game of the goose) in which players move their counters inwards round a spiral track to square sixty-three in the center, hoping to avoid penalties and benefit from concessions.[12] The small cartoons scattered along the route exhibit figures and scenery. If square twenty-three represents Pamina's place of captivity, she awaits her prince in a medieval turret. The traditional "death" square (fifty-eight) hosts the two men in black armor. Papageno appears twice with a dulcimer, striking it with tremendous vigor. A rite of passage, this operatic version of the game ends with a series of extra squares: three depict the trial of fire, one the magic flute, and four the trial of water. Although the rules of play are not known, landing on the square of the magic flute must in some way have facilitated admission to the Grecian "Tempel der Weisheit."

A popular party game, described in several social entertainment manuals of the late 1790s, was simply entitled *Papageno*.[13] Rife with sexual innuendo, the improvised drama required a bird-catcher, selected from the company, to trap a bird and by extension a partner for life, sight unseen. The rules of the game leave the manner of performance entirely open; as described, it could sit anywhere on a spectrum from innocent diversion to drunken sex caper. Blindfolded, Papageno is led back into the room, where a circle is formed to whirl round him while two strophes are sung to the tune of "Ein Mädchen oder Weibchen." He sounds his pipes to stop the dance, makes a "V" sign with his forefinger and middle finger, points in a random direction, and then begins to "lure" an unknown person. The victim approaches and inserts a finger into his "Klobe" (the fowler's cleft-stick trap represented by the "V"), which promptly snaps shut. Papageno must now divine the gender of the captive, which he does with obvious parody: "Ein Männchen! Ein Männchen! Oder Ein Weibchen! Ein Weibchen!"[14] If he gets it wrong, he is ribbed, especially if he has let an attractive partner escape. The next stage parodies the bird-catcher's checklist of Pamina's personal characteristics, as further details of the unknown person are elicited: either in one-word responses to a question ("schön oder häßlich?"), or through the use of innuendo ("auf eine verblümte Art"). Papageno now has to name the "little bird" he has captured, and if he is successful, the two will switch places in a manner to be determined by the full company.[15] The game is a re-enactment of the moment when Papageno, faced with the reality of life with an ugly crone, allows himself briefly to dream of a more beautiful alternative. Another *Zauberflöte* game, rules unknown but probably involving pairing as even numbers are required, was advertised as a suitable gift for Christmas or New Year in 1793.[16]

A version of *Papageno* for children, with sexual innuendo removed, featured birds, as the participants each select a songster such as a "Nachtigall," a "Lerche," or a "Stiglitz" (goldfinch).[17] A bird able to perform a tune from the opera appears in a tiny playlet, also for children. Jensen boasts to Lennchen that the bullfinch ("Gimpel") with which he hopes to make a fortune can whistle four tunes, including a little piece from *Die Zauberflöte*. Easily trapped – hence its name "sucker" – but valuable (once trained to perform a song), the bullfinch is mentioned by Papageno during his long conversation with Tamino after "Der Vogelfänger"; if the prince asks such stupid questions, he will be "trapped like a bullfinch in my aviary" ("wie einen Gimpel in mein Vogelhaus").[18]

The opulent Königsberg production (1794) exemplified the opera's debt to the world of fashion and its influence on it. An early review began with an account of the costumes, treating the singers as models on a catwalk: Sarastro with a silver undergarment and a wrap of glazed gold, attendants clad in "Mousselin" (satin); the Queen of the Night with an embroidered red gown; Tamino, in Japanese costume, with a hose of glazed gold and a bodice embroidered "à quatre couleurs," set off by a wrap of green atlas weave; Pamina with a garment of white atlas weave and a ponceau (poppy-colored) wrap.[19] Papageno's outfit caused a great sensation as his feathers gave the illusion of flight in response to the slightest movement. There was no need for Monostatos to black up as he wore a black leather mask, very natural looking! But substandard costumes would usually attract criticism. A review of the 1793 Passau production took Pamina to task for looking like a seventeenth-century German woman "quite in the manner of a - marionette."[20] The *Zauberflöte* "look" proved very marketable. As the *Journal des Luxus* report noted, little Papageno flutes ("Papageno-Pfeiffchen") were all the rage among the lads. Fashionable accessories, these items could have been sold as badges to be sewn on clothing, as pin-on brooches, or as sounding whistles to be slung round the neck. Papageno masks were available for balls.[21] For women who wanted to self-identify with a character, there were hair styles, headbands, muffs, and workbags *à la Papagena*, presumably not contributing to the representation of an aging hag![22]

The visual magnificence of the sets was a big factor in attracting audiences. A celebrated series of engravings by Joseph Schaffer, dating from around 1794 and published in the *Allgemeines europäisches Journal* in 1795, may represent the sets used in the Brünn production: one shows a snake, tastefully trisected; another features Sarastro's entry on a throne drawn by lions, his attendants clad in Turkish garb (see Figures 4.3–4.8

earlier in this volume). The scene in which Tamino and Pamina submit themselves for testing is presented with due solemnity. A challenge both to painters and machine designers, this set piece was often seen as a test of the effectiveness of the opera's scenography overall. A generally weak production in Cassel was redeemed by the speedy transformation achieved in the test of fire, a feat credited to "Mechanikus Moretti."[23] When Schikaneder transferred his production to the new Theater an der Wien, all went well: the audience witnessed a "sea of fire and a column of flames, steam and smoke which rises in billowing waves against the clouds, and is instantly transformed into a raging, plunging stream to great effect."[24] In *Der gestiefelte Kater* (Puss in Boots), Ludwig Tieck satirized inadequate staging when at the end of the play recourse has to be had to Mozart's music for the trials by fire and water in order to produce a memorable climax.[25]

Die Zauberflöte was created in a world fascinated by high-quality human automata. Shortly before Mozart's death, Carl Enslen advertised a theatrical performance embodying a union of music, painting, and sculpture with technology.[26] His show offered the intriguing spectacle of robots able to communicate expressively.[27] Musical automata also featured prominently in displays of waxwork figures. Joseph Müller was quick to incorporate in his celebrated show a "künstliche Stahl Harmonika," which played the most enjoyable melodies from the opera.[28] The Salzburg entrepreneur Bartholomäus Lemminger went further in a display in the Lichtensteg in Vienna that featured a wax model of "Der Vogelfänger Papageno."[29] Some early productions of *Die Zauberflöte* were influenced by the automata on display in these very popular shows. In Königsberg, an inventor came up with a two-octave "Glockeninstrument," the sound of which was supposed to resemble that of a harmonica.[30]

Part of Papageno's charm is that he sings in an unaffected mechanical style, a robotic topic taken by Richard Middleton to represent rational classicism reduced to its "nuts and bolts."[31] His musical box numbers presented retailers everywhere with an opportunity to rake in the cash. Small aural mementos were manufactured on an industrial scale: clocks, miniature barrel organs, whistles, figurines, and musical toys incorporating clockwork. Their timbre varied but not their reliance on machine-generated sound. The glockenspiel's distinctive tones came to define the opera.[32] At the other end of the technological spectrum, the great mechanized orchestra developed by Johann Georg Strasser for St. Petersburg began, symbolically, with the arresting chords of the overture.[33]

By early 1794, the darkening political landscape across Europe was starting to have a discernible effect on the reception of *Die Zauberflöte*.

This was evident both in the emergence of allegorical interpretations with a political slant and in the detail of some staged versions. In the wake of the occupation of the Rhinelands by French armies, an unambiguously pro-Jacobin reading of the work gained currency. It cast the Queen of the Night as an embodiment of the *Ancien Régime* and Pamina as freedom itself, "a daughter of despotism."[34] Acknowledging that the French Revolution formed no part of the original conception, it argued that, in the spirit of the times, the work could now be viewed as "Propagande der Freiheit."

A rival reading of *Die Zauberflöte* was offered in Weimar.[35] It sees the work as a universal allegory of man's progress from darkness into light and hints that "certain orders" might recognize this journey in their own ceremonies. Whether or not Schikaneder and Mozart took Masonic ritual as a model for some scenes in Act II, the craft was quick to claim the ethos of Sarastro's realm, adapting the music to its own fraternal context. In *Freymaurer Lieder mit Melodien*, Papageno's "Ein Mädchen oder Weibchen," shorn of its sprightly dotted rhythms and marked moderately slow, is set to Ludwig Hölty's famous hymn to loyalty: "Uebt immer Treu und Redlichkeit" (Always practice truth and honesty). It includes a choral da capo for the assembled brethren, as does the arrangement of "Seid uns zum zweiten Mal willkommen."[36] In this and other published collections a mood of benevolence prevails, but sharper political point-scoring sometimes intrudes. An advertisement for the second edition of a Masonic collection of choruses and songs by "O. Br. W. E. Mozart" alerted purchasers to a comment denigrating the emperor himself. A "freedom-mad Franz" is scathingly identified as Monostatos, the opera's imprisoner-in-chief.[37] In a nifty bit of textual editing, the two stanzas of Sarastro's Act 2 aria are blended to telling effect: "In ächten Maurer Hallen steht Tugend felsenfest" (In true *Masonic* halls virtue stands rock-solid).

In the pervasive atmosphere of crisis gripping revolutionary Europe, all sides saw *Die Zauberflöte* as an irresistible resource for the expression of their views. Doubtless thanks to its association with "Ueb immer Treu," "Ein Mädchen oder Weibchen" established itself at the heart of the Prussian military establishment when the carillon of the Garnisonkirche in Potsdam was reprogrammed in 1797 to facilitate hourly renditions of it.[38] At the opposite end of the political spectrum, Papageno's tunes were quick to infiltrate the fast-proliferating republican song repertoire. *Liederlese für Republikaner*, a collection of song texts, includes a setting of Sarastro's aria.[39] But the favored tune from the opera (allocated to three songs) is "Ein Mädchen oder Weibchen"; Papageno's signature piece thus rubs shoulders with overtly political melodies such as "God save great

George our King" and the *Marseillaise*.[40] Even more striking is the use of "Der Vogelfänger bin ich ja!" as the tune for "Das Lied des freien Mannes," the unofficial Rhinelands ode to equality.[41] In sentiment close to Robert Burns's contemporaneous "A Man's a Man for a' That," the song proclaims that everyone in the new order, pimp or count, slave or king, will be able to sing: "Ich bin und bleib ein freier Mann!"[42] The author Friedrich Lehne, who signs himself simply as "Lehne: Republikaner von Mainz," credits "Mozzart" with the tune and identifies the opera. On the other hand, the version published in *Humaniora* in 1798 makes no mention of the composer or the opera; as with a true folksong, the tune title alone is sufficient for identification.[43] "Das Lied des freien Mannes" to Papageno's tune is followed in this source by two ardent republican songs: a celebration of Joseph Warren's heroism at the Battle of Bunker Hill, his sword colored with "Brittenblud"; and an ode entitled "Dem Helden Napoleon Buonaparte," which begins with the optimistic accolade "Friedegeber!"[44]

By the mid-1790s, republican themes were starting to infiltrate new translations of the opera. A telling example comes in the three-act version prepared by Christian August Vulpius for Mannheim and Weimar.[45] In Mannheim, the first performance had been scheduled for January 6, 1794, but events upstream, the loss of Alsace to the French in the Second Battle of Wissembourg on December 26, 1793, led to a state of emergency and the temporary closure of the theaters. Once things had calmed down, *Die Zauberflöte* in the "more palatable" translation by Vulpius was given on March 29.[46] By then, the Weimar premiere had taken place.[47] Vulpius reworded the first line of the Queen of the Night's rage aria as a direct plea for assassination: "Es sterbe der Tirann von deinen Händen."[48] The echo of a well-known revolutionary slogan celebrating the regicide of Louis XVI could hardly have been missed. The demise of "Ludwig Capet" (the commoner's name assigned to the king) was reported in typically understated fashion on January 29, 1793, by the republican journal *Argos*, edited by Eulogius Schneider in Strasbourg, but there was nothing understated about the accompanying ode which begins in triumph: "Es sterbe der Tyrann, der Volksverrätther!"[49]

The short-lived journal *Rheinische Musen*, our main source for the opera's progress in this highly politicized region, sometimes looked further afield, while maintaining its distinctive focus on the political backstory. It credited *Il flauto magico*, the Italian translation presented by Domenico Guardasoni in Prague, Dresden, and Leipzig in 1794, to Scipione Piattoli, a priest closely associated with a large expatriate community of Poles. In the aftermath of the Polish-Russian War of 1792, thousands had taken refuge in Saxony under the leadership of Tadeusz Kościuszko and Ignacy Potocki. The former had passed through Lemberg, now Lviv in the western Ukraine, where he is likely to have encountered the Polish translation of Wolfganga Amade Mozarta's new opera. The premiere of *Die Zauberflöte* in Lemberg on September 21, 1792, is the first known performance of the work outside Vienna, a clear reflection of the speed with which it spread through the Austrian monarchy.

By the time *Il flauto magico* opened in Leipzig, its author Piattoli was already under arrest, his French sympathies attracting scrutiny.[50] The radical, Masonic views espoused by the leaders of this expatriate community left their mark on the Italian translation. Its "argomento" identifies the work's main allegory as a platitude: "misfortunes" (unidentified) may in the end still turn out well. In the circumstances, Poles exiled in Saxony might well have read that as a coded political comment.[51] The most significant change in Act 1 is the incorporation of an aria for Pamina ("Infelice, sconsolata"), an impassioned if thoroughly conventional lament that resonates with the reading of her as a political prisoner.[52]

In a sharply divided Europe, even attendance at this most escapist of operas could become a pointed signal of political allegiance. In the summer of 1796, the situation in the Rhinelands was deteriorating fast, as a French army under the command of General Jean Victor Marie Moreau began to push into south Germany along the Neckar. A traveler from Regensburg was surprised when the bombardment of Cannstadt was paused so that *Die Zauberflöte* could go ahead in nearby Stuttgart. But the audience was unusually limited. The unknown observer noted with evident satisfaction that local "women of class" were boycotting the performance, prompting French members of the audience to make fun of the timidity of the fair sex in the city.[53]

During his long association with the opera, Goethe acted as a powerful advocate of its universality. In *Hermann und Dorothea* (1797), an idyll set in an era of revolutionary war, a young man is sent with supplies for refugees in the Mainz area. He meets and falls for a young woman who is assisting the destitute and has just helped at a roadside birth. His father, though, wishes him to marry well. As instructed, he sets his cap at the daughter of a well-to-do neighbor. He listens to her singing at the piano but is puzzled by references to "Tamino" and "Pamina."[54] Having thus exposed his total ignorance of the opera, he is ridiculed. Later, he learns that the household has awarded him the ironic nickname "[Mr.] Tamino." In 1797, a real-life Hermann might well have assumed that the young lady was calling her lapdogs, given the current vogue for naming pets after characters from the opera![55] In this story, *Zauberflöte* pointedly represents affluent domesticity with its comfortable musical soirées, a world untouched by the unfolding human catastrophe.

Yet Goethe believed that the soundscape of *Die Zauberflöte* was just as appropriate for victims of poverty and war on their stages: the open road and the temporary camp. Accordingly, when he began work on his unfinished sequel, he modified the portrayal of Papageno, refashioning him as an altogether less cozy symbol of humanity's place in the world than the original child of nature. Jane K. Brown sees the characterization of the bird-catcher and his wife as the "glummest" feature of this fragment: "They come onstage carrying rabbits by their ears and birds by their wings." As if the commodification of the fuzzy friends of *Die Zauberflöte* was not bad enough, Papageno and Papagena are still childless.[56] The absence of any of the "Kinderlein" so joyfully anticipated in the original amounted to a striking rebuttal of the warmth of its tone.

The *Journal des Luxus* had already been struck by the way that the opera's melodies were permeating the lowest strata of German musical society. It was not surprising that its sonic reach should have colonized middle-class safe spaces: "Bädern, Gärten, Caffeehäusern, Gasthöfen, Redouten und Ständchen." More striking was its presence on the streets, represented by a procession of itinerant entertainers and vagrant fiddlers: "Unsern Stadtpfeifern, Prager-Musikanten, Bänkelsängern, und Marmotten-Buben." Two of these generic vagabonds – the ballad singer and the marmot knave, an itinerant beggar boy who performs tricks with his animal to the sound of a hurdy-gurdy – had appeared earlier in Goethe's farce *Das Jahrmarktsfest zu Plundersweilern* (1773).[57] There is nothing cute about this picture of a furry animal jumping through a hoop; its antics have (so far) staved off its owner's starvation ("und immer was zu essen fand"). Prague musicians are wandering players, fiddlers like those in Wilhelm Müller's "Der Prager Musikant," who travel with instrument on the back.

Other outdoor beneficiaries of the opera were presenters of "Laterne-Magique" shows. Goethe was much moved by engravings of street entertainers, self-employed in their chosen genre; such images, he thought, expressed the humanity of the poor. A well-known example is the woman player of the "L'orgue de Barbarie," a striking visual counterpart to Papageno with his basket.[58] The bird-catcher is relatively unencumbered by his lofty wicker cage, but she, with a living to make and no tenure in the realm of the Queen of the Night, has serious weight to carry: a substantial barrel organ slung in front of her and on her back a peep show. In effect she transports her own stage.[59]

In October 1813, the apocalyptic Battle of the Nations signaled the approaching end of the carnage of the Napoleonic era, and the music of *Die Zauberflöte* was on hand to celebrate its passing. A remarkable satire, *Politisches Quodlibet, oder Musikalisches Probechart*, was published in Hannover on November 21, a month after this epic defeat for the French.[60] Cast in the form of a typical Viennese quodlibet, it consists of texts from five Mozart operas and works by Salieri, Martín y Soler, Dittersdorf, Wranitzky, and others.[61] Also stitched together in this patchwork quilt are many folksongs, national songs, and political pieces.[62] *Die Zauberflöte* is a primary source, and Napoleon quits the European theater of war using its language, interspersed with several utterances from his favorite composer Paisiello. Extremely bitter, he exclaims "Der Hölle Rache kocht in meinem Herzen." An accompanying cartoon depicts a fire-breathing dragon. He defiantly taunts the Allies: "Tod und Verzweiflung sey eu'r Lohn." To their suggestion, derived from the words of Monostatos, that he should shut his eyes if he does not like what he sees, he replies with some Grétry: "Non, non, non, non, non, non, j'ai trop de fierté." His response to Jérôme Buonaparte's pathetic plea for help ("Zur Hilfe! Zur Hilfe!" – Tamino's words at the start of the opera) draws on the same character's refusal to assist in the quintet ("Ich kann nichts thun").[63] This piece also supplies the moment of farewell, as Napoleon's ship sets sail back across the Rhine:

> NAPOLEON *(drohend sich umsehend)*   *(looking around menacingly)*
> Auf Wiedersehn!
> DIE ALLIIRTEN *(mit Nachdruck)*   *(emphatically)*
> Auf Wiedersehn!

Notes

1. "Ueber Mozarts Oper die Zauber-Flöte," *Journal des Luxus und der Moden*, vol. 9 (August 1794), 364–66.
2. For an excellent survey of the opera's early reception, see COH, 152–67.
3. I aim to develop a comment by Rachel Cowgill, "New Light and the Man of Might: Revisiting Early Interpretations of Mozart's *Die Zauberflöte*," in *Art and Ideology in European Opera: Essays in Honour of Julian Rushton*, ed. Rachel Cowgill, David Cooper, and Clive Brown (Woodbridge: Boydell, 2010), 194–221, at 199: "the immediate context for *Die Zauberflöte* was a Europe wracked with conflict and revolution."
4. ". . . ein künstlich aufgeführter Berg darstellte, in welchem Bergknappen unter einer schönen Musik eben beschäftiget waren." *Kurfürstlich gnädigst privilegirte*

Münchner Zeitung 160 (October 11, 1792): 838. If the source of the music was Ignaz Umlauf's *Die Bergknappen*, a politically inspired reference to the inaugural *Singspiel* of Joseph II's troupe in 1778 may have been intended.

5. *Bayreuther Zeitung* 132 (October 25, 1792): 897.

6. Ibid.

7. John Rice, *Empress Marie Therese and Music at the Viennese Court* (Cambridge: Cambridge University Press, 2003), 130–39. Music from *Die Zauberflöte* can be deciphered in a watercolor of one of the wallpapers.

8. These are reproduced in Martin Nedbal, *Prague's Estates Theater, Mozart, and Bohemian Patriotism* (Mozart Society of America, 2018), 8–10.

9. Brigitte Richter, "'Sehr gut und mit allem beyfall gegeben': Erstaufführungen von Mozarts Opern auf dem Leipziger Theater des 18. Jahrhunderts," in *Mozart in Kursachsen*, ed. Brigitte Richter and Ursula Oehme (Leipzig: Stadtgeschichtliches Museum, 1991), 63–88, at 77–83.

10. Such products helped to ensure that the vivid language of the libretto became an integral part of the opera's identity, a counterbalance to the scathing literary criticism that Schikaneder's "wretched" effort usually attracted.

11. *Historisches Taschenbuch für Liebhaber der Trierischen Geschichte auf das Jahr 1797*. The illustrations are reproduced in Hans-Ulrich Seifert, "Tamino ist zum Malen schön," *Kurtrierisches Jahrbuch* (1991), 159–71.

12. Jan Assmann, "Kunst und Ritual: Mozarts *Zauberflöte*," in *Die neue Kraft der Rituale*, ed. Axel Michaels (Heidelberg, 2007), 87–116. On Mozart's fondness for *Zwicken*, a popular gambling game, see David J. Buch, "Three Posthumous Reports Concerning Mozart in His Late Viennese Years," *Eighteenth-Century Music* 2/1 (2005): 125–26.

13. A short description appears in *Tempel der Musen und Grazien: Ein Taschenbuch zur Bildung und Unterhaltung* (Mannheim, 1795). Much more detail is given in the *Jahrbuch der Freude* (Leipzig, 1797), 108, where it is preceded by another social game entitled, perhaps with a nod to Dittersdorf, "Der Doktor und Apotheker."

14. Self-identification with Papageno's quest for a wife is seen in the letters of Joseph Friedrich zu Racknitz on January 10, 1796, and again on June 2, two days after his marriage. He quotes the first four lines of "Ein Mädchen." *A Rare Treatise on Interior Decoration and Architecture: Joseph Friedrich zu Racknitz's Presentation and History of the Taste of the Leading Nations*, trans. and ed. Simon Swynfen Jervis (Los Angeles: Getty Research Institute, 2019), 10–11.

15. A description in *Ganz neues allgemeinnütziges Unterhaltungsbuch für muntere Gesellschaften jedes Standes, Alters und Geschlechts* (Graz, 1799) recommends a parting kiss.

16. *Bayreuther Zeitung* 152 (December 19, 1793): 1071. Another pairing game "Venus und Pomona," described in *Jahrbuch der Freude* (1797), at 88, makes

use of "Der Vogelfänger." This manual also offers a birthday song to the tune of "Das klinget so herrlich" (at 88).

17. *Unterhaltungen ausser der Schule oder gesellschaftliche Jugendspiele* (Munich, 1818), 3.

18. *Neue Kinderspiele* (Böhme: Leipzig, 1799), 16. A trained bullfinch can easily master a complete stanza in Papageno style! www.youtube.com/watch?v=9a18bdYx-XU.

19. *Rheinische Musen* 2/5 (1794): 114–15.

20. *Rheinische Musen* 2/1 (1794): 10.

21. *Steyermärkische Intelligenz-Blätte zu Nro. 6 der Gräzer Zeitung* (January 7, 1795).

22. *Journal des Luxus* 9 (August 1794), 365.

23. *Rheinische Musen* 3/8 (1795): 176.

24. *Allgemeine musikalische Zeitung* 5/2 (October 6, 1802): cols. 26–27. Cited by Carol Padgham Albrecht, "Music in Public Life in Viennese Reports from the *Allgemeine musikalische Zeitung*, 1798–1804" (PhD diss., Kent State University, 2008), 118.

25. Ludwig Tieck, *Der gestiefelte Kater: Ein Kindermärchen in drey Akten* (Berlin, 1797), 136. The "pacifier" ("Besänftiger"), who addresses audience dissatisfaction, enters to sing Sarastro's aria, incongruously accompanying himself on a glockenspiel.

26. An inventive entertainer, Enslen presented aerostatic spectaculars in the Prater. The *Wiener Zeitung* (November 26, 1791), at 3036, reported his new venture.

27. Well-known opera arias were ideal for demonstrations of this kind, although individual tunes are rarely identified. An exception was an automaton "couple," programmed to perform the celebrated duet "Pace, mio caro sposo." *Bayreuther Zeitung* 83 (July 12, 1788): 562: "Die Figuren werden dabey, statt der bisher gesungenen Arien, wechselweise ein Duett aus Cosa rara singen."

28. "Ankundigung neuer Kunstwerke, welche in Herrn Müllers Kunst-Kabinet, so dermahlen auf dem Kohlmarkt, Nro. 167. im ersten Stock befindlich ist, zugewachsen sind," Wienbibliothek im Rathaus (digital library), www.digital.wienbibliothek.at/wbrobv/content/titleinfo/1933908.

29. "Mit gnädigster Erlaubniß wird der Unterzeichnete die Ehre haben, während der Marktzeit allhier eine Sammlung von Naturalien, Kunstwerken, und von verschiedenen Gruppen, Figuren und Portraiten in Wachs ...," Wienbibliothek im Rathaus (digital library), www.digital.wienbibliothek.at/wbrobv/content/titleinfo/1933916.

30. "Der Ton ist schön und voll – inwendig gleicht es einer Harmonika." *Rheinische Musen* 2/5 (1794): 116.

31. Richard Middleton, "Musical Belongings: Western Music and Its Low-Other," in *Western Music and Its Others: Difference, Representation, and Appropriation in Music*, ed. Georgina Born and David Hesmondhalgh (Berkeley: University

of California Press, 2000), 59–85, at 64. Mechanical features include: "tick-tock rhythms, elementary tonic-dominant progressions, predictable melodic sequences, and banal phrase-structure." To this list might be added a rhythmic figure in which pairs of quavers frame and articulate a four semiquaver turn. In "Der Leierman" Schubert's hurdy-gurdy beggar repeatedly cranks his drone into action but can manage no more than this "nuts and bolts" fragment. When he summons up the strength to extend it, the result is memorably expressive; he is a human after all, not a mechanical contraption.

32. *Journal der practischen Artzneykunde und Wundartzneykunst*, ed. Christoph Wilhelm Hufeland, vol. 5 (Jena: In der academischen Buchhandlung, 1797), 327, describes a case of severe memory loss; a music-loving patient could recall nothing of *Die Zauberflöte* but the sound of the "Glöckchen." Upon recovery, she was able to experience the opera as for the first time.

33. Anon., "Strasser's (sehr merkwürdiges) mechanisches Orchester," *Zeitung für die eleganter Welt* 2 (1802): cols. 297–303, at 300; Emily I. Dolan, *The Orchestral Revolution* (Cambridge: Cambridge University Press, 2013), 180–83.

34. *Rheinische Musen* 1/1 (1794): 11. See also Andrea Klitzing, *Don Giovanni unter Druck: Die Verbreitung der Mozart-Oper als instrumentale Kammermusik im deutschsprachigen Raum bis 1850* (Göttingen: Vandenhoeck & Ruprecht, 2020), 62–64.

35. *Journal des Luxus* 9 (August 1794): 367–71. Ludwig von Batzko's interpretation, dated April 19, 1794, follows a detailed account of the Jacobin reading.

36. *Freymaurer Lieder mit Melodien* (Berlin, 1795), nos. 1, 5. There is also a setting of "In diesen heilgen Hallen" (no. 2).

37. "Der Mohr Monostatos (der Zauberflöte) ist das Bild eines Freiheitstollen Franzen." *Litteratur-Zeitung* (Erlangen, September 1800): col. 1456. The first edition of this collection appeared in 1795. Thanks to my colleague Dr. David Robb for helpful comments on this passage, which evokes the commoner phrase "freedom-mad French."

38. The carillon was destroyed in an air raid on April 15, 1945. A new one has since been constructed, although restoration of the church itself has provoked endless controversy. A recording of the original bells has survived. www .youtube.com/watch?v=yC9OBj-vnwk.

39. *Liederlese für Republikaner* (Hamburg, 1797), no. 20. Herbert Schneider, "Revolutionäre Lieder und vaterländische Gesänge," in *Volk – Nation – Vaterland*, ed. Ulrich Hermann (Hamburg, 1996), 279–90.

40. No. 12 ("Harmonie und Freude") and no. 26 ("Geselliges Vergnügen auf dem Land") fit Mozart's melody, composed for line lengths of 76769988 syllables, but no. 15 ("Ruf der Natur"), with its strophes of 76767766, would require some melisma.

41. Mozart had set this song's refrain "Wohl mir! Ich bin ein freier Mann" in 1786 as the final line of Alois Blumauer's *Lied des Freiheit* (K. 506). After the composer's death, his creation Papageno took up the cudgels on behalf of freedom!

42. *Rheinische Zeitung* 126, suppl. (June 9, 1796): 561.

43. *Humaniora* 8 (1798): 358–61. The title alone also suffices for the version in *Allgemeingültiges Gesellschaftsgesangbuch* (Bayreuth, 1798), 52. In *Auswahl der schönsten Lieder und Gesänge für fröhliche Gesellschaften* (Nuremberg, 1815), the common formulation "in bekannter Melodie" (to a familiar tune) introduces two arias from the opera, each supplied with a title ("Die heil'gen Hallen" and "Die Liebe"). This collection also includes a remarkable skit on Papageno, introduced by the Boys' trio "Seid uns," the fourth line of which is adapted to "Zu singen euch ein Quodlibet." Their admonition "Du Papageno, schweige still, still, still, schweige still" is followed by a host of allusions, including a play on the word mouse, a line imported from Monostatos ("O so mach die Augen zu"), and, very appropriate for Papageno although not sung by the character, "Ein Weib ist das herrlichste Ding."

44. "Der Vogelfänger" was deeply embedded in early nineteenth-century German song. In *Schöne neue Opern-Arien* (n.d.), it even seems to substitute for the name of the opera when "Ein Mädchen" is described as an "Arie aus dem Vogelfänger." In this small collection, "Der Vogelfänger" itself is provided with a refrain "Stigliz Seisla" (goldfinch siskin). In *Vier neue auserlesene Lieder* (n.d.), Zenomide's romance from *Der wohltätige Derwisch* ("Ein Jüngling frisch wie Milch und Blut") is sung to the tune of "Ein Vogelfänger." In the final stanza a young maiden tries to identify a bird, her main rival for the lad's affections; it is not a sparrow ("Sperling"), nor a parrot ("Papagay"), nor a talking starling ("ein Starr, der spricht"), but a bullfinch.

45. His translation (Leipzig: Johann Samuel Heinsius, 1794) also reflects a general desire for Papageno to flaunt his knowledge of bird species. He initially identifies Pamina as a little goldfinch ("Goldfinkchen"). Following "Ein Mädchen," he embarks upon a running "bird" gag in his banter with the "old woman"; she is, in turn, a sweet little thrush ("Drosselchen"), a loveable bittern ("Rohrdommel"), a little bird of paradise ("Paradiesvögelchen"), a beloved woodlark ("Haidelerche"), and a sweet little blackbird ("Aemselchen").

46. "Herr Vulpius hat das Originalwerk des Hrn Schikaneder geniessbarer gemacht." *Annalen des Theaters* 14 (1794): 21.

47. The first performance was on January 16, 1794. In the preface of the Weimar libretto Vulpius discloses that his translation was also due to be performed in Mannheim.

48. The supplement to *Rheinische Musen* 1/12 (1794), entitled *Geschichte der schönen, besonders der zeichnenden und bildernden Künste*, at 24, depicts the Queen of the Night in a highly dramatic pose, wielding a dagger as though about to strike.

49. *Argos, oder der Mann mit hundert Augen* 8 (January 29, 1793): 64. Both Mozart's aria and Schneider's ode use stanzas with lines of eleven-ten-eleven-ten syllables. Their mutual recourse to the rhyme scheme Natur/Schwur seems coincidental.

50. "Der Uebersezzer des Stücks ist der bekannte Abbate Piatoli, welcher sich im vorigen Jahre mit den Pohlen Potoki, Kosciusko und Madalinski hier aufhielt." *Rheinische Musen* 2/2 (1794): 47. Piattoli's authorship and his arrest are also noted in *Oberdeutsche allgemeine Litteraturzeitung im Jahre 1794*, issue 2 (1794): 1083.

51. A translation of the "argomento" is given in Rachel Cowgill, "Mozart Productions and the Emergence of *Werktreue* at London's Italian Opera House, 1780–1830," in *Operatic Migrations*, ed. Roberta Montemorra Marvin and Downing A. Thomas (Aldershot: Ashgate, 2006), 145–86, at 159–60. On the conflicting claims of authorship, see Nedbal, *Prague's Estates Theater*, 9.

52. The lack of an Act I entrance aria for Pamina was another consideration for revisers of the opera. This lacuna had already been addressed in an extraordinary small-stage reworking in Passau (1793). In this version, Pamina is the recipient of the Queen of the Night's Act 2 rage aria. The review in *Rheinische Musen* 2/1 (1794), 10, was fiercely critical of the whole conception, and the author of the essay in *Oberdeutsche allgemeine Litteraturzeitung im Jahre 1794*, issue 2 (1794), 1083–87, also poked fun at it.

53. *National-Zeitung der Deutschen* (July 21, 1796): cols. 942–43.

54. Jane K. Brown, "Classicism and Secular Humanism: The Sanctification of *Die Zauberflöte* in Goethe's 'Novelle,'" in *Religion, Reason, and Culture in the Age of Goethe*, ed. Elisabeth Krimmer and Patricia Anne Simpson (Rochester, NY: Camden House, 2013), 120–40. See also Klitzing, *Don Giovanni unter Druck*, 64–70.

55. An illustrated almanac, *Der Freund der Schoosshündchen: Ein Neujahrs-Geschenk für Damen* (Königsberg, 1797), at 97, discusses the fashion for *Zauberflöte* dog naming. No longer were ladies calling their pets "jolie," "charmant," "joujou," (plaything), or "minette," but Papageno, Monostatos, Sarastro, Tamino, Pamina, Papagena. In the poem "Tamino und Pamina," in *Minerva: Taschenbuch für das Jahr 1810* (Leipzig: Gerhard Fleischer d. Jüng., 1810), Tamino is a greyhound ("Windhund"), who steals a roast joint and retires to a gazebo in the garden, and Sarastro an elderly poodle ("ein betagter Pudel").

56. Jane K. Brown, "'The Monstrous Rights of the Present': Goethe and the Humanity of *Die Zauberflöte*," *Opera Quarterly*, 28 (2012): 1–19, at 13.

57. The young Beethoven set the first stanza of Goethe's song text for the boy ("Ich komme schon") as the seventh piece in Op. 52 ("Marmotte"). In *Die Zauberflöte*, Act 2, scene 19, Papageno, obsessed by food and unable to keep silent, makes use of "Ich komme schon" as a temporary catchphrase.

58. Eric Hadley Denton, "The Technological Eye: Theater Lighting and *Guckkasten* in Michaelis and Goethe," in *The Enlightened Eye: Goethe and Visual Culture*, ed. Evelyn K. Moore and Patricia Anne Simpson (Amsterdam: Rodopi, 2007), 239–64, at 253.

59. In a fictional account of an "outdoor" performance of *Die Zauberflöte* given by an itinerant troupe in a barn, the humanity on display transcends the ragged production values. "Die Schwäger," in *Taschenbuch für Damen auf das Jahr 1801* (Tübingen: J. G. Gotta'schen Buchhandlung, 1801). For all its limitations, this ad hoc troupe offered a "sublime beggar's painting" ("erhabene Bettlergemählde"), a true and touching image of the human race.

60. It describes itself as a "Schwank [farce] in drey Acten." Another version, published in 1814, claims to be "Eine neue Oper mit alten Gesängen." In *Die Franzosen im Gedränge* it is a *Singspiel* "performed in Europe for the good of mankind."

61. The cited texts are identified and in any case are easily recognizable. Some are lightly amended for satirical purposes: "Sey uns zum zweytenmal willkommen / Willkommen in Germaniens Reich!" Other quodlibets make use of the music of *Die Zauberflöte*. In *Die Familie Pumpernickel* (Vienna, 1811), at 104, the duet for Pamina and Papageno is fashioned into a sextet. In the same work, at 92, a quartet, effectively a quodlibet-within-a-quodlibet, stitches together fragments from many sources, including four from *Die Zauberflöte*. The solemnity of Sarastro's "In diesen heilgen Hallen" is irreverently undermined by its continuation into Wenzel Müller's *Das neue Sonntagskind*.

62. One surprise is Napoleon's use of the folksong "Ich bin ein armer Teufel," identified as a "Canon, von Mozart."

63. The feeble Jerome is pilloried with Papageno's words "O wär' ich eine Maus" together with an appropriate cartoon.

The Magic Flute in Biography, Criticism, and Literature

SIMON P. KEEFE

Beyond the majestic open spaces of the adjoining Residenz Platz and Mozart Platz in Salzburg, an innocuous alleyway leads – surprisingly for the uninitiated – to another tiny square, Papageno Platz, graced by twentieth-century Austrian artist Hilde Heger's modest statue of the dedicatee. It is a salutary reminder that *The Magic Flute* makes its lighthearted and serious musical, philosophical, literary, and physical presence felt in all kinds of (often unusual) places. Up to the early twentieth century, its arias and ensembles provided material for variation sets by the likes of Anton Eberl, Joseph Gelinek, Fernando Sor, Ludwig van Beethoven (WoO 46 and Op. 66), Étienne Jean François Gebauer, Bartolomeo Campagnoli, and Charles Grobe, as well as potpourri, medleys of tunes, and transcriptions by Johann Christian Stumpf, Louis Boiledieu, Louis Spohr, Jacques-Louis Battmann, Carl Czerny, Charles Samuel Bovy-Lysberg, Joachim Raff, Sigismond Thalberg, and Ferrucio Busoni. The opera also occupied the minds of many great artists of the twentieth century, including Max Slevogt, Oskar Kokoschka, Marc Chagall, and David Hockney, who produced costumes and stage sets for productions, *Magic Flute*-themed paintings, murals, and – in Chagall's case – a segment of the repainted ceiling of the Paris Opéra (Palais Garnier).[1]

A single chapter can account for only a small portion of the impact of a work as culturally rich and influential as *The Magic Flute*. I shall look initially at critical writings on the opera, focusing on the different periods in which it first came to prominence in Germanic, French, and anglophone countries, as well as at contributions made by Mozart's major nineteenth-century biographers. I then turn to a representative sample of nineteenth- and twentieth-century literary works and visual media that reference or are inspired by *The Magic Flute*.

The Early Biographical and Critical Reception of *The Magic Flute*

The Magic Flute enjoyed remarkable success in Germanic countries in the 1790s, probably contributing more than any other individual work to Mozart's meteoric reputational rise in the decade or so after his death. Performances were numerous, and work and performers critically lauded; many published arrangements, as well as unpublished ones for dances, for serenading lovers, for fairs, and so on, also enabled musicians to get to know and appreciate the opera in whole or in part outside the theater.[2] Early biographer Franz Niemetschek (1798) asked rhetorically whether anyone in Germany was as yet unfamiliar with it and called it "our national work" (*unser Nationalstück*).[3] (In a later edition from 1808, he explained that *The Magic Flute* "announced [Mozart's] greatness abroad," stimulating interest in other Mozart works.[4]) Even as early as 1793 a reviewer of a piano reduction considered discussion of the opera's quality superfluous.[5] The aesthetician Johann Heinrich Gottlob Heusinger (1797) held up *The Magic Flute* – always admired by the Germans, he wrote – as a gold standard for musical "unity" (*Einheit*), remarking that a feeling of calm striving toward an elevated goal pervaded individual numbers and the opera in its entirety.[6] Anticipating the diverse interpretations of later years, one critic considered *The Magic Flute* to have been conceived (to his mind unfortunately) as an allegory of the French Revolution, with the Queen of the Night representing the *Ancien Régime*, Pamina freedom (though still the daughter of a despot), Tamino the people, Sarastro the wisdom of a better law, and the Priests the national assembly. Mozart as creator of the excellent, beautiful music was not to blame, we are told, and was probably unaware of the allegorical content in any case.[7]

German writings by Johann Friedrich Rochlitz (1798) and Ignaz Arnold (1803) are respectively the most influential and important from the first dozen years of *The Magic Flute*'s life. Criticism of librettist Emanuel Schikaneder's work had surfaced before Rochlitz's famous anecdotes about Mozart's life and works: in addition to negativity about the purported allegory reported above, Niemetschek explained that Mozart greatly improved and enhanced texts in the act of setting them to music, including the "wretched" (*elend*) one for *The Magic Flute*.[8] Rochlitz intensified hostility toward Schikaneder by impugning his moral conduct: Schikaneder is accused of exploiting Mozart's goodwill to dig himself out of a serious financial hole and then of reneging on a commitment allowing Mozart (who was said to have composed the opera for free) exclusive rights to resell the score after the first production.[9] As with Rochlitz's dramatized story of the commissioning and composition of the Requiem and subsequent review of the first edition, initially ignoring then attempting to marginalize and trivialize Franz Xaver Süßmayr's involvement, he views Schikaneder in effect as an unwelcome distraction: Süßmayr and Schikaneder meddle at their peril with remarkable achievements that are Mozart's and Mozart's alone.[10] Arnold is slightly critical of Schikaneder, such as when imputing his probable desire to have a big bravura aria where Pamina contemplates suicide in Act 2 rather than the musically sensitive and subtle response provided by Mozart.[11] But it is only Mozart's participation that really interests him. *The Magic Flute*, recipient of Arnold's longest chapter on an individual opera, is identified as Mozart's greatest work, with inner beauty, perfection, pure feeling, and quiet and inner joy communicated in individual numbers and at the level of the whole opera. Inspired musical depiction of individual characters is witnessed throughout: the noble simplicity and gentleness of Sarastro's "In diesen heil'gen Hallen"; Pamina's continual projection of inner feelings, eschewing passionate outbursts; Tamino's utmost delicacy and certainty of feeling in "Dies Bildnis," properly developed and never overwrought, a model of emotional expression to all young composers; and the boiling, raging, and frothing of the Queen of the Night in "Der Hölle Rache."[12] Arnold's enthusiastic homage to *The Magic Flute* marks a fitting conclusion to early Germanic veneration. And in keeping with the larger narrative of his book, Arnold contributes thoughts on the opera's aesthetic import, in particular Mozart's use of orchestral instruments as expressive support for the text.

Admiration for *The Magic Flute* came later in France than in Germany, but when viewed in context was just as noteworthy. At the Paris Opéra in 1801, Mozart's work was transformed at the hands of E. Morel de Chédeville and Ludwig Wenzel Lachnith into *Les Mystères d'Isis*, with excerpts from *Figaro*, *Don Giovanni* and *La clemenza di Tito* placed alongside substantial reworking of the dramatic structure and much of the music of *The Magic Flute*. While this was a controversial adaptation from the start, critics agreed about the redeeming quality of Mozart's music. One writer identified the music as the truly new and enchanting feature of *Les Mystères* (accepting that dancing and scenery also contributed to the production's success), Mozart taking us back to nature with his melodic purity and simplicity and superbly communicating somber and melancholy emotions in the Priests' marches and ceremonies.[13] Another was enraptured by Mozart's music alone, enthusing that originality, truth, freshness, and grace, in harmony and melody, rendered it irresistible.[14] The adaptation could be faulted, but Mozart's contributions could not.[15] And the popularity of *Les Mystères*, in the short and long terms, went hand in hand with growing French interest in Mozart's biography.[16] Rochlitz's anecdotes were translated into French in 1801, and reviewed and partially reproduced in various publications; Théodore-Frédéric Winckler's *Notice biographique sur Mozart*, also from 1801 and widely distributed, began by observing that Mozart had been a subject of public attention since the premiere of *Les Mystères*.[17]

England, in the grip of a different *Magic Flute* at the turn of the nineteenth century (a version of Christoph Martin Wieland's *Oberon* where a flute replaced the original magical horn),[18] did not encounter Mozart's opera on stage until 1811, translated into Italian. But various numbers were already familiar to the public through published arrangements before the British premiere.[19] And more would follow in the years immediately after the premiere, including for piano and flute; for piano alone; for harp; for piano, flute, and cello; and for two pianos.[20]

Early nineteenth-century anglophone criticism engaged with a number of themes and predilections crystallizing around the opera. The overture was repeatedly singled out for special praise: "an effort of human genius, which . . . will command the admiration of ages to come"; a "masterpiece of composition [that] still electrifies all classes of auditors"; a "universal favorite, and most spirited composition"; "an inimitable masterpiece, which will forever be the model of overtures, and the despair of composers."[21] Combined veneration of music and deriding of text and plot characterized writings in both the United States and Britain. "It is very curious," mused one American critic citing *The Magic Flute* as a prime example, "how often beautiful music has been composed by men of the most eminent musical genius to poems void of all probability in their events, of all correctness or distinctness in their delineation of character, and of all elevation in their language." In Britain, another described *The Magic Flute* more bluntly as "the most divine music . . . allied to the most stupidly absurd story, if indeed it be a story at all, and not a monstrous vision of a sick dream." For George Hogarth, "in our apprehension, it must ever be a matter of regret that [Mozart's] most enchanting strains should not have been called forth by a subject more fitted to rouse the feelings and sympathies of our nature."[22] A critic in 1832, citing Schikaneder as "a bye-name of ridicule," considered the text so bad that the (incomplete) sequel from Goethe surely came about only under duress: "One might fancy, had

Goethe been a Catholic, that this composition had been a penance imposed on him by his confessor."[23]

Narratives around *The Magic Flute* also connected a peak of creative achievement with a fatal physical decline in the final months of life. (The idea that Mozart experienced physical decline for a protracted period in 1791 is now widely understood as an exaggeration.) In *The Percy Anecdotes*: "It was composed by him in his last illness, and he was frequently excited and exhausted during the composition of it, even to fainting. He loved it beyond all his other pieces; and when it was brought out at Vienna, he attended the ten first representations, until his health became so feeble that he could not go to the theatre."[24] While he wrote, his "wife and friends would try to win him out from his infatuated abstraction in which he was fast tending to realize his own presentiment, by getting him out to walk . . . But in vain . . . It seemed a miracle how he completed it. He said that the whole second act was conceived in one day in a stage-coach, and that he only wanted more hands to write it down fast enough."[25] Mozart, we are told, worked on the score "so freely given to one in distress . . . for sixteen and eighteen hours a-day; and if we consider the exhausting nature of his employment, and the corroding anxieties of a pecuniary nature which still beset him, we can not wonder that he was becoming prematurely old, and prey to the most painful nervous disorders."[26] Plainly, the legend of the Requiem, including feverish and obsessive composition in the immediate run-up to Mozart's death, influenced descriptions of *The Magic Flute*, a work completed just a month or two earlier.[27]

The major nineteenth-century biographers of Mozart – in German, French, and English – promoted these (and related) critical themes. Georg von Nissen (1828) considered the music of *The Magic Flute* so superior to the text as to render the latter almost insignificant, regarded the overture as a magical piece of the highest mastery, and deemed Schikaneder a bungler who made unreasonable demands on Mozart.[28] Alexandre Oulibicheff (1843) tried to reconcile high admiration for the music with a low opinion of the libretto and plot, which seemed the product of a sick mind, featuring trivial dialogue, dreadful verses, and absurd buffoonery. The shortcomings of the text, he thought, were partially mitigated: by the tradition in which Schikaneder worked (including a need to engage the "rabble" [*populace*]); by the advantageous inclusion of Masonic symbolism, with battles between wisdom and madness, virtue and reason, light and darkness; and by the inspiration Mozart clearly derived from it at various points. According to Oulibicheff, bringing together the biographical position and musical quality of *The Magic*

Flute, it was not unusual for a severely ill young artist like Mozart to attain the greatest strength in spiritual and poetic respects as a direct consequence of physical exhaustion.[29] Edward Holmes (1845) joined anglophone colleagues in regarding Schikaneder's contributions as universally poor and Mozart's as consistently brilliant, as well as in linking work on the opera to Mozart's ultimate demise: "It was during the composition of the 'Zauberflöte' that the eruption of those symptoms which portend decay of the vital powers, and a general breaking up of the constitution, first appeared. As usual, he grew interested in his work, and wrote by day and night . . . . He sunk over his composition into frequent swoons, in which he remained for several minutes before consciousness returned."[30]

Elsewhere, Otto Jahn (1856) offers glimpses of positivity on Schikaneder's work, including issuing credit to him for creating Papageno. But he toes the standard line about Schikaneder's general disreputability and shoddy libretto, regarding *The Magic Flute* in fundamental respects as Mozart's achievement alone. The classic trope of Mozart's serenity when (supposedly) sensing imminent death is also aired: "there is revealed a perfected spirit at peace with itself, which having fought and overcome all opposition from within, has no longer to dread that which comes from without."[31] For Ludwig Nohl (1863), who continued to promote literary and moral distrust of Schikaneder, Mozart's spiritual journey to a higher plane – in advance of and while recognizing impending death – coincided with work on *The Magic Flute*: beyond the "joys of life," having "closed his account with life's gifts," Mozart turned to the highest matters on earth in *The Magic Flute*, before heavenly ones occupied his attention in the Requiem.[32] Ultimately, a decisive change in Schikaneder's critical fortunes would have to wait until the publication of Hermann Abert's biography (1919–21), which impressively refuted notions of incompetence – moral and literary – and malign influence on Mozart,[33] and thereby provided a foundation upon which sensitive and incisive libretto- and text-led research could build. While Schikaneder's contribution to *The Magic Flute* is usually valued highly now and deemed worthy of Mozart's musical setting, lingering doubts about it continued to be expressed into the late twentieth century.[34]

Responses to *The Magic Flute* in Literature and Other Fiction

The sequels, parodies, and adaptations of *The Magic Flute* in the decades after the premiere are further evidence of the opera's remarkable early popularity.[35] In addition to *Les Mystères d'Isis* (discussed above), the most famous is Goethe's *Magic Flute Part Two*, unfinished and abandoned by 1800; it is darker than the original, perhaps in response to the deeply disconcerting social implications of events in France.[36] Comprising an incomplete libretto, which includes instructions for musical setting and staging, Goethe invoked popular elements of the original: the stagecraft (most importantly, the trials of fire and water); the contrast between the respectively earthy and lofty pairings of Papageno–Papagena and Tamino–Pamina; and the magic of the magic flute, which is now played by Papageno and alleviates Tamino's and Pamina's distress, only for despair to return immediately (and comically) when the flute is not played during Papageno's breaks. Goethe takes the ideological struggle between the Queen of the Night and Sarastro/Tamino to the next generation in the battle over Tamino and Pamina's son, whom Monostatos and the Queen have imprisoned underground in a casket protected by fire and water. In similar fashion to the original *Magic Flute*, Tamino and Pamina have to work hard to achieve their goal (the son's release), while Papageno and Papagena – disgruntled at their childlessness – see their own problems solved in a flash by Sarastro planting eggs in their dwelling and having children emerge from them.

A cross section of nineteenth-century fiction captures the diversity of literary work inspired by *The Magic Flute* and by those associated with it. Schikaneder makes a number of appearances, including in an imaginary dialogue "Mozart und Schikaneder: Ein theatralisches Gespräch über die Aufführung der *Zauberflöte* im Stadt-Theater" (1801), in which he and the spirit Mozart muse on the popularity of *The Magic Flute*, their coauthorship, and the work's continued success in Vienna and further afield.[37] In line with prevailing critical negativity, he is a villainous character in other sources. "The Story of 'the Requiem'" (ca. 1850) describes him as "one of the greatest rascals in the ranks of German managers ... always in debt," a rogue who carried out "tricks which might have sent him to a gaol and a guillotine." One such trick, a wager with Anton Stadler (the virtuoso recipient of Mozart's Clarinet Concerto) that he could "half kill Mozart with fright" in order to "convince all Vienna of his foolish belief in supernatural agency," involved instructing Hofer (cousin of Mozart's brother-in-law, musician Franz de Paula Hofer) to commission the Requiem in a mysterious way. Deeply affected by the strange circumstances, Mozart died shortly after completing the work and before being able to write three operas requested of him: "Schickaneder [*sic*] knew that he was liable to heavy punishment for what he had done ... and the triumph of possessing Mozart's *last* opera was too profitable a pleasure to be given up to another. Unless Mozart wrote another opera, nothing could eclipse the *Zauberflöte*; and he might hold all audiences captive with Mozart's last work, if Mozart died. If he lived, the scene would be changed. I [Hofer] believe that a diabolical prudence made Schickaneder poison him."[38] In his biographical romance about Mozart, Heribert Rau (1858) is scarcely more generous toward Schikaneder, portraying him as an unprincipled, conniving, luxury-living theater director who bleeds Mozart dry. Schikaneder abuses his position by setting himself up to take advantage of a poor young girl, a profoundly unsettling turn of events for the principled, generous, and sensitive Mozart, who is inspired to write the song "Das Veilchen" after meeting her. Then, Schikaneder spreads all kinds of exaggerated gossip about the staging of *The Magic Flute* in order to heighten anticipation of the premiere, ensure a large and eager audience, and maximize ticket receipts, safe in the knowledge that Mozart's music would win everyone over at the eventual staging of the opera, with exaggerations consequently being forgotten.[39]

In a story of Beethoven's youth (1842), Mozart passes the compositional baton on to Beethoven when working on *The Magic Flute*; Beethoven's only encounter with him happens in Vienna at that time. (In reality, Mozart and Beethoven may have met when Beethoven visited Vienna in spring 1787, but not in 1791.) In the same account, Schikaneder, ridiculed for his appearance and pompous manner, is also presented as a malign influence on Mozart; following a strain of nineteenth-century criticism, he – like Süßmayr in the case of the Requiem – is a mediocrity meddling with a genius.[40] Away from Schikaneder, Heinrich Smidt (1841) wrote a morality tale for children, *The Magic Flute*, inspired by the characters and events of the opera. A boy called Love Truth, thrown in jail for speaking the truth and now free, is sent with a flute to seek his way in the world by his mother, the Goddess of Truth. Encountering a wise and kind King and entering his service, Love Truth makes people speak honestly by playing his flute, which is helpful to the King. But when the Princess (the King's beloved daughter) reveals herself to be in love with him, Love Truth is tempted to lie about having noble parentage – the condition for marriage – in order to win her. But before so doing, he has a dream that frighteningly reveals to him the consequences of such immoral conduct. When recalled to the court and offered the Princess's hand, he refuses it on the grounds that he was born a peasant. The King is delighted: it had been a test for Love Truth, who has passed! Love Truth is knighted and marries the Princess.[41]

Two works from the interwar years that could not be more different in subject matter, orientation, and seriousness capture in microcosm the diversity of inspirations drawn from *The Magic Flute* in the twentieth century. Lotte Reiniger's "Papageno" (Germany, 1935) is a charming, ten-minute animated film about the eponymous character's exploits, accompanied by music from the opera. Birds are Papageno's life – friends who bring him food and drink, play his magic bells, rescue him from a serpent, and save him from suicide (after an ostrich had taken Papagena away during the serpent attack). In the animated silhouette genre, Reiniger is able to play visually and psychologically with fluid human and avian forms: during "Ein Mädchen oder Weibchen," birds turn into women then back into birds and fly off; three birds stand in for the Three Boys and prevent Papageno from hanging himself; and as Papageno and Papagena in "Pa, pa, pa" imagine having lots of children, birds break eggs on cue and children jump out (possibly in reference to Goethe's sequel to *The Magic Flute*). In contrast to Reiniger's lighthearted film, a novel by G. Lowes Dickinson (1920) uses *The Magic Flute* as inspiration for its allegory of one of the twentieth century's greatest challenges: rebuilding after the horrors of World War I. Tamino assumes the position of the world's conscience: after providing the stimulus for war, in calling for Monostatos and his army following an unproductive first encounter with Pamina, Tamino participates willingly in it, comes to hate it, tries passionately to persuade everyone to abandon it, and then (in effect) reconstructs society through a spiritual journey and pursuit of truth in re-examining fundamental principles of religion, sophistry, and skepticism. The flute itself, protecting Tamino during the fire and water trials, conveying positive messages, and providing a moment of spiritual bliss at Tamino's final encounter with Pamina, symbolizes social enlightenment in the rebuilding process.[42]

The Magic Flute inspired a number of twentieth-century cinematic endeavors in addition to Reiniger's animation, most often alongside narratives about the end of Mozart's life. *Whom the Gods Love* (1935, director Basil Dean), tracing Mozart's successes and failures, represents *The Magic Flute* as the apogee of his popularity, understood by the public at last. As Constanze explains to a threatening aristocratic patron toward the end of the opera's performance, "No one can hurt him now; he has done what he was born to do [achieving great esteem through *The Magic Flute*] ... We [Mozart and Constanze] can never be like other people, we have so little time. .... I've known it for some months, and he knows it too. We have to live a lifetime in a few years." A German film by the same title, *Wen die Götter Lieben* (1942, director Karl Hartl) interweaves accounts of *The*

Magic Flute and the Requiem. Schikaneder, frustrated at Mozart's slow progress on the opera, tries to interest Mozart in the aria "Ein Mädchen." But after playing the opening bar or two, Mozart puts it away dejectedly and turns to the Recordare from the Requiem instead. On his deathbed, immediately before the final rehearsal of the Requiem, Mozart proudly imagines numbers from the opera being performed at that moment; with family and rehearsal participants later standing solemnly to acknowledge his passing, Schikaneder races in ebulliently, recounting tales of the extraordinary success of the opera performance that evening, unaware that Mozart is now dead. Hartl revisited the composer's final months in *The Life and Loves of Mozart* (1955), but now with *The Magic Flute* and its circle of characters as the primary subject matter, rather than the Requiem. It imagines a love affair between Mozart and inspirational muse Anna Gottlieb (the original Pamina) during the composition of *The Magic Flute*; only when she is with him can he finish the opera.

In *Amadeus* (1984, director Miloš Forman), *The Magic Flute* and Requiem are again brought together in memorable musical and dramatic fashion, as representatives of the light and dark in Mozart's world, the former ultimately and inevitably ceding precedence to the latter.[43] As a prime example of a work where "the crowd of spectators take pleasure in what is obvious, [and] the initiated will detect the higher meaning" in Goethe's famous formulation, *The Magic Flute* will no doubt continue to provide material for fictional, critical, musical, artistic, and dramatic inspiration and interpretation for generations to come.[44]

Notes

1. See *Mozart in Art, 1900–1990* (Munich: Bayerische Vereinsbank, 1991).
2. For a flavor of *The Magic Flute*'s success up to 1795, see MDL, 410–11, 413; MDB, 468–69, 472, 477. On the multiple arrangements by 1803 – including more than six for piano alone and those for popular contexts – see Ignaz Arnold, *Mozarts Geist* (Erfurt: Henningschen Buchhandlung, 1803), 247–49.
3. Niemetschek, *Leben des K. K. Kapellmeisters Wolfgang Amadeus Mozart* (Prague: Herrlische Buchhandlung, 1798), 74; for a different translation, see *Life of Mozart*, trans. Helen Mautner (London: Hyman, 1956), 83.
4. Niemetschek, *Lebensbeschreibung des K. K. Kapellmeisters Wolfgang Amadeus Mozart*, 2nd edn. (Prague: Herrlische Buchhandlung, 1808), 61 ("seine Grösse dem Auslande zu verkünden").

5. See *Politische Annalen*, ed. Christoph Girtanner, vol. 1 (Berlin: Unger 1793), "Ankündigungen" (n.p.).

6. Heusinger, *Handbuch der Aesthetik*, vol. 1 (Gotha: Justus Perthes, 1797), 147–49.

7. *Geheime Geschichte der Verschwörungs-Systems der Jakobiner in den österreichischen Staaten* (London, 1795), 47–49.

8. See Niemetschek, *Leben*, 69; *Life of Mozart*, 78 (different translation).

9. For the translated anecdotes, and refutation of much of their content, see Maynard Solomon, "The Rochlitz Anecdotes," in *Mozart Studies*, ed. Cliff Eisen (Oxford: Clarendon Press, 1991), 1–59, at 20–23, 30.

10. On Rochlitz's contributions to the Requiem legend and criticism in this respect, see Simon P. Keefe, *Mozart's Requiem: Reception, Work, Completion* (Cambridge: Cambridge University Press, 2012), 16–19, 44–49.

11. Arnold, *Mozarts Geist*, 268.

12. See Arnold, *Mozarts Geist*, chap. *"Die Zauberflöte,"* 246–83, esp. 249, 252, 255–56, 262–67, 270–72, 274–75.

13. M. Peltier, *Paris, pendant l'année 1801*, vol. 32 (London: Baylis, 1801), 474–79.

14. *Année théatrale: Almanach* (Paris: Courcier, 1801), 184.

15. *Briefe aus Frankreich geschrieben im Sommer 1801*, vol. 2 (Tübingen, 1803), 244.

16. *Les Mystères d'Isis* was staged 134 times between 1801 and 1835; see COH, 165.

17. See *Anecdotes sur W.G. Mozart*, trans. Ch. Fr. Cramer (Paris, 1801); reviewed in *Journal général de la littérature de France*, vol. 4 (Paris: Treuttel and Würtz, 1801), 306 and reviewed and partially reproduced in *La Décade philosophique, littéraire et politique*, vol. 1 (Paris: Panckoucke, 1802), 403–14. It was also blandly reviewed in *Allgemeine musikalische Zeitung* 4/45 (August 4, 1802): col. 736, where an assumption was made about German readers' familiarity with the content. See also Winckler, *Notice biographique sur Mozart* (Paris, 1801); republished in *Magasin encyclopédique, ou Journal des sciences, des lettres et des arts*, ed. A. L. Millin, vol. 3 of 7 (Paris, 1801), 29–72, and *L'esprit des journaux françois et étrangers*, vol. 3 (Brussels, 1801), 147–93. This book is heavily derived from Friedrich Schlichtegroll's 1793 obituary of Mozart.

18. For positive reception of this adaptation of Wieland, see *Monthly Mirror* 10 (1800): 55. By 1801 it had been performed so frequently as to become tiresome in some quarters; see *Lady's Monthly Museum*, vol. 6 (London, 1801): 488.

19. See *Monthly Magazine*, vol. 9 (London, 1800): 480; *Monthly Magazine*, vol. 11 (London, 1801): 436.

20. See *The Repository of Arts, Literature, Commerce*, vol. 7 (1812), 359, 288; vol. 9 (1813), 100; series 2, vol. 8 (1819), 351; series 2, vol. 10 (1820), 362.

21. *Repository of Arts, Literature, Commerce*, vol. 8 (1819): 351; *New Monthly Magazine*, vol. 7 (London: Colburn, 1823): 300; *American Monthly Magazine*, vol. 1 (Philadelphia: Clarke, 1833): 192; François-Joseph Fétis, *Music Explained to the World*, trans. anon. (Boston: Perkins, 1842), 182. For examples of early praise of the overture in Germanic writings, see Heusinger, *Handbuch der Aesthetik*, 148; Arnold, *Mozarts Geist*, 278.

22. See *Musical Magazine*, vol. 3 (Boston: Otis and Broaders, 1842): 91; *Fraser's Magazine for Town and Country*, vol. 26 (London: Nickisson, 1842): 123; Hogarth, *Memoirs of the Musical Drama*, vol. 2 of 2 (London: Bentley, 1838), 257. Many comments along similar lines were made earlier in the nineteenth century in journals such as *The London Literary Gazette*, *The New Monthly Magazine*, *The American Monthly Magazine*, *Harmonicon*, and *The Court Journal*.

23. *Monthly Repository* 42 (1832): 687.

24. *The Percy Anecdotes*, ed. Sholto and Reuben Percy, vol. 11 of 20 (London: Cumberland, 1826), 85.

25. *United States Magazine and Democratic Review* (New York: Langley, 1843): 469.

26. William and Robert Chambers, *Chambers's Edinburgh Journal* (Edinburgh: Chambers, 1844), 310–13, at 312. Article also given in E. Littel, *Littel's Living Age*, vol. 4 (Boston: T. H. Carter, 1845), 28–31; *The Family Instructor, or Digest of General Knowledge*, ed. Robert Sears (New York: Sears, 1852), 309–14.

27. On the Requiem legend in the nineteenth century, see Keefe, *Mozart's Requiem*, 11–24.

28. Nissen, *Biographie W. A. Mozarts* (Hildesheim: Georg Olms, 1991; orig. pub. 1828), 549–51.

29. Oulibicheff, *Nouvelle biographie de Mozart*, vol. 3 of 3 (Moscow: Auguste Semen, 1843), 330–74, esp. 333–35, 340, 342, 346. For laudatory discussion of Mozart's individual numbers, see ibid., 349–65.

30. Edward Holmes, *The Life of Mozart* (London: Folio Society, 1991; orig. pub. 1845), 283–88 (quotation at 283).

31. Otto Jahn, *Life of Mozart* (1856), trans. Pauline D. Townsend, vol. 3 of 3 (London: Novello, 1891), 282–86, 302–52 (quotation, from critic David Strauss, at 346). On this late-style trope (serenity, reticence, resignation) and its misleading connotations extending into twentieth-century criticism, see Simon P. Keefe, *Mozart's Viennese Instrumental Music: A Study of Stylistic Re-Invention* (Woodbridge: Boydell Press, 2007), 84–85.

32. Nohl, *The Life of Mozart* (1863), trans. Lady Wallace, vol. 1 of 2 (London: Longmans, 1877), 239–75 (quotations at 267, 275).

33. Abert, *W. A. Mozart* (1919–21), trans. Stewart Spencer, ed. Cliff Eisen (New Haven, CT: Yale University Press, 2007), 1245–1304.

34. On the latter point, reporting some continued negativity, see Joscelyn Godwin, "Layers of Meaning in *The Magic Flute*," *Musical Quarterly* 65 (1979), 471–92, at 472. For a well-known late twentieth-century criticism of the libretto, see Wolfgang Hildesheimer, *Mozart*, trans. Marion Faber (New York: Vintage, 1983), 313–32.

35. On sequels and parodies, see COH, 164–67; *Mozarts "Zauberflöte" und ihre Dichter: Schikaneder, Vulpius, Goethe, Zuccalmaglio*, ed. Werner Wunderlich, Doris Überschlag, and Ulrich Müller (Anif: Müller-Speiser, 2007). For more

on literary responses in general, see Peter Branscombe, "The Literary Afterlife of *Die Zauberflöte*," in *Words on Music: Essays in Honor of Andrew Porter on the Occasion of His 75th Birthday*, ed. David Rosen and Claire Brook (Hillsdale, NY: Pendragon Press, 2003), 14–29.

36. On the darkness of Goethe's sequel in this respect, see Jane K. Brown, "'The Monstrous Rights of the Present': Goethe and the Humanity of *Die Zauberflöte*," *Opera Quarterly* 28 (2012): 5–19.

37. "Mozart and Schikaneder, A Theatrical Dialogue on the Performance of *Die Zauberflöte* at the Stadt-Theater," trans. Adeline Mueller, *Opera Quarterly* 28 (2012): 108–21. Attention is drawn to its publication in *Allgemeine musikalische Zeitung* 3/28 (April 8, 1801): col. 484.

38. "The Story of 'the Requiem,'" *Fraser's Magazine for Town and Country*, vol. 41 (London: John W. Parker, 1850): 539–50 (quotations at 545, 547, 550). For further discussion of this story, see Keefe, *Mozart's Requiem*, 27–28.

39. Heribert Rau, *Mozart: A Biographical Romance* (1858), trans. E. R. Sill (Boston: Oliver Ditson, 1870), chaps. "The Violet" and "The Magic Flute," 284–90, 298–307.

40. Mrs. E. F. Ellet, "Beethoven: A Tale of Art," pt. II, "The Youth," *Ladies' Companion*, vol. 16 (New York: William W. Snowden, 1842), 299–302.

41. Heinrich Smidt, "*The Magic Flute*: A Moral Tale" (taken from Smidt's book, *Der Zaubergarten*), in *Chambers's Miscellany of Useful and Entertaining Tracts* (Edinburgh: Chambers, 1847), 1–25.

42. G. Lowes Dickinson, *The Magic Flute: A Fantasia* (London: George Allen and Unwin, 1920).

43. For further evaluation of *Amadeus*, see Simon P. Keefe, "Beyond Fact and Fiction, Scholarly and Popular: Peter Shaffer and Miloš Forman's *Amadeus* at 25," *Musical Times* 150 (2009): 45–53.

44. See *Conversations with Goethe, from the German of Eckermann*, trans. S. M. Fuller (Boston: Hilliard Gray, 1839), 199 (from a conversation dated January 29, 1827). On recent influences of *The Magic Flute* across the globe, see citations in Adeline Mueller, "Mythmaking," in *Mozart in Context*, ed. Simon P. Keefe (Cambridge: Cambridge University Press, 2019), 283–88.

19 | The Elusive Compositional History of *The Magic Flute*

DANIEL R. MELAMED

The compositional history of *The Magic Flute* remains shrouded in mystery, especially when compared with Mozart's other famous stage works for which we are fortunate to have sources, sometimes in abundance. The genesis of this opera has attracted interest since the early nineteenth century, but its study has been hindered by the absence of many of the kinds of evidence that inform our understanding of the creation and revision of Mozart's other operas: letters, sketches, evidence of revision, and alternate arias or ensembles composed later. As a result, until recently, much that has been claimed, especially about the libretto, has been based on speculation, misreadings of the sources, or outright fraud.

To take just one common assumption about the work as an example: it is paradoxical that precisely because we lack the evidence normally associated with late eighteenth-century operas – Mozart's other operas are obvious examples of the tendency for contemporary stage works to change in the course of their first productions, in restagings, and in moves from one city to another – Mozart and Schikaneder's magic opera has appeared to be the most fixed of all of Mozart's mature stage pieces. (*La clemenza di Tito* is a possible exception.) This is unlikely, doubly so for a work for a suburban theater with strong ties to the Hanswurst tradition of low musical comedy, and for one centered on a leading comic actor who was also the author of its libretto and director of the company that created it. The work does draw on musical conventions of more elevated opera, but even the pieces heard at the Burgtheater were subject to constant revision. *The Magic Flute* must have been entirely at home in the Theater auf der Wieden, and it is difficult to imagine that a work conceived for that house was more fixed in its text and music than those staged at the court theater.

To appreciate and understand the real compositional history of *The Magic Flute* we need to identify and set aside many dubious stories told in the past and many still-influential assumptions. We also need to consider expanding our definition of a source and to recognize that the opera's apparent stability is an artifact of its transmission and an accident of its chronology. There is a lot to undo in examining the various artifacts, assumptions, and myths that make up the compositional history of *The Magic Flute*, but also some genuine starting points for understanding the work's creation.

What We Do and Do Not Know

The paucity of sources for *The Magic Flute* has created problems for those wishing to study its genesis and premiere, in contrast to the rich variety of sources that document Mozart's other operas and their revision under the composer's supervision. The evidence begins with his own letters. Mozart's long-distance collaboration on *Idomeneo* with his librettist Giambattista Varesco was chronicled in letters through his father, which supply some of Mozart's most famous comments on opera composition. So do the letters written when he and his librettist Johann Gottlieb Stephanie created *Die Entführung aus dem Serail*; these are even more telling because of the extensive rethinking of their plans along the way. By contrast, Mozart wrote little about the genesis of *The Magic Flute*. Several letters mention the routine work of an assistant (Franz Xaver Süßmayr) in copying materials, and a couple bask in the work's warm reception once it found its way onto the stage. Other than that, we do not hear much from Mozart: he composed one (unidentified) aria out of boredom; he quoted a line of text ("Tod und Verzweiflung war sein Lohn") to his wife; and on two occasions he met or dined with Schikaneder.

The lack of information in letters is largely a feature of circumstance. Mozart was beyond busy during the composition of *The Magic Flute*, with the sudden commission of *La clemenza di Tito*, an opportunity he surely could not pass up, coinciding with his collaboration with Schikaneder. He presumably had little time to write at length about his work – and his principal correspondent on topics like this, his father, was no longer alive. Communication between librettist and composer must have been close and direct. (This is also true, of course, of his work with Lorenzo Da Ponte.)

Mozart needed no introduction to the Theater auf der Wieden, nor any intermediary with Schikaneder, and this probably contributed to a gap in the record of *The Magic Flute*'s creation. Indeed, Mozart's role in the composition of *Der Stein der Weisen* (The Philosopher's Stone) suggests that he may have been a regular in the social and professional company of the Theater auf der Wieden's musical staff. His sister-in-law Josepha Hofer (the first Queen of the Night) was a member of Schikaneder's troupe, and

Mozart probably also had connections through Anna Gottlieb (his first Barbarina and Pamina) and her parents, who worked for the court theater.

There is also almost nothing on the work's origins from Schikaneder's side, just a comment in the preface to his opera *Der Spiegel von Arkadien* (The Mirror of Arcadia, 1794). Objecting to changes that had been made to *The Magic Flute* in a recent production, he asked in the preface how somebody could "have thought of mutilating an opera which I thought through diligently with the late Mozart."[1] This tells us little beyond confirming Schikaneder's authorship and collaboration with the composer.

Unlike Mozart's many stage works for which there was an operatic or literary model, *The Magic Flute* was not based on a play or an existing libretto. It does draw on tales from Christoph Martin Wieland's collection *Dschinnistan*, but those stories are third-person narratives, not spoken dramas with interpolated poetry. And although they contribute the work's fairy-tale type,[2] its exotic locale, some character names, and a few plot devices, the stories do not represent the kind of direct literary starting point we have for other Mozart operas. Some colorful Egyptian detail evidently came from Jean Terrasson's novel *Sethos* and Ignaz von Born's *On the Mysteries of the Egyptians*, but *The Magic Flute* as a drama is almost wholly newly invented.

Musical materials in Mozart's hand illuminate the genesis of many of his operas. For *Die Entführung* we have sketches, the draft of a discarded ensemble, and late compositional cuts in several numbers. Autograph materials for *Le nozze di Figaro* likewise reveal some aspects of its compositional process; for example, some draft material survives, including the planned rondò, "Non tardar, amato bene," ultimately abandoned in favor of a different aria. The autograph score of *Così fan tutte* documents the replacement of a second-act aria for Francesco Benucci during the course of production. For *The Magic Flute,* there is nothing comparable. A few sketches survive, but the autograph score is remarkably clean. Overall, the autograph materials reveal relatively little about the work's creation and much less than for other operas.

For most of Mozart's operas we also know about revisions made to original productions as they were coming together and to later stagings: the last-minute deletion of arias in *Idomeneo*, and revisions to that work made for Mozart's later performances of music from it in Vienna; traces of deleted music in *Figaro*, substantial cuts made in the course of its Vienna run, and revisions for a new production in Prague in which Mozart and Da Ponte may have had a hand; and new arias and a duet for *Don Giovanni's* move from Prague to Vienna, along with the elimination of the *scena ultima*.

But Mozart's death soon after *The Magic Flute*'s initial production meant, of course, that no revival with the participation of the composer ever took place. This leaves us without evidence of the sort of revisions that were regularly undertaken in his stage works when they were remounted. In addition, there are no surviving musical sources that can be confidently associated with the first production, depriving us of evidence of its realization in any form that was directly connected with Mozart.

Overall, then, we have much less evidence on the genesis of *The Magic Flute* than we do for many of Mozart's other operas. But that does not mean that the work did not have a compositional history, or did not undergo revisions in the course of its composition, staging, and performance. The lack of evidence is potentially misleading; we need to be careful not to assume that the work, in the form we have it, was created as a perfect, unified, and organic whole by its composer and librettist.

False Histories and Theories

The picture that emerges of *The Magic Flute*'s creation is thus much vaguer than for his other mature operas. At the same time, or maybe for that reason, commentary and scholarship on the genesis of *The Magic Flute* have been plagued by false histories that have obscured the picture even further. Foremost among them is the claim that Karl Ludwig Giesecke was jointly or even completely responsible for the opera's libretto. The assertion, reported second- or thirdhand well after the fact and with potentially suspect motivations, has no reliable evidentiary support – there is nothing to sustain an assertion that anyone other than Schikaneder was responsible for *The Magic Flute*'s libretto.[3] And a letter ostensibly from Schikaneder to Mozart touching on the composition of the Papageno-Papagena duet in the Act 2 finale is itself strongly suspected of being a forgery.

Also weighing down the study of the work's genesis is a theory, promoted for decades by one scholar, that the original text of the opera was not the one found in the libretto and in Mozart's autograph score, but rather an alternative that appears in the earliest published full score issued by Simrock in 1814. The arguments for this view depend largely on aesthetic claims of the superiority of the alternative text's relationship to the music and an overconfident acceptance of the publisher's claim to have based his edition on Mozart's materials.[4] It is easy to show that the textual changes originated in Hamburg performances that took place after the opera's Vienna premiere. The text transmitted in Mozart's score and in the printed Viennese libretto is the original; the variants, while documents of the work's performance and reception, are not part of its compositional history.[5] (The revised text arguably fits better in some places; if so, that might tell us something about Mozart's and Schikaneder's priorities in creating the work.)

So many commentators found fault with the perceived inconsistencies in the *Magic Flute* libretto – especially the apparently stark change of perspective between Acts 1 and 2 involving the characterization of the Queen and Sarastro – that this tendency gave rise early in the opera's reception history to a theory of a midstream change of plan on the part of Mozart and Schikaneder. According to this hypothesis, known in German as the *Bruchtheorie*, librettist and composer altered their plan for Act 2 after Act 1 was complete; this change is said to explain supposed contradictions and inconsistencies.[6] A historical reason has even been put forward: Mozart and Schikaneder's purported concern over competition from *Kaspar der Fagottist*, a new work staged at a rival theater in June of 1791, which likewise drew on Wieland's *Dschinnistan*. The starting point for the story is a letter, probably penned around 1840, reporting a recollection that cannot be confirmed. It is especially telling that the theory was quickly accepted in many quarters in light of literary and dramatic reservations about the libretto.

There is, however, no evidence to support a radical change of plan, and some manuscript evidence that contradicts it. To this, one can add that a sudden change of perspective is unsurprising in this repertory. Act 1 of Schikaneder's *Der Stein der Weisen* ends with a decision to board ship for an island to which a central character has been abducted, apparently nothing more than an excuse for a storm and shipwreck (favorite stage effects) that open Act 2. And with the change of setting to the familiar theatrical environs of a magic island come doubts about whether the white demigod Astromonte is indeed good, or the black demigod Eutifronte really is evil. It is no more necessary to postulate a change in plan for *The Magic Flute* than for this work.[7]

The comparison of *The Magic Flute* with the collaborative *Der Stein der Weisen* points up a broader problem in evaluating theories about the genesis of Mozart's work, and in judging interpretive theories as well. The piece is singular in Mozart's output: there are no other magic operas, no other works for a suburban theater, and no other operatic collaborations with Schikaneder (aside from Mozart's small contributions to *Der Stein der*

Weisen and one lost insertion aria from 1780).[8] We cannot measure theories about this work against Mozart's usual practices because we do not have any comparable pieces by the composer. This situation has allowed for or even encouraged all kinds of speculation; even the most implausible theory has flourished, in part because it cannot be evaluated in the context of Mozartean norms.

The compositional history of *The Magic Flute* also became entangled with myths about Mozart's supposed debauchery and Schikaneder's purported role in his moral and eventual physical decline. David Buch has shown how writers from Friedrich Schlichtegroll to Otto Jahn, repeating dubiously sourced anecdotes, implied that Mozart came under the influence of a morally loose community at the Theater auf der Wieden while composing *The Magic Flute*. Along the way they also advanced the undocumented claims that Mozart wrote much of the opera in a shack in the Freihaus, and that he made compositional choices under the inappropriate influence of Barbara Gerl, the first Papagena. None of this appears to be supported by reliable evidence, and these stories represent yet another layer of fiction.[9]

The misinformation and falsehoods associated with *The Magic Flute*, the relative lack of evidence concerning its genesis, and its character as Mozart's only magic opera may together be responsible for the unusual interpretive traditions that are now commonly associated with it. In many ways these traditions are not merely unique but extreme, especially those that take the work to be a secretly coded allegory of the power of music, or of Enlightenment, or of Masonry, or of musical politics in Vienna. Often such interpretations offer not just a way of understanding the opera but a theory of its origin – a precompositional plan on the part of Mozart and Schikaneder designed to make a particular allegorical point. For the more thoughtful interpreter, these speculations are as dubious as guides to the work's origins as they are to its intended meanings. I would suggest that such coded readings have flourished in part because of the relative absence of evidence concerning the work's creation. For many, they fill a void.[10]

Reviewing the Sources

Despite the obstacles to writing a compositional history of *The Magic Flute*, including the absence of many kinds of information, there is some reliable evidence that has been carefully considered in a number of admirable studies. We can begin with the libretto. Although Schikaneder's reliance on stories from *Dschinnistan* was limited, the ones he drew on for *The Magic Flute* (1791) – together with those from the same collection he used for *Oberon* (1789), *Der Stein der Weisen* (1790), *Der wohltätige Derwisch* (The Beneficent Dervish, 1791), and the *Magic Flute* sequel *Das Labyrinth* (1798) – do offer insight into the sort of fairy-tale exotic settings that evidently appealed to the Viennese suburban-theater audience. *The Magic Flute* might best be regarded as a commercially conceived amalgam of many operatic elements – Eastern exoticism, a rescue plot, spectacles of ritual, low comedy, magic, fairy tales, and so on – and materials like *Dschinnistan* represent resources from which Schikaneder and Mozart drew. The same might be said with respect to the influence of Masonic ritual; just because it is unlikely that *The Magic Flute* is a through-and-through Masonic allegory, that does not mean that Mozart and Schikaneder did not draw on Masonic imagery (or on the public's idea of it).

Then there are the autograph musical materials, which offer a great deal of useful information. At the earliest stage of Mozart's work are sketches of varying degrees of detail. A surviving draft of the overture records a very different opening for the opera, later rejected. Particularly notable are two sketches for the most complex segments of the two finales. One is the long exchange in accompanied recitative between Tamino and a Priest in Act 1. Most extraordinarily, we have a complete continuity draft in which Mozart worked out the unfolding of the entire scene in minimal scoring before copying the number (almost without change) into his full score. The other is the song of the two Armored Men in the Act 2 finale, where we can see Mozart drafting a contrapuntally supported cantus firmus setting.[11]

The main musical source is, of course, Mozart's autograph composing score, a document that has been the subject of fascination for almost two centuries. As early as 1829 the publisher Johann André issued the overture "in exact agreement with the composer's manuscript as he drafted, orchestrated, and completed it."[12] Mozart's compositional process is depicted by the use of two inks: black mostly for the leading violin lines and for the orchestral bass, and red for the instrumentation in between. This corresponds to the two colors of ink discernible in Mozart's scores, and to the two customary phases of his creative work. The first involved the drafting of essential lines that defined a movement (this included the vocal lines in a sung piece). Mozart then sent his assistants segments of the score in this skeletal state for a head start in copying role books from which singers could begin to learn their parts. Only when Mozart's first layer was returned to him did he complete the second stage – the work's instrumentation – and this full version was the basis for the copying of instrumental parts. André's 1829 score reproduces these layers in the overture in two colors of ink.

Several studies have since attempted, with mixed success, to go beyond these two layers to a more detailed reconstruction of Mozart's process: by ink color (up to seventeen supposedly discernible shades),[13] by distinguishing inks through infrared reflectography and x-ray fluorescence spectography,[14] and by the identification of the various papers Mozart used.[15] To a degree, these studies do suggest the order in which Mozart undertook various movements. And aligning details of the manuscript with Mozart's few comments in his letters does offer some insight.[16] Mozart also distinguished two stages of composition in the entries in his work catalogue, a main one for twenty-two numbers on September 3, 1791, and a second on September 28 for the Priests' march and the overture.

But there are limits to what we can know, and some attempts fall short of their claims, such as the assertion that manuscript evidence suggests that Mozart tackled movements and sections by character, and that this, in turn, informs our interpretation of the work's meaning. Besides the unlikely specificity of the eleven distinct stages the study claims to identify, there is a problem in the implication that characters and their musical-dramatic depiction were Mozart's priority. This is a view that resonates more with nineteenth-century opera than with works from Mozart's time, and we do not know what (if anything) Mozart's particular focus was in composing.[17] Other attempts to interpret details of the score give similarly dubious results, like a close study of the grammatical punctuation marks in the vocal lines.[18] These do not appear to shed much light on the work's compositional history or on Mozart's understanding of his settings.

Although Mozart's score and the printed libretto agree for the most part, there are a few lines present in the printed libretto that Mozart did not set to music: a four-line stanza for Pamina and Papageno in the Act 1 finale; a handful of substituted words; a few lines reassigned to different characters; and an aria with chorus (Sarastro's "O Isis und Osiris") that was originally designated just "Chorus" in the libretto. Together, they suggest an original plan for these places and Mozart's somewhat different realization of them in the end.

Mozart's autograph score occasionally shows the composer's rethinking and revision of a drafted movement. (Of course, pieces he discarded or restarted on a fresh page are invisible to us.) Most famous in this regard are his revisions to Pamina and Papageno's duet No. 7 "Bei Männern welche Liebe fühlen." Remarkably, he completed the movement (including the filling-out stage) and then, as an afterthought, shifted the bar lines through-out, moving the music from one half of each measure to the other.

The rebarring of the movement may also be connected with a detail of its opening. In Mozart's autograph, the brief instrumental introduction con-sists only of an initial gesture from the strings; the answering phrase in the woodwinds, now infinitely familiar, is not present. The missing measures (if that is what they are) are known from other eighteenth-century sources, and this points to the value of early secondary copies of the work that are potential witnesses to lost sources connected with the Theater auf der Wieden.[19] The earliest sources that transmit the additional woodwind measure, for example, are score copies and a printed piano-vocal score thought to have originated in Vienna. Viennese copyists, including some with direct connections to Schikaneder's theater, may have had access to authentic materials reflecting Mozart's revisions. Definitive answers to the questions here depend on establishing the origins of each of the sources of *The Magic Flute* and their relationship to each other, an ongoing task involving many uncertainties. To the extent that these differences represent changes made in the course of staging the work, they document the opera's compositional history.

Evidence from Early Performances

Other sources may offer evidence of early performances of *The Magic Flute* and additional insight into its earliest history. For example, some early manuscript copies were apparently connected with productions in Frankfurt and other places. Although changes made there are too distant from Mozart and Schikaneder to be considered part of the work's genesis – they represent its early reception instead – the demonstrable origin of the scores or their ultimate models from Vienna opens the possibility that they are derived from sources close to the original production. More directly, some manuscript materials – a score copy from 1796 and some performing parts – have been identified as stemming from the Theater auf der Wieden itself.[20] It is difficult to know how many of the numerous changes reflected in them might stem from the first production or even from 1796 (given the long use to which these parts were put). But they do show how this sort of opera – and this piece in particular, in the theater in which it was created – underwent changes once it hit the stage.

And this material raises an important question: Do alterations made by Schikaneder after Mozart's death represent part of the work's genesis and authorized revision, or are they, too, part of its early reception? For example, Mozart's autograph and the printed libretto each provide only two stanzas of Papageno's first song, "Der Vogelfänger bin ich ja." But as early as 1792 or 1793 Viennese copies of the score include a third stanza. Is this third stanza an authentic part of *The Magic Flute*? The answer depends somewhat on one's view of the fixity of the opera's text. It has been argued that the addition of stanzas to strophic songs like Papageno's was part of the improvisational tradition of comic theater in Vienna. Indeed, there are surviving printed texts from 1795, 1801, and 1802 that document Schikaneder's continuous addition to and substitution of verses in this number; one writer has gone so far as to suggest that we cannot perform *The Magic Flute* as "originally as possible" without introducing some creative variation like this.[21] But we do not have to believe in the concept of an "original" performance to take seriously the contributions of Mozart's co-creator of the opera even after the composer was gone.

There are two lessons to be drawn from the evidence of *The Magic Flute*'s early performances. One is that the kind of stability we might be tempted to associate with a work as venerated as this opera is not borne out by its history; it changed even in the hands of its creators. The other is that we probably need to take Schikaneder's revisions seriously, even though they were made after Mozart's death. If things had unfolded the other way around, with Schikaneder predeceasing Mozart, we would presumably consider changes made by Mozart alone in later Viennese performances to be part of the work's compositional history. At the least, we need to keep in mind how quickly works like this changed and to refine our sense of where composition and creation end and performance history starts.

In some cases, evidence of early performances has been misinterpreted. A particularly interesting example involves a printed libretto annotated by Giesecke, believed to be a prompter's copy from the Theater auf der Wieden. The term "quodlibet" appears twice in its annotations, before scenes 2 and 20 of Act 2. Various interpreters have suggested that the word may have indicated the site of inserted or optional musical numbers, reflecting variety from performance to performance.[22] This is especially tempting because of the near-contemporary popularity of musical quod-libets that combined tunes from favorite operas,[23] and of the Viennese stage genre itself known as the quodlibet that flourished not long after the time of *The Magic Flute*, both of which use the term to refer to music with sung text.[24]

But the placement of the term "quodlibet" in the prompt book makes it far more likely that the word refers to stage décor, not to an inserted musical number. Contemporary dictionaries first define "quodlibet" as referring to things juxtaposed without order or coherence, to miscellanies, or to mishmashes. "Quodlibet" in the prompt book was almost certainly a shorthand reference to a set or backdrop depicting ruins and debris, a sort of setting documented in contemporary magic operas in Vienna. This understanding lines up with the mysterious frontispiece engraving of *The Magic Flute*'s printed libretto (see Figure 4.9 earlier in this volume), which depicts just such a scene, and with the text's description of a half-stage setting in Act 2 as "a short courtyard of the temple, where are seen ruins of fallen columns and pyramids." Although some variation from performance to performance is possible, it does not appear that this was intended by the word "quodlibet" in the prompt book.

There is some further evidence hinting at the opera's original staging and décor. The printed libretto contains an engraved illustration of Schikaneder in his Papageno costume, but the background of the illustration is also potentially informative: it aligns strikingly with elements of stage décor described in the libretto, including "climbable mountains" and a round temple (see Figure 4.2 earlier in this volume). The Egyptian theme shared with *Der Stein der Weisen* and the likelihood that some of that opera's decorations were reused for *The Magic Flute* might give further hints of its appearance onstage. And it raises the possibility that the available sets from *Der Stein der Weisen*, themselves almost certainly adaptations of stock settings, were part of the raw material of *The Magic Flute* – that is, part of its compositional history.

Some early interventions in the opera raise interesting questions about later changes to the work. In 1802 Schikaneder announced the addition of two new numbers to a revival of *The Magic Flute*. The status of these pieces would be complex enough if they were known to have been composed by somebody else, but Schikaneder claimed that they were by Mozart. It is not known for certain what these two numbers might have been. One was possibly a surviving duet for Tamino and Papageno, "Pamina, wo bist du?," but the duet is generally regarded as not by Mozart.[25] These added numbers potentially challenge several assumptions: that everything that happened to *The Magic Flute* after Mozart's death represents inauthentic tampering with the work; that additions to the opera, even those authored by Schikaneder, do not constitute a part of the work's compositional history if they took place after December 1791; and that additions to the opera authorized by Schikaneder (with texts presumably by him) are not part of the work's genesis if their settings are not by Mozart.

In fact, Schikaneder was credited with the music of various stage pieces, though whether as composer or arranger is sometimes not clear. Sources associated with the Theater auf der Wieden, for example, occasionally attribute either a number or its tune to him; and a large collection of anecdotes whose authenticity is difficult to evaluate describes his musical collaboration with composers, Mozart included.[26] It thus seems possible that some music in *The Magic Flute*, while unquestionably Mozart's in its fully realized form, may have started with melodic ideas from Schikaneder, particularly the strophic songs and duets in which his character participates. However it might have unfolded, this process is surely a potential part of the work's genesis, though one that is difficult to trace in sources.

The elusiveness of *The Magic Flute*'s genesis and the misleading impression of its fixed text has contributed to the interpretive burden that has been laid on the opera. Even if we turn away from various invented chapters in the story of the work's creation, and from critical judgments that condemn the work from the start (a flawed collaborative libretto reflecting a sudden change in plans, a work of Mozartean genius contaminated by demands of a comic actor, and so on), we are still left with the assumption, frequently made by critics and commentators, that the opera sprung fully formed from the minds of Schikaneder and Mozart. The resulting tendency to regard the work as a perfect and unified whole has opened the door to a host of dubious symbolic or allegorical readings that are not supported by the sources or by what we know about late eighteenth-century opera.

A recent discovery suggests the extent to which aspects of the work were, in fact, in flux. A newspaper report of the opera's premiere published in the *Münchner Zeitung* gave its title not as *The Magic Flute* but as *The Egyptian Mysteries*.[27] This title's emphasis on the opera's Oriental Egyptianness is striking – it is, after all, a work with two prayerful numbers addressed to Isis and Osiris, an invocation of the "Mysteries of Isis" by the two Armored Men, and repeated references to pyramids in the stage directions. But the report (admittedly second-hand) suggests that elements of the work, right down to its title, were fluid throughout its creation. And it reminds us that our view of the opera's creation is severely limited by the lack of sources. At the same time, this discovery can remind us that there is more to learn and that we are indeed capable of enlightenment on the topic of *The Magic Flute*'s compositional history.

Notes

For assistance with this essay, I am grateful to Jessica Waldoff, Neal Zaslaw, Edmund Goehring, Miguel Arango Calle, and Paul Corneilson.

1. In COH, 89, cited by Martin Nedbal, "Mozart as a Viennese Moralist: *Die Zauberflöte* and Its Maxims," *Acta Musicologica* 81 (2009): 123–57.

2. David J. Buch, "Fairy-Tale Literature and *Die Zauberflöte*," *Acta Musicologica* 64 (1992): 30–49.

3. See Peter Branscombe, "*Die Zauberflöte*: Some Textual and Interpretive Problems," *Proceedings of the Royal Musical Association* 92 (1966): 45–63; Gerd Ibler, "Betrachtungen und historische Feststellungen zur Urheberschaft des Textbuches zur deutschen Oper *Die Zauberflöte*," *Acta Mozartiana* 59 (2012): 45–61.

4. Most fully in Michael Freyhan, *The Authentic* Magic Flute *Libretto: Mozart's Autograph or the First Full-Score Edition?* (Lanham, MD: Scarecrow Press, 2009). See the review by Paul Corneilson, "Conspiracy Theory," *Newsletter of the Mozart Society of America* 14/2 (2010): 18–19.

5. Some stories about *The Magic Flute*'s genesis are not so much false as fantastically speculative. Erik Smith's essay in COH, for example, explains the overture's fugal texture as the result of an imagined conversation between Schikaneder and Mozart, an invented anecdote that both denigrates Schikaneder's musical sophistication and simultaneously credits him with the inspiration for the overture. See COH, 139–40.

6. See Günter Meinhold, Zauberflöte *und* Zauberflöten-Rezeption: Studien zu Emanuel Schikaneders Libretto Die Zauberflöte *und seiner literarischen Rezeption* (Frankfurt am Main: Peter Lang, 2001), 51–56.

7. It is possible to take parallels with *Der Stein der Weisen* too far, though; one important study calls it the (singular) model for *The Magic Flute*. See *Der Stein der Weisen*, ed. David J. Buch (Middleton, WI: A-R Editions, 2007); Martin Nedbal, "Mozart as a Viennese Moralist."

8. Dexter Edge, "A newly discovered autograph source for Mozart's aria, K. 365a (Anh. 11a)," *Mozart-Jahrbuch* 1996, 177–96.

9. See the citations and detailed history of this thread in Mozart biography in David J. Buch, "Mozart's Bawdy Canons, Vulgarity and Debauchery at the Wiednertheater," *Eighteenth-Century Music* 13 (2016): 283–308. Many of the dubious claims appear together in the anonymous "Die Entstehung der 'Zauberflöte,'" *Monatschrift für Theater und Musik* 3 (1857): 444–46.

10. For a really interesting view of the nature of allegory in *The Magic Flute*, see Jane K. Brown, *The Persistence of Allegory: Drama and Neoclassicism from Shakespeare to Wagner* (Philadelphia: University of Pennsylvania Press, 2007), 193–201.

11. Robert L. Marshall proposed that behind this sketch is the possibility of Mozart's exposure to motet-style movements by J. S. Bach. Marshall, "Bach and Mozart's Artistic Maturity," in *Creative Responses to Bach from Mozart to Hindemith*, ed. Michael Marissen (Lincoln, NE: Nebraska University Press, 1998), 71. And Markus Rathey has argued in favor of the hypothesis that Mozart's source was a treatise by Johann Philipp Kirnberger. Rathey, "Mozart, Kirnberger and the Idea of Musical Purity: Revisiting Two Sketches from 1782," *Eighteenth-Century Music* 13 (2016): 235–52. In some sense, these materials could be considered sources for *Die Zauberflöte*.

12. *Partitur der W. A. Mozart'schen Ouverture zu seiner Oper Die Zauberflöte in genauer Übereinstimmung mit dem Manuscript des Komponisten, so wie er solches entworfen, instrumentiert und beendet hat*, ed. A. André (Offenbach: J. André, 1829).

13. Karl-Heinz Köhler, "Zu den Methoden und einigen Ergebnissen der philologischen Analyse am Autograph der "Zauberflöte," *Mozart-Jahrbuch* 1980–83, at 283–87.

14. Oliver Hahn and Claudia Maurer Zenck, "Die Tinten des Zauberflöten-Autographs: Möglichkeiten und Grenzen neuer Analyseverfahren: Ein Nachtrag zur Chronologie und biographische Pointe," *Acta Mozartiana* 50 (2003): 3–22.

15. NMA, II/5/19 KB; Christoph Wolff, "Musicological Introduction," in FACS.

16. Wolff, "Musicological Introduction."

17. Köhler, "Zu den Methoden."

18. Gernot Gruber, "Das Autograph der 'Zauberflöte': Eine stilkritische Interpretation des philologischen Befundes," *Mozart-Jahrbuch* 1967, 127–49, largely reproduced in the critical commentary to his edition for the NMA.

19. David J. Buch, "Eighteenth-Century Performing Materials from the Archive of the Theater an der Wien and Mozart's *Die Zauberflöte*," *Musical Quarterly* 84 (2000): 287–322.

20. David J. Buch, "A Newly Discovered Source for Mozart's *Die Zauberflöte* from the Copy Shop of Emanuel Schikaneder's Theater auf der Wieden (1796)," *Studia Musicologica* 45 (2004): 269–79.

21. Ulrich Müller, "'O Mozart Steig Hernieder': Das Rätsel von Papagenos dritter Strophe in der 'Zauberflöte,'" *Neue Zeitschrift für Musik* 153/7–8 (1992): 27–34.

22. See, for example, David J. Buch, "Eighteenth-Century Performing Materials," 297, 306; COH, 92–98.

23. Including one by W. Müller, *Quodlibet (Alles fühlt der Liebe Freuden) aus der Zauberposse: Amosa* (Vienna: A Diabelli, [1825]) that begins with a phrase from Mozart's aria.

24. See Lisa Feurzeig and John Sienicki, *Quodlibets of the Viennese Theater* (Middleton, WI: A-R Editions, 2008).

25. There is no evidence that the other was an aria for Pamina, despite the unexplained claim by Gernot Gruber, editor of *Die Zauberflöte* for the NMA. See the discussion in COH, 207–09.

26. David J. Buch, "Emanuel Schikaneder as Theater Composer, or Who Wrote Papageno's Melodies in *Die Zauberflöte*?," *Divadelní Revue* 26 (2015): 160–67.

27. *Münchner Zeitung*, no. 158 (Friday, October 7, 1791). See Dexter Edge, "The earliest published report on the premiere of *Die Zauberflöte* (1 October 1791)," in *Mozart: New Documents*, ed. Dexter Edge and David Black (first published March 16, 2015; updated December 6, 2017), www.mozartdocuments.org/documents/1-october-1791/.

Staging *The Magic Flute*

KATE HOPKINS

The Magic Flute is at once a witty operatic fairy tale and a celebration of love, wisdom, and self-discovery as serious as Shakespeare's *The Tempest*. It is both a "popular entertainment with songs"[1] and a work of spiritual intensity that Nicholas Till infers may express Mozart's disenchantment with "the shallowness of the Enlightenment's secularized ethical systems."[2] It movingly explores the emotional development of a serious and a comic pair of lovers, as Edward Dent pointed out.[3] And, as Brigid Brophy[4] among others has painstakingly researched, it is in part a Masonic allegory, which also refers to the Classical myth of Orpheus. *The Magic Flute*'s dramatic and musical variety has made it one of the world's most popular operas. But it has often challenged directors, who have worried about supposedly nonsensical, racist, or sexist elements in the libretto and struggled to mold the opera's fantastical, comic, and serious aspects into a visually and dramatically coherent whole.

Mozart's letters to his wife during the first weeks of performances imply that he at least was wholly satisfied with Schikaneder's libretto and with the opera's combination of comedy and profundity. He was delighted that his seven-year-old son Carl enjoyed the piece, and he himself relished its humor and playfulness, as he related in a letter to his wife, Constanze, on October 8–9, 1791:

> . . . during Papageno's aria with the glockenspiel I went behind the scenes, as I felt a sort of impulse today to play it myself. Well, just for fun, at the point where Schikaneder has a pause, I played an arpeggio. He was startled, looked behind the wings and saw me. When he had his next pause, I played no arpeggio. This time he stopped and refused to go on. I guessed what he was thinking and again played a chord. He then struck the glockenspiel and said "*Shut up*." Whereupon everyone laughed.[5]

This anecdote makes it clear that Mozart intended *The Magic Flute* to be entertaining and had great fun in helping to make it so himself. But it is equally clear, from earlier passages in this letter and from two other letters to Constanze, that he considered the opera to be far more than a lighthearted, popular entertainment. Its serious aspects mattered deeply to him. He was keen that his mother-in-law, who, because of either musical ignorance or poor hearing, would "*see* the opera, but not *hear* it,"[6] should read the libretto in advance. He was enraged by a "know-all . . . Bavarian"[7] who found the solemn opening scene of Act 2 funny, despite the composer's attempts to explain it to him. He was thrilled when Salieri and the soprano Caterina Cavalieri admired both *The Magic Flute*'s libretto and its music and declared it "an *operone* [grand opera] – worthy to be performed for the grandest festival and before the greatest monarch."[8] And what pleased Mozart most was not the fact that Schikaneder's theater was invariably packed, nor the encores for some numbers, nor even the success of the comic scenes, but the "silent approval"[9] that conveyed how seriously the audience took the piece.

The initial production of *The Magic Flute* remained a popular triumph despite some criticism from connoisseurs, notably Count Karl von Zinzendorf, who declared the opera "an incredible farce" while admitting that its music was "pretty."[10] *The Magic Flute* went on to enjoy great success in German-speaking countries, where audiences appreciated its music and story, and its serious and comic elements, alike. Both Goethe (who attempted to write a sequel) and E. T. A. Hoffmann considered the work a masterpiece, while at the Berlin Court Opera in 1816 Karl Friedrich Schinkel was inspired by its magical-mythic ambience and Schikaneder's detailed stage instructions to create stunning designs, including a star-swept sky and a majestic Egyptian temple. But even in Germany and Austria the opera underwent some striking transformations. These included a 1793 Passau production that presented Tamino as an Arthurian knight; a Weimar staging in 1794 for which Christian August Vulpius (Goethe's brother-in-law) rewrote much of the libretto and made Sarastro the Queen's brother-in-law; a Dresden and Prague production in Italian the same year; and parodies such as Schikaneder's mockery of the unlucky Vienna Court Opera production (Theater an der Wien, 1801) and Karl Meisl and Wenzel Müller's *Die falsche Zauberflöte* (Theater in der Leopoldstadt, Vienna, 1818–19), which featured Sarastro's brotherhood riding an early version of the bicycle.

In countries unused to German *Singspiel*, *The Magic Flute* underwent more drastic alterations. Paris Opéra audiences first heard it in 1801, transformed into a four-act French *grand opéra*, *Les Mystères d'Isis*. The score, arranged by Ludwig Wenzel Lachnith, consisted of heavily edited extracts from *The Magic Flute* and other Mozart operas plus part of Haydn's "Drumroll" Symphony, while librettist Étienne Morel de Chédeville maintained only the bare bones of Schikaneder's plot and renamed most of the characters. *Les Mystères* remained in repertory for more than twenty years, to the fury of Berlioz, who admired the original's "religious splendours"[11] and felt that "Mozart a été assassiné par Lachnith."[12] In England, impresarios tended to dislike the comic Papageno scenes, which James Robinson Planché cut to a minimum in his 1838 English-language version,[13] and *The Times* (1851) was not alone in sneering at "the stupidity of Schikaneder and the *libretto*."[14] For years, London chiefly staged *Die Zauberflöte* as a vehicle for star singers such as Giulia Grisi and her husband Mario (Pamina and Tamino at Covent Garden in 1851) and performed it in Italian as *Il flauto magico*, with recitatives replacing the dialogue. Only with Edward Dent's 1911 English-language version with the dialogue restored, first staged in Cambridge by Clive Carey, did critics begin to appreciate the opera: *The Times* finally admitted that Mozart's music "binds the story into a coherent psychological whole."[15] Carey's production, in Dent's translation, was later staged at the Old Vic by Lilian Baylis's company in 1920, and went on to become a staple of Sadler's Wells Opera. *The Magic Flute* also received productions at Covent Garden (generally sung in English) in the 1920s and 1930s and made its Glyndebourne debut in 1935 sung in German. However, it was only after World War II that the opera began to achieve the popularity in the United Kingdom and other non-German-speaking countries that it enjoys today.

The Magic Flute's growing international success from the 1950s onwards was partly due to several beautiful productions designed by distinguished artists. Oscar Kokoschka's uncharacteristically playful visuals for the Salzburg Festival (1955) included a dancing donkey, cockerel, goat, and cat. At the Metropolitan Opera, New York (1967), Marc Chagall's richly colored designs featured his characteristic Russian fairy-tale imagery and fantastical creatures (the closest *The Magic Flute* has come visually to *The Firebird!*). Maurice Sendak, who felt Chagall had imposed a "shtetl symbolism" on the work,[16] created inventive designs for the Houston Grand Opera (1980) that blended fairy-tale imagery reminiscent of his children's books with Egyptian and Enlightenment elements.[17] And at Glyndebourne (1978), David Hockney – inspired both by Schinkel's 1816 Berlin designs and a visit to the ancient sites of Egypt – made an entire magical world from thirty-five painted backdrops plus minimal scenery and props.[18] Directors during this period tended to concentrate on straightforward storytelling. Andrew Porter praised Günther Rennert's direction at the Metropolitan Opera in 1967 for its "directness, naturalness . . . supple response to all the diverse elements."[19] Much the same can be said of the directing style of

John Cox at Glyndebourne and of Jean-Pierre Ponnelle in his elegant, yet playful, Salzburg production to his own designs (both 1978) and of Göran Järvefelt in his Welsh National Opera staging designed by Carl Friedrich Oberle (1979), which "balanced human comedy simultaneously with deep seriousness" and emphasized the characters' humanity.[20]

However, some discomfort about Schikaneder's libretto remained. W. H. Auden and Chester Kallman found it "peculiarly silly"[21] and made major edits in their 1956 English-language version for an American television production. They cut much of the dialogue and transformed the rest – adding their own new material – into heroic rhyming couplets. They reordered some musical numbers in Act 2, so that the Queen's "Der Hölle Rache" followed Pamina's aria and her trio with Sarastro and Tamino, as "the effect of Monostatos and her mother upon [Pamina] would be a much greater temptation to suicidal despair if she had to endure [their cruelty] after she imagines her lover has deserted her . . . ."[22] They also added a lengthy metalogue for Sarastro to declaim between the acts – in which he muses on the opera's enduring appeal in 1956 ("Though Papageno, one is sad to feel/Prefers the juke-box to the glockenspiel"[23]) – and a wry postscript for Astrafiammante (the Queen of the Night). These, though witty, can come close to sending up the opera, while the incessant heroic couplets seem excessively florid.

Ingmar Bergman, who adored *The Magic Flute*, made a subtler attempt to address the libretto's problems in his joyful 1975 Swedish-language television film *Trollflöjten*, a celebration of eighteenth-century stagecraft set chiefly in a studio replica of the Drottningholm Court Theater. His most significant change was to make the Queen of the Night and Sarastro into Pamina's estranged parents: this makes Sarastro's actions easier to understand and eradicates any sense that Mozart and Schikaneder changed their minds about which was the "good" character.[24] In addition, Bergman gave his benign Sarastro a Wagnerian dimension by having him retire in favor of Tamino and Pamina and, as in Goethe's planned sequel, leave his community to become a wanderer. (Bergman further stressed the Wagnerian connection by showing the singer of Sarastro studying *Parsifal* in the interval.) He also removed explicit Masonic and Egyptian references to focus on more universal themes of love, wisdom, and compassion, expunged mentions of Monostatos's dark skin, and reordered and cut parts of Act 2.[25]

Despite these changes, Bergman, like Auden and Kallman, had great respect for *The Magic Flute*'s essential scenario and left it, for the most part, intact. But, with the rise of *Regietheater* in the 1980s and 1990s, directors began to take greater liberties as they sought to demystify the work. At the Scottish Opera in 1983 Jonathan Miller (who had no love for myth) transformed the enmity between the Queen and Sarastro into a battle between the Catholic Church and the eighteenth-century Freemasons, presented as the dream of an Enlightenment scholar who falls asleep in a library and imagines himself as Tamino. While this interpretation may have shed light on the opera's historical-political context, Robert Grant felt that it reduced *The Magic Flute* to merely "a quaint memorial to bygone ideology."[26] More iconoclastic still was Peter Sellars's Glyndebourne production (1990). Sellars, who saw the opera as a scary "confused power struggle,"[27] relocated the action to contemporary Los Angeles, with Tamino as a hippy dropout, Papageno as a beach bum, the Queen of the Night as a bourgeois housewife, and Sarastro as a cult leader. This was not wholly perverse; as *Times Literary Supplement* critic Christopher Wintle pointed out, the 1776 American Declaration of Independence expressed ideals similar to those of eighteenth-century Freemasonry, while the Los Angeles setting articulated "the perpetual quest of the deracinated for exotic cults."[28] However, Sellars's decisions to omit all dialogue and replace it with explanatory neon signs; to combine the contemporary setting with stylized gestures inspired by Indian, Indonesian, and Japanese theater; to make Tamino's flute-playing seem ridiculous; and to turn Sarastro's brotherhood into a "collection of morally ambiguous drop-outs" ultimately reduced the production to little more than "a lampoon by a sparky student."[29] Its disastrous reception led Glyndebourne's artistic director Peter Hall to resign.

In the twenty-first century, directors have responded in an extraordinary variety of ways to *The Magic Flute*'s mixture of knockabout comedy, spiritual seriousness, and magic, and its potentially racist and misogynist elements. A few have explored the opera's serious themes in a secular, modern context. Kenneth Branagh – perhaps inspired by Goldsworthy Lowes Dickinson's *The Magic Flute: A Fantasia* – set his 2006 film *The Magic Flute* at the height of World War I, with Tamino as a frontline soldier and Sarastro the chief doctor in a field hospital. Peter Brook's free, much-abridged adaptation *A Magic Flute* (2011) pared back the opera's magical and pantomime aspects to focus on the emotional development of its two young couples. And Robert Carsen (Baden-Baden and Opéra Bastille, 2013–14) staged *The Magic Flute* as a rite of passage from adolescence to adulthood in which the younger generation came to terms with death – which Carsen noted is mentioned sixty times in Schikaneder's libretto.[30] Everyone wore simple black and white contemporary clothes (except Papageno and Papagena, who looked like hippy backpackers), and the Queen of the Night and Sarastro worked together to guide the lovers through trials in what appeared to be a woodland cemetery and crypt. Throughout, Carsen minimized the opera's fantasy elements to focus on humanitarian themes of community and compassion.

Other recent directors have had less optimistic visions – particularly as regards Sarastro. Netia Jones (Garsington, 2018) portrayed him as a pompous modern Freemason,[31] who kept the women at his lodge (dressed in costumes reminiscent of Margaret Atwood's *The Handmaid's Tale*) in servitude. Martin Kušej (Zurich Opera, 2007) made Sarastro into a dubious guru (though the nymphomaniac Queen of the Night was still worse) based in a charmless grey basement. During Act 2 he submitted Pamina and Tamino – here, a couple separated on their wedding day and presumably rendered amnesiac – to harrowing ordeals culminating in a trial by water in which they escaped from a submerged car. In the finale he dispassionately proclaimed victory as they recovered on hospital beds before returning to their initial bridal pose, which implied the entire opera was their hallucination. David Pountney offered an equally disturbing, if more fantastical, interpretation in his 2013 Bregenz Festival production, set on a primitive island ruled by a villainous, brutal Sarastro. (Pountney stated that, unlike Mozart and Schikaneder, he believes Sarastro "belongs in jail."[32]) Everything about the island was frightening, not least the grotesque life-sized marionettes symbolizing the Three Ladies and the Three Boys, sung offstage. In the finale, the Queen and Sarastro murdered each other, while Tamino and Pamina escaped with relief into the audience's modern world.

If Pountney criticized *The Magic Flute*'s philosophical and mystical aspects, another set of directors have cheerfully ignored them and staged the work as pantomime. Achim Freyer followed his Salzburg Festival production (1997), set in a circus tent with the characters as clowns, with a 2006 Semperoper Dresden staging to his own designs with more clown imagery and brightly colored, inflated costumes that drew comparisons with the Teletubbies.[33] Pierre Audi and COBRA artist Karel Appel created an equally colorful Dutch National Opera (1995) and Salzburg Festival (2006) *Magic Flute*, with mock-primitive sculptures, mountaineering Ladies and a dreadlocked Papageno in an orange car accompanied by yellow birds reminiscent of *Sesame Street*. In Adrian Noble's 2004 Glyndebourne production, cheerful animal imagery dominated so much that *The Observer*'s Anthony Holden complained Sarastro's court was "reduced to an outtake from *The Lion King*."[34] And Moshe Leiser and Patrice Caurier's postmodern Vienna State Opera staging (2013) included Three Ladies from vaudeville, levitating musical instruments and Boys, pyrotechnics, a comic menagerie, and ballet-dancing policemen, and reduced Sarastro's noble brotherhood to dark-suited, handshaking businessmen (perhaps an ironic reference to Freemasonry). Pantomimic productions can have serious aspects – Audi movingly depicted Pamina's conflicted feelings about her mother and Sarastro, while Leiser and Caurier made Papageno touching rather than imbecilic. But at worst they reduce *The Magic Flute* to farce, as with Jonathan Moore's updated 2003 Scottish Opera production, which started on the moon with an astronaut Tamino and ended at Sarastro's multifaith Isis and Osiris Mission; or Yuval Sharon's 2019 Berlin Opera staging, in which the characters were puppets inspired by pop culture, the cast performed uncomfortable acrobatics, and the opera was revealed to be a play staged by children whose prerecorded voices spoke the dialogue. Sharon's production, which also featured a nonsinging actor as Papageno, was so disliked that one critic dubbed it "the tragic flute."[35]

Technology has played a major part in several reinventions of *The Magic Flute*. In his 2012 Dutch National Opera production (which replaced Nicholas Hytner's 1988 classic staging at the English National Opera in 2013), Simon McBurney used video projections, puppetry, and live sound art to create a contemporary equivalent to Schikaneder's much-admired 1791 stage effects. Sometimes he succeeded, as in the trial by water, where Tamino and Pamina appeared to swim. However, McBurney's eagerness to rid the work of "confectionery"[36] through a single, minimalist set and plain, modern costumes – Sarastro and Papageno looked like a 1970s French intellectual and a tramp, while the Queen was a crippled black-clad crone – resulted in a rather drab staging that *The Guardian*'s Martin Kettle felt fell "frustratingly short of the great enlightenment experience that Mozart's music demands."[37] Projections dominated to an even greater extent in William Kentridge's 2005 staging for La Monnaie, Brussels, subsequently performed by several international companies, including La Scala, Milan (with a recording in 2011). The South African artist-director used his characteristic black-and-white animated drawings throughout, not only to illustrate the opera's story but also to explore his own lifelong preoccupation with colonialism: his Sarastro was an overbearing nineteenth-century imperialist overlord.[38]

But the most radical use of video art came from Barrie Kosky, working with Paul Barritt and Suzanne Andrade from London theater group 1927 at the Komische Oper Berlin (2012). Kosky believes that *The Magic Flute* is not an opera but "end-of-the-pier meets panto meets Mozart's profound music meets vaudeville,"[39] and he and 1927 reworked it as a mixture of animated film and live action inspired by cartoons and 1920s silent cinema. The innumerable animations included a dancing black cat, baying dogs, a nude fairy (the flute), flowers, hearts, bells, and pink elephants. The singers often sang frozen in movie spotlights. Pamina became a Louise Brooks lookalike, Papageno Buster Keaton, the Queen was a fiendish cartoon spider, and the serious Sarastro was banished to a high shelf at the back of the stage. To heighten the silent-movie ambiance, Kosky removed the spoken dialogue and replaced it with libretto extracts projected on screens, accompanied by Mozart fantasias performed on a fortepiano. The production's inventive visuals have made it a worldwide success, but at the Edinburgh Festival in 2015 Kate Molleson noted that erasing the dialogue left little space for character development,[40] while *The Observer*'s Fiona Maddocks found the perpetual animations exhausting and felt that "Mozart's music [was] knocked into the background."[41]

Kosky's is one of several productions that feels conceptually a long way from Mozart and Schikaneder's scenario. Dominic Cooke's 2005 Welsh National Opera staging was an homage to René Magritte. Radical theater group La Fura dels Baus (Ruhr Triennale, 2003/Opéra Bastille, 2005) set *The Magic Flute* inside a brain, with twelve giant inflatable blocks symbolizing "the units of memory,"[42] and replaced the dialogue with text by poet Rafael Argullol, declaimed by actors. Lydia Steier (Salzburg Festival, 2018) turned it into a fairy tale that was narrated to well-off Viennese siblings by their grandfather on the eve of World War I. James Brining (Opera North, 2019) made it the sinister dream of a small girl who falls asleep playing a record of *The Magic Flute* and imagines her parents' dinner guests as the characters. Inspired by the conflict between religious and secular education since the French Revolution, Damiano Michieletto (La Fenice, Venice, 2015) set the action in a modern school. Tamino, Pamina, and Monostatos were pupils, Papageno the illiterate janitor, the Queen of the Night a pious Catholic mama attended by three nuns, and Sarastro a kindly humanist headmaster, who devised trials including a woodland camping trip and a spelling test. And at Glyndebourne in 2019 André Barbe and Renaud Doucet, who denounced *The Magic Flute* as "racist and mostly very sexist,"[43] offered an irreverent feminist interpretation set in Vienna's Hotel Sacher in 1900, and possibly the dream of a hotel guest (Tamino). The Queen was modelled on the eccentric hotelier Anna Sacher, Sarastro was her head chef, and Monostatos the soot-dyed boilerman. Suffragettes turned up in Act 2 to highlight the misogyny of Sarastro's kitchen realm, and Pamina defiantly donned a male suit for the trials of fire and water, described by *The Stage*'s opera critic George Hall as a "period edition of Masterchef Vienna"[44] – with Tamino doing the washing-up.

While many recent productions of *The Magic Flute* are ingeniously inventive, they rarely capture the rich variety of Mozart and Schikaneder's opera. The dramatic pathos and noble music that dominate Act 2 make little sense in sinister productions such as Pountney's, or farcical ones such as Freyer's or Sharon's. Humanist stagings such as Carsen's may capture the opera's compassion, but invariably lack the original's imaginative scope and element of fantasy. And more radical reworkings of the piece, such as Kosky's or Barbe and Doucet's, often appear to tell a story very different from the original and give credence to Robert Grant's statement that, "far from clarifying or expanding [an opera's] meaning, the 'concept production' actually narrows and obscures it."[45] Above all, many *Magic Flute* productions since the 1980s lack what Ingmar Bergman felt was the opera's essential appeal: its unique combination of "childish magic and exalted mystery."[46]

Fortunately, a few directors have relished these aspects of *The Magic Flute* – to the delight of their audiences. Julie Taymor's exotic fairy-tale production for the Metropolitan Opera (2004) was hailed by *The New Yorker*'s Alex Ross as "a shimmering cultural kaleidoscope, with all manner of mystical and folk traditions blending together."[47] Taymor believes *The Magic Flute* is "like Shakespeare … it's like an elevator … you can get off on any level …. You can enjoy it for … the basic magical fairy-tale outline, or you can sit there and ponder the deeper thoughts behind it."[48] Her witty staging included playful life-sized puppets such as the silk bears who danced to Tamino's flute, Papageno's prancing birds, and the Three Boys' bird-kite. But George Tsypin's designs also paid tribute to the work's solemn Masonic and Egyptian aspects, and Taymor depicted Pamina and Tamino's emotional ordeals very movingly. Her production and a subsequent cut-down English-language version of it for children have been regularly staged at the Met for years. Peter Stein's 2016 production for La Scala's Accademia training program was equally well received. Unlike many contemporary directors, Stein admires the libretto – which he notes explores themes that also feature in Greek tragedy, Shakespeare, and Wagner operas – and feels that Pamina's position as Tamino's fellow-initiate and guide through the trials ensures that the piece is not sexist.[49] His simple, concept-free staging follows Schikaneder's stage instructions precisely, even to the lions that pull Sarastro's chariot. While his grass-skirted savage

Monostatos raised a few critics' eyebrows, Stein's production was a sellout success at its premiere and moved a subsequent Amazon reviewer of its DVD recording to give it a standing ovation.[50]

Mozart's anger at the Bavarian who laughed at the opening of Act 2 implies that *The Magic Flute*'s idealistic and spiritual aspects had personal significance for him. The two productions – still going strong as of 2020 – that best capture this, and a general sense of late-Enlightenment idealism, are David McVicar's (Royal Opera House, Covent Garden, 2003) and the late August Everding's (Bavarian State Opera, 1978), which both present Sarastro and his Priests not as austere mythical figures but, to quote Everding's designer Jürgen Rose, as "human beings who could have been Mozart's contemporaries."[51] The directors' insightful depictions of the young couples' emotional development – particularly Pamina's progress from victim to courageous heroine – and their radiantly joyous Act 2 finales likewise encourage us to feel the enlightenment espoused by Sarastro is worth striving for. But neither director neglects the opera's fantastical and funny elements: both include spectacular appearances for the otherworldly Queen of the Night and for the Three Boys in their flying machine, a genuinely magical flute and bells, charming dancing animals, laugh-out-loud humor in the Papageno scenes, and prominent parts for children – including delightful little Papageni – that remind one of *The Magic Flute*'s appeal for all ages.

In some respects, these two productions are very different – there is, after all, no definitive way to stage *The Magic Flute*. Everding uses Jürgen Rose's exquisitely detailed backdrops and scenery to adhere closely to Schikaneder's many scene changes and staging instructions, does not depart significantly from the original story – Monostatos remains a Moor, for example – and primarily sticks to a mixture of fairy-tale and eighteenth-century imagery. (Both Everding and McVicar, like Bergman in his film, avoid explicit Egyptian references.) McVicar and his designer John Macfarlane choose a simpler look – a single dark, marble set that periodically opens to reveal colored backdrops such as a starry sky, a flowering tree, or a golden sunrise – and playfully mix periods by having Papageno and Papagena in more modern dress than the other characters. They go for a stylized rather than literal staging of the animals dancing to Tamino's flute and the trials of fire and water, with actors who don animal heads onstage and illustrate the trials through movement. And McVicar excises any racism by making Monostatos a creepy eighteenth-century European dandy, and highlights the potential misogyny in Sarastro's court more than

Everding[52] by showing how the women there are marginalized until Pamina's initiation.

But what Everding and McVicar crucially have in common is their willingness to engage with Schikaneder's story as seriously as did Mozart, rather than alter it substantially, mock it, or largely discard it for their own new concept. Equally, they pay constant attention to how the musical score informs characterization and action, something McVicar says is key to all his opera productions,[53] so that there is no disjunction between what one sees and what one hears. As with Taymor and Stein, past directors such as Cox and Järvefelt, or Bergman in his ever-popular film, they thus allow audiences to enjoy the opera's comic, fantastical, and profound aspects equally, and to feel it all makes perfect sense, just as, to quote novelist Barbara Trapido, "a dream makes sense ... deeply, at the center of [your] being."[54] Mozart, who relished *The Magic Flute*'s unique mixture of wit and profundity so much, would surely would have been delighted.

Notes

1. Arthur Jacobs and Stanley Sadie, "*Die Zauberflöte,*" in *The Wordsworth Book of Opera* (Ware: Wordsworth Editions, 1996), 91.
2. Nicholas Till, *Mozart and the Enlightenment* (New York: W.W. Norton, 1993), 305.
3. Edward J. Dent, *Mozart's Operas* (London: Oxford University Press, 1960; orig. pub. 1913), 259–63.
4. Brigid Brophy, *Mozart the Dramatist* (London: Libris, 1988), 131–202.
5. LMF, 969; MBA, IV:160.
6. Ibid.
7. Ibid.
8. LMF, 970 (October 14, 1791); MBA, IV:161–62.
9. LMF, 967 (October 7–8, 1791); MBA, IV:157.
10. COH, 154.
11. Sarah Lenton, "Staging the *Flute,*" Royal Opera program for *Die Zauberflöte* (London: Royal Opera House, 2011 reprint), 35.
12. COH, 165.
13. See Rachel Cowgill, "New Light and the Man of Might," in *Art and Ideology in European Opera: Essays in Honour of Julian Rushton*, ed. Rachel Cowgill, David Cooper, and Clive Brown (Woodbridge: Boydell and Brewer, 2010), 219.
14. COH, 169.
15. Ibid., 170.

16. Julia Felsenthal, "Marc Chagall's Wild Designs for Mozart's *The Magic Flute* Are at the Fennimore Art Museum," *Vogue*, July 6, 2015, https://www.vogue.com/article/marc-chagall-mozart-the-magic-flute.

17. Sendak's designs remain in repertory today; they were most recently used by Washington National Opera in November 2019 in a production directed by Neil Peter Jampolis, warmly reviewed by Anne Midgette in the *Washington Post* (November 3, 2019).

18. Hockney subsequently enlarged his designs for performances at La Scala, San Francisco Opera, and the Metropolitan Opera.

19. COH, 174.

20. Tom Sutcliffe, *Believing in Opera* (London: Faber and Faber, 1996), 363.

21. W. H. Auden and Chester Kallman, *Libretti*, ed. Edward Mendelson (London: Faber and Faber, 1993), 129.

22. Ibid., 131.

23. Ibid., 154.

24. For more on Mozart and Schikaneder's potential "change of plan," see COH, 205–7.

25. Cuts included the misogynist Priests' duet "Bewahret euch vor Weibertücken" (this heightened the sense of the Priests' essential benignity) and the trio "Soll ich dich, Teurer," in which Pamina and Tamino bid farewell and Sarastro reassures them, sometimes seen as making little sense bearing in mind Pamina's subsequent suicide attempt.

26. Robert Grant, "The Disenchanted Flute," in *The Politics of Sex and Other Essays: On Conservatism, Culture and the Imagination* (Basingstoke: Macmillan, 2000), 71.

27. Sutcliffe, *Believing in Opera*, 216.

28. Christopher Wintle, "Wunderkind in the Modern Wilderness," *Times Literary Supplement* (June 1–7, 1990).

29. Ibid.

30. See George Loomis, "'Zauberflöte' in a New Easter Home," *New York Times* (March 27, 2013), www.nytimes.com/2013/03/27/arts/27iht-loomis27.html.

31. Few contemporary *Magic Flute* directors have staged explicitly Masonic productions, perhaps because they feel Freemasonry means little to today's audiences.

32. Steph Power, "David Pountney in Conversation at the Bregenz Festival," *Wales Arts Review* (August 28, 2014), www.walesartsreview.org/david-pountney-in-conversation-at-the-bregenz-festival-a-unique-event-in-a-unique-location/.

33. Freyer also staged a *Zauberflöte* for Hamburg State Opera in 1982, in which the opera was Tamino's dream. His Dresden production originated at the Schwetzingen Festival in 2002. It remained in repertory at the Semperoper Dresden until November 2020. The reference to the characters resembling Teletubbies was made in "*Die Zauberflöte* in Dresden," Intermezzo (March 1,

2013), https://intermezzo.typepad.com/intermezzo/2013/03/die-zauberfl%C3%B6te-dresden-achim-freyer.html.

34. Anthony Holden, "Glyndebourne's Flute Salad," *The Observer* (May 23, 2004), www.theguardian.com/music/2004/may/23/classicalmusicandopera.mozart.

35. Jesse Simon, "The Tragic Flute" (March 8, 2019), www.mundoclasico.com/articulo/31954/The-Tragic-Flute.

36. Simon McBurney, Interview trailer for *Die Zauberflöte*, Metropolitan Opera, New York, Metropolitan Opera channel, www.youtube.com/watch?v=MfAwIei_15A. The Metropolitan Opera premiere of McBurney's production was postponed due to the coronavirus pandemic; it eventually opened in May 2023.

37. Martin Kettle, "*The Magic Flute* Review: Happy Return of an Exhilaratingly Inventive Production," *The Guardian* (February 7, 2016), www.theguardian.com/music/2016/feb/07/the-magic-flute-review-eno-coliseum-review-mozart-lucy-crowe.

38. Kentridge emphasized Sarastro's unappealing characteristics by showing a film of African colonialists, presumably his men, shooting a rhinoceros during "In diesen heil'gen Hallen."

39. Tom Service, "Barrie Kosky: When I First Saw *The Magic Flute* I Didn't Get It and I Didn't Like It," *The Guardian* (July 13, 2015), www.theguardian.com/music/2015/jul/13/barrie-kosky-the-magic-flute-i-was-like-euggh.

40. Kate Molleson, "*The Magic Flute* at Edinburgh Festival Review: All the Makings of a Classic," *The Guardian* (August 28, 2015), www.theguardian.com/stage/2015/aug/28/magic-flute-festival-theatre-edinburgh-1927-barrie-kosky-paul-barritt-makings-of-a-classic.

41. Fiona Maddocks, "*The Magic Flute* at Edinburgh Festival Review: Unforgettable and Exhausting," *The Observer* (August 30, 2015), www.theguardian.com/stage/2015/aug/30/magic-flute-edinburgh-festival-review-barrie-kosky-1927-komische-oper-berlin.

42. "*La flauta màgica*," https://lafura.com/en/works/la-flauta-magica/.

43. Michael Church, "*Die Zauberflöte*, Glyndebourne Festival Opera Review: The Show Breaks Free of Renaud Doucet's Contrived, PC Rewrites," *The Independent* (July 22, 2019), www.independent.co.uk/arts-entertainment/classical/reviews/the-magic-flute-review-glyndebourne-festival-review-renaud-doucet-racism-sexist-a9015206.html.

44. George Hall, "*Die Zauberflöte* at Glyndebourne Review: A Trivial Staging of Mozart's Comedy," *The Stage* (July 19, 2019).

45. Grant, "The Disenchanted Flute," 60.

46. Peter Cowie, *Ingmar Bergman* (New York: Limelight Editions, 1982), 297.

47. Alex Ross, "Taymor's Mythology," *New Yorker* (October 24, 2004), www.therestisnoise.com/2004/10/julie_taymors_e.html.

48. "Julie Taymor on *The Magic Flute*," interview on the Metropolitan Opera Youtube channel, www.youtube.com/watch?v=0DSmNlCdJeg (December 14,

2016) (excerpts). Taymor staged two versions of her production for the Metropolitan Opera: a German-language full-length version and a 100-minute version for young audiences in a new English translation by J. D. McClatchy.

49. "*Il flauto magico/Die Zauberflöte*: Intervista a Peter Stein," interview (in Italian) on the La Scala, Milan's Youtube channel, www.youtube.com/watch? v=NGZirmjlGCo (August 30, 2016).

50. Luis Pena, "Spectacular and Fascinating," review (from the United States) of Peter Stein's Accademia Teatro alla Scala production of *Die Zauberflöte* on DVD, Amazon (September 21, 2018), www.amazon.com/gp/customer-reviews/R4PWVK2APTSQ0?ref=pf_vv_at_pdctrvw_srp.

51. Interview with Jürgen Rose, "The Joy of Drawing Has Remained," by Hella Bartnig, translated by Donald Arthur (https://operamylove.com/2015/12/31/the-magic-flute-in-munich/). Everding's production was originally a coproduction with the Royal Opera House, where it remained in repertory from 1979 to 1991. Everding staged three other successful productions of *The Magic Flute*: for Savonlinna Festival (1973), for Lyric Opera of Chicago (1986) and for Berlin State Opera (1994, to his own designs modeled on Karl Friedrich Schinkel's from 1816). The latter remains in repertory, alongside Yuval Sharon's.

52. Everding lessened the misogyny in Sarastro's temple by cutting the Priests' antiwoman duet. His other major change was to move the trio "Soll ich dich, Teurer" before "O Isis und Osiris," for clearer dramatic continuity.

53. Richard Fairman, "Radical Reconnection," interview with David McVicar, *Opera News*, December 2017, www.operanews.com/Opera_News_Magazine/2017/12/Features/Radical_Reconnection.html.

54. Barbara Trapido, *Temples of Delight* (London: Penguin Books, 1991), 292. The novel explores how the heroine Alice's fascination with *The Magic Flute* informs her life choices.

21 | Ingmar Bergman's Film Version of *The Magic Flute*

DEAN DUNCAN

Any discussion about *The Magic Flute* and film will quite naturally concern itself with Ingmar Bergman's celebrated 1975 production. *The Magic Flute* is a very distinct entry in Bergman's *oeuvre*. Further, it is a distinct, distinguished example of a very rare and particular kind of movie. It stands with so much of Georges Méliès, with the first Marx Brothers features, with René Clair's *Le Million*, Sacha Guitry's *Story of a Cheat*, Laurence Olivier's *Henry V*, Carné/Prévert's *Children of Paradise*, Powell and Pressburger's *The Red Shoes* and *Tales of Hoffman*, Chaplin's *The Circus* and *Limelight*, and Jean Renoir's *The Golden Coach* as one of the preeminent and most beautiful examples of what we might call the theatrical film. The theatrical film is no simple adaptation, no mere derivation, nor is it a case of cinema subordinating itself to a parent art. In his *Images*, Bergman himself describes and celebrates this merging of the theatrical and the cinematic as he recollects his own youthful visit to Stockholm's eighteenth-century Drottningholm Court Theater, and a dear ambition that was seeded there.

In my imagination I have always seen *The Magic Flute* living inside that old theater, in that keenly acoustical wooden box, with its slanted stage floor, its backdrops and wings. Here lies the noble, magical illusion of theater. Nothing *is*; everything *represents*. The moment the curtain is raised, an agreement between stage and audience manifests itself. And now, together, we'll create![1]

The theatrical film, like its ancestor the *Singspiel*, can be simultaneously heightened and plain, artificial and conversational. It emphasizes equally the tale and its telling. In doing so it contemplates and integrates notions of artifice and reality, creation and reception, even nature and culture.

Bergman's *Magic Flute* does all that, and more. Mozart's *Figaro* and *Così* stand as supreme examples of a comic tradition that boasts countless other supreme examples. His last opera is much more singular. For many, it is the preeminent specimen of its genre, and as such it has been performed and celebrated through the centuries. But Theodor Adorno, famously, makes a case for a more complex view: "*The Magic Flute*, in which the Utopia of the Enlightenment and the pleasure of a light opera comic song precisely coincide, is a moment by itself. After *The Magic Flute* it was never again possible to force serious and light music together."[2]

In this oft-cited quotation lies much of the melancholy burden of modernity, and of Adorno's and the Frankfurt School's intractable integrity. And yet, as is well known, Adorno never really accounted for so much of the post-WWII popular culture that might have challenged this brave, dire assertion. It may indeed be that the Utopias of Enlightenment, of reconciled binaries, and of the Brotherhood of Man, are forever beyond our reach. (Were they ever really within it?) Still, *The Magic Flute*, and Bergman's theatrical film version of it especially, most certainly did manage to combine noble seriousness and joyful lightness, even going so far as to bind up some of our most painful historical and cultural wounds.

On the face of it, Ingmar Bergman is an unlikely contributor to this conciliatory project. His early films were angst-ridden melodramas, drawing upon the inspiration of his spiritual forebear, August Strindberg, to portray the painful incompatiblities that so often exist between men and women. As Bergman gained confidence, as he found his voice and style, these conflicts went on to reflect and represent a deeper alienation, speaking to what he saw as the fundamental solitude of life, the irreducible suffering of the human condition.

Bergman would extend these explorations into the arenas of faith and religion, going on to hold forth on the subject of God's silence, or outright nonexistence. As he did so, he established and refined a more rigorous set of cinematic strategies. This particular brand of modernism would become emblematic of the period's sense of discontinuity, anxiety, and absurdity. Bergman was an articulate witness to anguished times, and to the existential agony that transcends time.

But if Bergman's sensibility was compelling and resonant, it also invited – even demanded – interrogation and critique. He lacked ideological concern, and even awareness.[3] And at times his morbidity and defeatism seemed to border on the pathological. A young Bergman planned for his staging of a Strindberg play to be "a vision of toiling, weeping, evil-smitten humanity … in all its grotesqueness, its terror and its beauty."[4] In middle age, upon receiving a major award at the height of his power and influence, he had this to say about the world and the artist's place in it:

To be an artist for one's own sake is not always pleasant. But it has one enormous advantage: the artist shares his condition with every other living being who also exists solely for his own sake. When all is said and done, we doubtless constitute a fairly large brotherhood, which thus exists within a selfish community on our warm and dirty earth, beneath a cold and empty sky.[5]

Bergman's very sympathetic critical biographer, Peter Cowie, quite justly observed that his "rigid, some would say inflexible, view of the world leads to a certain repetition of themes, doubts, and aspirations. The unremitting obsession with death and betrayal, belief and disillusionment, produced in the fifties and sixties a style ripe for parody . . . ."[6] The American film critic Jonathan Rosenbaum, who had very much admired many of Bergman's films, could still, finally, look back at and characterize his work as "solipsistically self-pitying, spiritually constipated, and utterly without interest in overcoming these flaws."[7]

All that said and given its due, it is important to note that Bergman's films are not without their infusions of high spirits, humor, and, especially, tenderness. These latter episodes (i.e., the clown Jof's luminous vision of the Virgin and Child in *The Seventh Seal*, the sisters' placid walk through the park at the conclusion of *Cries and Whispers*, etc.) are the more uncommonly affecting because of their comparative infrequency and because of the way they leaven the darker films, which in turn brighten the dark times that produced them.

With remarkably few exceptions, Bergman's *Magic Flute* is a celebrated, beloved film. It is also quite strikingly distinct from the rest of his *oeuvre*. On a number of occasions Bergman gave exquisite expression to impulses and impressions that provide a context for understanding what drew him to this opera and what connects this film to moments in his other films. For example, he wrote the following during the production of *The Seventh Seal* (1957): "I believe a human being carries his or her own holiness, which lies within the realm of the earth; there are no other-worldly explanations. So in the film lives a remnant of my honest, childish piety lying peacefully alongside a harsh and rational perception of reality."[8]

A decade later he wrote the following in a notebook while preparing for the production of *Persona* (1966):

My parents spoke of *piety*, of *love*, and of *humility*. I have really tried hard. But as long as there was a God in my world, I couldn't even get close to my goals. My humility was not humble enough. My love remained nonetheless far less than the love of Christ or of the saints or even of my own mother's love. And my piety was forever poisoned by grave doubts. Now that God is gone, I felt that *all this* is mine; *piety* toward life, *humility* before my meaningless fate, and *love* for the other children who are afraid, who are ill, who are cruel.[9]

In another passage he expresses his hopes for what would in many ways be his testament film, *Fanny and Alexander*, but this statement might also be applied to his entire work:

Through my playing, I want to master my anxiety, relieve tension, and triumph over my deterioration. I want to depict, finally, the joy that I carry within me in spite of everything, and which I so seldom and so feebly have given attention to in my work. To be able to express the power of action, decisiveness, the vitality, and the kindness.[10]

These seemingly atypical, wonderfully refreshing comments indicate qualities that are also important parts of Bergman's sensibility, and of his work. And as it turns out, music – and Mozart – are crucial to the implementation of these ideas.

Alexis Luko provides a thorough study of Bergman's extensive, detailed, and purposeful use of previously composed classical music in the films.[11] Luko had observed, of course, that the intense close-ups for which Bergman has been so noted are very often rife with confrontation, alienation, and agony. She contrasts these familiar qualities with what she calls the "aural closeup," which is generally marked by the featured, foregrounded presence of classical music on the soundtrack.[12] These aural close-ups often run counter to the harrowing nature of so much of Bergman's work, featuring as they do these same characters now courteously listening, experiencing brief, incandescent moments of comprehension and connection.[13]

In Bergman's films these moments are powerful, but glancing. Significantly, they constitute the near entirety of *The Magic Flute*, which is the only completely concentrated, utterly unmitigated example of harmonious concord in his entire *oeuvre*.[14] Since Bergman was such a lightning rod, such an uncommonly versatile, prolific, acclaimed, and excoriated artist, his *Magic Flute* ended up being more than just a striking contrast to the main body of one individual's film output. It would emerge as a galvanizing contrast to, and even a bright beacon for, international film in general, as well as for the tumultuous decade that it bisected.

Writing toward the end of Bergman's active career as a film director, Peter Cowie said that "*The Magic Flute* may well take its place among the five or six greatest films that [he] has directed,"[15] in part because "Bergman's own predilection for chilly metaphysics had been tempered by Mozart's sense of wonder."[16] Jeremy Tambling (in a generally critical analysis) saw the film as an attempted "corrective to the tortured mind of the twentieth century."[17]

All of this was by design, and a consequence of a very particular attitude and process. As mentioned earlier, the theatrical film is not simply a matter of cinematic subordination to a parent art. Bergman's *Magic Flute*, for instance, is precisely aware of, and becomes a sophisticated essay about, the relationship between theater/opera and film, and of film's early grammatical evolution.

That said, Bergman's *Magic Flute* is also, decidedly, a modest adaptation, in which its brilliant, morose, and often seething adaptor submits to the sensibilities of the original authors (Schikaneder and Mozart), their inspirations, and the institutions that allowed them to communicate.

The Magic Flute's opening montage sets the tone for this important, encouraging act of obeisance, and it does so in a couple of important ways.[18] Eight serene, sunsetting establishing shots of the Drottningholm Court Theater[19] and its environs give way to an image of the spectators whom we presume to be sitting inside, and to a shot of one spectator in particular. The camera frames and then zooms in on a red/golden-haired girl of some eight or nine years. It comes to, and holds on, a close-up of her face, which lasts for a full forty-five seconds.

This is Bergman and Liv Ullmann's daughter, Linn,[20] to whom we will return with some frequency throughout the course of the film. She is listening to the opening Adagio of Mozart's overture. She is also looking, off-frame. Presently, the camera cuts to what she is looking at – namely, an eighteenth-century winged putto painted on the closed curtain at the front of the stage. We cut back to Linn, who now glances over to a draped and helmeted Muse figure seated in billowing clouds. To Linn, again, and now a last cut to the expanse of the curtain in its entirety.

This back-and-forth is known as cinematic suture, and *The Magic Flute* establishes Linn Ullmann as the site thereof. Suture is a standard technique through which classical (commercial) film spectators are brought into the film space and under the conventions and assumptions that inform and structure it.[21] It is accomplished by shot-reverse shot sequences in which we see a person looking, cut to what or who she is looking at, then return for her response to the thing she has just seen. In this construction we are introduced to the character with whom we will identify, come to share her space and perspective, see through her eyes, and feel as she feels.

To a degree, Linn is looking at, and about to bear witness to, "the noble, magical illusion of theater."[22] But there is something more, something much more, to her presence here. The deeper significance of this first suturing in *The Magic Flute* is that we are not completely, or even primarily, being invited to identify with a character in the opera proper. Instead, we identify with a spectator, and with a child at that. This is the sensibility that our suddenly, surprisingly humble director expects or perhaps invites us to assume, at least for the duration of this film.

At a basic level, Bergman's *The Magic Flute* is a story for children, and a reflection of the guileless, hopeful spirit of childhood. As in:

Then were there brought unto [Jesus] little children, that he should put his hands on them, and pray: and the disciples rebuked them. But Jesus said, Suffer little children, and forbid them not, to come unto me: for of such is the kingdom of heaven.[23]

And again:

The wolf also shall dwell with the lamb, and the leopard shall lie down with the kid; and the calf and the young lion and the fatling together; and a little child shall lead them.[24]

These moving statements, combined, evoke childhood's exemplary qualities and redemptive, paradisiacal power. These are manifest as Mozart's serene expository Adagio gives way to the electrifying Allegro, and as the last close-up of this beloved child resolves into what could well be her own bright vision. Now comes *The Magic Flute*'s celebrated assembly of attentive faces, juxtaposed and multiplying, comprising an impressive, practically comprehensive litany of bone structures and expressions, ages, and ethnicities. This striking, raptly listening legion of facial types is all bound together by the score on the soundtrack.

Motion picture soundtracks are traditionally tasked with binding together a film's disparate and often disharmonious images. In the nature of its production and assembly, film is a very fragmented medium. Conventional film music, so smooth and flowing, distracts the spectator from this fact. And it has further labors to perform. Most film music is subordinated to the narrative, as well as to the other ideological and commercial functions that motion pictures perform.[25] The overture sequence in *The Magic Flute* reverses this standard hierarchy: its images actually accompany the music and serve to secure and exemplify the story that the music tells.

In some ways, Mozart himself is the story in question. He has not only written this score, but he also represents the musical and cultural ideal that embraces and unites all of these spectators. Since viewers of the film have seen in this opening sequence almost every kind of person that they might imagine – since they have almost certainly seen someone who looks like them – then they too are invited to become part of this communion.

A waggish commentator once suggested that "Ingmar Bergman presented the overture to *The Magic Flute* (1975) as if it was a Coca-Cola commercial . . . ."[26] This is quite funny, but it is not quite fair. In the context of Bergman's customary alienation, not to mention 1968, absurdism, Allende, Baader-Meinhof, the cataclysmic end of the Vietnam War, constant clouds of nuclear threat, the FLQ, intractable instability in the Middle East, the implosion of an American presidential administration, if not of American democracy itself, the Khmer Rouge (and East Timor, and on and on), Munich, the OPEC oil embargo, rampant industrial pollution, and the threat of environmental cataclysm, rapacious capitalism with its resultant recessions and oppressions, revolutions, and totalitarianisms all around – surely, in this calamitous context (to say nothing of Bergman's constant, perpetual sickness unto death), a modest measure of sentiment and even calculated simplicity is not just to be dismissed.[27]

It is in part because of the tortured twentieth century that Bergman stages his *Magic Flute* as a story for children. But his staging is not merely escapist, nor at all childish. As its Masonic traces suggest, the opera also contains lessons that both youthful spectators and guileless protagonists can share as together they trace its archetypal passage from guileless innocence, through fiery trial and abiding love, to outright exaltation.

Once again, Ingmar Bergman has with some justice been taken to task for the consistent lack of political engagement in his films. Better, say some, the artist hit nails right on the head, fashioning narratives and even making outright declarations that directly address some aspect of social reality, that raise awareness and lead to needful change. But it could just as much be argued that Bergman left ideological interrogation in other capable hands as he ably explored his own alternative courses for illuminating the human condition.

In his autobiography he describes what he felt to be the opera's central scene, the one that moved him most profoundly, the one that most motivated him to undertake this adaptation. Tamino, the protagonist, the aspirant, the young hero who is passing through necessary trials on the way to his eventual, glorious apotheosis, is downcast (in the Act 1 finale). He has encountered deceit and dishonor, is discouraged by all the gaps that exist between appearance and reality, between his ardent aspiring and the obstacles that stand in his way:

Tamino is left alone . . . He cries: "Oh, dark night! When will you vanish? When shall I find light in the darkness?" The chorus answers pianissimo from within the temple: "Soon, soon or never more!" Tamino: "Soon? Soon? Or never more.

Hidden creatures, give me your answer. Does Pamina still live?" The chorus answers in the distance: "Pamina, Pamina still lives."

These twelve bars involve two questions at life's outer limits – but also two answers. When Mozart wrote his opera, he was already ill, the spectre of death touching him. In a moment of impatient despair, he cries: "Oh, dark night! When will you vanish? When shall I find light in the darkness?" The chorus responds ambiguously. "Soon, soon or never more." The mortally sick Mozart cries out a question into the darkness. Out of this darkness, he answers his own question – or does he receive an answer?

Then the other question: "Does Pamina still live?" The music translates the text's simple question into the greatest of all questions. "Does Love live? Is Love real?" The answer comes, quivering but hopeful in a strange division of Pamina's name: "Pa-mi-na still lives!" It is no longer a matter of the name of an attractive young woman, but a code word for love: "Pa-mi-na still lives." Love exists. Love is real in the world of human beings.[28]

Bergman had previously used this very sequence in his 1968 horror film, *Hour of the Wolf*. There, it is performed on the stage of a marionette theater, witnessed by a disintegrating artist and the group of demons who will ultimately consume him. This 1968 quotation was sincere and unsarcastic. It provided a real respite, real refreshment, and it ended, and gave way once again to, despair.

Following this *Magic Flute*'s bright ascendence, Bergman would in some ways do the very same thing, returning in part, or at least alternatingly, to his dire and even demonic melancholy. The Mozart film was preceded by the exquisite dissolutions of *Scenes from a Marriage* (1974; also, subsequently, adapted for the stage), succeeded by the marital entropy of *Face to Face* (1976). On the stage, it was back to Ibsen's *A Doll's House* and Strindberg's *Miss Julie*.[29]

But no matter. *The Magic Flute* provided a refreshing contrast to its director's deeply resonant but sometimes burdensome output. It provided a refreshing contrast to the troubled films that abounded during that troubling decade. Since that time, *The Magic Flute* has been continuously available and has become only increasingly visible.[30] This is so much the case that it really has begun to pose a serious challenge to Adorno's previously quoted statement about the Mozart/Schikaneder original. If the opera, as originally produced, was "a moment by itself," then Bergman's modest and self-effacing theatrical film has become an ever-renewing, ever-present moment of reconciliation and pleasure.

Notes

1. Ingmar Bergman, *Images: My Life in Film*, trans. Marianne Ruuth (New York: Arcade Publishing, 2007), 353.
2. In *Essays on Music: Theodor W. Adorno*, ed. Richard Leppert, trans. Susan H. Gillespie (Berkeley: University of California Press, 2002), 290.
3. On the cause and consequence of this disengagement, see Peter Cowie, *Ingmar Bergman: A Critical Biography* (New York: Scribners, 1982), 16, 133–34. For a particularly blistering critique, see Robert Phillip Kolker, *The Altering Eye: Contemporary International Cinema* (Oxford: Oxford University Press, 1983), 11, 163–65, 220, 327–28.
4. Quoted in Cowie, *Ingmar Bergman*, 21.
5. From "The Snakeskin," presented in 1965; in Bergman, *Images*, 51.
6. Cowie, *Ingmar Bergman*, 341.
7. Rosenbaum, reviewing Bergman's 2003 release, *Sarabande*, www .chicagoreader.com/chicago/saraband/Content?oid=919560.
8. Bergman, *Images*, 238.
9. Ibid., 56–58 (emphasis in original).
10. Ibid., 366.
11. Alexis Luko, *Sonatas, Screams, and Silence: Music and Sound in the Films of Ingmar Bergman* (New York: Routledge, 2016), 71–105.
12. Ibid., 74.
13. See Ingmar Bergman, *The Magic Lantern: An Autobiography*, trans. Joan Tate (New York: Viking Penguin, 1988), 43, 281–82, for a few of the very moving reasons for his frequent, fervent use of Bach.
14. But what, one might say, of Monostatos and the Queen of the Night? Quite right: these complicated characters, along with their many contradictory resonances and implications, give serious challenge to the point made above. That challenge is fully and fairly considered elsewhere in this volume, allowing for and in light of which I continue to urge this point.
15. Cowie, *Ingmar Bergman*, 295.
16. Ibid., 299.
17. Jeremy Tambling *Opera, Ideology, and Film* (Manchester: Manchester University Press, 1987), 136.
18. Parts of this analysis of the film proper are adapted from Dean W. Duncan, "Interpretation and Enactment in Ingmar Bergman's 'The Magic Flute,'" *BYU Studies* 43/3 (2004): 229–50.
19. As indicated earlier, Bergman had long imagined, then actually planned, his enactment of *The Magic Flute* with reference to the dimensions and accoutrements of the eighteenth-century court theater in Stockholm's Drottningholm Palace. It turned out that though still extant, the theater was too delicate to withstand the presence of a film crew. So designer Henny

Noremark, in close consultation with his director, replicated the original space, together with all of its apparatus and devices, in the studios of the Swedish Film Institute. This was partly, certainly, for the sake of homage. It also gave the collaborators full control of the filming space and allowed them to demonstrate their fascinating ideas about the early evolution of the language of cinema. In this, it is evident that Olivier's *Henry V* informed Bergman's film, which would subsequently inspire productions like Louis Malle/André Gregory's *Vanya on 42nd Street* (1994) and others.

20. As identified in Rose Laub Coser, "The Principle of Patriarchy: The Case of The Magic Flute," *Signs* 4/2 (1978): 337–48, esp. 340; William Moritz, Review of *The Magic Flute, Film Quarterly* (Fall 1976): 45–49, esp. 47. Linn Ullmann has become a major critic and novelist in her own right.

21. See Daniel Dayan, "The Tutor-Code of Classical Cinema," *Film Quarterly* 28/1 (1974): 22–31.

22. See note 1.

23. Matthew 19:13. Also Mark, 10:14, Luke 18:15.

24. Isaiah 11:6.

25. Note the title, and then the overarching thesis, of film music scholar Claudia Gorbman's *Unheard Melodies: Narrative Film Music* (Bloomington: Indiana University Press, 1987).

26. Ronald Bergan, "How to Use Classical Music Properly in a Film," *The Guardian* (November 19, 2008), www.theguardian.com/film/filmblog/2008/nov/19/classical-music-in-film. Bergan is referring to the famous 1971 Coca-Cola commercial that would have liked to teach the world to sing. See also Moritz's salutary review in *Film Comment*, which takes the things we are praising here to be silly, more childish than childlike.

27. There are many touching examples of alienated, even hell-hounded artists seeking refuge, or at least a brief respite, in the tender visions of children. The fact that their reaching is not always quite convincing may make the gesture all that much more touching. Think of Bergman, again (his novel, *Sunday's Children*), Cormac McCarthy (*The Road*), Roman Polanski (*Oliver Twist*, still infernal), Nicolas Roeg (*The Witches* [but not *Walkabout*]), Martin Scorcese (*Hugo*), Wim Wenders (*Alice in the Cities*).

28. Bergman, *Magic Lantern*, 216–17.

29. Egil Törnqvist, *Between Stage and Screen: Ingmar Bergman Directs* (Amsterdam: Amsterdam University Press, 1995), 69.

30. For example, as a much remarked-upon part of the 2018 centenary celebrations of Bergman's birth and its recent rerelease on DVD in the prestigious Criterion Collection.

Further Reading

The literature on *The Magic Flute* and its surrounding context is vast and has grown enormously in recent decades. The list provided here is highly selective and focuses mainly on works that are readily accessible. I have made no attempt to be comprehensive or to duplicate the recommendations authors have made on specific topics in the notes for individual chapters. Instead, this list is organized in the following way: (1) reference works, (2) biographies and books on Mozart of both recent and historic interest, (3) books on Mozart's operas aimed at different types of readers, (4) books devoted entirely to *The Magic Flute*, and (5) further reading on the topics covered in Parts I–IV of this volume. With very few exceptions, I have listed items only once, even where they may be relevant to several sections. Readers will find a wide range of issues and diversity of opinions as well as works of historical interest that have shaped and continue to shape the opera's reception.

Reference Works

Anderson, Emily, trans. and ed. *The Letters of Mozart and His Family*. 3rd edn. Revised and edited by Stanley Sadie and Fiona Smart. London: Macmillan, 1985. (LMF)

Bauer, Wilhelm A., Otto Erich Deutsch, and Joseph Heinz Eibl, eds. *Mozart: Briefe und Aufzeichnungen, Gesamtausgabe*. 8 vols. Kassel: Bärenreiter, 1962–2005. (MBA)

Clive, Peter. *Mozart and His Circle: A Biographical Dictionary*. New Haven, CT: Yale University Press, 1993.

Deutsch, Otto Erich. *Mozart: Die Dokumente seines Lebens*. Neue Mozart-Ausgabe, Series 10: Supplement, Workgroup 34. Kassel: Bärenreiter, 1961. (MDL)

   Mozart: A Documentary Biography. Translated by Eric Blom, Peter Branscombe, and Jeremy Noble. 3rd edn. London: Simon & Schuster, 1990. (MDB)

Edge, Dexter and David Black. *Mozart: New Documents*. www.mozartdocuments.org

Eisen, Cliff, ed. *New Mozart Documents: A Supplement to O. E. Deutsch's Documentary Biography*. Stanford, CA: Stanford University Press, 1991.

   Wolfgang Amadeus Mozart: A Life in Letters. Translated by Stewart Spencer. London: Penguin Books, 2006.

Eisen, Cliff and Simon P. Keefe, eds. *The Cambridge Mozart Encyclopedia.* Cambridge: Cambridge University Press, 2006.

Landon, H. C. Robbins, ed. *The Mozart Compendium: A Guide to Mozart's Life and Music.* London: Thames and Hudson, 1990.

Link, Dorothea. *The National Court Theatre in Mozart's Vienna.* Oxford: Clarendon Press, 1998.

Marshall, Robert L., ed. *Mozart Speaks: Views on Music, Musicians, and the World.* New York: Schirmer, 1991.

Mozart, Wolfgang Amadeus. *"Die Zauberflöte," K. 620: Facsimile of the Autograph Score.* With essays by Hans Joachim Kreuzer and Christoph Wolff. 3 vols. Los Altos, CA: The Packard Humanities Institute, 2009. (FACS)

   Neue Ausgabe sämtlicher Werke. Kassel: Bärenreiter, 1955–2007. Available at Digital Mozart Edition: https://dme.mozarteum.at. (NMA)

Spaethling, Robert, ed. and trans. *Mozart's Letters, Mozart's Life.* New York: Norton, 2000.

Warburton, Ernest, ed. *The Librettos of Mozart's Operas.* 7 vols. New York: Garland, 1992.

Selected Biographies and Books on Mozart

Abert, Hermann. *W. A. Mozart* (1919–21; 3rd edn. 1955–56). Translated by Stewart Spencer and edited by Cliff Eisen. New Haven, CT: Yale University Press, 2007.

Braunbehrens, Volkmar. *Mozart in Vienna: 1781–1791.* Translated by Timothy Bell. New York: Grove Weidenfeld, 1990. Originally published in German as *Mozart in Wien* (Munich: R. Piper, 1986).

Einstein, Alfred. *Mozart: His Character, His Work.* Translated by Arthur Mendel and Nathan Broder. New York: Oxford University Press, 1945.

Glover, Jane. *Mozart's Women: His Family, His Friends, His Music.* London: Macmillan, 2005.

Halliwell, Ruth. *The Mozart Family: Four Lives in a Social Context.* New York: Oxford University Press, 1998.

Keefe, Simon P. *Mozart in Vienna: The Final Decade.* Cambridge: Cambridge University Press, 2017.

Keefe, Simon P., ed. *The Cambridge Companion to Mozart.* Cambridge: Cambridge University Press, 2003.

   Mozart in Context. Cambridge: Cambridge University Press, 2019.

Knepler, Georg. *Wolfgang Amadé Mozart.* Translated by J. Bradford Robinson. Cambridge: Cambridge University Press, 1994. Originally published in German as *Wolfgang Amadé Mozart: Annäherungen* (Berlin: Henschel Verlag, 1991).

Küster, Konrad. *Mozart: A Musical Biography*. Translated by Mary Whittall. Oxford: Clarendon Press, 1996. Originally published in German as *Mozart: Eine musicalische Biographie* (Stuttgart: Deutsche Verlags-Anstalt, 1990).

Landon, H. C. Robbins. *1791: Mozart's Last Year*. New York: Schirmer, 1988.
  Mozart: The Golden Years, 1781–1791. New York: Schirmer, 1989.

Rushton, Julian. *Mozart*. Oxford: Oxford University Press, 2006.

Solomon, Maynard. *Mozart: A Life*. New York: HarperCollins, 1995.

Stafford, William. *The Mozart Myths: A Critical Reassessment*. Stanford, CA: Stanford University Press, 1991.

Wolff, Christoph. *Mozart at the Gateway to His Fortune: Serving the Emperor, 1788–1791*. New York: Norton, 2012.

Selected Books on Mozart's Operas

Angermüller, Rudolf. *Mozart's Operas*. Translated by Stewart Spencer. New York: Rizzoli, 1988. Originally published in German as *Mozart: Die Opern von der Uraufführung bis heute* (Frankfurt am Main: Ullstein, 1988).

Brophy, Brigid. *Mozart the Dramatist*. New York: Da Capo, 1968.

Brown-Montesano, Kristi. *Understanding the Women of Mozart's Operas*. Berkeley: University of California Press, 2007.

Cairns, David. *Mozart and His Operas*. Berkeley: University of California Press, 2006.

Dent, Edward J. *Mozart's Operas* (1913). 2nd edn. London: Oxford University Press, 1947.

Heartz, Daniel. *Mozart's Operas*. Edited, with contributing essays, by Thomas Bauman. Berkeley: University of California Press, 1990.

Hunter, Mary. *Mozart's Operas: A Companion*. New Haven, CT: Yale University Press, 2008.

Kunze, Stefan. *Mozarts Opern*. Stuttgart: Philipp Reclam, 1984.

Nagel, Ivan. *Autonomy and Mercy: Reflections on Mozart's Operas*. Translated by Marion Faber and Ivan Nagel. Cambridge, MA.: Harvard University Press, 1991. Originally published in German as *Autonomie und Gnade: Über Mozarts Opern* (Munich: Carl Hanser Verlag, 1988).

Nedbal, Martin. *Morality and Viennese Opera in the Age of Mozart and Beethoven*. London: Routledge, 2017.

Rice, John A. *Mozart on the Stage*. Cambridge: Cambridge University Press, 2009.

Till, Nicholas. *Mozart and the Enlightenment: Truth, Virtue and Beauty in Mozart's Operas*. London: Faber and Faber, 1992.

Waldoff, Jessica. *Recognition in Mozart's Operas*. New York: Oxford University Press, 2006.

Selected Books on *The Magic Flute*

Assmann, Jan. *Die Zauberflöte: Oper und Mysterium*. Munich: Carl Hanser Verlag, 2005.

Berk, M. F. M. van den. *The Magic Flute: An Alchemical Allegory*. Translated by J. Berkhout. Leiden: Brill, 2004.

Branscombe, Peter. *W. A. Mozart: "Die Zauberflöte."* Cambridge Opera Handbooks. Cambridge: Cambridge University Press, 1991. (COH)

Buch, David J. *Magic Flutes & Enchanted Forests: The Supernatural in Eighteenth-Century Musical Theater*. Chicago: Chicago University Press, 2008.

Chailley, Jacques. *The Magic Flute: Masonic Opera*. Translated by Herbert Weinstock. New York: Knopf, 1971. Originally published in French as *La flûte enchantée: Opéra maçonnique* (Paris: Robert Laffont, 1968). The most recent reprint is entitled *The Magic Flute Unveiled: Esoteric Symbolism in Mozart's Masonic Opera* (Rochester, VT: Inner Traditions International, 1992).

Eckelmeyer, Judith A. *The Cultural Context of Mozart's "Magic Flute": Social, Aesthetic, Philosophical*. Lewiston, NY: Edwin Mellen Press, 1991.

Evenden, Michael. *Silence and Selfhood: The Desire of Order in Mozart's "Magic Flute."* New York: Peter Lang, 1999.

Freyhan, Michael. *The Authentic* Magic Flute *Libretto: Mozart's Autograph or the First Full-Score Edition?* Lanham, MD: Scarecrow Press, 2009.

Gammond, Peter. *"The Magic Flute": A Guide to the Opera*. London: Barrie and Jenkins, 1979.

Irmen, Hans-Josef. *Mozart's Masonry and "The Magic Flute."* Translated by Ruth Ohm and Chantal Spenke. Essen: Prisca, 1996.

Kahn, Gary, ed. *"Die Zauberflöte": Wolfgang Amadeus Mozart*. Overture Opera Guides in association with English National Opera. Richmond: Alma Books, 2019.

Mueller, Adeline, guest ed. *After "Die Zauberflöte."* Special issue, *Opera Quarterly* 28/1–2 (2012).

Nicholas, John, ed. *The Magic Flute*. English National Opera Guide No. 3. London: River Run Press, 1980.

Rosenberg, Alfons. *"Die Zauberflöte": Geschichte und Deutung von Mozarts Oper*. Munich: Prestel, 1972.

Part I: Conception and Context

Baker, Evan. *From the Score to the Stage: An Illustrated History of Continental Opera Production and Staging*. Chicago: University of Chicago Press, 2013.

Bauman, Thomas. *North German Opera in the Age of Goethe*. Cambridge: Cambridge University Press, 1985.

Brauneis, Walther. "Wolfgang Amadé Mozarts 'Zauberflöte' und Innsbruck: Neue Quellen zum Erstaufführungsdatum im National-Hoftheater gegenüber der Innsbrucker Hofburg und zu den sechs Szenenbildern des Innsbrucker Zeichners und Kupferstechers Joseph Schaffer," *Wissenschaftliches Jahrbuch der Tiroler Landesmuseen* 2/43 (2009): 43–61.

Buch, David J. "The Choruses of 'Die Zauberflöte' in Context: Choral Music at the Theater auf der Wieden." *Choral Journal* 46/12 (2006): 6–21.

"Eighteenth-Century Performing Materials from the Archive of the Theater an der Wien and Mozart's *Die Zauberflöte*." *Musical Quarterly* 84 (2000): 287–322.

"The House Composers of the Theater auf der Wieden in the Time of Mozart (1789–91)." *Min-Ad: Israel Studies in Musicology Online* 5/2 (2006): 14–19.

"Mozart and the Theater auf der Wieden: New Attributions and Perspectives." *Cambridge Opera Journal* 9/3 (1997): 195–232.

"A Newly-Discovered Manuscript of Mozart's *Die Zauberflöte* from the Copy Shop of Emanuel Schikaneder's Theater auf der Wieden." *Studia Musicologica Academiae Scientiarum Hungaricae* 45/3–4 (2004): 269–79.

"*Der Stein der Weisen*, Mozart, and Collaborative Singspiels at Emanuel Schikaneder's Theater auf der Wieden." *Mozart-Jahrbuch* 2000, 89–124.

Cole, Malcolm. "Mozart and Two Theaters in Josephinian Vienna." In *Opera in Context: Essays on Historical Staging from the Late Renaissance to the Time of Puccini*, edited by Mark A. Radice. Portland, OR: Amadeus Press, 1998, 111–45.

Corneilson, Paul. "Josepha Hofer: First Queen of the Night." *Mozart Studien* 25 (2018): 477–88.

DelDonna, Anthony R. and Pierpaolo Polzonetti, eds. *The Cambridge Companion to Eighteenth-Century Opera*. Cambridge: Cambridge University Press, 2009.

Edge, Dexter. "Mozart's Viennese Orchestras." *Early Music* 20/1 (1992): 63–88.

Glatthorn, Austin. *Music Theatre and the Holy Roman Empire: The German Musical Stage at the Turn of the Nineteenth Century*. Cambridge: Cambridge University Press, 2022.

Honolka, Kurt. *Papageno: Emanuel Schikaneder, Man of the Theater in Mozart's Time*. Translated by Jane Mary Wilde. Portland, OR: Amadeus Press, 1990.

Joubert, Estelle. "Genre and Form in German Opera." In *The Cambridge Companion to Eighteenth-Century Opera*, edited by Anthony R. DelDonna and Pierpaolo Polzonetti. Cambridge: Cambridge University Press, 2009, 184–201.

Komorzynski, Egon. *Emanuel Schikaneder: Ein Beitrag zur Geschichte des deutschen Theaters* (1901). 2nd edn. Vienna: Ludwig Doblinger, 1951.

Link, Dorothea. *The National Court Theatre in Mozart's Vienna: Sources and Documents, 1783–1792*. Oxford: Oxford University Press, 1998.

Mueller, Adeline. "Who Were the Drei Knaben?" *Opera Quarterly* 28/1–2 (2012): 88–103.

Nedbal, Martin. "Mozart as a Viennese Moralist: *Die Zauberflöte* and Its Maxims." *Acta Musicologica* 81/1 (2009): 123–57.

Schikaneder, Emanuel. *Die Zauberflöte: Eine große Oper in zwey Aufzügen*. Vienna: Alberti, 1791.

Sonnek, Anke. *Emanuel Schikaneder: Theaterprinzipal, Schauspieler und Stückenschreiber*. Kassel: Bärenreiter, 1999.

Warrack, John. *German Opera: From the Beginnings to Wagner*. Cambridge: Cambridge University Press, 2001.

Woodfield, Ian. *Cabals and Satires: Mozart's Comic Operas in Vienna*. New York: Oxford University Press, 2019.

Yates, W. E. *Theatre in Vienna: A Critical History, 1776– 1995*. Cambridge: Cambridge University Press, 1996.

Zenck, Claudia. "German Opera from Reinhard Keiser to Peter Winter." Translated by Anke Caton and Simon P. Keefe. In *The Cambridge History of Eighteenth-Century Music*, edited by Simon P. Keefe. Cambridge: Cambridge University Press, 2009, 331–84.

Part II: Music, Text, and Action

Abert, Hermann. "*Die Zauberflöte*." In *W. A. Mozart*, translated by Stewart Spencer and edited by Cliff Eisen. New Haven, CT: Yale University Press, 2007, 1245–304.

Albrecht, Theodore. "Anton Dreyssig (c. 1753/4–1820): Mozart's and Beethoven's *Zauberflötist*." In *Words about Mozart: Essays in Honor of Stanley Sadie*, edited by Dorothea Link and Judith Nagley. Woodbridge: Boydell Press, 2005, 179–92.

Batley, E. M. "Textual Unity in *Die Zauberflöte*." *Music Review* 27 (1966): 81–92.

Bauman, Thomas. "At the North Gate: Instrumental Music in *Die Zauberflöte*." In Daniel Heartz, *Mozart's Operas*, edited, with contributing essays, by Thomas Bauman. Berkeley: University of California Press, 1990, 277–97.

Branscombe, Peter. "*Die Zauberflöte*: Some textual and interpretive problems." *Proceedings of the Royal Musical Association* 92 (1965–66): 45–64.

Chapin, Keith. "Strict and Free Reversed: The Law of Counterpoint in Koch's *Musikalisches Lexikon* and Mozart's *Zauberflöte*." *Eighteenth-Century Music* 3/1 (2006): 91–107.

Cole, Malcolm S. "*The Magic Flute* and the Quatrain." *Journal of Musicology* 3 (1984): 157–76.

Everett, Walter. "Voice Leading, Register, and Self-Discipline in Mozart's *Die Zauberflöte*." *Theory and Practice* 16 (1991): 103–26.

Farnsworth, Rodney. "Tamino at the Temple's Portals: A Literary-Musical Analysis of a Key Passage from *Die Zauberflöte*." *Canadian Review of Comparative Literature* 8 (1981): 483–507.

Heartz, Daniel. "*Die Zauberflöte.*" In *Mozart, Haydn and Early Beethoven, 1781–1802.* New York: W. W. Norton, 2009, 270–88.

Joubert, Estelle. "Songs to Shape a German Nation: Hiller's Comic Operas and the Public Sphere." *Eighteenth-Century Music* 3/2 (2006): 213–30.

Keefe, Simon P., ed. *The Cambridge History of Eighteenth-Century Music.* Cambridge: Cambridge University Press, 2009.

King, A. Hyatt. "The Melodic Sources and Affinities of *Die Zauberflöte.*" In *Mozart in Retrospect: Studies in Criticism and Bibliography.* London: Oxford University Press, 1955, 141–63. Originally published in *Musical Quarterly* 36 (1950): 241–58.

Kunze, Stefan. "*Die Zauberflöte:* Theater als Sinnbild." In *Mozarts Opern.* Stuttgart: Philipp Reclam, 1984, 554–646.

Laskowski, Larry. "Voice Leading and Meter: An Unusual Mozart Autograph." In *Trends in Schenkerian Research,* edited by Allen Cadwallader. New York: Schirmer, 1990, 41–50.

Nowotny, Rudolf. "Das Duett Nr. 7 aus der Zauberflöte: Periode und Takt." *Mozart-Jahrbuch* 1996, 85–125.

Platoff, John. "Musical and Dramatic Structure in the Opera Buffa Finale." *Journal of Musicology* 7 (1989): 191–230.

Rathey, Markus. "Mozart, Kirnberger and the Idea of Musical Purity: Revisiting Two Sketches from 1782." *Eighteenth-Century Music* 13 (2016): 235–52.

Smith, Erik. "The Music." In Peter Branscombe, *W. A. Mozart: "Die Zauberflöte."* Cambridge Opera Handbooks. Cambridge: Cambridge University Press, 1991.

Tyson, Alan. "Two Mozart Puzzles: Can Anyone Solve Them?" *Musical Times* 129/1741 (1988): 126–27.

Waldoff, Jessica. "Operatic Enlightenment in *Die Zauberflöte.*" In *Recognition in Mozart's Operas.* New York: Oxford University Press, 2006, 17–43.

Webster, James. "The Analysis of Mozart's Arias." In *Mozart Studies,* edited by Cliff Eisen. Oxford: Clarendon Press, 1991, 101–99.

"Cone's 'Personae' and the Analysis of Opera." *College Music Symposium* 29 (1989): 44–65.

"Mozart's Operas and the Myth of Musical Unity." *Cambridge Opera Journal* 2 (1990): 197–218.

"To Understand Verdi and Wagner We Must Understand Mozart." *19th-Century Music* 11 (1987): 175–93.

Wolff, Christoff. "'O ew'ge Nacht! Wann wirst [du] schwinden?' Zum Verständnis der Sprecherszene im ersten Finale von Mozarts 'Zauberflöte.'" In *Analysen: Beiträge zu einer Problemgeschichte des Kompanierens: Festschrift für Hans Heinrich Eggebrecht,* edited by Werner Breig, Reinhold Brinkmann, and Elmar Budde. Stuttgart: F. Steiner, 1984, 234–47.

Part III: Approaches and Perspectives

Abbate, Carolyn. "Magic Flute, Nocturnal Sun." In *In Search of Opera*. Princeton: Princeton University Press, 2001, 55–106.

Allanbrook, Wye Jamison, Mary Hunter, and Gretchen A. Wheelock. "Staging Mozart's Women." In *Siren Songs: Representations of Gender and Sexuality in Opera*, edited by Mary Ann Smart. Princeton: Princeton University Press, 2000, 46–66.

Baker, P. G. "'Night into Day': Patterns of Symbolism in Mozart's *The Magic Flute*." *University of Toronto Quarterly* 49 (1979/80): 95–116.

Bartel, Kate. "Pamina, Portraits, and the Feminine in Mozart and Schikaneder's *Die Zauberflöte*." *Musicology Australia* 22/1 (1999): 31–45.

Berger, Karol. "*Die Zauberflöte*, or the Self-Assertion of the Moderns." In *Bach's Cycle, Mozart's Arrow: An Essay on the Origins of Musical Modernity*. Berkeley: University of California Press, 2007, 280–91.

Brown, Jane K. "'The Monstrous Rights of the Present': Goethe and the Humanity of *Die Zauberflöte*." *Opera Quarterly* 28/1–2 (2012): 5–19.

"The Queen of the Night and the Crisis of Allegory in *The Magic Flute*." *Goethe Yearbook* 8 (1996): 142–56.

Buch, David J. "*Die Zauberflöte*, Masonic Opera, and Other Fairy Tales." *Acta Musicologica* 76/2 (2004): 193–219.

"Fairy-Tale Literature and *Die Zauberflöte*." *Acta Musicologica* 64/1 (1992): 30–49.

Cohen, Mitchell. *The Politics of Opera: A History from Monteverdi to Mozart*. Princeton: Princeton University Press, 2017.

Cole, Malcolm S. "Monostatos and His 'Sister': Racial Stereotype in *Die Zauberflöte* and Its Sequel." *Opera Quarterly* 21/1 (2005): 2–26.

Corse, Sandra. "The Magic Flute." In *Opera and the Uses of Language: Mozart, Verdi, and Britten*. Rutherford, NJ: Fairleigh Dickinson University Press, 1987, 46–68.

Coser, Rose Laub. "The Principle of Patriarchy: The Case of *The Magic Flute*." *Signs* 4/2 (1978): 337–48.

Fischer, Petra. "Die Rehabilitierung der Sinnlichkeit: Philosophische Implikationen der Figurenkonstellation der *Zauberflöte*." *Archiv für Musikwissenschaft* 50/1 (1993): 1–25.

Frese, Annette. "'Das Theater verwandelt sich . . .': Bühnenbilder, Figurinen und Illustrationen zur Zauberflöte." In *Theater um Mozart*, edited by Bärbel Pelker. Heidelberg: Universitätsverlag Winter, 2006, 143–208.

Gilman, Sander L. "The Figure of the Black in German Aesthetic Theory." *Eighteenth-Century Studies* 8/4 (1975): 373–91.

Godwin, Jocelyn. "Layers of Meaning in The Magic Flute." *Musical Quarterly* 65/4 (1979): 471–92.

Head, Matthew. *Orientalism, Masquerade and Mozart's Turkish Music*. London: Royal Musical Association, 2000.

Heartz, Daniel. "La Clemenza di Sarastro: Masonic Beneficence in the Last Operas." In *Mozart's Operas*, edited, with contributing essays, by Thomas Bauman. Berkeley: University of California Press, 1990, 254–75.

Howards, Alyssa. "Beyond the Glockenspiel: Teaching Race and Gender in Mozart's *Zauberflöte*." *Die Unterrichtspraxis/Teaching German* 47/1 (2014): 1–13.

Howarth, Peter. "Symbolism in *Die Zauberflöte*: Origin and Background of the Symbolism of 'Sevenfold,' 'Mighty,' and 'All-Consuming Sun Disk.'" *Opera Quarterly* 8/3 (1991): 58–85.

Kerry, Paul E. "'Initiates of Isis Now, Come, Enter into the Temple!': Masonic and Enlightenment Thought in *The Magic Flute*." *Brigham Young University Studies* 43/3 (2004): 104–36.

Koenigsberger, Dorothy. "A New Metaphor for Mozart's *The Magic Flute*." *European Studies Review* 5 (1975): 229–75.

Küster, Konrad. "Machinery, Symbolism, Music: *Die Zauberflöte*, K. 620." In *Mozart: A Musical Biography*, translated by Mary Whittall. Oxford: Clarendon Press, 1996, 356–69.

Locke, Ralph. *Music and the Exotic from the Renaissance to Mozart*. Cambridge: Cambridge University Press, 2015.

Lösel, Steffen. "Monostatos: Racism in *Die Zauberflöte*." *Soundings* 102/4 (2019): 275–324.

Nettl, Paul. *Mozart and Masonry*. New York: Dorset Press, 1957.

Rumph, Stephen. *Mozart and Enlightenment Semiotics*. Berkeley: University of California Press, 2002.

Scott, Derek B. "A Problem of Race in Directing *Die Zauberflöte*." In *Musical Style and Social Meaning*. London: Routledge, 2010, 295–301.

Spaethling, Robert. "Folklore and Enlightenment in the Libretto of Mozart's *Magic Flute*." *Eighteenth-Century Studies* 9/1 (1975): 45–68.

Stucky, Priscilla. "Light Dispels Darkness: Gender, Ritual, and Society in Mozart's *The Magic Flute*." *Journal of Feminist Studies in Religion* 11/1 (1995): 5–39.

Subotnik, Rose R. "Whose *Magic Flute*? Intimations of Reality at the Gates of Enlightenment." In *Deconstructive Variations: Music and Reason in Western Society*. Minneapolis: University of Minnesota Press, 1996.

Tettlebaum, Marianne. "Whose Magic Flute?" *Representations* 102/1 (2008): 76–93.

Werner, Eric. "Leading or Symbolic Formulas in *The Magic Flute*: A Hermeneutic Explanation." *Music Review* 18 (1957): 286–93.

Wheelock, Gretchen A. "*Schwarze Gredel* and the Engendered Minor Mode in Mozart's Operas." In *Musicology and Difference: Gender and Sexuality in Music Scholarship*, edited by Ruth A. Solie. Berkeley: University of California Press, 1993), 201–21.

Wolff, Larry. *The Singing Turk: Ottoman Power and Operatic Emotions on the European Stage from the Siege of Vienna to the Age of Napoleon*. Stanford, CA: Stanford University Press, 2016.

Zech, Christina. "'Ein Mann muß eure Herzen leiten': Zum Frauenbild in Mozarts 'Zauberflöte' auf musikalischer und literarischer Ebene." *Archiv für Musikwissenchaft* 52/4 (1995): 279–315.

Part IV: Reception, Interpretation, and Influence

Auden, W. H. and Chester Kallman. *The Magic Flute: An Opera in Two Acts; Music by W. A. Mozart; English Version after the Libretto of Schikaneder and Giesecke*. London: Faber and Faber, 1957.

Branscomble, Peter. "The Literary Afterlife of *Die Zauberflöte*." In *Words on Music: Essays in Honor of Andrew Porter on the Occasion of His 75th Birthday*, edited by David Rosen and Claire Brook. Hillsdale, NY: Pendragon Press, 2003, 14–29.

Brown, Jane K. "Classicism and Secular Humanism: The Sanctification of *Die Zauberflöte* in Goethe's 'Novelle.'" In *Religion, Reason, and Culture in the Age of Goethe*, edited by Elisabeth Krimmer and Patricia Anne Simpson. Rochester, NY: Camden House, 2013, 120–40.

Citron, Marcia J. "Vococentrism and Sound in Ingmar Bergman's *The Magic Flute*." In *Voicing the Cinema: Film Music and the Integrated Soundtrack*, edited by James Buhler and Hannah Lewis. Urbana: University of Illinois Press, 2020, 91–107.

Cowgill, Rachel. "New Light and the Man of Might: Revisiting Early Interpretations of Mozart's *Die Zauberflöte*." In *Art and Ideology in European Opera: Essays in Honour of Julian Rushton*, edited by Rachel Cowgill, David Cooper, and Clive Brown. Woodbridge: Boydell Press, 2010, 194–221.

Dickinson, G. Lowes. *The Magic Flute: A Fantasia*. London: George Allen and Unwin, 1920.

Duncan, Dean W. "Adaptation, Enactment, and Ingmar Bergman's *Magic Flute*." *Brigham Young University Studies* 43/3 (2004): 229–50.

Freyhan, Michael. *The Authentic "Magic Flute" Libretto: Mozart's Autograph or the First Full-Score Edition?* Lanham, MD: Scarecrow Press, 2009.

Goethe, Johanne Wolfgang von. *Der Zauberflöte zweiter Teil/The Magic Flute, Part II*, in the original German and with simultaneous translation by Eric Blom. In Robert Spaethling, *Music and Mozart in the Life of Goethe*. Columbia, SC: Camden House, 1987, 175–231. Originally published in *Music and Letters* 23 (1942): 234–54.

Grant, Robert. "The Disenchanted Flute." In *The Politics of Sex and Other Essays: On Conservatism, Culture and the Imagination*. Basingstoke: Macmillan, 2000, 59–74.

Henderson, Donald G. "The 'Magic Flute' of Peter Winter." *Music and Letters* 64/3–4 (1983): 193–205.

Ibáñez-Garcia, Estela. "Displaying the Magician's Art: Theatrical Illusion in Ingmar Bergman's *The Magic Flute* (1975)." *Cambridge Opera Journal* 33/3 (2021): 191–211.

Kauffman, Stanley. "The Abduction from the Theater: Mozart Opera on Film." In *On Mozart*, edited by James M. Morris. New York: Woodrow Wilson Center Press, 1994, 227–39.

Kohler, Karl-Heinz. *Das Zauberflötenwunder: Odyssee einer Handschrift.* Weimar: Wartburg, 1996.

Kramer, Lawrence. "Value and Meaning in *The Magic Flute.*" In *Musicological Identities: Essays in Honor of Susan McClary*, edited by Stephen Baur, Raymond Knapp, and Jacqueline Warwick. Burlington, VT: Ashgate, 2008, 3–16.

Levi, Erik, "Mozart and the Freemasons: A Nazi problem." In *Mozart and the Nazis: How the Third Reich Abused a Cultural Icon.* New Haven, CT: Yale University Press, 2010, 33–52.

Meinhold, Günter. Zauberflöte *und* Zauberflöten-*Rezeption: Studien zu Emanuel Schikaneders Libretto* Die Zauberflöte *und seiner literarischen Rezeption.* Frankfurt am Main: Peter Lang, 2001.

Müller, Ulrich. "'O Mozart steig hernieder': Das Rätsel von Papagenos dritter Strophe in der 'Zauberflöte.'" *Neue Zeitschrift für Musik* 153/ 7–8 (1992): 27–34.

Nedbal, Martin. "Live Marionettes and Divas on the Strings: *Die Zauberflöte*'s Interactions with Puppet Theater." *Opera Quarterly* 28/1–2 (2012): 20–36.

Niemetschek, Franz Xaver. *Lebensbeschreibung des K. K. Kapellmeisters Wolfgang Amadeus Mozart, aus Originalquellen.* Prague: Herrlischen Buchhandlung, 1798. For an English translation, see *Mozart: The First Biography*, translated by Helen Mautner with an introduction by Cliff Eisen. Oxford: Berghahn Books, 2007.

Nissen, Georg Nikolaus von. *Biographie W. A. Mozarts*, edited by Rudolph Angermüller. Hildesheim: Georg Olms, 2010. Originally published in 1828 by Breitkopf and Härtel, Leipzig.

Perinet, Joachim. "Mozart and Schikaneder, A Theatrical Dialogue on the Performance of *Die Zauberflöte* at the Stadt-Theater," translated with an introduction by Adeline Mueller. *Opera Quarterly* 28 (2012): 104–21.

Rasmussen, James P. "Sound and Motion in Goethe's 'Magic Flute.'" *Monatshefte* 101/1 (2009): 19–36.

Wunderlich, Werner, Doris Überschlag, and Ulrich Müller, eds. *Mozarts "Zauberflöte" und ihre Dichter: Schikaneder, Vulpius, Goethe, Zuccalmaglio; Faksimiles und Editionen von Textbuch, Bearbeitungen und Fortsetzungen der Mozart-Oper.* Anif: Müller-Speiser, 2007.

Index